The Scarecrow Author Bibliographies

1. John Steinbeck (Tetsumaro Hayashi). 1973.
2. Joseph Conrad (Theodore G. Ehrsam). 1969.
3. Arthur Miller (Tetsumaro Hayashi). 2d ed. 1976.
4. Katherine Anne Porter (Waldrip & Bauer). 1969.
5. Philip Freneau (Philip M. Marsh). 1970.
6. Robert Greene (Tetsumaro Hayashi). 1971.
7. Benjamin Disraeli (R. W. Stewart). 1972.
8. John Berryman (Richard W. Kelly). 1972.
9. William Dean Howells (Vito J. Brenni). 1973.
10. Jean Anouilh (Kathleen W. Kelly). 1973.
11. E. M. Forster (Alfred Borrello). 1973.
12. The Marquis de Sade (E. Pierre Chanover). 1973.
13. Alain Robbe-Grillet (Dale W. Frazier). 1973.
14. Northrop Frye (Robert D. Denham). 1974.
15. Federico Garcia Lorca (Laurenti & Siracusa). 1974.
16. Ben Jonson (Brock & Welsh). 1974.
17. Four French Dramatists: Eugène Brieux, François de Curel, Emile Fabre, Paul Hervieu (Edmund F. Santa Vicca). 1974.
18. Ralph Waldo Ellison (Jacqueline Covo). 1974.
19. Philip Roth (Bernard F. Rodgers, Jr.). 1974.
20. Norman Mailer (Laura Adams). 1974.
21. Sir John Betjeman (Margaret Stapleton). 1974.
22. Elie Wiesel (Molly Abramowitz). 1974.
23. Paul Laurence Dunbar (Eugene W. Metcalf, Jr.). 1975.
24. Henry James (Beatrice Ricks). 1975.
25. Robert Frost (Lentricchia & Lentricchia). 1976.
26. Sherwood Anderson (Douglas G. Rogers). 1976.
27. Iris Murdoch and Muriel Spark (Tominaga & Schneidermeyer). 1976.
28. John Ruskin (Kirk H. Beetz). 1976.
29. Georges Simenon (Trudee Young). 1976.
30. George Gordon, Lord Byron (Oscar José Santucho). 1976.
31. John Barth (Richard Vine). 1977.
32. John Hawkes (Carol A. Hryciw). 1977.
33. William Everson (Bartlett & Campo). 1977.
34. May Sarton (Lenora Blouin). 1978.
35. Wilkie Collins (Kirk H. Beetz). 1978.
36. Sylvia Plath (Lane & Stevens). 1978.
37. E. B. White (A. J. Anderson). 1978.
38. Henry Miller (Lawrence J. Shifreen). 1979.
39. Ralph Waldo Emerson (Jeanetta Boswell). 1979.
40. James Dickey (Jim Elledge). 1979.
41. Henry Fielding (H. George Hahn). 1979.
42. Paul Goodman (Tom Nicely). 1979.
43. Christopher Marlowe (Kenneth Friedenreich). 1979.
44. Leo Tolstoy (Egan & Egan). 1979.
45. T. S. Eliot (Beatrice Ricks). 1980.
46. Allen Ginsberg (Michelle P. Kraus). 1980.
47. Anthony Burgess (Jeutonne P. Brewer). 1980.
48. Tennessee Williams (Drewey Wayne Gunn). 1980.

Scarecrow Author Bibliographies,
No. 45

T. S. Eliot:

A bibliography of secondary works

compiled by

BEATRICE RICKS

*The Scarecrow Press, Inc.
Metuchen, N.J., & London
1980*

Library of Congress Cataloging in Publication Data

Ricks, Beatrice.
T. S. Eliot, a bibliography of secondary works.

(Scarecrow author bibliographies ; 45)
Includes indexes.
1. Eliot, Thomas Stearns, 1888-1965--
Bibliography. I. Title.
Z8260.5.R5 [PS3509.L43] 016.821'9'12 79-21305
ISBN 0-8108-1262-2

Manufactured in the United States of America

Dedicated to the Staff of the
Ward Edwards Library
of
Central Missouri State University

PREFACE

This bibliography is intended as a strictly utilitarian compilation of secondary references. Since Eliot was a poet, playwright, and critic, the compilation is therefore divided into three divisions: Drama, Poetry, and Criticism, in which the secondary material is arranged alphabetically under the titles of Eliot's works. Each section is as complete as possible. Although completeness may result in some repetition, an effort has been made to keep this to a minimum. However, if an item is an analysis of Eliot's works in general, it will be found under General Criticism.

The sections entitled Interviews, Lectures, and Letters are also compilations of secondary materials, that is, items involving comment, analysis, or reactions to Eliot's views.

An effort has been made to obtain material from various time periods, from critics important in certain decades, from British as well as American journals, and also from some foreign journals, although the latter category is a minority in quantity because of the unavailability to this compiler of many such items.

Annotation has been given only to advise the student of the nature of an item, or when apropos, a brief quotation from the author to advise the critical slant of an analysis.

Material has not been divided into separate sections of articles and books for the reason that very frequently a notable article will be revised and reissued as the basic theme of a book, or possibly, merely reprinted as the leading chapter of a book devoted to the same critical analysis.

The Topical Index, in which cross references are given by item numbers, has been designed to suggest facets of study, persons important in the life and work of T. S. Eliot, authors whose influence on Eliot has been noted, authors influenced by Eliot, or whatever area of interpretation or technique critics have considered.

Acknowledgment is made of the assistance and encouragement particularly of Dr. Edward Harris, Mrs. Kathryn Erisman, and Mrs. Eloise Kibbie, as well as many others of the staff of Ward Edwards Library of Central Missouri State University.

B. R.

TABLE OF CONTENTS

Preface v

Abbreviations of Publications ix

BIOGRAPHY 1

DRAMA

The Cocktail Party 7
The Confidential Clerk 15
The Elder Statesman 18
The Family Reunion 21
Murder in the Cathedral 27
The Rock 41
Sweeney Agonistes 42
Miscellaneous [Drama] 44

POETRY

Ash Wednesday 60
Ariel Poems: 65
    Animula 66
    Journey of the Magi 66
    Marina 68
    A Song for Simeon 69
Aunt Helen 70
The Boston Evening Transcript 70
Burbank with a Baedeker: Bleistein with a Cigar 70
A Cooking Egg 72
Coriolan 72
The Cultivation of Christmas Trees 73
Dans le Restaurant 74
La Figlia che Piange 74
Four Quartets 74
    Burnt Norton 89
    East Coker 93
    The Dry Salvages 95
    Little Gidding 97
Gerontion 99
The Hippopotamus 104
The Hollow Men 104
Hysteria 107
Lines to Ralph Hodgson Esqre 107
Mr. Apollinax 108

Mr. Eliot's Sunday Morning Service 108
New Hampshire 109
Old Possum's Book of Practical Cats 109
    Macavity: The Mystery Cat 109
    Gus: The Theatre Cat 109
    Skimbleshanks: The Railway Cat 110
Portrait of a Lady 110
Preludes 111
Prufrock and Other Observations 112
Rhapsody on a Windy Night 123
Sweeney Among the Nightingales 123
Sweeney Erect 125
To the Indians Who Died in Africa 126
The Waste Land 126
    I. The Burial of the Dead 164
    II. A Game of Chess 166
    III. The Fire Sermon 166
    IV. Death by Water 167
    V. What the Thunder Said 167
Whispers of Immortality 168
Collected Poems, 1909-1935; 1909-1962 168

CRITICISM

After Strange Gods 170
Dante 171
Essays, Ancient and Modern 172
Ezra Pound: His Metric and Poetry 173
For Lancelot Andrewes 173
Hamlet and His Problems 174
Homage to John Dryden 175
The Idea of a Christian Society 176
Knowledge and Experience in the Philosophy of F. H. Bradley 179
The Metaphysical Poets 179
Notes Toward the Definition of Culture 180
On Poetry and Poets 183
The Sacred Wood 184
Selected Essays, 1917-1932 186
Three Voices of Poetry 188
To Criticize the Critic and Other Writings 189
Tradition and the Individual Talent 190
The Use of Poetry and the Use of Criticism 192

INTERVIEWS 195

LECTURES 198

LETTERS 199

GENERAL CRITICISM 200

BIBLIOGRAPHY 321

Topical Index 327

Index of Critics 339

ABBREVIATIONS OF PUBLICATIONS

AAS	Asian and African Studies
ABC	American Book Collector
ABR	American Benedictine Review
AFF	Annali Facoltà di Lingue Letterature Straniere di Feltre
AI	American Imago
AInt	Art International
AION-SG	Annali Instituto Universitario Orientale, Napoli, Sezione Germanica
AKML	Abhandlungen zur Kunst-, Musik- und Literaturwissenschaft
AL	American Literature
AmBk	American Bookman
AmMerc	American Mercury
AmNep	American Neptune
AmQ	American Quarterly
AmR	American Review
AmSch	American Scholar
AN&Q	American Notes and Queries
AntigR	Antigonish Review
AnUBLUC	Analele Universitatu Bucuresti. Literatura universala si comparata
AP&P	American Poetry and Poetics
ApSTC	Appalachian State Teachers College Faculty Publications
AR	Antioch Review
Archiv	Archiv für das Studium der neueren Sprachen und Literaturen
ArielE	Ariel: A Review of International English Literature
ArlQ	Arlington Quarterly

ArQ	Arizona Quarterly
AryP	Aryan Path (Bombay)
ASUI	Analele Stuntifice ale Universitatu Iasi
Atl	Atlantic Monthly
AUB-LG	Analele Universitatii, Bucuresti, Limbi Germanice
AUB-LUC	Analele Universitatii, Bucuresti, Literatura Universale Comparata
AUC	Anales de la Universidad/de Chile
AUMLA	Journal of the Australasian Universities Language and Literature Association
AWR	The Anglo-Welsh Review (Pembroke Dock, Wales)
AylR	The Aylesford Review (Aylesford, Kent)
BA	Books Abroad
B&B	Books and Bookmen
BardR	Bard Review
BB	Bulletin of Bibliography
BC	Book Collector
BDEC	Bulletin of Department of English, Calcutta
BJA	British Journal of Aesthetics (London)
BLM	Bonniers Litterara Magasin (Stockholm)
BNYPL	Bulletin of New York Public Library
BP	Banasthali Patrika
BRMML	Bulletin of the Rocky Mountain Modern Language Association
BSJ	Baker Street Journal
BSNotes	Browning Society Notes
BSTCF	Ball State Teachers College Forum
BSUF	Ball State University Forum
BuR	Bucknell Review
BUSE	Boston University Studies in English
BuUS	Bucknell University Studies
CalcR	Calcutta Review
CamJ	Cambridge Journal
CamQ	Cambridge Quarterly
CamR	Cambridge Review
CanA&B	Canadian Author and Bookman

C&L	Christianity and Literature
CanF	Canadian Forum
CanL	Canadian Literature
CarQ	Carolina Quarterly
CaSE	Carnegie Studies in English
CathQ	Catholic World
CBull	Classical Bulletin
CC&C	College Composition and Communication
CdMN	Cahiers du Monde Nouveau (Paris)
CDr	Comparative Drama
CdS	Cahiers du Sud
CE	College English
CEA	CEA Critic
CEJ	California English Journal
CEKWJC	Collected Essays: Kyoritsu Women's Junior College
CentR	The Centennial Review (Michigan State University)
CeyJH	Ceylon Journal of the Humanities
CHA	Cuadernos Hispanoamericanos (Madrid)
ChiR	Chicago Review
ChrC	Christian Century
ChrNL	Christian News Letter
ChS	Christian Scholar
CimR	Cimarron Review
CJ	Classical Journal
CJR	Contemporary Jewish Record
CL	Comparative Literature
CLAJ	College Language Association Journal (Morgan State College, Baltimore)
CLit	Contemporary Literature
CLS	Comparative Literature Studies (University of Illinois)
CMC	Crosscurrents/Modern Critiques
CMF	Casopis promoderni filologii
CollL	College Literature
ColQ	Colorado Quarterly
ColuF	Columbia Forum
CompD	Comparative Drama

ConL	Contemporary Literature (supersedes WSCL)
ConnR	Connecticut Review
ConR	Contemporary Review
ContempE	Contemporary Education
ContempR	Contemporary Reader
Conv	Convivium (Barcelona)
CP	Classical Philology
CR (& CritR)	Critical Review (Melbourne)
CRAS	The Centennial Review of Arts & Science (Michigan State)
CRCL	Canadian Review of Comparative Literature
CritQ	Critical Quarterly: Poetry Supplement (London)
CritR	Critical Review (Melbourne)
CritS	Critical Survey (Hull University)
CSMM	Christian Science Monitor Magazine
CSR	Christian Scholar's Review (supersedes Gordon Review)
CUF	Columbia University Forum
Cw	Commonweal
DA, DAI	Dissertation Abstracts, Dissertation Abstracts International
DCLB	Dartmouth College Library Bulletin
DilR	Diliman Review
DownsideR	Downside Review
DR	Dalhousie Review
DramaCrit	Drama Critique
DramS	Drama Survey (Minneapolis)
DRs	Deutsche Rundschau
DSARDS	Dante Studies with the Annual Report of the Dante Society
DubM	Dublin Magazine
DubR	Dublin Review
DUJ	Durham University Journal
DWB	Dietsche Warande en Belfort
EA	Etudes Anglaises
EA&A	Etudes Anglaises et Americaines (formerly Travaux du Centre d'Etudes Anglaises et Americaines)

E&S(T)	Essays and Studies in British and American Literature (Tokyo Woman's Christian College)
EDH	Essays by Divers Hands (Published by the Royal Society of Literature of the United Kingdom, London)
EFL	Essays in French Literature (University of Western Australia)
EG	Etudes Germaniques
EIC	Essays in Criticism (Oxford)
EIE	English Institute Essays
EigoS	Eigo Seinen [The Rising Generation] (Tokyo)
EIHC	Essex Institute Historical Collections
EJ	English Journal
ELH	Journal of English Literary History
ELLS	English Language and Literature (English Literary Society of Korea)
ELN	English Language Notes (University of Colorado)
EM	English Miscellany: A Symposium of History, Literature and the Arts (Rome)
EngRec	English Record (New York State English Council)
EngRev	English Review
ES	English Studies (Amsterdam)
ESA	English Studies in Africa (Johannesburg)
ESPSL	O Estado de São Paulo, Suplemento Literário
ESQ	Emerson Society Quarterly
ESRS	Emporia State Research Studies
EStudien	Englische Studien
ETJ	Educational Theatre Journal
EUQ	Emory University Quarterly
EurH	Europäische Hochschulschriften
E-WR	East-West Review (Doshisha University, Kyoto)
Expl	Explicator
FH	Frankfurter Hefte
FJS	Fu Jen Studies (Republic of China)
FL	Figaro Littéraire (Paris)
FLe	La Fiera Letteraria (Italy)
FMLS	Forum for Modern Language Studies (University of St. Andrews, Scotland)

FMod	Filología Moderna (Madrid)
FnR	Fortnightly Review
FordUQ	Fordham University Quarterly
Forum&C	Forum and Century (New York)
ForumH	Forum (Houston)
FQ	Four Quarters
FR	French Review
GaR	Georgia Review
GL&L	German Life and Letters
GordonR	Gordon Review
GR	Germanic Review
GRM	Germanisch-romanische Monatsschrift, neue Folge
GSE	Graduate Student of English
GuG	Gestalt und Gedanke: Ein Jahrbuch
GyS	Gypsy Scholar
HA	Harvard Advocate
HAB	Humanities Association Bulletin (Canada)
H&H	Hound and Horn
HeM	Hommes et Mondes
HemN	Hemingway Notes
HES	Harvard English Studies
HINL	History of Ideas Newsletter
HistA	Historical Abstracts
HJ	Hibbert Journal
HolbornR	Holborn Review
HR	Hiboshi Ronbunshu (Keio Gijiju University)
HSE	Hungarian Studies in English (L. Kossuth University, Debrecen)
HSELL	Hiroshima Studies in English Language and Literature (Japan)
HudR	Hudson Review
HumB	Humanities Bulletin
HUSL	Hebrew University Studies in Literature
HussR	Husson Review
HZM	Handelingen van de Zuidnederlandse Maatschappij voor Taal--en Letterkunde en Geschiedenis

ICS	L'Italia che scrive
IEY	Iowa English Yearbook
IJES	Indian Journal of English Studies (Calcutta)
IJSLP	International Journal of Slavic Linguistics and Poetics
IJSym	International Journal of Symbology
ILA	International Literary Annual (London)
IllQ	Illinois Quarterly
IndL	Indian Literature
InR	Intercollegiate Review (Bryn Mawr)
IowaR	Iowa Review
IrishM	Irish Monthly
ISE	Ibadan Studies in English
Ital	Italica
IUHS	Indiana University--Humanities Series
JA	Jahrbuch für Amerikastudien
JAAC	Journal of Aesthetics and Art Criticism
JAAR	Journal of the American Academy of Religion
JAmS	Journal of American Studies
JAOS	Journal of the American Oriental Society
JBalS	Journal of Baltic Studies
JCHist	Journal of Contemporary History
JEGP	Journal of English and Germanic Philology
JES	Journal of European Studies
JewQ	Jewish Quarterly
JF	Jewish Frontier
JGE	Journal of General Education
JHI	Journal of the History of Ideas
JHR	Journal of Human Relations
JJCL	Jadavpur Journal of Comparative Literature
JJQ	James Joyce Quarterly (Tulsa University)
JKU	Journal of Karnatak University
JML	Journal of Modern Literature
JO'LW	John O'London's Weekly
JUB	Journal of the University of Baroda
JWS	Journal of Western Speech

KanoS	Kano Studies (Ahmadu Bello University, Nigeria)
KN	Kwartalnik Neofilologiczny (Warsaw)
KogK	Kirke og Kultur (Oslo)
KP	Kritika Phylla
KR	Kenyon Review
KSV	Kirjallisuudenlukijain Seuran Vuosikirja (Helsinki)
L&I	Literature and Ideology (Montreal)
L&L	Life and Letters
L&LT	Life and Letters Today
L&P	Literature and Psychology (University of Hartford)
LanM	Les Langues Modernes
LaurelR	Laurel Review
LCritM	Literary Criterion, Mysore
LCUT	Library Chronicle of the University of Texas
LE&W	Literature East and West
LeS	Lingua e Stile (Bologna)
Let	Litteratura (Italy)
LetF	Lettres Françaises
LetM	Letterature Moderne (Milan)
LHR	Lock Haven Review
LHY	The Literary Half-Yearly (Bangalore Central)
LibJ	Library Journal
List	Listener
Lit	Die Literatur
LitC	Literary Collector
LiteraryR	Literary Review
LitEW	Literature East and West
LitMod	Littérature Moderne
LittleR	The Little Review
LivAge	Living Age
LonMag	London Magazine
LonMerc	London Mercury
LonQt	London Quarterly
LSUSHS	Louisiana State University Studies, Humanities Series
Luceafărul	Luceafărul: Revista a Uniunii scriitorilor din

LugR	Lugano Review
LuthChQt	Lutheran Church Quarterly
LWU	Literatur in Wissenschaft und Unterricht
MalR	Malahat Review
MassR	Massachusetts Review
McMaster Qt	McMaster Quarterly
MD	Modern Drama
MdF	Mercure de France
MFS	Modern Fiction Studies
MichA	Michigan Academician
MidwQ	Midwest Quarterly
MiltonQ	Milton Quarterly
MissQ	Mississippi Quarterly
MLA	Modern Language Association
MLN	Modern Language Notes
MLQ	Modern Language Quarterly
MLR	Modern Language Review
ModA	Modern Age (Chicago)
ModM	Modern Monthly
ModQt	Modern Quarterly
ModRev	Modern Review (Calcutta)
Mon/AnTu	Annales Universitatis Turkuensis (Turku, Finland)
Mon/Aug	Augustana College Press Monograph Series (Rock Island, Ill.)
Mon/FlH	University of Florida Monographs: Humanities
Mon/HES	Monographs: Harvard English Studies
MonLMW	Literary Monographs: University of Wisconsin
Mon/TuMS	Tulsa Monograph Series: University of Tulsa
Mon/WSUBUS	Wichita State University Bulletin: University Studies
MoOc	Modern Occasions
MP	Modern Philology
MQR	Michigan Quarterly Review
MSE	Massachusetts Studies in English
MSpr	Moderna Språk (Stockholm)
MW	The Muslim World (Hartford)
NA	Nuova Antologia (Rome)

N&Q	Notes and Queries
NAR	North America Review
NassauRev	Nassau [New York] Community College
NatlR	National Review
NConL	Notes on Contemporary Literature
NCRMM	La Nouvelle Critique, Revue du Marxisme Militant
NDH	Neue Deutsche Hefte
NDQ	North Dakota Quarterly
Neophil	Neophilologus (Groningen)
NEQ	New England Quarterly
NewEW	New English Weekly
NewL	New Leader
NewSt	New Statesman
NineC	Nineteenth Century
NL	Nouvelles Littéraires
NM	Neuphilologische Mitteilungen (Helsinki)
NMQ	New Mexico Quarterly
NMQR	New Mexico Quarterly Review
NR	New Republic
NRF	La Nouvelle Revue Française
NRs	Die Neue Rundschau
NS	Die Neueren Sprachen
NS&N	New Statesman and Nation
NsM	Neusprachliche Mitteilungen aus Wissenschaft und Praxis
NSt	New Statesman
NT	Nuestro Tiempo
NW	New Yorker
NYRB	New York Review of Books
NYTBR	New York Times Book Review
NYTMS	New York Times Magazine Section
NZ	Neuphilologische Zeitschrift
NZZ	Neue Zürcher Zeitung
Obs	Observer
Occi	Occident
OJES	Osmania Journal of English Studies (Osmania University, Hyderabad)

OL	Orbis Litterarum (Copenhagen)
OPL	Osservatore Politico Letterario
OUR	Ohio University Review (Athens)
ParisR	Paris Review
PartisanR	Partisan Review
PBA	Proceedings of the British Academy
PBSA	Papers of the Bibliographical Society of America
PE&W	Philosophy East and West (University of Hawaii)
PeI	Le Parole e le Idee (Naples)
PhoenixK	Phoenix (Korea University)
PLL	Papers on Language and Literature
PMLA	Publications of the Modern Language Association of America
PN	Poe Newletter (Washington State University)
PoetA	Poetry Australia
Poet&C	Poet and Critic
PoetryJ	Poetry Journal
PoetryQt	Poetry Quarterly
PoetryR	Poetry Review (London)
PP	Philologica Pragensia
PPR	Philosophy and Phenomenological Research
PQ	Philological Quarterly
PrS	Prairie Schooner
PubW	Publishers' Weekly
PULC	Princeton University Library Chronicle
PURBA	Punjab University Research Bulletin
QQ	Queen's Quarterly
QRL	Quarterly Review of Literature
RdM	Revue des deux mondes
RdP	Revue de Pari
RE: A&L	Re: Arts & Letters
REL	Review of English Literature
REngL	Review of English Literature (Kyoto University, Japan)
RES	Review of English Studies
Rev	Review (Oxford)

RGB	Revue Générale Belge (Brussels)
RHL	Revue d'Histoire Littéraire de la France
RL	Revista de Literatura
RLC	Revue de Littérature Comparée
RLitC	Readings in Literary Criticism
RLM	Rivista di Letterature Moderne
RLV	Revue des Langues Vivantes
RMMLAB	Rocky Mountain MLA Bulletin
RN	Revue Nouvelle (Brussels)
RNC	Revista National de Cultura (Caracas)
RNL	Review of National Literatures
RockyMR	Rocky Mountain Review
RRAL	Rikkyo Review Arts and Letters (Tokyo)
RSWSU	Research Studies: Washington State University
RUCR	Revista de la Universidad de Costa Rica
RusR	Russian Review
SA	Studi Americani
SAB	South Atlantic Bulletin
SAmH	Studies in American Humor
S&S	Science & Society
SAQ	South Atlantic Quarterly
SatR	Saturday Review [of Literature]
SB	Studies in Bibliography: Papers of the Bibliographical Society of the University of Virginia
SCR	South Carolina Review
SDD-UW	Summaries of Doctoral Dissertations--University of Wisconsin
SdZ	Stimmen der Zeit (Freiburg)
SEL	Studies in English Literature, 1500-1900
SELit	Studies in English Literature (English Literary Society of Japan)
SELL	Studies in English Literature and Language (Kyushu University, Fukuoka, Japan)
SGF	Stockholmer Germanistische Forschungen
SGG	Studia Germanica Gandensia
SHR	Southern Humanities Review
SJ	Shakespeare-Jahrbuch

SLRJ	St. Louis University Research Journal of the Graduate School of Arts and Sciences
SLT	Svensk Litteraturtidskrift
SLU	Studii de litteraturǎ universalǎ (Bucharest)
SoF	Samtid och Framtid
SoLit	Southern Literature
SoQ	Southern Quarterly (Hattiesburg, University of Southern Mississippi)
SoR	Southern Review (Louisiana State University)
SoRA	Southern Review: An Australian Journal of Literary Studies (University of Adelaide)
SPe	Lo Spettatore Italiano
SR	Sewanee Review
SRAQ	Studia Romancia et Anglica Zagrabiensia
SSF	Studies in Short Fiction
StLouisR	St. Louis Review
STwenC	Studies in the Twentieth Century
SUS	Susquehanna University Studies (Selinsgrove, Pa.)
SWR	Southwest Review
TamarackR	Tamarack Review
T&T	Time and Tide
TC	Twentieth Century
TCAus	Twentieth Century (Australia)
TCBS	Transactions of the Cambridge Bibliographical Society
TCI	Twentieth Century Interpretations
TCL	Twentieth Century Literature
TDR	Tulane Drama Review
TeM	O Tempo e o Modo
ThA	Theatre Arts
TkR	Tamkang Review
TLS	Times Literary Supplement (London)
TM	Les Temps Modernes
TP	Terzo Programma (Rome)
TPr	Tempo Presente
TQ	Texas Quarterly (University of Texas)
TriQ	TriQuarterly (Evanston, Ill.)

TSE	Tulane Studies in English
TSEN	T. S. Eliot Newsletter
TSER	T. S. Eliot Review
TSLL	Texas Studies in Language and Literature
TVUB	Tydschrift van de Vrije Universiteit van Brussel
UCSLL	University of Colorado Studies in Language and Literature
UDQ	University of Denver Quarterly
UDR	University of Dayton Review
UES	Unisa English Studies
UFMH	University of Florida Monographs, Humanities Series
UKCR	University of Kansas City Review
Univ	Universitas (Stuttgart)
UR	University Review (Kansas City, Mo.)
UTQ	University of Toronto Quarterly
UTSE	University of Texas Studies in English
UWR	University of Windsor Review (Windsor, Ont.)
VeP	Vita e Pensiero
VIndJ	Vishveshvaranand Indological Journal
VlG	De Vlaamse Gids
VLit	Voprosy Literatury
VMU	Vestnik Moskovskogo Universiteta. Filologiya
VP	Victorian Poetry
VQR	Virginia Quarterly Review
VS	Victorian Studies
VWQ	Virginia Woolf Quarterly
WASAL	Wisconsin Academy of Sciences, Arts and Letters
WBEP	Wiemer Beiträge zur englischen Philologie
WestR	Western Review
WHR	Western Humanities Review
WindsorQt	The Windsor Quarterly
WiOr	Windless Orchard
WisSL	Wisconsin Studies in Literature
WLWE	World Literature Written in English
Wn	A Wake Newsletter (Newcastle University College, N. S. W., Australia)

WorldR	World Review
WSCL	Wisconsin Studies in Contemporary Literature
WTW	Writers and Their Work
WuW	Welt und Wort
WWR	Walt Whitman Review
WZ	Wort in der Zeit (Vienna)
XR	X, A Quarterly Review
XUS	Xavier University Studies
YFS	Yale French Studies
YGen	Y Genhinen
YR	Yale Review
YULG	Yale University Library Gazette
Ź	Źycie
ZAA	Zeitschrift für Anglistik und Amerikanistik (East Berlin)
Žovten'	Žovten': Literaturno-Xudožnij Žurnal

BIOGRAPHY

1 Aiken, Conrad. "An Anatomy of Melancholy," T. S. Eliot: The Man and His Work. Allen Tate, ed. New York: Delacorte Pr., 1966, pp. 194-202.

2 _______. "Homage to T. S. Eliot," HA, 125, #3 (1938), 17.

3 _______. "King Bolo and Others," T. S. Eliot: A Symposium. Richard March and Tambimuttu, comps. Freeport, N.Y.: Books for Libraries Pr., 1968, pp. 20-23.

4 _______. Ushant: An Essay. New York: Duell, Sloan & Pearce, 1952, passim.

5 Aldington, Richard. Life for Life's Sake: A Book of Reminiscences. New York: Viking Pr., 1941, passim.

6 Auden, W. H. "T. S. Eliot: A Tribute," List, 73 (January 7, 1965), 5.

7 Bell, Clive. "How Pleasant to Know Mr. Eliot," T. S. Eliot: A Symposium. Richard March and Tambimuttu, comps. Freeport, N.Y.: Books for Libraries Pr., 1968, pp. 15-19.

8 Bergonzi, Bernard. T. S. Eliot. (Masters of World Literature Series) New York: Macmillan, 1972.

9 Blackmur, R. P. "Homage to T. S. Eliot," HA, 125, #3 (December, 1938), 20. "What is to me most remarkable about Eliot's mind is its seminal quality.... It is partly that quality which causes his verse ... to become gradually a part of our experience...."

10 Blanshard, Brand. "Eliot in Memory," YR, 54 (June, 1965), 635-640.

11 Braybrooke, Neville, ed. Introduction. T. S. Eliot: A Symposium for His Seventieth Birthday. New York: Farrar, Straus & Cudahy, 1958, passim.

12 _______. "T. S. Eliot at Seventy," Norseman, 16 (September-October, 1958), 331-334. Notes Eliot's "development as a

poet, dramatist, and critic" and "the shift of public opinion by which the leader of one generation has become the prophet of another."

13 Breit, Harvey. "An Unconfidential Close-up of T. S. Eliot," NYTBR (November 21, 1948); NYTMS (February 7, 1954), 16, 24-25.

14 Brestin, James. "Too Far and Not Far Enough," VQR, 50 (Autumn, 1974), 632-637. A critical essay-review of T. S. Matthews' Great Tom. New York: 1974.

15 Davies, H. S. "Mistah Kurtz: He Dead," SR, 74 (Winter, 1966), 349-357; repr., from Eagle (Cambridge, England), 60 May, 1965), #264; repr., in T. S. Eliot: The Man and His Work. Allen Tate, ed. New York: 1966, pp. 355-363.

16 Day Lewis, C. "At East Coker" [poem], SR, 74 (January-March, 1966), 134-135; repr., in T. S. Eliot: The Man and His Work. Allen Tate, ed. New York: 1966, pp. 114-115.

17 Department of English. "The Eliot Family and St. Louis," St. Louis: Washington U. Studies, No. 23, 1953.

18 Dobrée, Bonamy. "T. S. Eliot: A Personal Reminiscence," SR, 74 (January-March, 1966), 85-108; repr., in T. S. Eliot. Allen Tate, ed. New York: 1966, pp. 65-88.

19 Dozier, Thomas. "Would the Real Mr. Eliot Please Stand Up?" Month, 5 (October, 1972), 309-313.

19a Ellmann, Richard. "Eliot's Conversion," TriQ, #4 (1965), 77-80.

19b Ezekiel, Nissim. "T. S. Eliot: A Personal Review," Quest, #45 (Spring, 1965), 17-22.

20 Frye, Northrop. Introduction. T. S. Eliot. New York: Barnes & Noble, 1966, pp. 1-6.

20a Garçon, Maurice. "Compliment à T. S. Eliot," MdF, 335, #1145 (janvier, 1959), 16-25.

20b George, R. E. Gordon. "The Return of the Native," Bookman, 75, #5 (September, 1932), 423-431.

21 Gerber, Richard. "In Memoriam T. S. Eliot," NRs, 76 (1966), 150-155.

22 Giroux, Robert. "A Personal Memoir," SR, 74 (Winter, 1966), 331-338; repr., in T. S. Eliot: The Man and His Work. Allen Tate, ed. pp. 337-344.

22a Gordon, Lyndall. Eliot's Early Years. Oxford and New York: Oxford U. Pr., 1977.

23 Grobler, P. du P. "In Memoriam: T. S. Eliot," Theoria, #25 (1965), 41-46.

24 Hall, Donald. "The Art of Poetry I: T. S. Eliot," ParisR, 21 (Spring-Summer, 1959), 47-70.

25 Hawkins, Desmond. "The Pope of Russell Square," T. S. Eliot: A Symposium. Richard March and Tambimuttu, comps. [item #3], pp. 44-47.

26 Hewes, Henry. "T. S. Eliot at Seventy," SatR, 41, #37 (September 13, 1958), 30-32.

27 Holroyd, Michael. Lytton Strachey. Vol. II, London; New York: Holt, Rinehart, & Winston, 1968, pp. 364-367, passim.

28 Howarth, Herbert. Notes on Some Figures Behind T. S. Eliot. Boston: Houghton Mifflin, 1964, passim.

29 ________. "T. S. E. and the 'Little Preacher,'" AmQ, 13 (Summer, 1961), 179-187.

29a Kenner, Hugh. "T. S. Eliot, RIP: Death of a Poet," NatlR, 17, #4 (January 26, 1965), 63-65.

30 Kirk, Russell. "The Youngest Eliot of St. Louis," Eliot and His Age: T. S. Eliot's Moral Imagination in the Twentieth Century. New York: Random House, 1971, pp. 22-26.

31 Levy, William Turner, and Victor Scherle. Affectionately, T. S. Eliot: The Story of a Friendship, 1947-1965. London: Dent; Philadelphia: Lippincott, 1968.

32 Lewis, Wyndham. "Early London Environment," T. S. Eliot: A Symposium. Richard March and Tambimuttu, eds. [item #3, pp. 29-30.

33 ________. "First Meeting with T. S. Eliot," Blasting and Bombardiering. 2nd rev. ed. Berkeley: California U. Pr., 1967, pp. 282-289.

34 ________. The Letters of Wyndham Lewis, W. K. Rose, ed. Norfolk, Conn.: New Directions, 1964, passim.

35 ________. "T. S. Eliot: The Pseudo-Believer," Men without Art. London: Cassell; New York: Russell & Russell, 1964, pp. 65-91, 92-100.

36 Lowell, R. T. S. "Homage to T. S. Eliot," HA, 125, #3 (December, 1938), 20, 41.

36a Lowenfels, Walter. "Farewell to T. S. Eliot," American Dialog, 2, #1 (Spring, 1965), 35-37.

37 Ludwig, Richard M. "Biography," Fifteen Modern American Authors. Jackson R. Bryer, ed. Durham, NC: Duke U. Pr., 1969, pp. 145-148.

37a ________. "Biography," Sixteen Modern American Authors. Jackson R. Bryer, ed. Durham, NC: Duke U. Pr., 1974, pp. 187-190, 217-218.

38 MacLeish, Archibald. "Homage to T. S. Eliot," HA, 125, #3 (December, 1938), 18.

39 Madge, Charles. "In Memoriam T. S. E.," New Verse, 31 (1938), 18-21.

40 Mairet, Philip. "Memories of T. S. E.," T. S. Eliot: A Symposium for His Seventieth Birthday. Neville Braybrooke, ed. [item #11], pp. 36-44.

41 March, Richard, and Tambimuttu, comps. Foreword. T. S. Eliot: A Symposium [item #3], pp. 11-12.

42 Matthews, Thomas Stanley. Great Tom: Notes Toward the Definition of T. S. Eliot. London; New York: Harper & Row, 1974.

43 Matthiessen, Francis Otto. "Biographical Note," The Achievement of T. S. Eliot. 3rd ed., rev. & enl. New York: Oxford U. Pr., 1959, pp. xix-xxi.

43a Montgomery, Marion. "Eliot's Autobiography," IllQ, 37, ii (1974), 57-64.

44 Morley, Frank. "A Few Recollections of Eliot," SR, 74 (Spring, 1966), 110-133; repr., in T. S. Eliot: The Man and His Work. Allen Tate, ed. [item #15], and T. S. Eliot: A Symposium, Richard March, and Tambimuttu, comps. [item #3], pp. 60-70.

45 Nuhn, Ferner. "Orpheus in Hell: T. S. Eliot," The Wind Blew from the East: A Study in the Orientation of American Culture. London; New York: Harper & Bros., 1942, pp. 195-255. "...It is a Puritan, Calvinist, New England hell that this Orpheus sings...."

46 Patmore, Brigit. "Dancing with the Eliots," LonMag, 6, #10 (January, 1967), 82-86.

47 ________, ed. Introduction. My Friends When Young. London: Heinemann, 1968.

47a Pound, Ezra. "For T. S. E.," SR, 74, #1 (Spring, 1966),

109; repr., in T. S. Eliot: The Man and His Work. Allen Tate, ed. [item 15], p. 89.

48 Powel, Harford Willing Hare, Jr. Notes on the Life of T. S. Eliot, 1888-1910. Diss., Brown U., 1954.

48a Rago, Henry. "T. S. Eliot: A Memoir and a Tribute," Poetry, 105, #6 (March, 1965), 392-395.

48b ________. T. S. Eliot: A Memoir and a Tribute. Chicago: U. of Chicago Printing Dept., 1965.

49 Read, Herbert. "T. S. E.: A Memoir," SR, 74, #1 (January-March, 1966), 31-57; repr., in T. S. Eliot: The Man and His Work. Allen Tate, ed. [item #15], pp. 11-37.

49a ________. T. S. E.: A Memoir. Middletown, Conn.: Center for Advanced Studies, Wesleyan U., 1966.

50 Regnery, Henry. "Eliot, Pound and Lewis: A Creative Friendship," ModA, 16 (1972), 146-160.

51 Richards, I. A. "On TSE: Notes for a Talk at the Institute of Contemporary Arts, London, June 29, 1965," SR, 74, #1 (Spring, 1966), 21-30; repr., in T. S. Eliot: The Man and His Work. Allen Tate, ed. [item #15], pp. 1-10.

52 Richardson, Joanna. "T. S. Eliot," LHY, 3 (January, 1962), 9-12.

53 Richman, Robert. "The Day of Five Signs: An Elegy for Eliot: 5 January 1965 (Georgetown & Estero Island) [poem]," SR, 74 (Spring, 1966), 238; repr., in T. S. Eliot: The Man and His Work. Allen Tate, ed. [item #15], p. 244.

54 Russell, Bertrand. The Autobiography of Bertrand Russell, 1914-1944. Vol. II. Boston: Little, Brown, 1968, passim. Reminiscences.

55 Russell, Francis. "Some Non-encounters with Mr. Eliot," Horizon, 7, #4 (Autumn, 1965), 37-41.

56 Seferis, George. "T. S. E. (Pages from a Diary by George Seferis)," QRL, 15 (1967), 209-228.

57 Sencourt, Robert. T. S. Eliot: A Memoir. Donald Adamson, ed. New York: Dodd, Mead, 1971.

58 Soldo, John J. "The American Foreground of T. S. Eliot," NEQ, 45 (1972), 355-372.

59 Spender, Stephen. "How Pleasant to Know Mr. Eliot," JO'L, 57 (October 29, 1948), 515.

60 __________. "Meeting T. S. Eliot," The English-Speaking World," 33, #2 (1951), 13-15.

61 __________. "Remembering Eliot," Encounter, 24, #4 (April, 1965), 3-14.

61a __________. "Remembering Eliot," SR, 74, #1 (Winter, 1966), 58-84.

61b __________. "Remembering Eliot," T. S. Eliot: The Man and His Work. Allen Tate, ed. [item #15], pp. 38-64.

61c __________. "T. S. Eliot's London," SatR, 50 (March 11, 1967), 58-59, 87-88. Biographical sketch of Eliot's London years.

62 Stevens, Wallace. "Homage to Eliot," HA, 125 (December, 1938), 42ff.

63 Stock, Noel. "Eliot: The Early Years," PoetA, 20 (February, 1968), 43-47. Eliot's biography to May, 1917.

63a __________. "Eliot: The Early Years (II)," PoetA, 21 (April, 1968), 34-38. Eliot's biography from 1917 to 1925.

64 Stravinsky, Igor. "Memories of T. S. Eliot," Esquire, 64, #2 (August, 1965), 92-93. Descriptions of meetings with Eliot between December, 1956, and December, 1963.

65 Styler, W. E. "Eliot as an Adult Tutor," N&Q, 19, #2 (February, 1972), 53-54.

66 Tate, Allen. "Postscript by the Guest Editor," SR, 74 (January, 1966), 383-387.

66a __________, ed. T. S. Eliot: The Man and His Work. New York: Delacorte Pr., 1966.

67 Tinckom-Fernandez, W. G. "T. S. Eliot, '10," HA, 125, #3 (December, 1938), 5-10, 47-48. A classmate's remembrance of Eliot at Harvard.

68 Warren, Robert Penn. "Homage to T. S. Eliot," HA, 125, #3 (1938), 46.

69 Williams, William Carlos. "Homage to T. S. Eliot," HA, 125, #3 (1938), 42.

70 Woolf, Leonard. Beginning Again: An Autobiography of the Years 1911 to 1918. New York: Harcourt, Brace & World, 1964, pp. 240-245.

71 __________. Downhill All the Way: An Autobiography of the Years 1919 to 1939. New York: Harcourt, Brace & World, 1967, pp. 107-111, passim.

DRAMA

THE COCKTAIL PARTY

72 Adler, Jacob. H. "A Source for Eliot in Shaw," N&Q, 14, #7, n. s. (July, 1967), 256-257. Shaw's Arms and the Man a "highly probable source" for passage in The Cocktail Party describing the death of Celia Copplestone.

73 Anér, Kerstin. "Anglarna bid cocktailbricken," BLM (Stockholm), 8 (October, 1950), 593-602.

74 Arrowsmith, William. "Eliot and Euripides," Arion, 4, #1 (Spring, 1965), 21-35. Application of Euripides in analysis of The Cocktail Party.

74a ______________. "English Verse Drama (II): The Cocktail Party," HudR, 3 (Autumn, 1950), 411-430.

75 Bain, Donald. "T. S. Eliot's The Cocktail Party," Nine, 2, #1 (January, 1950), 16-21. The Cocktail Party as a dramatization of the Four Quartets.

76 Barrett, William. "Dry Land, Dry Martini," PartisanR, 17, (April, 1950), 354-359. A critical analysis.

77 Barry, Michael. "Televising The Cocktail Party," T. S. Eliot: A Symposium for His Seventieth Birthday. Neville Braybrooke, ed. [item #11], pp. 85-88.

78 Bayley, John. "The Collected Plays," Rev, #4 (November, 1962), 3-11. The Cocktail Party as "a difficult but marvelous birth of something that may well prove to be stillborn."

79 Brown, John Mason. "Honorable Intentions," SatR, 33 (February 4, 1950), 28-32; repr., in Still Seeing Things. New York: McGraw-Hill, 1950, pp. 167-174.

79a Brown, Ray C. B. "Alcoholic Allegory," Voices (Summer, 1950-51), 33-40.

80 Browne, E. Martin. "The Cocktail Party," The Making of T. S. Eliot's Plays. London; New York: Cambridge U. Pr., 1969, 172-248.

80a ______________. "The Making of a Play: T. S. Eliot's

The Cocktail Party," The Judith Wilson Lecture. [London]: Cambridge U. Pr., 1966.

81 Carter, Paul J. "Who Understands The Cocktail Party?" ColQ, 2 (Autumn, 1953), 193-205. The play criticized for "the mechanical tonelessness of his sterile verse."

82 Coghill, Nevill, ed. T. S. Eliot's The Cocktail Party. With Notes and Commentary. London: Faber & Faber, 1974.

83 Colby, Robert A. "The Three Worlds of The Cocktail Party: The Wit of T. S. Eliot," UTQ, 24 (October, 1954), 56-69. According to Eliot's "wit of ambivalence," his (Eliot's) conclusion shows three elements of Christian society: the Community of Christians, the Christian State, the Christian Community.

84 Davenport, Gary T. "Eliot's The Cocktail Party: Comic Perspective as Salvation," MD, 17 (September, 1974), 301-306. Finds that Eliot reconciles "two seemingly incompatible elements: high moral seriousness and 'light' comedy in the Noel Coward idiom."

85 Dickinson, Donald H. "Mr. Eliot's Hotel Universe," DramaCrit, 1 (February, 1958), 33-44. Comparison of Eliot's play with Philip Barry's Hotel Universe.

86 Donoghue, Denis. "The Cocktail Party," The Third Voice: Modern British and American Verse Drama. Princeton, N.J.: Princeton U. Pr., 1959, passim; abridged and repr., in T. S. Eliot: A Collection of Critical Essays. Hugh Kenner, ed. Englewood Cliffs, N.J.: Prentice-Hall, 1962, pp. 173-186.

87 Dunkel, Wilbur Dwight. "An Exchange of Notes on T. S. Eliot: A Rejoinder," Theology Today, 7, #4 (January, 1951), 507-508. Cf., R. Gregor Smith. "An Exchange of Notes on T. S. Eliot: A Critique," Theology Today, 7, #4 (January, 1951), 503-506.

87a ______________. "T. S. Eliot's Quest for Certitude," Theology Today, 7, #2 (July, 1950), 228-236.

88 Enright, D. J. "On Not Teaching The Cocktail Party: A Professorial Dialogue," The Apothecary's Shop: Essays on Literature. London: Secker & Warburg, 1957, pp. 206-211.

89 Fallon, Gabriel. "After the Party," IrishM, 79 (September, 1951-52), 389-393.

90 Fluchère, Henri. "Le Drame Poétique de T. S. Eliot: The Cocktail Party," EA, 5 (May, 1952), 122-135.

91 Gardner, Helen. "The Cocktail Party," T&T, 31 (March 25, 1950-51), 284-285.

92 ________. "The Comedies of T. S. Eliot," SR, 74, #1 (January-March, 1966), 153-175. The Cocktail Party, "built on the distinction between ... eros and agape," involves self-discovery.

92a ________. "The Comedies of T. S. Eliot," T. S. Eliot: The Man and His Work. Allen Tate, ed. New York: Delacorte Pr., 1966, pp. 169-170.

93 ________. "The Comedies of T. S. Eliot," EDH, 34 (1966), 55-73. "No other plays of our generation present with equal force, ... our almost ... unlimited powers of self-deception...."

94 Gassner, John. "T. S. Eliot: The Poet as Anti-Modernist," The Theatre in Our Times. New York: Crown Pubs., 1954, pp. 267-281.

95 Gillett, Eric. "Mr. Eliot Throws a Party," NatlR, 134 (February, 1950-51), 140-147.

96 Goldmann, Wilhelm. Mythos-Neuplatonismus-Mystik: Studien zur Gestaltung des Alkestisstoffes. Munich: Wilhelm Goldmann, 1972. Devotes a long chapter to The Cocktail Party and its relation to Euripides and others.

97 Hamalian, Leo. "Mr. Eliot's Saturday Evening Service," Accent, 10 (Autumn, 1950), 195-206. Says aim is to "illuminate the text of [The Cocktail Party] ... by showing how it is related to, and grows out of, ideas contained in his poems, essays, and other plays."

98 Hamilton, Iain. "Reflections on The Cocktail Party" [an interview and criticism], WorldR, n.s. #9 (November, 1949), 19-22.

99 Hanzo, Thomas. "Eliot and Kierkegaard: 'The Meaning of Happening' in The Cocktail Party," MD, 3 (May, 1960), 52-59. Kierkegaard's description of despair helps to understand what happens in The Cocktail Party.

100 Harding, D. W. "Progression of Theme in Eliot's Modern Plays," KR, 18, #3 (Summer, 1956), 337-360.

101 Hardy, John Edward. "An Antic Disposition," SR, 65 (Winter, 1957), 50-60. Examines the character Harcourt-Reilly in The Cocktail Party.

102 Heilman, Robert B. "Alcestis and The Cocktail Party," CL, 5 (Spring, 1953), 105-116.

103 Heywood, Robert. "Everybody's Cocktail Party," Renascence, 3, #1 (Autumn, 1950), 28-30.

104 Hobson, Harold. Verdict at Midnight. London: Longmans, Green & Co., 1952, pp. 183-185.

105 Hochwald, Ilse E. "Eliot's Cocktail Party and Goethe's Wahlverwandtschaften," GR, 29 (December, 1954), 254-259. Goethe's novel considered "a genuine source for The Cocktail Party."

106 Holland, Joyce M. "Human Relations in Eliot's Drama," Renascence, 22 (1970), 151-161.

107 Hollis, Christopher. "Saint of the Cocktail Bar?" List (August 30, 1951), 337-338.

108 Hovey, Richard P. "Psychiatrist and Saint in The Cocktail Party," L&P, 9 (Summer-Fall, 1959), 51-55. Eliot's inadequate understanding of "dynamic depth psychology" limits his insight into Christianity.

109 Inge, W. Motter. "The Bookshelf" (Review), ThA, 34 (May, 1950), 8-9.

110 Jones, David E. "Plays in a Contemporary Setting: The Cocktail Party," The Plays of T. S. Eliot. London: Routledge & Kegan Paul; Toronto U. Pr., 1960, pp. 123-154.

111 Kee, Howard C. "The Bible and the Work of Eliot and Sitwell," Friends Intelligencer, 109 (November, 1952), 641-642.

112 Kintanar, Thelma B. "T. S. Eliot's The Cocktail Party," DilR, 7 (October, 1959), 440-447. The play shows how the Chamberlaynes "find their place in the Christian order of things."

113 Klatt, Heinz Günther. Sanatorium einer Ehe. Versuch einer Deutung von T. S. Eliot's Cocktail Party. Hannover, Lutherhaus-Verlag, 1952.

114 Koch, Vivienne. "Programme Notes on The Cocktail Party," PoetryQt, 11 (Winter, 1949), 248-251.

115 Kramer, Hilton. "T. S. Eliot in New York (Notes on the End of Something)," WestR, 14 (Summer, 1950), 303-305. Critical review.

116 Lawlor, John. "The Formal Achievement of The Cocktail Party," VQR, 30, #3 (Summer, 1954), 431-451. Notes blending of satirical comedy and the high comedy of "Romance" in the consulting-room scene.

116a Lawrence, Seymour. "Review," WN, 9 (1950), 120-122.

117 Leggatt, Alison. "A Postscript from Mrs. Chamberlayne and Mrs. Guzzard," T. S. Eliot: A Symposium for His Seventieth Birthday. Neville Braybrooke, ed. New York: Farrar, Straus & Cudahy, 1958, pp. 79-80.

118 Levine, George. "The Cocktail Party and Clara Hopgood," GSE, 1, #2 (Winter, 1958), 4-11. A comparison.

119 Lightfoot, Marjorie Jean. "T. S. Eliot's The Cocktail Party: An Experiment in Prosodic Description," DA, 25 (Northwestern U., 1965), 6630.

120 ____________. "The Uncommon Cocktail Party," MD, 11, #4 (February, 1969), 382-395. "... In using 4-stress measured accentual verse, with variants, T. S. Eliot developed a verse form ... admirably suited for modern verse drama."

121 McLaughlin, John J. "A Daring Metaphysic: The Cocktail Party," Renascence, 3, #1 (Autumn, 1950), 15-28.

122 Mambrino, Jean. "Un Divertissement métaphysique: The Cocktail Party," Etudes (Paris), 273 (June, 1952), 351-362.

123 Morgan, Frederick. "Chronicles: Notes on the Theater," HudR, 3, #2 (Summer, 1950), 290-293.

124 Munz, Peter. "The Devil's Dialectic, or The Cocktail Party," HJ, 49 (April, 1950-51), 256-263.

125 Murry, J. Middleton. "Mr. Eliot's Cocktail Party," FnR, 1008, n.s. (December, 1950), 391-398. Relates the play to Family Reunion.

125a ____________. "The Plays of T. S. Eliot: The Cocktail Party," Unprofessional Essays. London: J. Cape, 1956, pp. 162-176.

126 Nathan, George Jean. "The Theatre: Clinical Notes," AmMerc, 70, #317 (May, 1950), 557-558.

127 Oberg, Arthur K. "The Cocktail Party and the Illusion of Autonomy," MD, 11 (September, 1968), 187-194. The role of language in the play.

128 Packard, William. "Poetry in the Theater--V," Trace, 66 (Fall, 1967), 447-455. Eliot's play one of the examples discussed.

128a Parsons, Geoffrey. "Solving Some of Eliot's Riddles," NYHT

(February 12, 1950), Sec. 5, pp. 1, 2. Interview with Martin Browne.

129 Paul, David. "Euripides and Mr. Eliot," TC, 152 (August, 1952), 174-180. Influence of Euripides on The Cocktail Party.

130 Peacock, Ronald. "Public and Private Problems in Modern Drama," Bulletin of John Rylands Library (Manchester), 36 (1953-54), 38-55; repr., in TDR, 3, #3 (March, 1959), 58-72.

131 Peschmann, Hermann. "The Cocktail Party: Some Links between the Poems and Plays of T. S. Eliot," Wind and Rain, 7, #1 (Autumn, 1950), 53-58.

132 Peter, John. "Sin and Soda: The Cocktail Party," Scrutiny, 17, #1 (Spring, 1950), 61-66.

133 Pick, John. "A Note on The Cocktail Party," Renascence, 3, #1 (Autumn, 1950), 30-32.

134 Popkin, Henry. "Theatre Letter," KR, 12, #2 (Spring, 1950), 337-339.

134a Porter, Thomas E. "The Old Woman, the Doctor, and the Cook: 'The Cocktail Party,'" Myth and Modern American Drama. Detroit: Wayne State U. Pr., 1969, pp. 53-76.

135 Quin, I. T. "The Cocktail Party," IrishMo, 79 (June, 1951-52), 259-263.

136 Rebora, Roberto. "La discussione continue: Cocktail Party commedia dell' uomo vuoto," FLe, 52 (December 31, 1950), 1, 8.

137 Reckford, Kenneth J. "Heracles and Mr. Eliot," CL, 16 (Winter, 1964), 1-18. Influence of Euripides's Alcestis on Eliot's play.

138 Reed, Henry. "Towards The Cocktail Party," List, 45 (May 10, and May 17, 1951), 763-764, 803-804.

139 Rexine, John E. "Classical and Christian Foundations of T. S. Eliot's Cocktail Party," BA, 39 (Winter, 1965), 21-26. The "... similarities [of the play] to Euripides' Alcestis are closely interwoven with Christian symbolism, other Greek myths, and similarities to Eliot's own The Waste Land."

140 Robbins, Rossell Hope. "A Possible Analogue for The Cocktail Party," ES, 34 (August, 1953), 165-167. Charles Williams' novel, Descent into Hell (London, 1937), suggested as an analogue.

141 ________. The T. S. Eliot Myth. New York: Schuman, 1951-52, pp. 97-112.

141a Russell, Peter. "A Note on Eliot's New Play," Nine, 1 (October, 1949), 28-29.

142 Schwartz, Edward. "Eliot's Cocktail Party and the New Humanism," PQ, 32, #1 (January, 1953), 58-68.

143 Scott, N. A., Jr. "T. S. Eliot's The Cocktail Party: Of Redemption and Vocation," Religion in Life, 20, #2 (Spring, 1951), 286-294.

144 Sena, Vinod. "The Ambivalence of The Cocktail Party," MD, 14 (February, 1972), 392-404. Though Eliot's Guardians are an aid in the structural pattern of the play, they weaken it as Christian drama.

145 Sherek, Henry. "On Giving a Cocktail Party," ThA, 34, #4 (April, 1950), 25-26.

146 Shuman, R. Baird. "Buddhistic Overtones in Eliot's The Cocktail Party," MLN, 72 (June, 1957), 426-427. Buddhistic elements appear in Sir Henry Harcourt-Reilly's advice and in the actions of Celia.

147 ________. "Eliot's The Cocktail Party," Expl, 17 (April, 1959), Item 46. Sir Henry Harcourt-Reilly as celebrant or high priest.

148 Simiot, Bernard. "La Cocktail Party," HeM, 9 (June, 1954), 432-435.

149 Smith, Carol H. "The Cocktail Party," T. S. Eliot's Dramatic Theory and Practice: From Sweeney Agonistes to The Elder Statesman. Princeton, N. J.: Princeton U. Pr., 1963, pp. 147-183.

150 Smith, Grover, Jr. "Hieronym's Mad Againe: The Cocktail Party," T. S. Eliot's Poetry and Plays. Chicago: U. of Chicago Pr., 1956, pp. 214-227.

150a Smith, R. G. "An Exchange of Notes on T. S. Eliot: A Critique," Theology Today, 7, #4 (January, 1951), 503-506. Cf., Wilbur Dwight Dunkel, "An Exchange of Notes on T. S. Eliot: A Rejoinder," Theology Today, 7, #4 (January, 1951), 507-508.

151 Speaight, Robert. "Sartre and Eliot," Drama, n. s., 17 (Summer, 1950), 15-17.

151a Spender, Stephen. "On The Cocktail Party," The Year's Work in Literature, 1950. John Lehmann, ed. London: Longmans, Green, 1951, pp. 17-23.

152 Steiger, Emil. "Gehalt and Gestalt des Dramas The Cocktail Party von T. S. Eliot," NS, 7/8 (1954), 311-318.

153 Stein, Walter. "After the Cocktails," EIC, 3 (January, 1953), 85-104.

154 Thrash, Lois G. "A Source for the Redemption Theme in The Cocktail Party," TSLL, 9 (Winter, 1968), 547-553. Charles Williams's The Greater Trumps suggested as source.

155 Thurber, James. "What Cocktail Party?" NY, 26 (April 1, 1950), 26-29.

156 Toms, Newby. "Eliot's The Cocktail Party: Salvation and the Common Routine," ChS, 47, #2 (Summer, 1964), 125-138. Considers The Cocktail Party both a comedy of manners and a morality play.

157 Valette, Jacques. "Dégustation d'un cocktail," MdF, 1049 (January, 1951), 140-142.

158 Vassilieff, Elizabeth. "Piers to Cocktails," Meanjin, 9, #3 (Spring, 1950), 193-203.

159 Vincent, C. J. "A Modern Pilgrim's Progress," QQ, 57, #3 (Autumn, 1950), 346-352.

160 Weisstein, Ulrich. "The Cocktail Party: An Attempt at Interpretation on Mythological Grounds," WestR, 16 (Spring, 1952), 232-240.

161 ____________. "Form as Content in the Drama of T. S. Eliot," WestR, 23 (Spring, 1959), 239-246. The Cocktail Party must be called "a failure rather than a success."

162 Williams, Raymond. "Tragic Resignation and Sacrifice," CritQ, 5, #1 (Spring, 1963), 5-19.

163 Wimsatt, W. K., Jr. "Eliot's Comedy," SR, 58 (October, 1950), 666-678; repr., in Hateful Contraries, Lexington: Univ. of Kentucky, 1965, pp. 184-200.

164 Winter, Jack. "'Prufrockism' in The Cocktail Party," MLQ, 22 (June, 1961), 135-148.

165 Wiseman, James. "Of Loneliness and Communion," Drama-Crit, 5, #1 (February, 1962), 14-21.

166 Wool, Sandra. "Weston Revisited," Accent, 10 (August, 1950), 207-212. The play interpreted in terms of Weston's From Ritual to Romance.

167 Worsley, T. C. The Fugitive Art. Dramatic Commentaries, 1947-51. London: John Lehmann, 1952, pp. 144-146.

168 Wren-Lewis, John. "The Passing of Puritanism," CritQ, 5 (Winter, 1963), 295-305. Modern society makes it possible to "avoid puritanism and world-denial without sacrificing personal sensitivity." The Cocktail Party exemplifies such a combination of denial and affirmation.

169 Wyatt, Euphemia Van Rensselaer. "Theater" (review), Catholic World, 170, #1020 (March, 1950), 466-467.

170 Yoklavich, John M. "Eliot's Cocktail Party and Plato's Symposium," N&Q, 196 (December 8, 1951), 541-542.

171 Zolotow, Maurice. "Psychoanalyzing the Doctor," NYT (February 26, 1950), Sec. 2, p. 3. Interview of Alec Guinness, who played Sir Henry Harcourt-Reilly in the original production.

THE CONFIDENTIAL CLERK

172 Appia, H. [The Confidential Clerk], LitMod, 49 (1955-1956), 274.

173 Arrowsmith, William. "Eliot and Euripides," Arion, 4, #1 (Spring, 1965), 21-35.

174 __________. "Menander and Milk Wood," HudR, 7, #2 (Summer, 1954), 291-296.

175 __________. "Transfiguration in Eliot and Euripides," SR, 63 (Summer, 1955), 421-442; repr., in English Stage Comedy. W. K. Wimsatt, Jr. New York: Columbia U. Pr., 1955, pp. 148-172. Analysis of Eliot and Euripides relative to "double reality."

176 Beaufort, John. "The Confidential Clerk on Broadway" CSMM, (February 20, 1954), 16.

177 Bellow, Saul. "Theatre Chronicle," PartisanR, 21, #3 (May-June, 1954), 313-315.

178 Brooke, Nicholas. "The Confidential Clerk: A Theatrical Review," DUJ, 46, #1 (December, 1953), 66-70.

179 Brown, Spencer. "T. S. Eliot's Latest Poetic Drama," Commentary, 17 (April, 1954), 367-372. The Confidential Clerk proves Eliot is a "second-rate playwright."

180 Browne, E. Martin. "The Confidential Clerk," The Making of T. S. Eliot's Plays. New York: Cambridge U. Pr., 1969, pp. 249-294.

181 ________. "From The Rock to The Confidential Clerk," T. S. Eliot: A Symposium for His Seventieth Birthday. Neville Braybrooke, ed. New York: Farrar, Straus & Cudahy, 1958, pp. 57-69.

182 Cazamian, L. "The Confidential Clerk," EA, 8 (1955-1956), 271-272.

183 Colby, Robert A. "Orpheus in the Counting House: The Confidential Clerk," PMLA, 72, #4 (September, 1957), 791-802. In the play, Eliot has analyzed the problems of twentieth-century man: "his loneliness ... his incommunicability ... his insecurity...."

184 Dobrée, Bonamy. "The Confidential Clerk," SR, 62 (Winter, 1954), 117-131.

185 ________. "On Two Plays by Eliot: The Confidential Clerk...." The Lamp and the Lute. New York: Barnes & Noble, 1964, pp. 122-141.

186 Donoghue, Denis. "The Confidential Clerk," The Third Voice. Princeton, N. J.: Princeton U. Pr., 1959, pp. 138-157.

187 Fergusson, Francis. "Three Allegorists: Brecht, Wilder, and Eliot," SR, 64 (October-December, 1956), 562-569, 571-572.

188 Findlater, Richard. "The Camouflaged Dream," TC, 154, #920 (October, 1953), 311-316. Considers the play a failure because it lacks "emotional unity."

189 Gardner, Helen. "The Comedies of T. S. Eliot," SR, 74, #1 (January-March, 1966), 153-175.

189a ________. "The Comedies of T. S. Eliot: The Confidential Clerk," EDH, 34 (1966), 55-73.

190 ________. [The Confidential Clerk], NS&N, 47, #1202 (March 20, 1954), 373-374.

191 Giudici, Giovanni, "La via della saggezza" [The Confidential Clerk] FLe, 9 (May 2, 1954), 1.

192 Harding, D. W. "Progression of Theme in Eliot's Modern Plays," KR, 18, #3 (Summer, 1956), 337-360.

192a Hartley, Anthony. "The Drama and Mr. Eliot," Spectator (March 26, 1954), 364-365.

193 Hewes, Henry. "T. S. Eliot: Confidential Playwright," SatR, 36, #35 (August 29, 1953), 26-28.

194 Hivnor, Mary. "Theatre Letter," KR, 16 (1954), 463-465.

195 Holland, Joyce M. "Human Relations in Eliot's Drama," Renascence, 22 (1970), 151-161. Eliot's view of human relationships in the plays. Celia's martyrdom is balanced by Edward's and Lavinia's revitalization.

195a Hynes, Sam. "Religion in the West End," Cw, 59, #19 (February 12, 1954), 475-578. Comparison of Confidential Clerk with Graham Greene's The Living Room.

196 Jones, David E. "Plays in a Contemporary Setting: The Confidential Clerk," The Plays of T. S. Eliot. London: Routledge & Kegan Paul, 1960, pp. 155-178.

196a Kirk, Russell. "Two Plays of Resignation," Month, 10 (October, 1953), 223-229.

197 Leggatt, Alison. "A Postscript from Mrs. Chamberlayne and Mrs. Guzzard," T. S. Eliot: A Symposium for His Seventieth Birthday. Neville Braybrooke, ed. New York: Farrar, Straus & Cudahy, 1958, pp. 79-80.

198 Melchiori, Giorgio. "The Baroque Theatre: The Confidential Clerk," The Tightrope Walkers: Studies of Mannerism in Modern English Literature. London: Routledge & Kegan Paul, 1956, pp. 248-254.

199 Mitchell, John D. "Applied Psychoanalysis in the Drama," AI, 14 (Fall, 1957), 263-280. Analysis of The Confidential Clerk.

200 Mosley, Nicholas. "Mr. Eliot's Confidential Clerk: The Importance of Being Amusing," European, 13 (March, 1954), 38-44.

201 Sampley, Arthur M. "The Woman Who Wasn't There: Lacuna in T. S. Eliot," SAQ, 67 (Autumn, 1968), 603-610. "... In the body of [Eliot's] work from the beginning through The Confidential Clerk one does not find a woman who has achieved a satisfying emotional relationship with a man."

202 Schlüter, Kurt. Der Mensch als Schauspieler. Bonn: 1962. A "study in the meaning of Eliot's social dramas," particularly The Confidential Clerk and The Elder Statesman.

203 Smith, Carol H. "The Confidential Clerk," T. S. Eliot's Dramatic Theory and Practice from Sweeney Agonistes to The Elder Statesman. Princeton, N. J.: Princeton U. Pr., 1963, pp. 184-213.

204 Smith, Grover, Jr. "His Father's Business: The Confidential Clerk," T. S. Eliot's Poetry and Plays. Chicago: U. of Chicago Pr., 1956, pp. 228-243.

205 Spelvin, George. "Confidentially, 'Clerk' Had 'em Confused," ThA, 38 (May, 1954), 77, 91. Review of the critics' estimate of the play.

206 Voisine, Jaques. "Le Problème du Drame Poétique selon T. S. Eliot," EA, 19 (October-December, 1956), 289-302. Eliot's theories of poetic drama expressed in various essays reach "fruition" in The Confidential Clerk.

207 Weightman, J. G. "Edinburgh, Elsinore and Chelsea," TC, 154, #920 (October, 1953), 306-308.

208 Wilkinson, Burke. "A Most Serious Comedy by Eliot," NYT (February 7, 1954), Sec. 2, p. 1, col. 5. An interview of E. Martin Browne.

209 Williamson, Audrey. "Eliot, Whiting and Fry: The Confidential Clerk," Contemporary Theatre, 1953-56. London: Rockliff, 1956; New York: Macmillan, 1956, pp. 22-26.

THE ELDER STATESMAN

210 Balakanian, Nona. "Affirmation and Love in Eliot," NewL, 42, #19 (May 11, 1959), 20-21. The Elder Statesman suggests Dante's Paradiso, "without strife or suffering, and in the presence of a loving, forgiving person, the penitent finds both freedom and bliss."

211 Boardman, Gwenn R. "Restoring the Hollow Man," Rev (Oxford), #4 (November, 1962), 35-45. "Lord Calverton finds peace at the end of The Elder Statesman in a symbolic gesture that expresses Eliot's recurrent theme of the restoration of the hollow man...."

212 Brien, Alan. "The Invisible Dramatist," Spectator, 201 (September 5, 1958), 305-306. Finds The Elder Statesman "a zombie play designed for the living dead."

213 Browne, E. Martin. "The Elder Statesman," The Making of T. S. Eliot's Plays. New York: Cambridge U. Pr., 1969, pp. 307-344.

214 Dobrée, Bonamy. "The Elder Statesman," The Lamp and the Lute. New York: Barnes & Noble, 1964, pp. 141-149.

215 ____________. "The London Stage," SR, 67, #1 (Winter,

1959), 109-115. Eliot's drama appeals to the conscience or "the consciousness of self," rather than to the passions or the intellect.

216 Donoghue, Denis. "The Elder Statesman," The Third Voice. Princeton, N.J.: Princeton U. Pr., 1959, pp. 158-168.

217 ________. "Eliot in Fair Colonus," Studies, 48 (Spring, 1959), 49-58. Analysis of The Elder Statesman shows that Eliot's plays "strive toward the condition of prayer," and that the play "bears some relation to Oedipus at Colonus."

218 Everett, Barbara. "The Elder Statesman," CritQ, 1 (1959), 163-164, 166.

219 Fleming, Rudd. "The Elder Statesman and Eliot's 'Programme for the Métier of Poetry,'" WSCL, 2, #1 (Winter, 1961), 54-64.

220 Gardner, Helen. "The Comedies of T. S. Eliot," SR, 74, #1 (January-March, 1966), 153-175.

221 Hewes, Henry. "His New Play: The Elder Statesman," SatR, 41, #37 (September 13, 1958), 30-31.

222 Holland, Joyce M. "Human Relations in Eliot's Drama," Renascence, 22 (1970), 151-161.

223 Jones, David E. "Plays in a Contemporary Setting: The Elder Statesman," The Plays of T. S. Eliot. London: Routledge & Kegan Paul, 1960, pp. 179-209.

224 Kenner, Hugh. "For Other Voices," Poetry, 95, #1 (October, 1959), 36-40. "... The verse of The Elder Statesman, like the language of Euclid, is coolly adequate to anything that requires saying...."

225 Kermode, Frank. "The Elder Statesman," Spectator (April 10, 1959), 513.

226 Melchiori, Giorgio. "L'ultima commedia di Eliot," SA, 5 (1959), 233-242.

227 Milward, Peter. "'In the End Is My Beginning': A Study of T. S. Eliot's The Elder Statesman in Comparison with The Waste Land," SELit, English No. (1967), 1-13.

228 Moffa, Marisa. "Ibsen e The Elder Statesman," SA, 8 (1962), 202-211.

229 Mudford, P. G. "T. S. Eliot's Plays and the Tradition of 'High Comedy,'" CritQ, 16 (Summer, 1974), 127-140.

In the tradition of high comedy, Eliot's plays provide "laughter at human folly."

230 Naik, M. K. "The Elder Statesman and An Ideal Husband: A Study in Comparison," Literary Studies. K. P. K. Menon, et al., eds. Aiyer: Trivandrum, 1973, pp. 70-77.

231 Okumura, Mifune. "T. S. Eliot's The Elder Statesman," SELit, 37 (October, 1960), 53-66. Study of the difficulty Eliot faces in trying to create poetic drama with the theme of faith.

232 Papajewski, Helmut. "Thomas Stearns Eliot: The Elder Statesman," Das moderne englische Drama. Horst Oppel, ed. Berlin: Erich Schmidt, 1963, pp. 332-344.

233 Salmon, Christopher, and Leslie Paul. "Two Views of Mr. Eliot's New Play," List, 60 (September 4, 1958), 340-341.

234 Sampley, Arthur M. "The Woman Who Wasn't There: Lacuna in T. S. Eliot," SAQ, 67, #4 (Autumn, 1968), 603-610.

235 Schlüter, Kurt. Der Mensch als Schauspieler: Studien zur Deutung von T. S. Eliots Gesellschaftsdramen. Bonn: Bouvier, 1962.

236 Smith, Carol H. "The Elder Statesman," T. S. Eliot's Dramatic Theory and Practice. Princeton, N.J.: Princeton U. Pr., 1963, pp. 214-239.

237 ____________. "From Sweeney Agonistes to The Elder Statesman: A Study of the Dramatic Theory and Practice of T. S. Eliot," DA, 23 (U. of Michigan: 1962), 635-636.

238 Smith, Grover, Jr. "The Ghosts in T. S. Eliot's The Elder Statesman," N&Q, 7, n.s. (June, 1969), 233-235. The ghosts cause Claverton to re-examine his past life.

239 Stanford, Derek. "Mr. Eliot's New Play," ConR, #1114 (October, 1958), 199-201; expanded in QQ, 65 (Winter, 1959), 682-689. "The world of 'the hollow men,' terminating with a whimper, now regenerates itself with a kiss."

240 Tbg [sic]. "Kritische Ruckschau," Forum (Austria), 8 (May, 1961), 178. Finds the play somewhat boring.

241 Unger, Leonard. "Deceptively Simple--and Too Simple," VQR, 35, #3 (Summer, 1959), 501-504. The major flaw seems to be in Eliot's too-simple view of love.

242 Voisine, Jacques. "The Elder Statesman," EA, 13 (1960), 73-74.

243 Weales, G. "The Elder Statesman," KR, 21 (1959), 473-478.

244 Weightman, J. G. "After Edinburgh," TC, 164, #980 (October, 1958), 342-344.

245 Willingham, John R. "The Elder Statesman," BA, 33 (1959), 410.

246 Worsley, T. C. "Mr. Eliot at Colonus," NS&N, 56, #1433 (August 30, 1958), 245-246.

THE FAMILY REUNION

247 Anthony, E. "The Family Reunion," SR, 47 (1939), 599-604.

248 Avery, Helen P. "The Family Reunion Reconsidered," ETJ, 17, #1 (March, 1965), 10-18. Considers that the technique and ideas of the play are closer to the avant garde theater of 1965 than to the drama of 1938, when it was written.

249 Barber, C. L. "T. S. Eliot after Strange Gods," SoR, 6, #2 (Autumn, 1940), 387-416; repr., in T. S. Eliot: A Selected Critique. Leonard Unger, ed. New York: Rinehart & Co., 1948, 415-443. "The exclusion of Christian terms in The Family Reunion is part of an effort to begin again at the beginning, at the point where the decay of faith has left modern men.... "

250 Barnes, T. R. "Poets and the Drama," Scrutiny, 4, #2 (1935), 189-195.

251 Battenhouse, Roy W. "Eliot's The Family Reunion as Christian Prophecy," Christendom, 10, #3 (Summer, 1945), 307-321.

252 Bland, D. S. "T. S. Eliot's Case-Book," MLN, 75 (January, 1960), 23-26. Thinks the play was influenced by the novels of Ivy Compton-Burnett.

253 Bodkin, Maud. "The Eumenides and the Present-day Consciousness," Adelphi, 15, #8 (May, 1939), 411-413.

253a __________. The Quest for Salvation in an Ancient and a Modern Play. London: Oxford U. Pr., 1941. Contrasts the Oresteia and The Family Reunion.

254 Brooks, Cleanth. "Sin and Expiation," PartisanR, 6, #4 (Summer, 1939), 114-116.

255 Brooks, Harold F. "The Family Reunion and Columbe's Birthday," TLS, #2654 (December 12, 1952), 819. Browning's play suggested as an influence.

256 Browne, E. Martin. "The Family Reunion," The Making of T. S. Eliot's Plays. New York: Cambridge U. Pr., 1969, pp. 90-151.

257 __________. Introduction. Four Modern Verse Plays. Harmondsworth, Middlesex, England: Penguin Books, 1957, pp. 8-10.

258 Carne-Ross, Donald. "The Position of The Family Reunion in the Work of T. S. Eliot," RLM, I, #2 (October, 1950), 125-139.

259 Cazamian, Louis. "The Family Reunion," EA, 4 (1940), 79-81.

260 Conrad, S. "The Family Reunion," SatR, 19 (April, 1939), 12.

261 Donoghue, Denis. "The Family Reunion," The Third Voice. Princeton, N.J.: Princeton U. Pr., 1959, pp. 94-113.

262 Fergusson, Francis. "Notes on the Theatre," SoR, 5, #3 (1939-40), 562-564.

263 Ferrara, Fernando. "Aspetti e significati della Family Reunion di T. S. Eliot," SA, 4 (1958), 247-294.

264 Floersheimer, Stephen. "Reply," EIC, 1 (July, 1951), 298-301. Cf., J. Middleton Murry, "A Note on The Family Reunion," EIC, 1 (January, 1951), 67-73.

265 Garrett, John. "Drama," The English-Speaking World, 21, #6 (June, 1939), 278-279.

266 Gaskell, Ronald. "The Family Reunion," EIC, 12 (July, 1962), 292-301.

267 Gassner, John. "Broadway in Review," ETJ, 11, #1 (March, 1959), 29-39.

268 Germer, Rudolf. "Thomas Stearns Eliot: The Family Reunion," Das moderne englische Drama. Horst Oppel, ed. Berlin: Erich Schmidt, 1963, pp. 220-241.

268a Greenwood, Ormerod. "T. S. Eliot's The Family Reunion," The Playwright: A Study of Form, Method and Tradition in the Theatre. London: Pitman, 1950, pp. 103-109.

269 Gregory, Horace. "The Unities and Eliot," L&LT, 23 (October-December, 1939), 53-60.

270 Hamalian, Leo. "Wishwood Revisited," Renascence, 12, #4 (Summer, 1960), 167-173. "The Eumenides are pivots in the pattern of [The Family Reunion] and not merely adjuncts to the action ... as most critics have maintained."

271 Harding, D. W. "Progression of Theme in Eliot's Modern Plays," KR, 18, #3 (Summer, 1956), 337-360.

272 Hausermann, H. W. "East Coker and The Family Reunion," L&LT, 47 (October, 1945), 32-38.

273 Horton, Philip. "Speculations on Sin," KR, 1, #3 (Summer, 1939), 330-333.

274 Inserillo, Charles R. "Wish and Desire: Two Poles of the Imagination in the Drama of Arthur Miller and T. S. Eliot," Eliot," XUS, 1 (Summer-Fall, 1962), 247-248.

275 Isaacs, Jennifer I. "Eliot the Poet-Playwright as Seen in The Family Reunion," English, 16, #93 (Autumn, 1966), 100-105. Despite two great scenes in the play, thinks cohesion is destroyed by idea.

276 Jack, P[eter] M[onroe]. "The Family Reunion," NYTBR (April 9, 1939), 2, 20.

277 Jamil, Maya. "Hamlet and The Family Reunion," Venture, 5, #1 (June, 1968), 21-29. Considers the two plays to be essentially the same in concept, theme, and structure, although Hamlet was misunderstood by Eliot as shown in his essay on that play.

278 Jones, David E. "Plays in a Contemporary Setting: The Family Reunion," The Plays of T. S. Eliot. London: Routledge & Kegan Paul, 1960, pp. 82-122.

279 Kelly, Bernard. [The Family Reunion], Blackfriars, 20, #231 (June, 1939), 469-471.

280 Knowlton, Edgar C. "A Playwright Preoccupied with Sin," SAQ, 38, #4 (October, 1939), 467-468.

281 Lightfoot, Marjorie J. "Purgatory and The Family Reunion: In Pursuit of Prosodic Description," MD, 7, #3 (December, 1964), 256-266. Influence of W. B. Yeats on Eliot's verse dramas.

282 Maccoby, H. Z. "Difficulties in the Plot of The Family

Reunion," N&Q, 15, #8 (August, 1968), 296-302. Notes that examination of chronology reveals contradictions and confusions.

283 ______. "The Family Reunion and Kipling's The House Surgeon," N&Q, 15 (n. s.), (February, 1968), 48-50.

284 MacNeice, Louis. "Original Sin: The Family Reunion," NR, 98, #1274 (May 3, 1939), 384-385.

285 Manuel, M. "The Family Reunion," Literary Studies: Homage to Dr. A. Sivaramasubramonia Aiyer. K. P. K. Menon, et al., eds. Aiyer Memorial Committee, 1973, pp. 229-255.

286 Moeller, Charles. "Religion and Literature: An Essay on Ways of Reading," Mansions of the Spirit. Melvin Zimmerman, tr. New York: Hawthorn Books, 1967, pp. 62-63.

287 Montgomerie, William. "Harry, Meet Mr. Prufrock (T. S. Eliot's Dilemma)," L&LT, 31, #51 (November, 1941), 115-128.

288 Mueller, William R. "Psychoanalyst and Poet: A Note," Psychoanalyst, 5 (Summer, 1957), 55-66. Psychoanalytic study of The Family Reunion.

289 Murry, J. Middleton. "Mr. Eliot's Cocktail Party," FnR, 1008, n. s., (December, 1950), 391-398. Relationship of the two plays, The Cocktail Party and The Family Reunion.

290 ______. "A Note on The Family Reunion," EIC, 1 (January, 1951), 67-73. Cf. Stephen Floersheimer. "Reply," EIC, 1 (July, 1951), 298-301.

291 Palmer, Richard E. "Existentialism in T. S. Eliot's The Family Reunion," MD, 5, #2 (September, 1962), 174-186. Four ways in which existentialism appears in the play.

292 Peacock, Ronald. "Public and Private Problems in Modern Drama," TDR, 3 (March, 1959), 58-72.

293 ______. "T. S. Eliot," The Poet in the Theatre. New York: Hill & Wang, 1946; repr., 1960, pp. 3-25.

294 Peter, John. "The Family Reunion," Scrutiny, 16 (September, 1949), 219-230.

295 Plewka, Kurt. "The Family Reunion, a Play by T. S. Eliot," NS, Heft 6 (1955), 264-276.

296 Porter, David H. "Ancient Myth and Modern Play: A Significant Counterpoint," CBull, 48, #1 (November, 1971), 1-9.

The Family Reunion named as one of the plays based on Greek myth in which there is tension between myth and play.

297 Pottle, Frederick A. "A Modern Verse Play," YR, 28 (June, 1939), 836-839.

298 Ransom, John Crowe. "T. S. Eliot as Dramatist," Poetry, 54, #5 (August, 1939), 264-271. In reviewing The Family Reunion, concludes that "[It] is not the Eliot we knew as a poet. It is that Eliot warmed over, for 'theatre.'"

299 Rezzano, Maria Clotilde. The Family Reunion: A Study. Argentine Association of English Culture. English Pamphlet Series No. 2, Buenos Aires, 1942.

300 Robbins, Rossell H. The T. S. Eliot Myth. New York: Schuman, 1951-52, pp. 97-112.

301 Roberts, Michael. "Mr. Eliot's New Play," LonMerc, 39, #234 (April, 1939), 641-642.

302 Russell, Peter. "A Note on Eliot's New Play," Nine, 1 (October, 1949), 28-29.

303 Schaeder, Grete, and Hans Heinrich Schaeder. "Mord im Dom," Ein Weg zu T. S. Eliot. Hameln: Verlag der Buchsterstube Fritz-Seifert, 1949, pp. 93ff. Mord im Dom in relation to The Family Reunion.

304 Schwartz, Delmore. "The Family Reunion," Nation, 148 (June, 1939), 676-677.

305 Scott, Nathan A., Jr. Rehearsals of Discomposure. New York: King's Crown Pr., 1952; London: John Lehmann, 1952, pp. 203-225, 230-238.

306 Scrimgeour, C. A. "The Family Reunion," EIC, 13 (1963), 104-106. Cf., Ronald Gaskell. EIC, 12 (1962), 292-301.

307 Sena, Vinod. "Eliot's The Family Reunion: A Study in Disintegration," SoR, n. s., #3 (Autumn, 1967), 895-921. The Family Reunion "fails to cohere as a work of art, adding up at every level, thematic, structural and verbal, to an excercise in disintegration and discontinuity."

308 Smith, Carol H. "The Family Reunion," T. S. Eliot's Dramatic Theory and Practice from Sweeney Agonistes to Elder Statesman. Princeton, N.J.: Princeton U. Pr., 1963, pp. 112-146.

309 Smith, Grover, Jr. "Bright Angels: The Family Reunion," T. S. Eliot's Poetry and Plays. Chicago: U. of Chicago Pr., 1956, pp. 196-213.

310 Spanos, William V. "T. S. Eliot's The Family Reunion: The Strategy of Sacramental Transfiguration," DramS, 4, #1 (Spring, 1964), 3-27. In this play Eliot pursues "the implications of a sacramental poetic, which reconciles poetry and everyday reality."

311 Spender, Stephen. "Books and the War--VII," Penguin New Writing. No. 8. John Lehmann, ed. Harmondsworth, England: Penguin, 1941, pp. 125-132.

312 Stamm, Rudolf. "The Orestes Theme in Three Plays by Eugene O'Neill, T. S. Eliot and Jean-Paul Sartre," ES, 30 (October, 1949), 244-255.

313 Suhrkamp, Peter. "T. S. Eliot und das Modell des antiken Dramas. Einführung in Der Familientag," Thema, No. 4 (1949), 21. [Hamburg]

314 Turnell, G. Martin. "Mr. Eliot's New Play," Scrutiny, 8, #1 (June, 1939), 108-114. With "the solitary exception of The Rock, The Family Reunion is the worst poem of any pretensions that Mr. Eliot has yet written."

315 Unger, Leonard. "T. S. Eliot's Rose Garden," SoR, 8 (1942), 667-689; repr., in T. S. Eliot: A Selected Critique. New York: 1948, pp. 374-394; The Man in the Name. Minneapolis: U. of Minnesota Pr., 1956, pp. 168-189.

316 Ward, Anne. "Speculations on Eliot's Time-World: An Analysis of The Family Reunion in Relation to Hulme and Bergson," AL, 21 (March, 1949), 18-34. "In Hulme's summary of Bergson's three-fold division of kinds of time-perception may be found a key to the structure of Eliot's time-world."

317 Wasson, Richard. "The Rhetoric of Theatre: The Contemporaneity of T. S. Eliot," DramS, 6, #3 (Spring, 1968), 231-243. Harry in The Family Reunion "is aware that he is a dramatic figure, a character in a play," and therefore, a study of Eliot's rhetoric enables us to "see more clearly the illusions of the presentational stage, and by implication the presentational world."

318 Weidlé, Wladimir. "Le renouveau du drame poétique en Angleterre et la Réunion de famille de T. S. Eliot," Le Mois, 9 (August, 1939), 147-156.

319 Wildi, Max. Die Dramen von T. S. Eliot. Kulture und Staatswissenschaftliche Schriften, Heft 97, Zurich: 1957. The Family Reunion and its background in Greek tragedy, especially Euripides.

319a Williams, Raymond. "Modern Experimental Drama: The Family Reunion," Drama in Performance. London: Frederick Muller, 1954; revised and extended, New York: Basic Books, 1968, pp. 134-148.

320 Williamson, Audrey. Contemporary Theatre, 1953-56. London: Rockliff, 1956, pp. 98-100.

321 Wood, Grace A. "Crime and Contrition in Literature," ConR, 198 (July, 1960), 391-397. Discussion of the Orestes theme in The Family Reunion.

322 Zabel, Morton Dauwen. "Two Years of Poetry, 1937-39," SoR, 5 (1939-40), 592. "Eliot's Family Reunion is a superior play by every measure ... superior in the central truth of its problem--the recovery of moral courage in a man who, by purging himself of a destroying sense of guilt, finds he must also destroy the sham ... of the decadent English gentility that bred him...."

MURDER IN THE CATHEDRAL

323 Adair, Patricia. "Mr. Eliot's Murder in the Cathedral," CamJ, 4, #2 (November, 1950), 83-95; excerpt, "Spokes of the Wheel: In the Cathedral," in Twentieth Century Interpretations. David R. Clark, ed. Englewood Cliffs, N.J.: Prentice-Hall, 1971, pp. 73-74.

324 Adams, John F. "The Fourth Temptation in Murder in the Cathedral," MD, 5, #4 (February, 1963), 381-388. Thomas must not take pride in his martyrdom--possibly the "fourth temptation." "Whether Thomas does or does not resist this final temptation" can never be known.

325 Anon. "Play for a Cathedral," CSMM, 28 (December 3, 1935), 30.

326 Arvin, Newton. "Murder in the Cathedral," NR, 85 (January, 1936), 290.

327 Auden, W. H. "The Martyr as Dramatic Hero," List, 79, #2023 (January 4, 1968), 1-6.

328 Barnes, T. R. "Poets and the Drama: Murder in the Cathedral," Scrutiny, 4, #2 (September, 1935), 189-191.

329 Battenhouse, Henry M. Poets of Christian Thought: Evaluations from Dante to T. S. Eliot. New York: Ronald Pr., (1947), pp. 167-170.

330 Beare, Robert L. "Notes on the Text of T. S. Eliot: Variants from Russell Square," SB, 9 (1957), 39-47.

331 Bengis, Nathan L. "Conan Doyle and T. S. Eliot," TLS (September 28, 1951), 613. In Murder in the Cathedral Eliot's use of the Musgrave Ritual is intentional.

332 Bischoff, Dietrich. "Der Mord im Münster," Die Sammlung [Göttingen], 3 (1948), 10-22.

333 Bittner, Anton. "Die Zeit in T. S. Eliots Mord im Dom," Pädagogische Provinz, 11 (1957), 381-389.

334 Blackmur, R. P. "T. S. Eliot: From Ash Wednesday to Murder in the Cathedral," T. S. Eliot: A Selected Critique. Leonard Unger, ed. New York: Rinehart, 1948, pp. 236-262.

335 Bland, D. S. "The Tragic Hero in Modern Literature," CamJ, 3 (January, 1950), 214-223.

336 Boulton, J. T. "The Use of Original Sources for the Development of a Theme: Eliot in Murder in the Cathedral," English, 11 (Spring, 1956), 2-8; excerpt, "Sources," Twentieth Century Interpretations of Murder in the Cathedral. David R. Clark, ed. Englewood Cliffs, N. J.: Prentice-Hall, 1971, pp. 74-79.

337 Bowers, John L. T. S. Eliot's Murder in the Cathedral. Cape Town: Cape Town U. Dept. of English, 1965.

338 Braybrook, Neville. T. S. Eliot: A Symposium for His Seventieth Birthday. London: Hart-Davis, 1958, passim.

339 Brooks, Cleanth, et al. An Approach to Literature. 3rd ed. New York: Appleton-Century-Crofts, 1952, pp. 754-757.

340 Brown, John Mason. "The High Excitements of Murder in the Cathedral," NYEPost (March, 1936), 18; repr., in Two on the Aisle. New York: Norton, 1938, pp. 124-126.

341 Browne, E. Martin. "The Dramatic Verse of T. S. Eliot," T. S. Eliot: A Symposium. Richard March and Tambimuttu, comps. Chicago: Regnery, 1949, pp. 196-207; excerpt, "The Priests," Twentieth Century Interpretations of Murder in the Cathedral. David R. Clark, ed. Englewood Cliffs, N.J.: Prentice-Hall, 1971, pp. 81-82.

342 ________. "From The Rock to The Confidential Clerk," in T. S. Eliot: A Symposium. Neville Braybrooke, ed. London: Hart-Davis, 1958, pp. 57-69.

343 ____________. "Henry II as Hero: Christopher Fry's New Play, Curtmantle," DramS, 2, #1 (Spring, 1962), 63-71. Comparison of Eliot's treatment of the story with that of Fry and Anouilh.

344 ____________. "A Most Serious Comedy by Eliot," NYT (February 7, 1954), Sec. 2, p. 1, col. 7. Describes Eliot's "team spirit" in work on the production.

345 ____________. "Murder in the Cathedral," The Making of T. S. Eliot's Plays. London: Cambridge U. Pr., 1969, pp. 34-79.

346 ____________. "Murder in the Cathedral--The Variations in the Text," Twentieth Century Interpretations of Murder in the Cathedral. David R. Clark, ed. Englewood Cliffs, N.J.: Prentice-Hall, 1971, pp. 99-106.

347 ____________. "T. S. Eliot in the Theatre: The Director's Memoirs," T. S. Eliot: The Man and His Work. Allan Tate, ed. New York: Delacorte, 1966, pp. 116-132.

348 Butler, John F. "Tragedy, Salvation and the Ordinary Man," LonQt and HolbornR, 162 (1937), 489-497.

349 Callahan, Elizabeth A. "The Tragic Hero in Contemporary Secular and Religious Drama," LHY, 8, #1-2 (January-July, 1967, 42-49. A study of the protagonists of Miller's The Crucible and Eliot's Murder in the Cathedral. Both are characteristic of the heroes of Greek tragedy.

350 Chang, Wang-Rok. "An Analysis of Murder in the Cathedral," ELLS, 10 (September, 1961), 280-291. A study of the theme, structure, Chorus, and sermon.

351 Chapman, Robert E. "Becket's Chameleon Character: An Analytical Study of the Universal Appeal of Thomas Becket's Dramatic Character," DAI, 33 (U. of So. Calif.: 1972), 848A.

352 Clark, David R., ed. Twentieth Century Interpretations of Murder in the Cathedral: A Collection of Critical Essays. Englewood Cliffs, N.J.: Prentice-Hall, 1971.

353 Clausen, Christopher. "A Source for Thomas Becket's Temptation in Murder in the Cathedral," N&Q, 21, #10 (October, 1974), 373-374. A suggested source is Sir Edwin Arnold's poem, "The Light of Asia," (1879).

354 Clutton-Brock, Alan. "T. S. Eliot and Conan Doyle," TLS (January 19, 1951-52), 37.

355 Colum, Mary M. "Life and Literature: Revival in the Theatre," Forum&C, 95, #6 (June, 1936), 344-345.

356 __________. "Spiritual and Temporal Order: Murder in the Cathedral," Forum&C, 95, #6 (June, 1936), 346-347. The theme is that "there are two orders in the world and that they can never coalesce--the spiritual order ... and the temporal order...."

357 Cutts, John P. "Evidence for Ambivalence of Motives in Murder in the Cathedral," CompD, 8 (Summer, 1974), 199-210. A study of Becket as "a character of ambiguous motives."

358 Dasgupta, Rabindrakumar. "T. S. Eliot's Murder in the Cathedral," CalcR, 69, #3 (December, 1938), 296-306.

359 Dean, Leonard F., ed. Nine Great Plays from Aeschylus to Eliot. Revised ed. New York: Harcourt, Brace, 1956, pp. 643-646.

360 Degroote, Gilbert. "Everyman en Murder in the Cathedral," HZM, 23 (1969), 42-46.

361 Dierickx, J. "King and Archbishop: Henry II and Becket from Tennyson to Fry," RLV, 28, #5 (1962), 424-435. A study of the Becket plays by Eliot, Fry, and Anouilh.

362 Donoghue, Denis. "Murder in the Cathedral," The Third Voice: Modern British and American Verse Drama. Princeton, N.J.: Princeton U. Pr., 1959), pp. 76-93.

363 Downey, Harris. "T. S. Eliot: Poet as Playwright," VQR, 12, #1 (January, 1936), 142-145.

364 Dukes, Ashley. "A Poet Turns Dramatist," NYT (February 20, 1938), Sec. 2, pp. 1, 3.

365 __________. "T. S. Eliot in the Theatre," T. S. Eliot: A Symposium. Richard March and Tambimuttu, comps. Freeport, N.Y.: Books for Libraries Pr., 1968, pp. 111-118.

366 Evans, R. Wallis. "Cymdeithaseg y Ddrama [A Sociology of the Drama, Part 2], YGen, 18, #1 (Winter, 1967-68), 42-46. Comparison of Eliot's play with Tennyson's Becket.

367 Farenc, J. "Murder in the Cathedral à la scène," EA (January, 1938), 27-35.

368 Fergusson, Francis. "Action as Passion: Tristan and Murder in the Cathedral," KR, 9, #2 (Spring, 1947), 201-221.

369 __________. "Murder in the Cathedral: The Theological Scene," The Idea of a Theater. Princeton, N.J.: Princeton U. Pr., 1949, pp. 222-234.

370 __________. "Notes on the Theater," SoR, 5 (1939), 562-564.

371 Ferrara, Fernando. Introduzione a Murder in the Cathedral di T. S. Eliot. Rome: Signorelli, 1957.

372 Fluchère, Henri. "Lettres étrangères," NRF, 47 (1936), 556-558.

373 __________. Meurtre dans la Cathédrale traduit de l'anglais et présenté par Henri Fluchere. (Les Cahiers du Rhône, Série Blanche.) Neuchatel: Éditions de la Baconnière, 1944, pp. 129-133.

374 Galinsky, Hans. "T. S. Eliot's Murder in the Cathedral," NS, Heft 7 (1958), 305-323.

375 Gardner, Helen. The Art of T. S. Eliot. New York: E. P. Dutton, 1959, pp. 127-139. Discusses the dramatic power of the Chorus.

376 Geraldine, Sister M. "The Rhetoric of Repetition in Murder in the Cathedral," Renascence, 19, #3 (Spring, 1967), 132-141. Discussion of three significant modes of repetition in Eliot's play.

377 Gerstenberger, Donna. "The Saint and the Circle: The Dramatic Potential of an Image," Criticism, 2, #4 (Fall, 1960), 336-341. Eliot's use of the image of the turning wheel and fixed point in Murder in the Cathedral shows the structural potentialities of an image.

378 Ghosh, P. C. "Poetic Drama and Murder in the Cathedral," CalcR, 2 (1961), 14-32.

379 Gielgud, Val. "Radio Play: In the Age of Television," ThA, 21 (February, 1937), 108-112. The success of Murder in the Cathedral as a radio play.

380 Goléa, Antoine. "The Modern Literary Opera," World Theatre, 7, #4 (Winter, 1958-59), 285-299. Ildebrando Pizzetti's setting of Eliot's Murder in the Cathedral.

381 Gregory, Horace. "Poets in the Theatre," Poetry, 48, #4 (July, 1936), 227-228.

382 Gross, John. "Eliot: From Ritual to Realism," Encounter, 24, #3 (March, 1965), 48-50. Considers Murder in the Cathedral Eliot's "high point."

383 Hoellering, George. "Filming Murder in the Cathedral," T. S. Eliot: A Symposium for His Seventieth Birthday. Neville Braybrooke, ed. New York: Farrar, Straus & Cudahy, 1958, pp. 81-84.

384 __________, and T. S. Eliot. The Film of Murder in the Cathedral. London: Faber & Faber; New York: Harcourt, 1952.

385 Holmes, John Haynes. "Murder in the Cathedral," Unity, 117 (August 3, 1936), 218.

386 Hönnighausen, L[othar]. "Die Verwendung der Dies Irae Sequenz in Eliots Murder in the Cathedral," NS, 14, #11 (November, 1965), 497-508.

387 Hübner, Walter. "T. S. Eliot und das neue Drama," NZ, 5 (1950), 337-352. Detailed analysis of Murder in the Cathedral.

388 Isaacs, Edith J. R. "Broadway in Review: Murder in the Cathedral," ThA, 22 (April, 1938), 254-255.

389 __________. "Saints and Law-Makers: Broadway in Review," ThA, 20, #5 (May, 1936), 341-343.

390 Isaacs, I. "T. S. Eliot and Conan Doyle," TLS (January 26, 1951-52), 53.

391 Jack, P. M. "Murder in the Cathedral," NYTBR (October 27, 1935), 11.

392 Jacobs, Arthur. "Murder in the Cathedral as an Opera," List, 59 (March 20, 1958), 504. 505.

393 Jennings, Humphrey. "Eliot and Auden and Shakespeare," New Verse, 18 (December, 1935), 4-7.

394 Jolivet, Philippe. "Le personnage de Thomas Becket dans Der Heilige de C. F. Meyer, Murder in the Cathedral de T. S. Eliot et Becket ou l'honneur de Dieu de Jean Anouilh, EG, 16 (July-September, 1961), 235-241.

395 Jones, David E. "Murder in the Cathedral," (1935); "Criticism of Murder in the Cathedral," The Plays of T. S. Eliot. London: Routledge & Kegan Paul; Toronto: Toronto U. Pr., 1960, pp. 50-81, 216-218.

396 Kantra, Robert A. "Satiric Theme and Structure in Murder in the Cathedral," MD, 10, #4 (February, 1968), 387-393.

397 Kazin, Alfred. "About T. S. Eliot: Murder in the Cathedral," NR, 85 (January 15, 1936), 290.

398 Kenner, Hugh. "Eliot's Moral Dialectic," HudR, 2 (Autumn, 1949), 421-428.

399 ________. "Murder in the Cathedral," The Invisible Poet: T. S. Eliot. New York: Obolensky, 1959, pp. 276-285.

400 Kivimaa, Kirsti. Aspects of Style in T. S. Eliot's Murder in the Cathedral. (Turun Yliopiston julkaisuja, Series B, 111). Turku, Finland: Turun Yliopisto, 1969.

401 Knieger, Bernard. "The Dramatic Achievement of T. S. Eliot," MD, 3, #4 (February, 1961), 387-392. Poetry in Murder in the Cathedral possesses "vividness of imagery and metaphor, portrayal of character ... by subtle shifts in poetic rhythms."

402 Koppenhaver, Allen J. "The Musical Design of T. S. Eliot's Murder in the Cathedral," HussR, 5, #1 (1971), 4-10.

403 ________. "T. S. Eliot's Murder in the Cathedral: A Study," DA, 25 (Duke U.: 1964), 2983.

404 Kornbluth, Martin L. "A Twentieth-Century Everyman," CE, 21, #1 (October, 1959), 26-29. Resemblances between Murder in the Cathedral and Everyman.

405 Kosok, Heinz. "Gestaltung und Funktion der 'Rechtfertigungsszene' in T. S. Eliots Murder in the Cathedral," NS, 12, #2 (February, 1963), 49-61. Discussion of the "justification" scene of the four knights and its function in the play.

406 Krieger, Murray. "The Critical Legacy of Matthew Arnold: Or the Strange Brotherhood of T. S. Eliot, I. A. Richards, and Northrop Frye," SoR, 5 (Spring, 1969), 457-474.

407 ________. "Murder in the Cathedral: The Limits of Drama and the Freedom of Vision," The Classic Vision: The Retreat from Extremity in Modern Literature. Baltimore: Johns Hopkins Pr., 1971, pp. 337-362.

408 ________. "Murder in the Cathedral: The Limits of Drama and the Freedom of Vision," The Shaken Realist: Essays in Modern Literature. Melvin J. Friedman and John B. Vickery, eds. Baton Rouge: Louisiana U. Pr., 1970, pp. 72-99.

409 ________. "T. S. Eliot: Expression and Impersonality," The New Apologists for Poetry. Minneapolis: U. of Minnesota Pr., 1956, pp. 46-56.

410 Krutch, Joseph Wood. "The Holy Blissful Martyr," Nation, 142, #3692 (April 8, 1936), 459-460.

411 Lally, Sister Mary A. "Comparative Study of Five Plays on the Becket Story: By Tennyson, Binyon, Eliot, Anouilh, and Fry," DA, 24 (Notre Dame: 1963), 2479.

412 Langslet, Lars Roar. "Tre dikteres mote med helgenen," KogK, 63, #7 (September, 1958), 406-415.

413 Lannes, Roger. "Les Spectacles de Paris," Fontaine, 45 (October, 1945), 733-735.

414 LeCroy, Anne. "Murder in the Cathedral: A Question of Structure," Essays in Memory of Christine Burleson in Language and Literature. Thomas G. Burton, ed. Johnson City: Res. Advisory Council, East Tennessee St. U., 1969, pp. 59-70.

415 Lemarchand, J. "Meurtre dans la Cathédrale au théâtre du Vieux-Colombier," Arche, 2 annee, No. 9, Vol. 3 (septembre, 1945), 121-123.

416 Lobb, K. Martyn. T. S. Eliot: Murder in the Cathedral. London: J. Brodie, 1950. Notes on chosen English texts.

417 Lodovici, C. V., tr. Assassino nella cattedrale. (Teatro dell' Università di Roma, Collezione di autori stranieri, I, pp. vii-xiv. [Introduction dates May, 1940.]

417a McCarthy, Patrick A. "Eliot's Murder in the Cathedral," Expl, 33, #1 (September 74), Item 7.

418 Maccoby, H. Z. "Two Notes on Murder in the Cathedral," N&Q, 14, #7 (July, 1967), 253-256; excerpt, "Thomas's Temptation," in Twentieth Century Interpretations of Murder in the Cathedral. David R. Clark, ed. Englewood Cliffs, N.J.: Prentice-Hall, 1971, pp. 93-96.

419 Martz, Louis L. "The Saint as Tragic Hero: Saint Joan and Murder in the Cathedral," Tragic Themes in Western Literature. Cleanth Brooks, ed. New Haven: Yale U. Pr., 1955, pp. 150-178.

420 ______________. "The Wheel and the Point: Aspects of Imagery and Theme in Eliot's Later Poetry," SR, 55 (Winter, 1947), 126-147; repr., in Twentieth Century Interpretations. David Clark, ed. Englewood Cliffs, N. J.: 1971, pp. 15-26; expanded in T. S. Eliot: A Selected Critique. Leonard Unger, ed. New York: Rinehart, 1948, pp. 444-462.

421 Mason, W. H. "Murder in the Cathedral." Oxford: Blackwell and Mott, 1962; New York: Barnes & Noble, 1963.

422 Matthiessen, F. O. "Murder in the Cathedral," SatR, 12 (October 12, 1935), 10-11.

423 ________. "Murder in the Cathedral," The Achievement of T. S. Eliot. New York: Oxford U. Pr., 1959, pp. 162-165.

424 Maxfield, Malinda R. "A Comparative Analysis of T. S. Eliot's Murder in the Cathedral and Jean Anouilh's Becket in light of Medieval and Contemporary Religious Drama in England and France," DAI, 30 (Vanderbilt: 1969), 4458A.

425 Maxwell, D. E. S. The Poetry of T. S. Eliot. London: Routledge & Kegan Paul, 1952; 3rd ed., 1958, pp. 181-189.

426 Melchiori, Giorgio. The Tightrope Walkers. London: Routledge & Kegan Paul, 1957, pp. 133, 138, passim.

427 Mickel, Wolfgang W. "Die Chorpartien in T. S. Eliots Murder in the Cathedral nach Gehalt, Stimmung und Stil," NS, 7 (November, 1958), 515-531.

428 Mineo, Adinolfa. "I tre misteri dell'arcivescovo," AION-SG, 12 (1969), 331-349. Dramas about Becket by Eliot, Anouilh, and Fry.

429 Moore, Marianne. "If I am worthy, there is no danger," Poetry, 47, #5 (February, 1936), 279-281.

430 Moseley, Edwin M. "Religion and the Literary Genres," Mansions of the Spirit: Essays in Literature and Religion. George Panichas, ed. New York: Hawthorn Books, 1967, pp. 91-92.

431 Mueller, W. R. "Murder in the Cathedral: An Imitation of Christ," Religion in Life, 27 (Summer, 1958), 414-426.

432 Muir, Edwin. "New Literature: Murder in the Cathedral," LonMerc, 32, #189 (July, 1935), 281-283.

433 "Murder in the Cathedral: Criticism," Life, 19 (October 1, 1945), 123-127.

434 Nicholas, Constance. "The Murders of Doyle [sic] and Eliot," MLN, 70 (April, 1955), 269-271. Assertion that Eliot borrowed "The Musgrave Ritual" from Conan Doyle's Sherlock Holmes story.

435 Nicholson, Norman. "Modern Verse-Drama and the Folk Tradition," CritQ, 2 (Summer, 1960), 166-170.

436 Nirula, S. C. "The Becket Fable in Tennyson, Eliot and Fry," IJES, 11 (1970), 34-53.

437 "The Old and New Plays in Manhattan: Murder in the Cathedral," Time, 31, #9 (February 28, 1938), 34.

438 Ould, Herman. The Art of the Play. (Pitman's Theatre and Stage Series.) London: Pitman, 1938, 2nd ed., 1948, pp. 124-128, 138.

439 Oxenford, Mabel A. Murder in the Cathedral: A Study. (Argentine Assn. of English Culture. English Pamphlet Series #2.) Buenos Aires [Talleres gráficos Contreras]: 1942.

440 Pacuvio, Giulio. "Assassino nella cattedrale e ritorno al teatro di poesia," Scenario, Anno. 9, N. 6 (giugno, 1940), 297-298.

441 Pankow, Edith. "The 'Eternal Design' of Murder in the Cathedral," PLL, 9, #1 (Winter, 1973), 35-47.

442 Peacock, Ronald. "T. S. Eliot," The Poet in the Theatre. New York: Hill & Wang, 1946; 1960, pp. 3-27.

443 Perselli, Luciano. "Relative e assoluto nel mito di Eliot," FLe, No. 30 (July 27, 1952), 8. Discussion of Josef Gielen's interpretation of Murder in the Cathedral.

444 Peter, John. "Murder in the Cathedral," SR, 61, #3 (Summer, 1953), 362-383; repr., in T. S. Eliot: A Collection of Critical Essays. Hugh Kenner, ed. Englewood Cliffs, N.J.: Prentice-Hall, 1962, pp. 155-172. The play is "lucid and integral in a way in which ... the later plays are not."

445 Pickering, Jerry V. "Form as Agent: Eliot's Murder in the Cathedral," ETJ, 20 (May, 1968), 198-207.

446 Püschel, Brita. "T. S. Eliot: Murder in the Cathedral," NsM, 21 (1968), 23-32.

447 Putt, S. Gorley. "This Modern Poetry," Voices, 85 (Spring, 1936), 58-60.

448 Rabut, Marguerite. "Le Thème de Thomas Becket dans Becket ou l'honneur de Dieu de J. Anouilh et Murder in the Cathedral de T. S. Eliot," Bulletin de l'Association Guillaume Budé, No. 4, 1964, pp. 494-554.

449 Ransom, John Crowe. "The Autumn of Poetry," SoR, 1 (1935-36), 619-623; excerpt, "A Cathedralist Looks at Murder," The World's Body. New York: Scribner's

1938; Port Washington, N.Y.: Kennikat Pr., 1964, pp. 166-172.

450 Rebmann, David R. "T. S. Eliot's Murder in the Cathedral: A Study of the Texts and Criticism," DAI, 32 (Minnesota: 1971), 2703A.

451 Rees, Richard. "Murder in the Cathedral. Adelphi, 11, #1, n.s. (October, 1935), 60-61.

452 Rehak, Louise Rouse. "On the Use of Martyrs: Tennyson and Eliot on Thomas Becket," UTQ, 33, #1 (October, 1963), 43-60.

453 Renner, Stanley. "Affirmations of Faith in Victory and Murder in the Cathedral," CSR, 4 (1974), 110-119.

454 Rickey, Mary Ellen. "'Christabel' and Murder in the Cathedral," N&Q, 10, #4 (April, 1963), 151. Notes parallels in the two works.

455 Román, M. C. "El pensamiento de Eliot a través de su teatro," RL, 15 (1959), 37-58.

456 Rosati, S., ed. Murder in the Cathedral. (Biblioteca di classici stranieri--Sezione inglese e americana diretta da E. Chinol.) Milan: U. Mursia & C. Edizioni A. P. E., 1960, p. 113.

457 Ross Williamson, Hugh. "Mediaeval Drama Redivivus," AmSch, 5, #1 (Winter, 1936), 49-63.

458 Roy, Emil. "The Becket Plays: Eliot, Fry, and Anouilh," MD, 8, #3 (December, 1965), 268-276. Finds the plays similar in subject matter and recurrent images, but different otherwise.

459 Sayers, M. "A Year in the Theatre," Criterion, 15, #61 (July, 1936), 653-655, 657.

460 Schaeder, Grete, and Hans Heinrich Schaeder. "Mord im Dom," Ein Weg zu T. S. Eliot. Hameln: Verlag der Buchsterstube Fritz-Seifert, 1948.

461 Shapiro, Leo. "The Medievalism of T. S. Eliot," Poetry, 56, #4 (July, 1940), 202-213.

462 Sharoni, Edna G. "'Peace' and 'Unbar the Door': T. S. Eliot's Murder in the Cathedral and Some Stoic Forebears," CompD, 6 (Summer, 1972), 135-153. Eliot has drawn on the dramas of Stoicism of Chapman, Shakespeare and Milton.

463 Shillito, Edward. "Murder in the Cathedral," ChrCen, 52, #51 (December 18, 1935), 1636-1637.

464 Shorter, Robert N. "Becket as Job: T. S. Eliot's Murder in the Cathedral," SAQ, 67, #4 (Autumn, 1968), 627-635; repr., in Twentieth Century Interpretations. David R. Clark, ed. Englewood Cliffs, N.J.: Prentice-Hall, 1971, pp. 86-93.

465 Siddiqui, M. N. "The Ambivalence of Motives in Murder in the Cathedral," OJES, 5 (1965), 1-11.

466 Smidt, Kristian. Poetry and Belief in the Work of T. S. Eliot. London: Routledge & Kegan Paul, 1961; excerpt, "A Shaft of Sunlight," in Twentieth Century Interpretations of Murder in the Cathedral. David R. Clark, ed. Englewood Cliffs, N.J.: Prentice-Hall, 1971, pp. 97-98.

467 Smith, Carol H. "The Rock and Murder in the Cathedral," T. S. Eliot's Dramatic Theory and Practice. Princeton, N.J.: Princeton U. Pr., 1963, pp. 104-109; excerpt, "Blessed Thomas," Twentieth Century Interpretations. David Clark, ed., Englewood Cliffs, N.J.: Prentice-Hall, 1971, pp. 82-86.

468 Smith, Grover. "Action and Suffering: Murder in the Cathedral," T. S. Eliot's Poetry and Plays: A Study in Sources and Meaning. Chicago: Phoenix Books, 1956, pp. 180-195.

469 __________. "Mr. Eliot's New Murder," NMQR, 22 (Autumn, 1952), 331-340.

470 __________. "T. S. Eliot and Conan Doyle," TLS (February 23, 1951-52), 117. See also TLS, January 19 and 26, 1951.

471 __________. "T. S. Eliot and Sherlock Holmes," N&Q, 193, #20 (October 2, 1948), 431-432. Imitation of "The Musgrave Ritual."

472 Smith, Stevie. "History or Poetic Drama?" T. S. Eliot: A Symposium. Neville Braybrooke, ed. New York: Farrar, Straus & Cudahy, 1958, pp. 170-175.

473 Sochatoff, A. Fred. "Four Variations on the Becket Theme in Modern Drama," MD, 12, #1 (May, 1969), 83-91. Because of "the clear-eyed vision" of Becket, Eliot's play has "an austerity and a unity," absent from the other Becket plays.

474 Spanos, William V. "Murder in the Cathedral: The Figure as Mimetic Principle," DramS, 3, #2 (Fall, 1963), 206-

223; repr., in Twentieth Century Interpretations of Murder in the Cathedral. David R. Clark, ed. Englewood Cliffs, N.J.: Prentice-Hall, 1971, pp. 54-72.

475 Speaight, Robert. "Interpreting Becket and Other Parts," T. S. Eliot: A Symposium. Neville Braybrooke, ed. New York: Farrar, Straus & Cudahy, 1958, pp. 70-78.

476 ________. "Marlowe: the Forerunner," REL, 7, #4 (October, 1966), 25-41.

477 ________. "With Becket in Murder in the Cathedral," SR, 74, #1 (January-March, 1966), 176-187.

478 ________. "With Becket in Murder in the Cathedral," T. S. Eliot: The Man and His Work. Allen Tate, ed. New York: Delacorte Pr., 1966, pp. 182-193.

479 Spencer, Theodore. "On Murder in the Cathedral," HA, 125, #3 (December, 1938), 21-22. Finds that the characters represent four levels of reality.

480 Spender, Stephen. "Murder in the Cathedral," T. S. Eliot: Modern Masters. New York: Viking, 1976, pp. 197-206.

480a Stone, Geoffrey. "Plays by Eliot and Auden," AmR, 6, #1 (November, 1935), 121-128.

481 Tardivel, Fernande. "Meurtre dans la Cathédrale," Culture, 2 (November, 1938), 92-99.

482 Thomas, Henri. "Le Théâtre dans l'oeuvre de T. S. Eliot," NRF, 9 (January, 1961), 30-40.

483 Troyat, Henri. "T. S. Eliot: Le Meurtre dans la cathédrale," La Nef, 2e annee, #8 (juillet, 1945), 157-159.

484 Turner, A. J. "A Note on Murder in the Cathedral," N&Q, n.s. 17, #2 (February, 1970), 51-53. The effect of Eliot's changes in the fourth edition.

485 Unger, Leonard, ed. T. S. Eliot: A Selected Critique. New York: Rinehart, 1948, pp. 444-462.

486 Van Doren, Mark. "The Holy Blisful Martir," Nation, 141 (October, 1935), 417; repr., in The Private Reader. New York: Henry Holt, 1942, pp. 210-212.

487 Virsis, Rasma. "The Christian Concept in Murder in the Cathedral," MD, 14, #4 (February, 1972), 405-407. Finds the Chorus a key to Eliot's concept of Christianity.

488 Watson, E. Bradlee and Benfield Pressey, eds. Introduction

and Notes. Contemporary Drama: Fifteen Plays. New York: Scribner's, 1959.

489 Whitlark, James S. "More Borrowings by T. S. Eliot from The Light of Asia," N&Q, 22, #5 (May, 1975), 206-207. Cf., Christopher Clausen, "A Source for Thomas Becket's Temptation," N&Q, 21 (1974), 373-374.

490 Wilder, Amos N. "Mr. T. S. Eliot and the Anglo-Catholic Option," The Spiritual Aspects of the New Poetry. New York: Harper, 1940, pp. 211-215.

491 Wildi, Max. Die Dramen von T. S. Eliot. (Kultur-und Staatswissenschaftliche-Schriften. Heft 97.) Zurich: Polygraphischer Verlag, 1957.

492 Wilhelm, Jean. T. S. Eliot's Murder in the Cathedral. Adelaide: Rigby, 1970.

493 Williams, Pieter D. "The Function of the Chorus in T. S. Eliot's Murder in the Cathedral," ABR, 23 (1972), 499-511.

494 Williams, Raymond. Drama from Ibsen to Eliot. London: Chatto & Windus, 1952, pp. 227-231.

495 ______. "Tragic Resignation and Sacrifice," CritQ, 5, #1 (Spring, 1963), 5-19.

496 Wilson, Frank. "Murder in the Cathedral," Six Essays on the Development of T. S. Eliot. London: Fortune Pr., 1948, pp. 46-51.

497 Wingate, Gifford W. "Murder in the Cathedral: A Step Toward Articulate Theatre," Greyfriar (1960), 22-35. Two levels of reality and two actions in the play: the inner and spiritual and the outer and temporal.

498 Wyatt, Euphemia V. "The Drama: St. Thomas à Becket," CathW, 143 (May, 1936), 207-211. "... the play that has been forced to extend its run three times--by popular demand."

498a Wyman, Linda. "Murder in the Cathedral: The Plot of Diction," MD, 19 (June, 1976), 135-145. "[T]o a very great extent, the words are what happens."

499 Yeats, William Butler. Introduction. The Oxford Book of Modern Verse. New York: Oxford U. Pr., 1936, pp. xxii-xxiii; repr., in T. S. Eliot: A Selected Critique. L. Unger, et al. New York: 1948, pp. 287-288.

500 Young, Stark. "Government and Guild: Murder in the Cathedral," NR, 86 (April 8, 1936), 253.

501 __________. "Murder in the Cathedral," NR, 94 (March 2, 1938), 101-102.

502 Zabel, M. D. "Two Years of Poetry, 1937-39," SoR, 5 (1939-40), 592.

503 Zanetti, Emilia. "Ricreato da Pizzetti l'Assassinio nella Cattedrale," FLe, 13 (March 16, 1958), 1-2

504 Zizola, Giancarlo. "Assassinio nella Cattedrale da Eliot a Pizzetti," Humanitas (Brescia), 13 (April, 1958), 313-316.

505 __________. "Orgoglio e santità nel Tommaso Becket di Eliot," Studium, 55 (1959), 649-658.

THE ROCK

506 Aiken, Conrad. "The Rock," Poetry, 45 (December, 1934), 161-165.

507 Anon. "The Rock: Ecclesiastical Revue," ThA, 18, #12 (December, 1934), 927-928.

508 Anon. "The Rock," TLS (June 7, 1934), 404.

509 Browne, E. Martin. "The Rock," The Making of T. S. Eliot's Plays. New York: Cambridge U. Pr., 1969, pp. 1-33.

510 Daniells, Roy. "The Christian Drama of T. S. Eliot," CanF, 16, #187 (August, 1936), 20-21.

511 Downey, Harris. "T. S. Eliot: Poet and Playwright," [The Rock], VQR, 12 (January, 1936), 142-145.

512 Harding, D. W. "The Rock," Scrutiny, 3, #2 (September, 1934), 180-183.

513 Jones, David E. "The Rock," The Plays of T. S. Eliot. London: Routledge & Kegan Paul; Toronto U. Pr., 1960, pp. 38-49.

514 Matthiessen, F. L. [The Rock], The Achievement of T. S. Eliot. New York: Oxford U. Pr., 1959, pp. 151-153, 161-162.

515 Moore, Harry Thornton. "The Rock," (Review), Adelphi, 9, #3 (December, 1934), 188-189.

516 Olshin, Toby A. "A Consideration of The Rock," UTQ, 39

(July, 1970), 310-323. Places Eliot in the Romantic tradition.

517 Smith, Carol. "The Rock and Murder in the Cathedral," T. S. Eliot's Dramatic Theory and Practice. Princeton, N.J.: Princeton U. Pr., 1963, pp. 76-111.

518 Smith, Grover, Jr. "Works and Days: The Rock," T. S. Eliot's Poetry and Plays. Chicago: U. of Chicago Pr., 1956, pp. 171-179.

519 Spender, Stephen. Modern Masters: T. S. Eliot. Frank Kermode, ed. New York: Viking, 1975, passim.

519a Strong, L. A. G. [The Rock], Obs (July 22, 1934).

520 Ullnaess, Sverre P. N. "T. S. Eliot--og poetisk reklame for kirkebygging," KogK, 63, #7 (September, 1958), 429-434. Concerns the Choruses in The Rock.

521 Zabel, M. D. "Poetry for the Theatre," Poetry, 45 (1934), 152-158.

SWEENEY AGONISTES

522 Barker, George. "Sweeney Agonistes," (Review), Adelphi, 5, #4 (January, 1933), 310-311.

523 Barrett, William. "Dry Land, Dry Martini," PartisanR, 17 (April, 1950), 354-359.

524 Coghill, Nevill. "Sweeney Agonistes: (An Anecdote or Two)," T. S. Eliot: A Symposium. Richard March and Tambimuttu, comps. Freeport, N.Y.: Books for Libraries Pr., 1968, pp. 82-87.

525 Dorris, George E. "Two Allusions in the Poetry of T. S. Eliot," ELN, 2, #1 (September, 1964), 54-57. The beginning of the "Fragment of Agon" in Sweeney Agonistes echoes a scene in James's Ambassadors, and Part III of The Waste Land has operatic allusions.

526 Freedman, Morris. "Jazz Rhythms and T. S. Eliot," SAQ, 51 (July, 1952), 419-435; excerpt repr., in A Collection of Critical Essays on The Waste Land. Jay Martin, ed. Englewood Cliffs, N.J.: Prentice-Hall, 1968, pp. 21-22.

527 ______. "The Meaning of T. S. Eliot's Jew," SAQ, 55 (April, 1956), 200-201.

528 Holt, Charles L. "On Structure and Sweeney Agonistes," MD, 10, #1 (May, 1967), 43-47. Discusses the "highly organized structure of two complex scenes."

529 Jayne, Sears. "Mr. Eliot's Agon," PQ, 34 (October, 1955), 395-414. Explication of two Themes: "the essential similarity of life to death in modern British life" and "the difficulty of communication among human beings...."

530 Jones, David E. "Eliot's Approach to Drama: The Experiments--Sweeney Agonistes (1926-27) and The Rock (1934)," The Plays of T. S. Eliot. London: Routledge & Kegan Paul, 1960, pp. 24-38.

531 Knust, Herbert. "Sweeney Among the Birds and Brutes," Arcadia, 2, #2 (1967), 204-217.

532 Moore, Marianne. "Sweeney Agonistes," Poetry, 42, #11 (May, 1933), 106-109.

533 Rao, G. Nageswara. "The Unfinished Poems of T. S. Eliot," LCrit, 9, #3 (Winter, 1970), 27-35.

534 Schneider, Elisabeth. "Sweeney Agonistes," T. S. Eliot: The Pattern in the Carpet. Berkeley: U. of California Pr., 1975, pp. 93-98.

535 Sitwell, Edith. Preface. The American Genius. London: Lehmann, 1951, pp. xvii-xix.

536 Smith, Carol H. "From Sweeney Agonistes to The Elder Statesman: A Study of the Dramatic Theory and Practice of T. S. Eliot," DA, 23 (U. of Michigan: 1962), 635-636.

537 ________. "Sweeney Agonistes," T. S. Eliot's Dramatic Theory and Practice. Princeton, N.J.: Princeton U. Pr., 1963, pp. 32-75.

538 Smith, Grover, Jr. "Across the Frontier: Sweeney Agonistes," T. S. Eliot's Poetry and Plays. Chicago: U. of Chicago Pr., 1956, pp. 110-118.

539 Spanos, William V. "'Wanna Go Home, Baby?' Sweeney Agonistes as Drama of the Absurd," PMLA, 85, #1 (January, 1970), 8-20.

540 Spender, Stephen. "T. S. Eliot in His Poetry," The Destructive Element. London: Cape, 1936; repr., in T. S. Eliot: A Selected Critique. L. Unger, ed. New York: Rinehart, 1948, pp. 274-275.

541 Thompson, T. H. "The Bloody Wood," LonMerc, 29 (1934), 233-239; repr., in A Selected Critique. L. Unger, ed.

New York: Rinehart, 1948, pp. 161-169.

542 Williamson, George. "Sweeney Agonistes," Reader's Guide to T. S. Eliot. New York: Noonday, 1953, pp. 191-195.

MISCELLANEOUS

543 Arrowsmith, William. "The Comedy of T. S. Eliot," English Stage Comedy. W. K. Wimsatt, Jr., ed. New York: Columbia U. Pr., 1955, pp. 148-172. (EIE, 1954).

544 ________. "Eliot and Euripides," Arion, 4, #1 (1965), 21-35.

545 ________. "Transfiguration in Eliot and Euripides," SR, 63, #3 (Summer, 1955), 421-442.

546 Ayling, Ronald. "The Poetic Drama of T. S. Eliot," ESA, 2 (September, 1959), 247-250. Eliot's technique possibly influenced by that of Sean O'Casey.

547 Barth, J. Robert, S. J. "T. S. Eliot's Image of Man: A Thematic Study of His Drama," Renascence, 14, #3 (Spring, 1962), 126-138, 165. The Theme: "... the problem of isolation from reality, leading to the thematic action of striving for union with reality--oneself, the world, other men, God."

548 Bassi, Emma. "Il teatro di T. S. Eliot," AION-SG, 1 (1958), 239-268.

549 Battenhouse, Henry M. Poets of Christian Thought. New York: Ronald Pr., 1947, pp. 167-170.

550 Bayley, John. "The Collected Plays," Rev, 4 (November, 1962), 3-11.

551 Birrell, Francis. "The Poetic Drama Once More," Nation & Athenaeum, 43, #14 (July, 1928), 470.

552 Blackmur, R. P. "T. S. Eliot: From Ash Wednesday to Murder in the Cathedral," The Double Agent. New York: Arrow Editions, 1935, pp. 184-218; repr., in A Selected Critique. L. Unger, ed. New York: Rinehart, 1948, pp. 236-262.

553 Bland, D. S. "The Tragic Hero in Modern Literature," CamJ, 3, #4 (January, 1950), 214-223.

554 Blau, Herbert. "W. B. Yeats and T. S. Eliot: Poetic Drama and Modern Poetry," DA, 14 (Stanford U.: 1954), 523-524.

555 Bloomfield, B. C. "An Unrecorded Article by T. S. Eliot," BC, 2 (Autumn, 1962), 350. An article about drama.

556 Blumenberg, Hans. "Rose und Feuer: Lyrik, Kritik und Drama T. S. Eliots," Hochland, 49 (1956), 109-126.

557 Bradbrook, M. C. "Eliot as Dramatist: The Nightmare Dream," English Dramatic Form: A History of Its Development. New York: Barnes & Noble, 1965, pp. 162-178.

558 __________. T. S. Eliot. London; New York: Longmans, Green, 1965, pp. 35-48, passim.

559 Branford, W. R. G. "Myth and Theme in the Plays of T. S. Eliot," Theoria, 7 (1955), 101-109.

560 Braybrooke, Neville, ed. T. S. Eliot: A Symposium for His Seventieth Birthday. New York: Farrar, Straus & Cudahy, 1958.

561 Brenner, Rica. Poets of Our Times. New York: Harcourt, Brace, 1941, pp. 193-197.

562 Brown, Spencer. "T. S. Eliot's Latest Poetic Drama," Commentary, 17 (April, 1954), 367-372.

563 Browne, E. Martin. "The Dramatic Verse of T. S. Eliot;" T. S. Eliot: A Symposium. Richard March and Tambimuttu, comps. London: Editions Poetry London, 1948, pp. 196-207.

564 __________. "From The Rock to The Confidential Clerk," T. S. Eliot: A Symposium. Neville Braybrook, ed. New York: Farrar, Straus & Cudahy, 1958, pp. 57-69.

565 __________. The Making of T. S. Eliot's Plays. New York; London: Cambridge U. Pr., 1969.

566 __________. "The Permanent Contribution of T. S. Eliot to the Drama," GordonR, 6, #4 (Winter, 1962-63), pp. 150-166.

567 __________. "The Poet and the Stage," The Penguin New Writing. John Lehmann, ed. No. 31 (1947), 81-92.

568 __________. "T. S. Eliot as Dramatist," Drama, 76 (Spring, 1965), 41-43.

569 __________. "T. S. Eliot in the Theatre: The Director's Memories," SR, 74, #1 (Winter, 1966), 136-152.

570 __________. "T. S. Eliot in the Theatre: The Director's Memories," T. S. Eliot: The Man and His Work. Allen Tate, ed. New York: Delacorte Pr., 1966, pp. 116-132.

571 __________. "Theatre Aims of T. S. Eliot," NYT (January, 1950), Sec. 2, p. 3.

572 Carnell, Corbin S. "Creation's Lonely Flesh: T. S. Eliot and Christopher Fry on the Life of the Senses," MD, 6 (September, 1963), 141-149.

572a Carpenter, Charles. "T. S. Eliot as Dramatist: Critical Studies in English, 1933-1975," BB, 33 (January, 1976), 1-12.

573 Chiari, Joseph. "The Plays," T. S. Eliot: Poet and Dramatist. New York: Barnes & Noble, 1972, pp. 115-143.

574 Chiaromonte, Nichola. "T. S. Eliot drammaturgo," Il Mondo, 10 (September 9, 1958), 14.

575 Chinol, Elio. "Teatro e poesia secondo T. S. Eliot," Comunita, 6 (October, 1952), 66-67.

576 Ciarletta, Lalla. "Christianesimo nel Teatro di Eliot," Approdo, 11, #1 (1965), 50-52.

577 Cookman, A. V. "The Verse Play," The Year's Work in the Theatre: 1949-1950. London: Published for the British Council by Longmans, Green, 1950.

578 Danby, John F. "Intervals during Rehearsals." CamJ, 2 (September, 1949), 707-720.

579 Daniells, R. "Christian Drama of T. S. Eliot," CanF, 16 (August, 1936), 20-21.

580 Darrell, Sherry Bevins. "Saint to Statesman: Structure and Theme in T. S. Eliot's Plays," DAI, 36 (Peabody U.: 1975), 2195A.

581 Davani, Maria Carmela C. Il Teatro di T. S. Eliot: Da Sweeney Agonistes a The Cocktail Party. Palermo: Flaccovio, 1973.

582 Dickinson, D. H. "Mr. Eliot's Hotel Universe," DramaCrit, 1 (1958), 33-44.

583 Dierickx, J. "T. S. Eliot, Dramaturge," RLV, 26, #2 (March-April, 1960), 96-123.

584 Drew, Elizabeth. Discovering Drama. Port Washington, N.Y.: Kennikat Pr., 1937; reissued, Norton & Co., 1968, passim.

585 Dukes, Ashley. "Re-enter the Chorus," ThA, 22 (May, 1938), 337, 340.

586 ________. "T. S. Eliot in the Theatre," T. S. Eliot: A Symposium. Richard March, et al., comps.; repr., Freeport, N.Y.: Books for Libraries Pr., 1968, pp. 111-118.

587 Engel, Claire-Eliane. Esquisses Anglaises. Collection: Les Essayistes. Editions "Je Sers," Paris: 1949.

588 Esch, Arno. "Das dramatische Werk T. S. Eliots," Anglia, 70 (1952), 405.

589 Evans, B. Ifor. "Contemporary Drama," A Short History of English Drama. Rev. Library ed. London: MacGibbon & Kee, 1965, pp. 188-191.

590 Findlater, Richard. The Unholy Trade. London: Gollancz, 1952, pp. 130-146.

591 Fluchère, Henri. "Un Théâtre poétique intérieur," CdSud, 51, #359 (February-March, 1961), 33-44.

592 Frankenberg, Lloyd. "Time and Mr. Eliot: The Plays," Pleasure Dome: On Reading Modern Poetry. Boston: Houghton Mifflin, 1949, pp. 78-96.

593 Freedman, Morris. American Drama in Social Context. (CMC) Carbondale: Southern Illinois U. Pr., 1971.

594 Fry, Edith M. "The Poetic Work of T. S. Eliot," The British Annual of Literature, Vol. 5 (1948), 11-12.

595 Gamberini, Spartaco. La Poesia di T. S. Eliot. Genova: Pubblicazioni dell'Instituto Universitario di Magistero, 1954.

596 Gardner, Helen. "The Comedies of T. S. Eliot," SR, 74, #1 (Winter, 1966), 153-175.

596a ________. "The Comedies of T. S. Eliot," EDH, 34 (1966), 55-73.

597 ________. "The Comedies of T. S. Eliot," T. S. Eliot: The Man and His Work. Allen Tate, ed. New York: Delacorte, pp. 159-181.

598 ________. "The Language of Drama," The Art of T. S.

Eliot. London: 6th ed., Faber & Faber, 1968, pp. 127-157.

599 Gassner, John. "English Poetic Drama: Eliot and Fry," Masters of the Drama. 3rd ed., rev. and enl. New York: Dover Pubs., 1954, pp. 729-731.

600 ___________. "T. S. Eliot: The Poet as Anti-Modernist," The Theatre in Our Times: A Survey of the Men, Materials and Movements in the Modern Theatre. New York: Crown Pub., 1954; 2nd pr., 1955, pp. 267-281.

601 Gerstenberger, Donna Lorine. "Formal Experiments in Modern Verse Drama," DA, 19 (U. of Oklahoma: 1959), 1757-58.

602 ___________. "The Saint and the Circle: The Dramatic Potential of an Image," Criticism, 2 (Fall, 1960), 336-341.

603 Glicksberg, Charles I. "The Journey That Must Be Taken: Spiritual Quest in T. S. Eliot's Plays," SWR, 40 (Summer, 1955), 203-210. "... Eliot concentrates on a special moment of crisis.... The hero must choose between the temporal realm and the eternal life: A choice, literally, between life and death."

604 ___________. "The Spirit of Irony in Eliot's Plays," PrS, 29 (Fall, 1955), 222-237.

605 Goldman, Michael. "Fear in the Way: The Design of Eliot's Drama," Eliot in His Time. A. Walton Litz, ed. Princeton, N.J.: Princeton U. Pr., 1973, pp. 155-180.

606 Graves, Robert. The Common Asphodel: Collected Essays on Poetry, 1922-49. London: Hamish Hamilton, 1949, 286-289.

607 Guidi, Augusto. "Il teatro di Eliot," Let (Italy), 3 (July-August, 1950), 76-78.

608 Hamalian, Leo. "The Voice of This Calling: A Study of the Plays of T. S. Eliot," DA, 15 (Columbia U.: 1955), 1398-99.

609 Harding, D. W. "Progression of Theme in Eliot's Modern Plays," KR, 18 (Summer, 1956), 339-360. The plays "all deal with human loneliness" and "examine the bearings that parental relations, marriage, religious faith and the response to vocation have upon this central experience...."

610 Harding, Joan N. "T. S. Eliot, O. M.," ConR, #1072 (April, 1955), 239-243. The humanist influence on Eliot.

610a Harlow, Agda Gronbech. "Lessons in Christian Love from the Four Last Plays of T. S. Eliot," DAI, 36 (Brigham Young U.: 1975), 1527A

610b Harris, Warren Meredith. "Theatrical Style and the Work of T. S. Eliot," DAI, 37 (Northwestern U.: 1976), 3988A.

611 Hassall, Christopher. Notes on the Verse Drama (The Masque No. 6). London: Curtain Pr., 1948), pp. 20-21, passim.

612 Hayman, Ronald. "T. S. Eliot and E. Martin Browne," Drama, #94 (Autumn, 1969), 45-46.

613 Heines, Henry. "Journey to Simplicity," SatR, 48 (January 23, 1965), 53-54.

614 Henn, Thomas Rice. "T. S. Eliot's Compromise," The Harvest of Tragedy. London: Methuen; New York: Barnes & Noble, 1956, pp. 217-232.

615 Hirsch, Foster L. "The Hearth and the Journey: The Mingling of Orders in the Drama of Yeats and Eliot," ArQ, 27 (1971), 293-307.

616 Hobson, Harold. "Enduring Drama of T. S. Eliot," EigoS, 115 (1969), 306-307.

617 ________. "The Paradoxical Public," CSMM, 42 (Spring, 1950), 10.

618 Holland, Joyce M. "Human Relations in Eliot's Drama," Renascence, 22 (1970), 151-161.

618a Homan, Richard Lawrence. "T. S. Eliot as a Dramatic Realist," DAI, 37 (U. of Minnesota: 1975), 37A-38A.

619 Howarth, Herbert. "Drama," Notes on Some Figures Behind T. S. Eliot. Boston: Houghton Mifflin, 1964, pp. 300-340.

620 Hübner, Walter. "T. S. Eliot und das neue Drama," NZ, 5 (1950), 337-352.

621 Inserillo, Charles R. "Wish and Desire: Two Poles of the Imagination in the Drama of Arthur Miller and T. S. Eliot," XUS, 1 (Summer-Fall, 1962), 247-258.

622 Isaacs, Jacob. "T. S. Eliot and Poetic Drama," An Assessment of Twentieth-Century Literature. London: Secker & Warburg, 1951; Port Washington, N.Y.: Kennikat Pr., 1968, pp. 133-160.

623 Jarrett-Kerr, Martin. "The Poetic Drama of T. S. Eliot,"

ESA, 2 (March, 1959), 16-33. Cf., Robert Ayline, "The Poetic Drama of T. S. Eliot," ESA, 2 (September, 1950), 247-250.

624 Jones, David E. The Plays of T. S. Eliot. London: Routledge & Kegan Paul, 1960; Toronto U. Pr., 1960.

625 Kaplan, Robert B. Major Poems and Plays of T. S. Eliot. Lincoln, Nebr.: Cliff Notes, 1965.

626 Kaul, R. K. "Rhyme and Blank Verse in Drama: A Note on Eliot," English, 15 (Autumn, 1964), 96-99.

626a Kennedy, Andrew K. Six Dramatists in Search of a Language: Studies in Dramatic Language. London: Cambridge U. Pr., 1975.

627 Kennedy, Richard S. "Working Out Salvation with Diligence: The Plays of T. S. Eliot," U. Wichita Bul, 40 (May, 1964), 1-11; Wichita, Kans.: Wichita U. Pr., 1964 (U. Studies, 57.)

628 Kerr, Walter. How Not to Write a Play. London: Max Reinhardt, 1956, pp. 230-231.

629 Kline, Peter. "The Spiritual Center in Eliot's Plays," KR, 21, #3 (Summer, 1959), 457-472. Eliot's "experience behind" the play is more important than "the dramatic format."

630 Knieger, Bernard. "The Dramatic Achievement of T. S. Eliot," MD, 3 (February, 1961), 387-392.

631 Krajewska, W. "Le Théâtre de T. S. Eliot," KN, 7, #24 (1960).

632 Kuma, Franz. T. S. Eliot. Velber bei Hannover: 1968.

633 Lambert, J. W. "The Verse Drama," Theatre Programme. J. C. Trewin, ed. London: Frederick Muller, 1954, pp. 63-66.

634 Langbaum, Robert. "The Mysteries of Identity as a Theme in T. S. Eliot's Plays," VQR, 49 (Autumn, 1973), 560-580.

635 Lanza, Guiseppe. "Eliot Drammaturgo," OPL, 11, #2 (1965), 23-28.

636 Lebel, M. "Actualité d'Eschyle," Revue de l'Université. Laval, 7 (October, 1952), 105-119.

637 Lee, Young G. "Other Echoes: Source Studies on the Poetry

and Plays of T. S. Eliot," DAI, 31 (St. Louis U.: 1971), 4125A.

638 Lightfoot, Marjorie J. "Charting Eliot's Course in Drama," ETJ, 20 (May, 1968), 186-197.

639 Lindenberger, Herbert. "Danton's Death and the Conventions of Historical Drama," CDr, 3, #2 (Summer, 1969), 99-109. T. S. Eliot among the English writers in this tradition.

640 Lindström, Göran. "T. S. Eliot som Dramatiker," Studiekamraten, 47 (1965), 24-26.

641 Lobb, Kenneth Martyn. The Drama in School and Church. London: George G. Harrap, 1955, pp. 115, 117-119.

642 Lucy, Seán. "Poetic Drama," T. S. Eliot and the Idea of Tradition. New York: Barnes & Noble, 1960, pp. 163-209.

643 Lumley, Frederick. "T. S. Eliot as Dramatist," Trends in Twentieth-Century Drama: A Survey since Ibsen and Shaw. London: Barrie & Rockliff, 1956; 2nd rev., 1960, pp. 80-91.

644 MacLeish, Archibald. "The Poet as Playwright," Atl, 195 (February, 1955), 49-52.

645 Madeleine, Sister M. Claire. "T. S. Eliot: Poet as Playwright," CEJ, 2, #3 (Fall, 1966), 65-76.

646 Mandel, Oscar. "Reactionary Notes on the Experimental Theatre," MassR, 11 (1970), 101-116. T. S. Eliot, the "only absolutely intelligent playwright America has begotten...."

647 March, Richard, and Tambimuttu, comps. T. S. Eliot: A Symposium. London: Editions Poetry, 1948; Freeport, N.Y.: Books for Libraries Pr., 1968.

648 Matlaw, Myron. "Eliot the Dramatist," CLAJ, 12, #2 (December, 1968), 116-122.

649 Matthiessen, Francis O. "For an Unwritten Chapter," HA, 125, #3 (1938), 22-24. Eliot's plays.

650 ______. "The Plays," The Achievement of T. S. Eliot. London: Oxford U. Pr., 1935; 2nd ed., 1947; rev. and enl., New York: 1958, pp. 155-176.

651 Maxwell, D. E. S. The Poetry of T. S. Eliot. London: Routledge & Kegan Paul, 1952; New York: Hilary House, 1959.

652 Melchiori, Giorgia. "La commedia degli equivoci," Spe, 7 (1954), 187-190, 239-243.

653 ______. "Eliot and the Theatre," EngMisc, 4 (1953), 187-233.

654 ______. "Eliot and the Theatre," The Tightrope Walkers. London: Routledge & Kegan Paul, 1956, 1957, pp. 104-149.

655 ______. "Tecnica e poetica nel teatro di Eliot," FLe, (November 14, 1948).

656 ______. "L'ultima commedia di Eliot," SA, 5 (1959), 233-242.

657 Merchant, W. M. "The Verse-Drama of Eliot and Fry," NS, 3 (1955), 97-106.

658 Miller, Arthur. "Morality and Modern Drama," ETJ, 10, #3 (October, 1958), 190-202. An interview granted to Phillip Gelb in which Miller comments upon his own work and that of Eliot and T. Williams.

659 Milstead, John. "The Structure of Modern Tragedy," WHR, 12, #4 (Autumn, 1958), 365-369.

659a Monis, Patricio V. "The Literary Symbol in Contemporary Poetry and Drama," Unitas, 48 (1975), 95-142.

660 Montgomery, Peter Cleghorn. Eliot's Urban Morality Plays. Diss., U. of Alberta, Canada, 1972.

661 Mudford, P. G. "T. S. Eliot's Plays and the Tradition of High Comedy," CritQ, 16 (Summer, 1974), 127-142.

662 Murry, John Middleton. "The Plays of T. S. Eliot," Unprofessional Essays. London: Jonathan Cape, 1956, pp. 149-191.

663 Naik, M. K. "The Characters in Eliot's Plays," Indian Essays in American Literature: Papers in Honour of Robert E. Spiller. Sujit Mukherjee, and D. V. K. Raghavacharyulu, eds. Bombay: Popular Prakashan, 1969, pp. 61-70.

664 ______. "Some Ambiguities in Eliot's Plays," PURBA, 3, #2 (October, 1972), 25-30.

665 Nichols, Dorothy. "Poets as Playwrights," SoQ, 4 (1968), 264-270.

666 Nicholson, Norman. Man and Literature. London: S. C. M. Press, 1943, pp. 197-201.

667 __________. "Modern Verse-Drama and the Folk Tradition," CritQ, 2 (Summer, 1960), 166-170.

668 Nicoll, Allardyce. "Drama in the Twentieth Century," British Drama. 5th ed. rev. New York: Barnes & Noble, 1963, pp. 320-321.

669 __________. "T. S. Eliot and the Revival of the Poetic Play in England," World Drama from Aeschylus to Anouilh. New York: Harcourt, Brace, 1950, pp. 871-873.

670 Oestreich, Marianne. Das Problem der Schuld bei T. S. Eliot. Versuch einer Deutung im lyrischen und dramatischen Werk. Diss., Berlin: 1955.

671 Orsini, Gian N. G. "T. S. Eliot and the Doctrine of Dramatic Conventions," WASAL, 43 (1954), 189-200.

672 __________. "T. S. Eliot e la teoria delle convenzioni drammatiche," LetM, 4 (November-December, 1953), 621-632.

673 Otten, Kurt. "Die Überwindung des Realismus im modernen englischen Drama," NS, 9 (June, 1960), 265-278.

674 Ozu, Jiro. T. S. Eliot's Poetic Drama. Tokyo: Hayakawashobo, 1953, p. 96.

675 Peacock, Ronald. "Public and Private Problems in Modern Drama," TDR, 3, #3 (March, 1959), 58-72.

676 __________. "T. S. Eliot," The Poet in the Theatre. New York: Hill & Wang, 1960, pp. 3-25.

677 Phillips, Rowena S. "Criticism of Verse Drama: An Organic Approach," DAI, 32 (U. of Southern California: 1972), 5749A.

678 Pietersma, H. "The Overwhelming Question," Folio, 21 (Summer, 1956), 19-32. A critique of Eliot's plays.

679 Policardi, Silvio. La Poesia di T. S. Eliot. Milan: Edizioni Universitarie, 1948-49, pp. 129-187.

680 Pottle, Frederick A. "Drama of Action," YR, n. s., 25, #2 (December, 1935), 426-430.

681 Powell, Dilys. "T. S. Eliot," Descent from Parnassus. London: Cresset Pr., 1934, pp. 74-75, 78-80.

682 Puhalo, Dušan. "Drame u stihu T. S. Eliota," Letopis Matice Srpske, 378, #6 (Novi Sad, 1956), 555-570.

683 Rahv, Philip. "T. S. Eliot: The Poet as Playwright," Literature and the Sixth Sense. Boston: Houghton Mifflin, 1969, pp. 350f.

684 Ransom, John Crowe. "T. S. Eliot as Dramatist," Poetry, 54, #5 (August, 1939), 264-271.

685 Read, Herbert. "A Point of Intensity: T. S. Eliot," The True Voice of Feeling: Studies in English Romantic Poetry. London: Faber & Faber; New York: Pantheon Books, 1953, pp. 139-150.

686 Richman, Robert. "The Quiet Conflict: The Plays of T. S. Eliot," NR, 127 (December 8, 1952), 17-18.

686a Robbins, Rossell Hope. The T. S. Eliot Myth. New York: Henry Schuman, 1951, passim. Attacks all of Eliot's plays.

687 Roby, Robert C. T. S. Eliot and Elizabethan and Jacobean Dramatists. Diss., Northwestern U., 1950.

688 Rogers, Daniel John. "Dramatic Use of the Liturgy in the Plays of T. S. Eliot: A Secular Evolution," DA, 24 (U. of Wisconsin: 1964), 4198.

689 Rosati, Salvatore, ed. Thomas Stearns Eliot: Teatro. Con un Saggio Introduttivo di Salvatore Rosati. Milan: Bompiani, 1958.

690 ____________. "Verso e linguaggio poetico nelle opere drammatiche di T. S. Eliot," Galleria, 1 (gennaio-febbraio, 1953), 21-24.

691 Russi, Antonio. "T. S. Eliot e il teatro," Spe, 3 (May, 1950), 110-114.

692 Sampson, George. The Concise Cambridge History of English Literature. Cambridge, England: Cambridge U. Pr., 1941, p. 1023.

693 Sarbu, Aladár. "Social Mask and Human Personality in T. S. Eliot's Plays," Studies in English and American Philology, 1 (1971), 208-226.

694 Schaeder, Grete. "T. S. Eliots dramatische Dichtungen, Sweeney Agonistes, The Family Reunion, Murder in the Cathedral," Neue Schweizer Rundschau, Heft Nr. 12 (April, 1948), 728-742.

695 ____________, and Hans Heinrich. Ein Weg zu T. S. Eliot. Hameln: Verlag der Buchsterstube Fritz-Seifert, 1948.

696 Schlüter, Kurt. Der Mensch als Schauspieler. Studien Zur Beutung von T. S. Eliots Gesellschaftsdramen. Bonn: Bouvier, 1962.

697 Schmidt, Gerd. "Die asketische Regel: Zum Verhaltnis von Poesie und Drama bei T. S. Eliot," NS, 14, #4 (April, 1965), 153-159.

698 ______. Die Struktur des Dramas bei T. S. Eliot. Diss., U. of Freiburg: 1962.

699 Semaan, Khalil I. H. "T. S. Eliot's Influence on Arabic Poetry and Theater," CLS, 6 (1969), 472-489. Eliot's influence on Salah 'Abd al-Sabur.

699a Sen, Asoke. "T. S. Eliot and the Revival of Poetic Drama in England," ModRev, 133, #5 (November, 1973), 377-380.

700 Shartar, I. Martin. "The Theater of the Mind: An Analysis of Works by Mallarmé, Yeats, Eliot, and Beckett," DA, 27 (Emory U.: 1966), 2161A.

701 Short, Ernest. "Expressionism and the Expressionist: The Poetical Plays: T. S. Eliot and Christopher Fry," Sixty Years of Theatre. London: Eyre & Spottiswoode, 1951, pp. 378-382.

701a Slawińska, Irena. "Dramaty T. S. Eliota," Dialog, #5 (1958), 87-98.

702 Smidt, Kristian. Poetry and Belief in the Work of T. S. Eliot. Skrifter utgitt av Det Norske Videnskaps-Akademi i Oslo; II Hist.-Filos. Klasse, 1949, #1 (Oslo, I. Kommisjon Hos Jacob Dybwad, 1949), p. 198, passim.

703 Smith, Carol H. "Eliot as Playwright," Nation, 203, #10 (October 3, 1966), 325-328. Relates Eliot's poetic drama to Eliot's belief in a supernatural order which gives meaning to the apparent disorder of nature and man.

704 ______. "From Sweeney Agonistes to The Elder Statesman: A Study of the Dramatic Theory and Practice of T. S. Eliot," DA 23 (U. of Michigan: 1962), 635-636.

705 ______. T. S. Eliot's Dramatic Theory and Practice from Sweeney Agonistes to The Elder Statesman. Princeton, N.J.: Princeton U. Pr., 1963.

706 Smith, Grover. T. S. Eliot's Poetry and Plays: A Study in Sources and Meaning. Chicago: U. of Chicago U. Pr., 1956; new 2nd ed., 1975.

707 Sochatoff, A. Fred. "The Use of Verse in the Drama of T.

S. Eliot," CaSE, 2 (1955), 59-75.

708 Sorial, F. I. A Study of Contemporary Verse Drama in England as Exemplified in the Plays of T. S. Eliot and Christopher Fry. Diss., Trinity College, Dublin: 1959-60.

708a Spanos, William. "God and the Detective: The Christian Tradition and the Drama of the Absurd," C&L, 20, #2 (1971), 16-22. Cf., Response by Nancy M. Tischler. "Sweeney, Absurdities, and Christians," C&L, 20, #3 (1971), 8-10.

709 Speaight, Robert. Drama Since 1939. London: Longmans, Green & Co., for the British Council, 1947, pp. 43-45.

710 ________. "Interpreting Becket and Other Parts," T. S. Eliot: A Symposium. Neville Braybrooke, ed. New York: Farrar & Straus, 1958, pp. 70-78.

711 ________. "The Plays of T. S. Eliot," Month, 30 (October, 1963), 209-213.

711a Srinath, C. N. "T. S. Eliot's Dramatic Theory and Practice," LCrit, 11, #4 (1975), 64-79.

712 Stamm, Rudolf. "The Orestes Theme in Three Plays by Eugene O'Neill, T. S. Eliot and Jean-Paul Sartre," ES, 30, #5 (1949), 244-255. A comparative study of employment of the Orestes theme.

713 Standop, Ewald. "A Note on the Dramatic Verse of T. S. Eliot," LWU, 5 (1972), 33-36.

714 Stelzmann, Rainulf A. "The Theology of T. S. Eliot's Dramas," XUS, 1, #1 (February, 1961), 7-17. Finds Eliot's theology unsatisfactory because it does not handle grace and free will.

715 Taborski, Boleslaw. "T. S. Eliot: pionier nowoczesnego dramatu poetyckiego," Teatr, #4 (1957), 20-21; #5, 21-22; #6, 20-21.

716 Talley, Jerry B. "Religious Themes in the Dramatic Works of George Bernard Shaw, T. S. Eliot and Paul Claudel," DA, 25 (U. of Denver: 1964), 3750.

717 Thomas, Henri. "Le théâtre dans l'oeuvre de T. S. Eliot," NRF, 17, #97 (January, 1961), 30-40.

718 Tordeur, Jean. A la Rencontre de T. S. Eliot: Un Classique vivant. Bruxelles: La Sixaine, 1946, pp. 36-41, 44-45.

719 Torrens, James. "T. S. Eliot and Shakespeare: 'This Music Crept By,'" BuR, 19, #1 (Spring, 1971), 77-96.

720 Trewin, J. C. Dramatists of Today. London: Staples Pr., 1953, passim.

721 __________. The Turbulent Thirties: A Further Decade of the Theatre. London: Macdonald, 1960, passim.

722 Tynan, Kenneth. "Prose and the Playwright," Atl, 194, #6 (December, 1954), 72-76.

723 Unger, Leonard. The Man in the Name: Essays on the Experience of Poetry. Minneapolis: Minnesota U. Pr., 1956, pp. 181-185, 211-215, 219-226, passim.

724 __________, ed. T. S. Eliot: A Selected Critique. New York: Rinehart, 1948.

725 Vallette, Jacques. "Remarques sur le théâtre de T. S. Eliot," La Nef, 2e année, 7 (juin, 1945), 119-124.

726 Vigée, Claude. "Les Artistes de la faim," CL, 9, #2 (Spring, 1957), 97-117. Eliot's plays and "symptoms of a new asceticism."

727 Visentin, Giovanni. "Teatro contemporaneo: Claudel, Eliot, Marcel," Idea, 6 (October 11, 1953), 3.

728 Voisine, Jacques. "Le Problème du drame poétique selon T. S. Eliot," EA, 9 (October-December, 1956), 289-302.

729 Wasson, Richard. "The Rhetoric of Theatre: The Contemporaneity of T. S. Eliot," DramS, 6 (Spring, 1968), 231-243.

730 Webster, C. J. "The Chorus: T. S. Eliot," McMasterQt (November, 1938), 40-49.

731 Weisstein, Ulrich. "Form as Content in the Drama of T. S. Eliot," WestR, 23, #3 (Spring, 1959), 239-246. "In all of Eliot's plays, rhythm, meter and rhyme serve to heighten the emotional and ... tragic impact of the action; they are co-ordinated with, not subordinated to, sheer content."

732 Wells, Henry W. New Poets from Old: A Study in Literary Genetics. New York: Columbia U. Pr., 1940, passim.

733 West, William Channing. "Concepts of Reality in the Poetic Drama of W. B. Yeats, W. H. Auden, and T. S. Eliot," DA, 25 (Stanford U.: 1965), 6120-21.

734 Whicher, George F. "Loopholes of Retreat," The Literature

of the American People: An Historical and Critical Survey. Arthur Hobson Quinn, ed. New York: Appleton-Century-Crofts, 1951, pp. 897-898.

734a White, Georgiana Donase. "The Theme of Guilt in the Poetry and Plays of T. S. Eliot," DAI, 37 (Fordham U.: 1976), 2906A.

735 Wildi, Max. Die Dramen von T. S. Eliot. (Kultur- und Staatswissenschaftliche-Schriften. Heft 97.) Zurich: Polygraphischer Verlag, 1957.

736 Williams, Raymond. "Criticism into Drama," EIC, 1, #2 (April, 1951), 120-138.

737 ______. Drama in Performance. New ed. New York: Basic Books, 1968, passim.

738 ______. "T. S. Eliot," Drama from Ibsen to Eliot. London: Chatto & Windus, 1952, pp. 223-246; New York: Oxford U. Pr., 1953, passim.

739 Williamson, Audrey. "Poetry in the Theatre: Eliot and Fry," Chrysalis, 4, #5-6 (1951), 3-12; repr., with additions in Theatre of Two Decades. London: Rockliff, 1951, pp. 127-130, 134-144.

740 Wilson, Edmund. Axel's Castle: A Study in the Imaginative Literature of 1870-1930. New York: Scribner's, 1931, passim.

741 Wilson, Frank. "The Plays," Six Essays on the Development of T. S. Eliot. London: Fortune Pr., 1948, pp. 41-53.

742 Wimsatt, William. "The Comedy of T. S. Eliot," English Stage Comedy. New York: U. of Columbia Pr., 1955, pp. 148-172.

743 ______. 'Eliot's Comedy," SR, 58 (Autumn, 1950), 666-678.

744 Wingate, Gifford W. Poetic Drama in the 1930's: A Study of the Plays of T. S. Eliot and W. H. Auden. Diss., Cornell U., 1954.

745 Worth, Katharine. 'Eliot and the Living Theatre," Eliot in Perspective: A Symposium. Graham Martin, ed. London: Macmillan; New York: Humanities, 1970, pp. 148-166; repr., T. S. Eliot: A Collection of Criticism. Linda W. Wagner, ed. New York: McGraw-Hill, 1974, pp. 105-123.

746 Wyman, Linda Lee. "'Where the Words Are Valid,': A

Study of the Language of T. S. Eliot's Plays," DAI, 33 (George Peabody: 1972), 1752A.

747 Wynn, Dudley. "The Integrity of T. S. Eliot," University of Denver Publications, Studies in Humanities, #1, A. M. I. Fiskin, ed. Denver U. Pr., 1950, pp. 59-78.

747a Yen, Yuan-shu. "Sound and Diction in T. S. Eliot's Verse Drama," FJS, 1 (1968), 119-144.

748 Zabel, M. D. "Poetry for the Theatre," Poetry, 45 (December, 1934), 152-158.

POETRY

ASH WEDNESDAY

749 Blackmur, R. P. "T. S. Eliot: From Ash-Wednesday to Murder in the Cathedral," The Double Agent. New York: Arrow Editions, 1935, pp. 184-218; repr., Language as Gesture: Essays in Poetry. New York: Harcourt, Brace & Co., 1952, pp. 168-171.

750 ____________. "T. S. Eliot: From Ash Wednesday to Murder in the Cathedral," T. S. Eliot: A Selected Critique. Leonard Unger, ed. New York: Rinehart, 1948, pp. 236-262.

751 Boardman, Gwenn R. "Ash Wednesday: Eliot's Lenten Mass Sequence," Renascence, 15, #1 (Fall, 1962), 28-36. The parallel structure of Eliot's poem and the six Lenten Masses of the Roman Catholic Church.

752 Bodelsen, C. A., and Merete Bodelsen. "T. S. Eliot's Jewelled Unicorns," ES, 35 (June, 1954), 125-126.

753 Brooks, Cleanth, and Robert Penn Warren. "The Reading of Modern Poetry," AmR, 7 (February, 1937), 445-446.

754 Chiari, Joseph. "Ash Wednesday," T. S. Eliot: Poet and Dramatist. New York: Barnes & Noble, 1972, pp. 75-80.

755 Cleophas, Sister M. "Ash Wednesday: The Purgatorio in a Modern Mode," CL, 11, #4 (Fall, 1959), 329-339. Finds Eliot's poem analogous to the "underlying spiritual Structure" of the Purgatorio of Dante.

756 Davidson, Clifford. "Types of Despair in Ash Wednesday," Renascence, 18, #4 (Summer, 1966), 216-218. Part I shows the despair is "ultimately opposed to hope and is thus 'the murderer of the soul,'" but despair then becomes a stage toward union with God. At last, "traditional despair is also united with modern concern about the existence of God...."

757 Davis, William V. "The Sound of Silence: Edward Lewis Wallant's The Children at the Gate," Cithara, 8, #1

(November, 1968), 3-25. Deals with parallels between Wallant's work and Eliot's poem.

758 Dolan, Paul J. "Ash Wednesday: A Catechumenical Poem," Renascence, 19 (Summer, 1967), 198-207.

759 Duncan Jones, E. E. "Ash Wednesday," Focus Three: T. S. Eliot, A Study of His Writings by Several Hands. B. Rajan, ed. London: Denis Dobson, 1947, pp. 37-56.

760 Dwyer, Daniel N. "Eliot's Ash Wednesday, IV, 1-4," Expl, 9 (October, 1950), Item 5. Significance of the colors.

761 Dzwonkoski, F. Peter, Jr. "The Hollow Men and Ash Wednesday: Two Dark Nights," ArQ, 30 (Spring, 1974), 16-42. Echoes of both The Divine Comedy and The Hollow Men in Ash Wednesday.

762 Eastman, Max. The Literary Mind. New York: Scribner's, 1931, pp. 20-23. Ash Wednesday "an oily puddle of emotional noises."

763 Foster, Genevieve W. "Archetypal Imagery of T. S. Eliot," PMLA, 60, #2 (June, 1945), 580-582.

764 Freimarck, Vincent. "Eliot's Ash Wednesday, III-V," Expl, 9 (October, 1950), Item 6.

765 Friar, Kimon, and John Malcolm Brinnin. "Ash Wednesday," Modern Poetry: American and British. New York: Appleton-Century-Crofts, 1951, pp. 459-498.

766 Fukuda, Rikutaro, and Yasuo Moriyama. "T. S. Eliot's Ash Wednesday," Kenkyu. Hiroshima: Bunka Hyoronsha. 1972.

767 Gardner, Helen. "The Landscapes of Eliot's Poetry," CritQ, 10 (1968), 325-326.

768 Gorman, William J. "Eliot's Ash Wednesday," Inlander, 11, #1 (November, 1930), 5-10.

769 Grubb, Frederick. "Ash-Wednesday," A Vision of Reality. New York: Barnes & Noble, 1965, pp. 60-61.

770 Hargrove, Nancy D. "Landscape as Symbol in T. S. Eliot's Ash Wednesday," ArQ, 30, (Spring, 1974), 53-62. The poem's landscape is important for symbolizing "the arduousness of the spiritual ascent as well as the final joy which awaits the determined soul."

771 Hester, Sister Mary. "The Lenten Liturgy as Objective Correlative for T. S. Eliot's Ash Wednesday," WisSL, 3 (1966), 43-56. Sixty of the sixty-seven scripture texts in

Ash Wednesday appear or are echoed in the Anglican Lenten liturgy.

772 Hewitt, Elizabeth K. "Structure and Meaning in T. S. Eliot's Ash Wednesday," Anglia, 83, #4 (1965), 426-450. An analysis of the sounds in Ash Wednesday an aid to understanding the meaning.

773 Howard, Brian. "Mr. Eliot's Poetry," NSt, 36 (1930), 146.

774 Jones, E. E. Duncan. "Ash Wednesday," T. S. Eliot: A Study of His Writing by Several Hands. B. Rajan, ed. London: Dennis Dobson, 1947, pp. 37-56.

775 Kenner, Hugh. "Ash Wednesday," The Invisible Poet: T. S. Eliot. New York: Ivan Obolensky, 1959, pp. 261-275.

775a ________. "Eliot's Moral Dialectic," HudR, 2 (Autumn, 1949), 439-446.

776 Kinnamon, Rebeccah A. "Eliot's Ash Wednesday and Maritain's Ideal for Poetry," GaR, 27, #2 (Summer, 1973), 156-165. Notes the parallels between Eliot's poem and an essay by Jacques Maritain which Eliot translated for The Criterion in 1927.

777 Koppenhaver, Allen J. "The Pattern in T. S. Eliot's Carpet," Cresset, 28, #5 (March, 1965), 15-17. In Ash Wednesday the speaker accepts "his suffering in order to arrive at fulfillment."

778 Leavis, Frank Raymond. "Blake and Ash Wednesday," Revaluation: Tradition and Development in English Poetry. London: Chatto & Windus, 1959, pp. 140-142.

778a ________. New Bearings in English Poetry. London: Chatto & Windus, 1932, pp. 117-128.

779 Little, Roger. "T. S. Eliot and Saint-John Perse," ArlQ, 2, #2 (Autumn, 1969), 5-17. Verbal echoes, as well as rhythms and imagery drawn from Saint-John Perse, are to be found in poems from Ash Wednesday onward.

780 Lozano Mompo, Mercedes. Significado de Ash Wednesday en T. S. Eliot. Diss., Madrid U.: 1970.

781 Maccoby, H. Z. "Two Notes on Ash Wednesday," N&Q, 13, n.s. #11 (November, 1966), 413-415. Aids to understanding Ash Wednesday are found in Murder in the Cathedral and The Dry Salvages.

782 Martin, Philip M. Mastery and Mercy: A Study of Two Religious Poems, The Wreck of the Deutschland by G. M.

Hopkins, and Ash Wednesday by T. S. Eliot. London; New York: Oxford U. Pr., 1957.

783 Morrison, Theodore. "Ash Wednesday: A Religious History," NEQ, 11 (June, 1938), 266-286. Finds William James's The Varieties of Religious Experience an aid to an understanding of the "experience of religious conversion" expressed in "images and symbols" of Ash Wednesday.

784 Oden, Thomas C. "Meditation for Ash Wednesday," CC, 15 (Winter, 1965), 1-8.

785 Peterson, R. G. "Our Debt to T. S. Eliot," Response (St. Louis), 6 (Easter, 1965), 158-164. Ash Wednesday is Eliot's declaration that the best course against inhumanity is acceptance of orthodox Christianity.

786 Pottle, Frederick Albert. The Idiom of Poetry. Ithaca: Cornell U. Pr., 1941; revised, 1946, pp. 89-91, 96-99.

787 Rajan, B. "The Overwhelming Question," SR, 74, Special Eliot Issue (Winter, 1966), 358-375. "The shape of Mr. Eliot's poetry is ... composed by two forces: the spiral of process and the circle of design ... both stipulate the search for reality as a condition of man's being."

788 Rodgers, Audrey T. "T. S. Eliot's Purgatorio: The Structure of Ash Wednesday," CLS, 7, #1 (March, 1970), 97-112. "Patterned simultaneously on the Sacrifice of the Mass and Dante's Purgatorio," Ash Wednesday's "final goal is the unitary objective of all myth."

789 Romer, Karen T. "T. S. Eliot and the Language of Liturgy," Renascence, 24, #3 (Spring, 1972), 119-135. Eliot's use of the language of the liturgy an aid to understanding Ash Wednesday and certain other poems.

790 Schneider, Elisabeth. "Ash Wednesday: The Time of Change," T. S. Eliot: The Pattern in the Carpet. Berkeley and Los Angeles: U. of California Pr., 1975, pp. 108-128.

791 Sencourt, Robert. "Ash Wednesday and Other Poems," T. S. Eliot: A Memoir. Donald Adamson, ed. London: Garnstone; New York: Dodd, Mead, 1971, pp. 140-144.

792 Sickels, Eleanor M. "Eliot's The Waste Land, I, 24-30, and Ash Wednesday, IV-VI," Expl, 9 (October, 1950), Item 4. The rock symbolism. Cf., Lyle Glazier, Expl, 8 (1950), Item 26.

793 Slattery, Sister Margaret Patrice. "Structural Unity in Eliot's Ash Wednesday," Renascence, 20 (Spring, 1968), 147-152. "[T]he over-all structure of the poem has a pattern of

regression and progression which reflects the essential meaning."

794 Smith, Grover, Jr. "Lady of Silences: Ash Wednesday," T. S. Eliot's Poetry and Plays. Chicago U. Pr., 1956, pp. 135-158.

795 Spender, Stephen. The Destructive Element: A Study of Modern Writers and Beliefs. Boston; New York: Houghton Mifflin, 1936, pp. 132-175.

796 Symes, Gordon. "T. S. Eliot and Old Age," FnR, 169 (March, 1951), 188-191.

797 Tate, Allen. "T. S. Eliot" [Ash Wednesday], Reactionary Essays on Poetry and Ideas. New York: Scribner's, 1936, pp. 210-220; repr., in On the Limits of Poetry. New York: Swallow & Morrow, 1948, pp. 344-349; excerpt in T. S. Eliot: Selected Criticism. L. Unger, ed. Englewood Cliffs, N.J.: Prentice-Hall, 1962, pp. 289-295.

797a ______. "T. S. Eliot: 1931," [Ash Wednesday], Collected Essays. Denver: Alan Swallow, 1959, pp. 341-349.

798 Torrens, James, S. J. "Charles Maurras and Eliot's 'New Life,'" PMLA, 89, #2 (March, 1974), 312-322. Finds Ash Wednesday a "mirror" of both Eliot's Dante essay and the esthetics of Charles Maurras.

799 Tschumi, Raymond. Thought in Twentieth-Century English Poetry. London: Routledge & Kegan Paul, Ltd., 1951, pp. 144-146.

800 Unger, Leonard. "Ash Wednesday," The Man in the Name: Essays on the Experience of Poetry. Minneapolis: U. of Minnesota Pr., 1956, pp. 141-167.

801 ______. "'The Hollow Men' and 'Ash Wednesday,'" T. S. Eliot: Moments and Patterns. Minneapolis: Minnesota U. Pr., 1956, pp. 65-71; repr., in T. S. Eliot: A Collection of Criticism. Linda W. Wagner, ed. New York: McGraw-Hill, 1974, pp. 65-71.

802 ______. "Notes on Ash Wednesday," SoR, 4, #4 (Spring, 1939), pp. 745-770.

803 ______. "T. S. Eliot's Rose Garden: A Persistent Theme," SoR, 7, #4 (Spring, 1942), 675-676. "In Ash Wednesday, more clearly than in earlier poems, restoration of the childhood experience is identified with the goal of religious life,...."

804 Vergmann, Finn. "Ash Wednesday: A Poem of Earthly and Heavenly Love," OL, 14 (Spring, 1959), 54-61.

805 Weatherhead, A. Kingsley. "Baudelaire in Eliot's Ash Wednesday, IV," ELN, 2 (June, 1965), 288-289. In Ash Wednesday, Part IV, Eliot was influenced by the cadences of Baudelaire's "Bohemiens en Voyage."

805a Webb, Eugene. "The Way Up and the Way Down: The Redemption of Time in T. S. Eliot's Ash Wednesday and Four Quartets," The Dark Dove: The Sacred and Secular in Modern Literature. Seattle: U. of Washington Pr., 1975, pp. 194-236.

806 Williams, William Carlos. "The Fatal Blunder," QRL, 2, #2 (Winter, 1944), 125-126.

807 Wilson, Frank. "The Middle Period," [Ash Wednesday], Six Essays on the Development of T. S. Eliot. London: Fortune Pr., 1948, pp. 36-40.

808 Wooton, Carl. "The Mass: Ash Wednesday's Objective Correlative," ArQ, 17, #1 (Spring, 1961), 31-42. Comparison of Catholic liturgy with Ash Wednesday indicates that the Mass is the controlling device of the poem.

809 Zabel, M. D. "T. S. Eliot in Mid-Career," Poetry, 36 (1930), 330-337.

ARIEL POEMS

810 Chiari, Joseph. "Ariel Poems and the First Dramatic Writings," T. S. Eliot: Poet and Dramatist. New York: Barnes & Noble, 1972, pp. 105-114.

811 Grubb, Frederick. [Ariel Poems], A Vision of Reality. London: Chatto & Windus; New York: Barnes & Noble, 1965, pp. 61-62.

812 Kenner, Hugh. "Ariel Poems," The Invisible Poet: T. S. Eliot. New York: Obolensky, 1959, pp. 239-260.

813 Schneider, Elisabeth. "The Ariel Poems and Coriolan," T. S. Eliot: The Pattern in the Carpet. Berkeley & Los Angeles: U. of Calif. Pr., 1975, pp. 129-148.

814 Smith, Grover, Jr. "Visions and Revisions: The Ariel Poems," T. S. Eliot's Poetry and Plays. U. of Chicago Pr., 1956, pp. 121-134.

815 Southham, B. C. "Ariel Poems," A Guide to the Selected Poems of T. S. Eliot. New York: Harcourt, Brace & Winston: 1969, pp. 119-126.

816 Williamson, George. "Ariel Poems," A Reader's Guide to T. S. Eliot. New York: Noonday, 1953, pp. 163-164, passim.

817 Zabel, M. D. "T. S. Eliot in Mid-Career," [Ariel Poems], Poetry, 36 (1930), 330-337.

"Animula" [Ariel]

818 Askew, Melwin W. "Form and Process in Lyric Poetry," SR, 72, #2 (April-June, 1964), 281-299. Sees Eliot's Animula as an example of the pattern and process to be found in English lyric poetry for over four hundred years.

819 Stroud, T. A. "Eliot's Animula," Expl, 28 (1969), Item 14. "The characters seem arranged, ... to suggest a movement up the levels of Hell...."

820 Williamson, George. "Animula," A Reader's Guide to T. S. Eliot. New York: Noonday, 1953, pp. 167-168.

820a Wilson, Frank. "The Middle Period," [Animula], Six Essays on the Development of T. S. Eliot. London: Fortune, 1948, pp. 35-36.

"Journey of the Magi" [Ariel]

821 Abel, Richard. "The Influence of St. John Perse on T. S. Eliot," ConL, 14 (1973), 213-239. An analysis of Journey of the Magi indicates not only "borrowing" but also technical experimentation.

822 Broes, Arthur T. "T. S. Eliot's Journey of the Magi: An Explication," XUS, 5, #3 (December, 1966), 129-131. Although the birth of Christ is the thematical center of the poem, notes allusions to other facets of the life of Christ.

823 Brown, R. D. "Revelation in T. S. Eliot's Journey of the Magi," Renascence, 24, #3 (Spring, 1972), 136-140. The realization of the Magus that the child is the Messiah "burns at the core of the work and its sources in the Old and New Testaments."

824 Church, Margaret. "Eliot's Journey of the Magi," Expl, 18 (June, 1960), Item 55. Study of the white horse as a symbol of "both birth in life and life in death, the reality of both the visible and the invisible."

825 Drew, Elizabeth. Poetry: A Modern Guide to Its Understanding and Enjoyment. New York: Norton, 1959, pp. 237-240.

826 Elmen, Paul. "The Magical Journey of T. S. Eliot," ChrCen, 82, #20 (May 19, 1965), 649-652. Journey of the Magi "has the merit of an epitaph, revealing frugally the whole life of the man,"--and perhaps Eliot's own spiritual journey.

827 Foster, Genevieve W. "Archetypal Imagery of T. S. Eliot," PMLA, 60 (June, 1945), 578-580.

827a Franklin, Rosemary. "The Satisfactory Journey of Eliot's Magus," ES, 49 (December, 1968), 559-561. "Satisfactory, ... becomes the pivotal word in the poem." It "marks the end of the Magus' quest for the Birth fulfilling history, and, ... it fits in appropriately with the symbols of the Passion."

828 Germer, Rudolf. "T. S. Eliot's Journey of the Magi," JA, 7 (1962), 106-132. A study of the use of sources and structure of the poem, and the "accumulation and digestion of experience."

829 ____________. "T. S. Eliot's Journey of the Magi," Die moderne englische Lyrik: Interpretationen. Oppel, Horst, ed. Berlin: E. Schmidt Verl. 1967, pp. 150-163.

830 Gish, Nancy. "The Meaning of the Incarnation in Two Ariel Poems," MichA, 6 (Summer, 1973), 59-69. Central to the meaning of Journey of the Magi and A Song for Simeon is the Incarnation and the quality of our emotional response.

831 Grahn, Heinz. "T. S. Eliot: Journey of the Magi," NS, n. s., 16, #7 (July, 1967), 341-349.

832 Joselyn, Sister M. "Twelfth Night Quartet: Four Magi Poems," Renascence, 16, #2 (Winter, 1964), 92-94. A comparative study of Eliot's Journey of the Magi, W. B. Yeat's The Magi, John Peale Bishop's Twelfth Night, and Edgar Bowers's The Wise Men.

833 Kaplan, Robert B., and Richard J. Wall. "Journey of the Magi," Expl, 19 (November, 1969), Item 8. Notes that the poem divides into two parts: birth and death, and death and rebirth.

834 Kenner, Hugh. "Ariel Poems," The Invisible Poet: T. S. Eliot. New York: Obolensky, 1959, pp. 239-260.

835 Mary Eleanor, Mother. "Eliot's Magi," Renascence, 10 (Autumn, 1957), 26-31.

836 Muir, Kenneth. "Kipling and Eliot," N&Q, n. s., 1 (September, 1954), 400-401. The influence of "The Man Who Would Be King" upon Journey of the Magi.

837 Scalise, Anna Maria. "T. S. Eliot: Due Composizioni Natalizie: 'La Coltivazione degli Alberi di Natale,' e 'Il Viaggio dei Magi,'" VeP, 48 (1965), 30-34.

838 Smailes, Thomas A. "Eliot's Journey of the Magi," Expl, 29 (1970), Item 18. The "old white horse" in Eliot's poem is used anachronistically to show that Advent brought about a change in loyalties indicated by "vine leaves over the lintel" of the tavern.

839 Standop, Ewald. "T. S. Eliot's Journey of the Magi," Archiv, 197 (November, 1960), 113-125. The poem is concerned with the death-in-life theme.

840 Thompson, A. C. "T. S. Eliot and the Journey of the Magi," Opinion (Adelaide), 7 (December, 1963), 8-12.

841 Williamson, George. "Journey of the Magi," A Reader's Guide to T. S. Eliot. New York: Noonday, 1953, pp. 164-165, passim.

842 Wills, John H. "Eliot's Journey of the Magi," Expl, 12 (March, 1954), Item 32.

"Marina" [Ariel]

843 Barnes, W. J. "T. S. Eliot's Marina," UKCR, 29, #4 (June, 1963), 297-305. "In Marina Eliot has re-created and re-presented the complex experience of regeneration by delineating ... the developing states of consciousness in a soul which is undergoing that experience in all its intensity."

844 Cameron, Elspeth. "T. S. Eliot's Marina: An Exploration," QQ, 77, #2 (Summer, 1970), 180-189. Though Shakespeare's Pericles and Seneca's Hercules Furens are sources for Eliot's Marina, the poem is not only about the religious experience, but is also an exploration of the creative process.

845 Cook, Harold E. "A Search for the Ideal: An Interpretation of T. S. Eliot's Marina," BuR, 5 (December, 1954), 33-41.

846 Cox, C. B., and A. E. Dyson. "T. S. Eliot: Marina," Modern Poetry: Studies in Practical Criticism. London: Ed. Arnold, 1963; repub., 1971, pp. 72-79.

847 Daiches, David, and William Charvat. "Marina," Poems in English, 1530-1940. New York: Ronald, 1950, pp. 741, passim.

848 Deutsch, Babette. Poetry in Our Time. New York: Henry Holt, 1952, p. 175.

849 Dolan, Paul J. "Eliot's Marina: A Reading," Renascence, 21 (Summer, 1969), 203-206. "Marina is a dramatic monologue in which the speaker having reached a new state of spiritual experience looks backward to what he has left and forward to try to discern what is ahead."

850 ________. "Milton and Eliot: A Common Source," N&Q, 13, n.s. (1966), 379-380. Line 1138 of Seneca's Hercules Furens seems to have been the source of both line 242, Book I, of Paradise Lost and the epigram to Eliot's Marina.

851 Foster, Genevieve W. "Archetypal Imagery of T. S. Eliot," PMLA, 60 (June, 1945), 582-583.

852 Jain, Narendra K. "An Appreciation of T. S. Eliot's Marina," BP, 10 (1968), 66-68.

853 Leavis, F. R. Education and the University. New York: Geo. Stewart, 1948, pp. 90-92.

854 ________. "Eliot's Later Poetry," Scrutiny, 11 (Summer, 1942), 61-63.

855 ________. New Bearings on English Poetry. London: Chatto & Windus, 1932, pp. 129-131.

856 Olsson, Y. B. "T. S. Eliot's Marina: A Study in Poetic Cohesion," DUJ, 33 (March, 1972), 115-119. The themes of the poem are interlocked, reflecting the affinity between poetry and music.

857 Vyas, H. K. "Lifting the Veil," BP, 16 (1971), 37-41. A comparative study of Marina and Tennyson's The Lady of Shalott.

858 Worthington, Jane. "The Epigraphs to the Poetry of T. S. Eliot," AL, 21 (March, 1949), 15-16.

"A Song for Simeon" [Ariel]

859 Gish, Nancy K. D. "The Meaning of the Incarnation in Two Ariel Poems," MichA, 6 (Summer, 1973), 59-69. A study of A Song for Simeon and Journey of the Magi with reference to the Incarnation.

860 Kenner, Hugh. "Eliot's Moral Dialectic," HudR, 2 (Autumn, 1949), 424-428.

AUNT HELEN

860a Hombitzer, Eleonore. "T. S. Eliot: 'Aunt Helen,'" NS, 24 (1975), 407-418.

860b Stemmler, Theo. "T. S. Eliot's Aunt Helen," NS, #10 (October, 1963), 477-481. "Aunt Helen ist mehr als das satirische Porträt einer alten Jungfer. In diesem Gedicht analysiert Eliot eine müde, sterile und konventionelle Welt, wie sie sich ihm in Neu-England,...."

THE BOSTON EVENING TRANSCRIPT

860c Brown, W. C. "'A Poem Should Not Mean but Be,'" UKCR, 15 (August, 1948), 61-62.

BURBANK WITH A BAEDEKER: BLEISTEIN WITH A CIGAR

861 Alter, Robert. "Eliot, Lawrence and the Jews," Commentary, 50, #4 (October, 1970), 81-86. Eliot's aloofness from European culture is suggested by the anti-Semitism of Burbank with a Baedeker: Bleistein with a Cigar.

862 Arms, G. W., J. P. Kirby, L. G. Locke, and R. W. Whidden. "Eliot's Burbank with a Baedeker: Bleistein with a Cigar," Expl. 3 (May, 1945), Item 53. The poem is "an expression of Eliot's evaluation of the modern age as ugly, decadent, unheroic, and unromantic," and this theme (lines 25-26) "is also in part a contrast between the romantic love of the past and the corrupt, concupiscent love of the modern age, as suggested particularly by the princess."

863 Bateson, F. W. "Burbank with a Baedeker, Eliot with a Laforgue," Rev. (Oxford), #4 (November, 1962), 12-15. Eliot's borrowed lines satirize his literary model, Jules Laforgue.

864 The Editors. "Eliot's Burbank with a Baedeker: Bleistein with a Cigar," Expl, 3, #3 (December, 1944), Item 53.

865 Espey, John J. "The Epigraph to T. S. Eliot's Burbank with a Baedeker: Bleistein with a Cigar," AL, 29 (January, 1958), 483-484. Notes possible association by Eliot of Henry James's Aspern Papers, but also notes the suggestion of Ford Madox Ford in Henry James: A Critical Study that Eliot utilized a phrase "Beautiful Genius" from another of James's stories, The Madonna of the Future.

865a Glenn, I. E. "T. S. Eliot's Burbank with a Baedeker: Bleistein with a Cigar: A Sociological Reading," Standpunte, 118 (1975), 39-44.

866 Goheen, Robert F. "Burbank with a Baedeker: The Third Stanza," SR, 61 (Winter, 1953), 109-119.

867 Locke, Louis G. "Eliot's Burbank with a Baedeker: Bleistein with a Cigar," Expl, 3 (1945), No. 53.

868 Loucks, James F. "A Second Browning Allusion in Eliot's Burbank poem," N&Q, 23, #1 (January, 1976), 18-19. "Line thirteen of Eliot's poem reads, 'But this or such was Bleistein's way: ...' This line bears a striking resemblance to the second line of Browning's 'How It Strikes a Contemporary': 'I only knew one poet in my life: / And this, or something like it, was his way.'"

869 Martin, B. K. "Prufrock, Bleistein and Company," N&Q, 14, #7 (July, 1967), 257. A possible source for the name of Bleistein.

870 Newton, Frances J. "Venice, Pope, T. S. Eliot and D. H. Lawrence," N&Q, 5, #3 (March, 1958), 119-120. "Eliot's Burbank with a Baedeker ..." recalls the Dunciad and Essay on Man (V, 291-2) in its use of Venice as a symbol of corruption.

871 Riding, Laura, and Robert Graves. A Survey of Modernist Poetry. New York: Doubleday, Doran, 1928, pp. 235-242.

872 Spencer, Theodore. "The Poetry of T. S. Eliot," Atl, 151 (January, 1933), 61-62.

873 Stanford, D. L. "Two Notes on T. S. Eliot," TCL, 1 (October, 1955), 133-134. Finds a source for a line in Burbank ("They were together, and he fell") from Tennyson's "The Sisters," ("They were together and she fell....")

874 Turner, Richard C. "Burbank and Grub Street: A Note on T. S. Eliot and Swift," ES, 52 (August, 1971), 347-348.

A COOKING EGG

875 Bateson, F. W. "A Cooking Egg," EIC, 4 (January, 1954), 106-108.

876 Drew, Elizabeth. "A Cooking Egg," Discovering Poetry. New York: Norton, 1933, pp. 113-115. 'It is clear that the poetic rhythm in A Cooking Egg is something quite different from anything we have yet examined...."

877 Howes, A. B. "T. S. Eliot's A Cooking Egg," The Humanities (Journal of the Yokahama National U.), (March, 1952), 1-5.

877a Loucks, James F. "T. S. Eliot's A Cooking Egg: An Echo from Thomas Hood," N&Q, 23, #7 (July, 1976), 299-300. The "Sidney-kidney" rhyme of stanza three "is evidently taken from a stanza of Thomas Hood's 'A Lament for the Decline of Chivalry.'"

878 Materer, Timothy. "A Note on T. S. Eliot's A Cooking Egg," TSER, 2 (Spring, 1975), 3.

879 Richards, I. A., and F. W. Bateson. "A Cooking Egg: Final Scramble," EIC, 4 (January, 1954), 103-108. An exchange of views about interpretation of A Cooking Egg.

880 Richards, I. A. Principles of Literary Criticism. London: 2nd ed., Kegan Paul, French, Trubner, 1926, pp. 293-294.

881 Vinograd, Sherna S. "The Accidental: A Clue to Structure in Eliot's Poetry," Accent, 9 (Summer, 1949), 231-232.

882 Worthington, Jane. "The Epigraphs to the Poetry of T. S. Eliot: A Cooking Egg," AL, 21 (March, 1949), 9-10. "... Life must, ... be different in heaven; there the pleasures denied the modern gentleman will be enjoyed...."

CORIOLAN

883 Bollier, E. P. "A Broken Coriolanus: A Note on T. S. Eliot's Coriolan," SoR, n.s., 3 (July, 1967), 625-633. "... since Coriolanus like its hero seems to say what it means and to mean what it says, to Eliot, 'Coriolanus' had come to be a private rubric for a personal poetic ideal."

883a Leavis, F. R. "Eliot's Later Poetry," Scrutiny, 11 (Summer, 1942), 63-64.

883b Martin, W. R. "A Possible Source for Eliot's 'Triumphal March,'" TSEN, 1 (Fall, 1974), 2-3. Heine's Riesebilder suggested as the source.

884 Rao, G. Nagaswara. "The Unfinished Poems of T. S. Eliot," LCrit, 9, #3 (1970), 27-35.

885 Romer, Karen T. "T. S. Eliot and the Language of Liturgy," Renascence, 24 (1972), 119-135. Coriolan and Ash Wednesday indicate use of consciousness in the liturgical experience.

885a Schmidt, A. V. C. "Crumpets in 'Coriolan,' Muffins in 'Pickwick,'" N&Q, 23 (July, 1976), 298-299.

886 Schneider, Elisabeth. "The Ariel Poems and Coriolan," T. S. Eliot: The Pattern in the Carpet. Berkeley; Los Angeles: California U. Pr., 1975, pp. 129-148.

887 Smith, Grover, Jr. "The Turning World: Coriolan," T. S. Eliot's Poetry and Plays. Chicago U. Pr., 1956, pp. 159-167.

888 Taranath, Rajeev. "Coriolanus, The Waste Land and Coriolan Poems," LCritM, 6 (Winter, 1963), 111-120.

889 Theall, Donald F. "Traditional Satire in Eliot's Coriolan," Accent, 11 (Autumn, 1951), 194-206. Coriolan is a satire of democracy and/or totalitarianism in government.

THE CULTIVATION OF CHRISTMAS TREES

889a Braybrooke, Neville. "Eliot's Search for a Lost Eden," CathW, (December, 1959), 151-156.

889b Combecher, Hans. "Zu Eliots The Cultivation of Christmas Trees," NS, 13, #11 (November, 1964), 530-534.

890 Kenner, Hugh. "A Plea for Metrics," Poetry, 86, #1 (April, 1955), 42-45. Discussion of the metrics in The Cultivation of Christmas Trees.

890a Maxwell, D. E. S. "The Cultivation of Christmas Trees," T. S. Eliot: A Symposium. Neville Braybrooke, ed. New York: 1958, 190-192.

DANS LE RESTAURANT

891 Frankenberg, Lloyd. Pleasure Dome: On Reading Modern Poetry. Boston: Houghton Mifflin, 1949, pp. 72-76.

891a Gent, Margaret. "The Drowned Phoenician Sailor: T. S. Eliot and William Morris," N&Q, n. s., 17 (February, 1970), 50-51. Comparison of Eliot's "Dans le Restaurant" with William Morris's "The Nymph's Song to Hylas" from the fourth Book of The Life and Death of Jason.

892 Unger, Leonard. The Man in the Name: Essays on the Experience of Poetry. Minneapolis: Minnesota U. P., 1956, pp. 169-171.

893 ____________. "T. S. Eliot's Rose Garden: A Persistent Theme," SoR, 7 (Spring, 1942), 669-671.

893a Whiteside, George. "T. S. Eliot's Dans le Restaurant," AI, 33 (Summer, 1976), 155-173.

LA FIGLIA CHE PIANGE

894 Hagstrum, J. H. English "A" Analyst, No. 3 (1947-49), 1-7.

895 Hall, Vernon, Jr. "Eliot's La Figlia che Piange," Expl, 5 (November, 1946), Item 16.

896 Worthington, Jane. "The Epigraphs to the Poetry of T. S. Eliot," AL, 21 (March, 1949), 4-5.

FOUR QUARTETS

897 Abrams, M. H. "Four Versions of the Circuitous Return: Marx, Nietzsche, Eliot, Lawrence," National Supernaturalism: Tradition and Revolution in Romantic Literature. New York: W. W. Norton, 1971, pp. 319-322.

898 Anderson, Paul Victor. "T. S. Eliot's Changing Dispositions of Thought," DAI, 37 (Washington: 1975), 977A-978A.

899 Bain, Donald. "T. S. Eliot's The Cocktail Party," Nine, 2, #1 (January, 1950), 16-22. The Cocktail Party as a dramatization of the Four Quartets.

900 Baron, C. E. "Lawrence's Influence on Eliot," CamQ, 5

(Spring, 1971), 235-248. Four Quartets may be an attempt to provide Christian answers to some of the religious questions raised by Lawrence's writing.

901 Beaver, Joseph. "T. S. Eliot's Four Quartets," Expl, 11 (March, 1953), Item 37. Comments on Eliot's images from science.

902 Bergonzi, Bernard, ed. T. S. Eliot, Four Quartets: A Casebook. London: Macmillan, 1969.

903 Bergsten, Staffan. Time and Eternity: A Study of the Structure and Symbolism of T. S. Eliot's Four Quartets. (Studia Litterarum Upsaliensia, #1.) Stockholm: Bonniers, 1960.

904 Bewley, Marius. "Aspects of Modern American Poetry," Scrutiny, 17, #4 (March, 1951), 350. "... Probably the greatest poetry in our time is the Four Quartets."

905 Bille, Finn. "The Ultimate Metaphor and the Defeat of Poetry in T. S. Eliot's Four Quartets," IJSym, 3, #1 (1972), 16-24.

906 Blackmur, R. P. "Unappeasable and Peregrine: Behavior and the Four Quartets," Thought, 26 (Spring, 1951), 50-76.

907 ___________. "Unappeasable and Peregrine: Behavior and the Four Quartets," Language as Gesture: Essays in Poetry. New York: Harcourt, Brace & Co., 1952, pp. 193-220. Eliot's Four Quartets, "a poem dense with behavior and brimming with order."

908 Blamires, Harry. Word Unheard: A Guide through Eliot's Four Quartets. London: Methuen, 1969; New York: Barnes & Noble, 1970.

909 Bland, D. S. "Mr. Eliot on the Underground," MLN, 68 (January, 1953), 27-28. The London underground railway as symbolism in Four Quartets.

910 Blisset, William. "The Argument of T. S. Eliot's Four Quartets," UTQ, 15, #2 (January, 1946), 115-126. Says that the Quartets deal primarily with "the basic Christian realities of sin and grace in terms of time and redeeming the time, and secondarily with poetry and the life of the poet."

911 Bluestein, Mary Kate. "'The Moment in the Arbour': Wordsworthian Qualities in Four Quartets," DAI, 35 (Boston: 1974), 3724A.

912 Bodelsen, C. A. "T. S. Eliot," Fremmede digtere i det 20 århundrede. Sven M. Kristensen, ed. Copenhagen: G. E. C. Gad, Vol. II, 1968, pp. 43-66.

913 ________. T. S. Eliot's Four Quartets: A Commentary. Copenhagen: Rosenkilde and Bagger, 1958.

914 ________. "Two 'Difficult' Poems by T. S. Eliot," ES (Amsterdam), 34 (February, 1953), 17-22. Explication of two passages in Four Quartets.

915 Bodgener, J. H. "Spiritual Life and Literary Trends," London Quarterly and Holborn Rev, 170 (1945), 321-327.

916 Bowra, C. W. The Creative Experiment. London: Macmillan, 1949; New York: Grove Pr., 1959, pp. 22-23. "... In his Four Quartets T. S. Eliot combines different forms of verse. If, on the whole, he uses a supple, sinuous verse of varying length and accent, at times he uses something much more traditional."

917 Bradbury, John M. "Four Quartets: The Structural Symbolism," SR, 59 (Spring, 1951), 254-270. "In the Quartets, as in all of Eliot's later poetry, the imagery is structural, and never so completely articulated as in the last poems of this group."

918 Bradford, Curtis B. "Journeys to Byzantium," VQR, 25 (Spring, 1949), 216-224.

918a Brady, Ann Patrick. "The Function of Lyrics in the Four Quartets," DAI, 36 (U. of North Carolina at Chapel Hill: 1974), 301A.

919 Braybrooke, Neville. "T. S. Eliot and Children," AryP, 41, #4 (April, 1970), 166-172. A survey of children's opinions in 1957-58 indicated they preferred the Four Quartets.

920 Brett, R. L. "Mysticism and Incarnation in Four Quartets," Eng, 16 (Autumn, 1966), 94-99. Four Quartets exemplifies the conjunction of Time and Eternity taken from the philosophy of F. H. Bradley and transformed by Christian tradition.

921 ________. Reason and Imagination: A Study of Form and Meaning in Four Poems. London; New York: Oxford U. Pr., for Univ. of Hull, 1960. Revs. TLS (January 29, 1960), 66; A. Alvarez, NSt, 59 (1960), 77-78; Bonamy Dobrée, CritQt, 2 (1960), 89, 91-92.

922 Brooks, Harold F. "Four Quartets: The Structure in Relation to the Themes," Eliot in Perspective: A Symposium. Graham Martin, ed. London: Macmillan; New York: Humanities, 1970, pp. 132-147.

923 Brotman, D. Bosley. "T. S. Eliot: 'The Music of Ideas,'" UTQ, 18 (October, 1948), 20-29. Notes analogy between musical forms and Eliot's Four Quartets.

924 Cambon, Glauco. "I Quartetti di Eliot," FLe, 16 (April 2, 1961), 5. Concerns the bilingual edition of Four Quartets, Filippo Donini, editor.

925 Cameron, Elspeth. "T. S. Eliot's Marina: An Exploration," QQ, 77 (1970), 180-189. Marina has themes which can be traced to Four Quartets.

926 Capellán Gonzalo, Angel. "Dimensiones metafísicas del tiempo en Four Quartets," Atlántida, 7 (1969), 51-68.

927 Carew, Rivers. "Georges Rouault and T. S. Eliot: A Note," HJ, 60, #3 (April, 1962), 230-235. Comparison of Rouault's Miserere and Eliot's Four Quartets as to themes of redemption through suffering.

928 Chaturvedi, B. N. "The Indian Background of Eliot's Poetry," English, 15, #90 (Autumn, 1965), 220-223. Notes the influence of Buddhism, the Bhagwat Gita, and the Upanishads, particularly as to Four Quartets.

929 Chiari, Joseph. "Four Quartets," T. S. Eliot: Poet and Dramatist. New York: Barnes & Noble, 1972, pp. 81-104.

930 Christie, Erling. "Mystikk og poesi i Four Quartets," Samtiden, 61 (1952), 301-309.

930a ________. "Mystikk og poesi i Four Quartets," Tendenser og profiler. Oslo: Aschehoug, 1955, pp. 41-54.

931 Cleophas, Sister M. "Notes on Levels of Meaning in Four Quartets," Renascence, 2 (1949-50), 102-116.

932 Clubb, Merrel D. "The Heraclitean Element in Eliot's Four Quartets," PQ, 40 (January, 1961), 19-33.

933 Coats, R. H. "An Anchor for the Soul (A Study of Mr. T. S. Eliot's Later Verse)," HJ, 44 (1946), 112-118.

934 Counihan, Sister Bernadette. "Four Quartets: An Ascent to Mount Carmel?" WisSL, 6 (1969), 58-71. The "still point" refers to the mystical experience at the moment when time falls away and the soul is in communion with God.

935 Dallas, Elizabeth S. "Canon Cancrizans and the Four Quartets," CL, 17 (Summer, 1965), 193-208. Resemblance in the Four Quartets to Guillaume de Machaut's rondeau.

936 Davie, Donald. "Anglican Eliot," SoR, 9, #1 (January, 1973), 93-104.

936a ______. "T. S. Eliot: The End of an Era," TC, 159, #950 (April, 1956), 350-362; repr., in T. S. Eliot: A Collection of Critical Essays. Hugh Kenner, ed. Englewood Cliffs, N.J.: Prentice-Hall, 1962, pp. 192-205.

937 De Masirevich, Constance. On the Four Quartets of T. S. Eliot. Foreword by Roy Campbell. New York: Barnes & Noble, 1965. A guide to the "inner meaning of an incomparable poem...."

938 De Sola Pinto, Vivian. Crisis in English Poetry, 1880-1940. London: Hutchinson's U. Library, 1951-52, pp. 170-175, 180-184.

939 Deutsch, Babette. "The Enduring Music of the Past," NYHTB (July 18, 1943), 6. Notes the music in the poems.

940 ______. Poetry in Our Time. New York: Henry Holt, 1952, pp. 164-167, 170-172.

941 Donini, Filippo, ed. and tr. Quattro Quartetti. Milan: Garzanti, 1959.

942 Donoghue, Denis. "A Reading of the Four Quartets," The Ordinary Universe: Soundings in Modern Literature. New York: Macmillan, 1968, pp. 241-266.

942a ______. "T. S. Eliot's Quartets: A New Reading," Studies, 54 (1965), 41-62. Calls attention to the shift in Quartets criticism and analyzes the cause.

943 Drew, Arnold P. "Hints and Guesses in Four Quartets," UKCR, 20 (Spring, 1954), 171-175. "These hints and guesses, these fragmentary, transitory flashes by which the poet sees the vague outline ... of the truth are to be found both in the imagery and in the argument of Four Quartets."

944 Ellis, Peter G. "T. S. Eliot, F. H. Bradley, and Four Quartets," RSWSU, 37, #2 (June, 1969), 93-111. The metaphysics of Bradley and Eliot as an aid in the understanding of this work.

945 Felstiner, John. "La danza inmóvil, el vendaval sostenido: Four Quartets de T. S. Eliot y Alturas de Macchu Picchu," AUC, 129, 157-160 (1971), 177-195.

946 Fletcher, J. G. "Poems in Counterpoint," Poetry, 63 (1943), 44-48.

947 Flint, R. W. "The Four Quartets Reconsidered," SR, 56 (Winter, 1948), 69-81.

948 Fowler, Russell T. "Krishna and the 'Still Point': A Study of the Bhagavad-Gita's Influence in Eliot's Four Quartets," SR, 79, #3 (Summer, 1971), 407-423. In this work of Eliot's, as in the Bhagavad-Gita, "the various abstract ideas and philosophical considerations of the poem are located by their relation to the progress of an individual protagonist who is both a particular 'traveller' and everyman."

949 Fowlie, Wallace. "Eliot and Tchelitchew," Accent, 5 (Spring, 1945), 166-170. Parallels of imagery and symbolism between Four Quartets and Pavel Tchelitchew's painting Cache-Cache (1942).

950 Frank, Joseph. "Force and Form: A Study of John Peale Bishop," SR, 55 (Winter, 1947), 102-103.

951 Frankenberg, Lloyd. "Four Quartets," Pleasure Dome: On Reading Modern Poetry. Boston: Houghton Mifflin, 1949, pp. 98-117.

952 Friar, Kimon, and John M. Brinnin. Modern Poetry: American and British. New York: Appleton-Century-Crofts, 1951, pp. 426-427, 459-461.

953 Fussell, B. H. "Structural Methods in Four Quartets," ELH, 22 (September, 1955), 212-241.

954 Fussell, Paul, Jr. "The Gestic Symbolism of T. S. Eliot," ELH, 22 (September, 1955), 194-211. "In these gestic symbols, ... it would appear that Eliot has presented the poetic emblem that is the most precise equivalent of his central concern with reunion and reintegration...."

955 Gardner, Helen. "Four Quartets," New Writing and Daylight, (Summer, 1942), 84-96.

956 __________. "Four Quartets: A Commentary," Focus Three: T. S. Eliot, A Study of His Writings by Several Hands. B. Rajan, ed. London: Dennis Dobson, 1947, pp. 57-77; repr., in Critiques and Essays in Criticism, selected by Robert W. Stallman. New York: Ronald Pr., 1949, pp. 181-197.

957 __________. "The Music of Four Quartets," The Art of T. S. Eliot. London; New York: Cresset, 1961, pp. 36-56.

958 Gerard, Sister Mary. "Eliot of the Circle and John of the Cross," Thought, 34 (Spring, 1959), 107-127.

959 Gordon, Sarah E. "The Great Dance: A Study of Eliot's Use of the Dance Metaphor in the Four Quartets," DAI, 34 (Texas Christian: 1973), 3394A. "As one of the central metaphors of the Four Quartets, the dance has its origins in the philosophy of Plato and Plotinus and is associated ... with the mystical apprehension of the divine and particularly with the mystic's attempt to convey his experience through language...."

960 Gowda, H. H. Anniah. "Four Quartets: An Aspect of Indian Thought," LHY, 3, #1 (January, 1962), 21-27.

961 Greenhill, Eleanor S. "The Child in the Tree: A Study of the Cosmological Tree in Christian Tradition," Traditio, 10 (1954), 323-371. See for a gloss on images in Four Quartets.

962 Gregory, Horace. "Fare Forward, Voyagers," NYTBR (May 16, 1943), 2. Compares The Quartets with Wordsworth's Prelude.

963 Grigorescu, Irina. "T. S. Eliot: 'Patru cvartete,' două versiuni romanesti." [T. S. Eliot: 'Four Quartets,' two Romanian versions], Orizont, 21, #10 (October, 1971), 79-81.

964 Grigsby, Gordon Kay. "The Modern Long Poem: Studies in Thematic Form," DA, 21 (Wisconsin: 1960), 622-623.

965 Gross, Harvey. "Four Quartets," The Contrived Corridor. Ann Arbor: Michigan U. Pr., 1971, pp. 58-73.

966 ________. "Music and the Analogue of Feeling: Notes on Eliot and Beethoven," CRAS, 3, #3 (Summer, 1959), 269-288. Compares Eliot's Four Quartets with some of Beethoven's work.

967 Grove, Robin. "Eliot's Four Quartets," CR, 10 (1967), 3-17. In Eliot's later work, such as the Four Quartets, he is shown as "a religious poet of an altogether new and completely compelling kind."

968 Grubb, Frederick. [Four Quartets], A Vision of Reality. New York: Barnes & Noble, 1965, pp. 63-69.

969 Guidacci, Margherita. "I Quartetti di Eliot," Let, 9 (July-October, 1947), 29-41.

970 Hamada, Kazuie. "A Viewpoint on T. S. Eliot's Four Quartets," Collected Essays by the Members of the Faculty, No. 16. Tokyo: Kyoritsu Women's Junior College, 1972, pp. 36-45.

971 Hamilton, Elizabeth. "Teaching the Four Quartets to Schoolgirls," T. S. Eliot: A Symposium for His Seventieth Birthday. Neville Braybrooke, ed. New York: Farrar, Straus & Cudahy, 1958, pp. 98-101.

972 Hayward, John. Notes to English Translation of the Quartets. Quatre Quatuors. Pierre Leyris, tr. Paris: 1950.

973 Hernigman, Bernard. "Two Worlds and Epiphany," BardR, 2 (May, 1948), 156-159. Compares Eliot's Four Quartets and Wallace Stevens' Ideas of Order, Parts of a World, and Transport to Summer.

974 Hirsch, David H. "T. S. Eliot and the Vexation of Time," SoR, 3 (July, 1967), 608-624. An analysis of Eliot's treatment of "time and timelessness" in Four Quartets and The Love Song of J. Alfred Prufrock.

975 Holden, Raymond. "The Dark Night of the Soul," SatR, 26 (July 24, 1943), 11.

976 Holland, Joyce M. "Human Relations in Eliot's Drama," Renascence, 22 (Spring, 1970), 151-161. As he was writing Four Quartets, Eliot turned toward drama which indicates his new interest in relationships.

977 Hough, Graham. "Vision and Doctrine in Four Quartets," CritQ, 15 (Summer, 1973), 107-127.

978 Howarth, Herbert. "Eliot, Beethoven, and J. W. N. Sullivan," CL, 9 (Fall, 1957), 322-332. Influence on Four Quartets of Beethoven's A Minor Quartet, Opus 132, and Sullivan's Beethoven: His Spiritual Development.

979 Ingalls, Jeremy. "The Epic Tradition: A Commentary," E-WR, 1, #1 (Spring, 1964), 42-69.

980 Iser, Wolfgang. "T. S. Eliot's Four Quartets," JA, 3 (1958), 192-204.

981 Iyengar, K. R. Srinivasa. "Understanding Four Quartets," Indian Essays in American Literature: Papers in Honour of Robert E. Spiller. Sujit Mukherjee and D. V. K. Raghavacharyulu, eds. Bombay: Popular Prakashan, 1969, pp. 195-207.

982 Jack, Peter Monro. "A Review of Reviews: T. S. Eliot's Four Quartets," AmBk, 1, #1 (Winter, 1944), 91-99.

983 Jahagirdar, C. J. "T. S. Eliot's Four Quartets: The Rhetoric of Impersonality," LCrit, 9, #2 (Summer, 1970), 65-69.

984 Johnson, Maurice. "The Ghost of Swift in Four Quartets," MLN, 64 (April, 1949), 273.

985 Juhasz, Suzanne H. "Patterns of Metaphor: Their Function in Some Modern Long Poems. Studies in Williams, Pound, Stevens, and Eliot," DAI, 32 (Berkeley, Calif.: 1971), 920A-21A.

986 Kenner, Hugh. "Four Quartets," The Invisible Poet: T. S. Eliot. New York: Obolensky, 1959, pp. 289-323.

987 Knox, George A. "A Quest for the Word in Eliot's Four Quartets," ELH, 18 (December, 1951), 310-321.

988 Kramer, Kenneth P. "The Waiting Self: A Study of Eliot's Quartets as Meditative Poetry," DAI, 32 (Temple: 1971), 3413A.

989 Lancaster, R. Y. "Symbols of the Journey in T. S. Eliot's Four Quartets," Philobiblon, 9 (1972), 32-40.

990 Langslet, Lars Roar. "Tidsopplevelsen i Eliots Four Quartets," KogK (Oslo), 61 (1956), 609-614.

991 Lasky, Melvin. "On T. S. Eliot's New Poetry," NewL, (June, 1943), 3.

992 Lea, Richard. "T. S. Eliot's Four Quartets," Adelphi, 21 (July-September, 1945), 186-187.

992a Leavis, F. R. "Four Quartets," The Living Principle: "English" as a Discipline of Thought. New York: Oxford U. Pr., 1975, pp. 155-264.

993 Lübker, Robert. "Vier Quartette von T. S. Eliot. Versuch zu einer Einführung," NS (1954), #2: 74-78; #3: 120-127; 4-5, 180-200.

994 MacCallum, H. Reid. "Time Lost and Regained," Imitation and Design. Toronto: 1953, pp. 132-161.

995 McCarron, William E. "An Approach to the Four Quartets," Poet&C, 2 (Winter, 1966), 39-45. The poem "is itself its own meaning: it has validity and meaning only in terms of the very subject it talks about."

996 Madhusudan, Reddy V. "The Concept of Time in T. S. Eliot's Four Quartets," OJES, 1 (1961), 31-38.

997 Mason, H. A. "Elucidating Eliot," Scrutiny, 14, #1 (Summer, 1946), 67-71. Review of Four Quartets Rehearsed by Raymond Preston. New York: Sheed & Ward, 1946.

998 Matthiessen, Francis Otto. "Eliot's Quartets," KR, 5, #2 (Spring, 1943), 161-178.

999 ________. "The Quartets," The Achievement of T. S. Eliot. New York: Oxford U. Pr., (Galaxy ed.), 1959, pp. 177-197.

1000 Maxwell, J. C. "Reflections on Four Quartets," Month, n. s., 4 (1950).

1001 Melchiori, Giorgio. "The Lotus and the Rose," The Tightrope Walkers. London: Routledge & Kegan Paul, 1957, pp. 89-103.

1002 ________. "The Lotus and the Rose, D. H. Lawrence and Eliot's Four Quartets," EngMisc, 5 (1954), 203-216.

1003 Miller, James E., Jr. "Whitman and Eliot: The Poetry of Mysticism," SWR, 43, #2 (Spring, 1958), 113-123. A comparison of "Song of Myself" and Four Quartets.

1004 ________. "Whitman and Eliot: The Poetry of Mysticism," Quests Surd and Absurd: Essays in American Literature. Chicago; London: Chicago U. Pr., 1967, pp. 112-136.

1005 Milward, Peter. A Commentary on T. S. Eliot's Four Quartets. Tokyo: Hokuseido, 1968.

1006 ________. "In Search of Four Quartets," EigoS, 113 (January, 1967), 34-37.

1007 Mizener, Arthur. "To Meet Mr. Eliot," SR, 65 (Winter, 1957), 45-49.

1008 Moynihan, William T. "Character and Action in the Four Quartets," Mosaic, 6, #1 (Fall, 1972), 203-228; repr., in T. S. Eliot: A Collection of Criticism. Linda W. Wagner, ed. New York: McGraw Hill, 1974, pp. 73-104.

1009 Murshid, K. S. "A Note on Eliot's Debt to the East," Venture, 5, #1 (June, 1968), 43-50. Eliot's view of reality in the Quartets corresponds to Indian philosophy.

1010 Musacchio, George L. "A Note on the Fire-Rose Synthesis of T. S. Eliot's Four Quartets," ES, 45, #3 (June, 1964), 238. Eliot's use of fire and rose imagery drawn from Dante's Commedia.

1010a Muth, John Barker. "The Patterned Pursuit: T. S. Eliot's Four Quartets and the Meditative Tradition," DAI, 37 (Rutgers U.: 1976), 3615A-16A.

1011 Ninomiya, Sondo. Eliot's Four Quartets. Tokyo: Nanundo, 1958.

1012 Noon, William T. "Four Quartets: Contemplatio ad Amorem," Renascence, 7 (1954), 3-10, 29.

1013 O'Connor, Daniel. T. S. Eliot: Four Quartets, A Commentary. New Delhi: Aarti Bk. Ctr; Mystic, Conn.: Verry, 1969.

1014 Ohashi, Isamu. "Jikan no Genzonsei to Ishiki--Yotsu no Shijuso boto ni tsuite," EigoS, 115 (1969), 222-224. ["Presence of Time and Consciousness--Four Quartets.]

1014a Olney, James. "Four Quartets," Metaphors of Self: The Meaning of Autobiography. Princeton, N. J.: Princeton U. Pr., 1972, pp. 260-316.

1015 Pagnini, Marcella. "La musicalità dei Four Quartets di T. S. Eliot," Belfagor, 13 (July, 1958), 421-440.

1016 Patrides, C. A. "The Renascence of the Renaissance: T. S. Eliot and the Pattern of Time," MQR, 12 (1973), 172-196. Cf., Marion Montgomery. "Through a Glass Darkly: Eliot and the Romantic Critics," SWR, 58 (1973), 327-335.

1017 Pearson, Norman Holmes. "T. S. Eliot: The Four Quartets," Yale Reports on the Arts and Sciences (March 4, 1959), pp. 1-4.

1018 Pellegrini, Allessandro. "Una conversazione Londonese con T. S. Eliot e i Four Quartets," Belfagor, 3 (July 31, 1948), 445-452.

1019 Perkins, David. "Rose Garden to Midwinter Spring: Achieved Faith in the Four Quartets," MLQ, 23, #1 (March, 1962), 41-45.

1020 Peschmann, Herman. "The Later Poetry of T. S. Eliot," English, 5 (Autumn, 1945), 180-188. The Four Quartets and their relationship to Eliot's earlier work.

1021 Porter, M. Gilbert. "Narrative Stance in Four Quartets: Choreography and Commentary," UR, 36, #1 (October, 1969), 57-66.

1022 Preston, Raymond. Four Quartets Rehearsed. New York: Sheed & Ward, 1947. Rev., by H. A. Mason, Scrutiny, 14 (1946), 67-71.

1023 Quinn, Sister M. Bernetta. The Metamorphic Tradition in Modern Poetry. New Brunswick, N.J.: Rutgers U. Pr., 1955, pp. 143-147.

1024 Rajan, B. "The Overwhelming Question," SR, 74 (Winter, 1966), 358-375.

1025 ______. "The Unity of the Quartets," Focus Three: T. S. Eliot, A Study of His Writings by Several Hands. B. Rajan, ed. London: Dennis Dobson, 1947, pp. 78-95.

1026 Rambo, Dorothy Ellen. "An Analysis of Four Quartets by T. S. Eliot with Particular Respect to Its Prosody," DA, 19 (Northwestern: 1958), 1476.

1027 Reddy, V. Madhusudan. "The Concept of Time in the Four Quartets," OJES, 1, #1 (1961), 31-38.

1028 Rees, Thomas R. "The Orchestration of Meaning in T. S. Eliot's Four Quartets," JAAC, 28 (Fall, 1969), 63-69.

1029 Reibetanz, Julia Maniates. "A Reading of Four Quartets," DA, 31 (Princeton: 1969), 766A.

1030 ______. "Traditional Meters in Four Quartets," ES, 56 (October, 1975), 409-420.

1031 Reinsberg, Mark. "A Footnote to Four Quartets," AL, 21 (1949-50), 342-344. " ... the architecture ... of the whole of Four Quartets is a sort of Odyssey, in which the return home (to reality) is delayed, ... until it can be tolerated by a protective, benevolent force.... "

1032 Rhoads, Kenneth W. "The Musical Elements of T. S. Eliot's Four Quartets," DAI, 30 (Michigan State: 1970), 5454A-55A.

1033 Rosenthal, M. L. "The Waste Land and Four Quartets," The Modern Poets: A Critical Introduction. New York: Oxford U. Pr., 1960, pp. 94-103.

1034 Salamon, Linda Bradley. "A Gloss on Daunsinge: Sir Thomas Elyot and T. S. Eliot's Four Quartets," ELH, 40 (Winter, 1973), 584-605.

1035 Schneider, Elisabeth. "Four Quartets," T. S. Eliot: The Pattern in the Carpet. Berkeley; Los Angeles: California U. Pr., 1975, pp. 168-208.

1036 Schwartz, Delmore. "Anywhere Out of the World," Nation, 157 (July 24, 1943), 102-103. Four Quartets compared with Beethoven's Quartets.

1036a Searl, Eva. "T. S. Eliot's Four Quartets and Wilson Harris's The Waiting Room," Commonwealth Literature and the Modern World. Hena Maes-Jelinek, ed. Brussels: Didier, 1975, pp. 51-59.

1037 Sen, S. C. "Four Quartets," BDEC, 3, #3 and 4 (1962), 1-12.

1038 Sergeant, Howard. "Religion in Modern British Poetry: The Influence of T. S. Eliot," Aryan Path (Bombay), 37 (February, 1966), 71-76. "Much modern poetry has been concerned with a sense of timelessness or inner state of being.... Eliot's Four Quartets provide an excellent example of this preoccupation...."

1039 Sexton, James P. "Four Quartets and the Christian Calendar," AL, 43, #2 (May, 1971), 279-281. Four Quartets allude to four holy days of the Christian calendar: Ascension Day, Good Friday, Annunciation, and Pentecost.

1040 Shepherd, T. B. "The Four Quartets Re-examined," London Quarterly and Holborn Rev, 175 (July, 1950), 228-239.

1041 Sheppard, R. W. "Rilke's Duineser Elegien: A Critical Appreciation in the Light of Eliot's Four Quartets," GL&L, 20, #3 (April, 1967), 205-217.

1042 Simister, O. E. "The Four Quartets--and Other Observations," AWR, 10 (1960), 39-45.

1043 Sinha, Krishna Nandan. "The Intimate and the Unidentifiable: Feeling in T. S. Eliot's Four Quartets," LCrit, 5, #3 (Winter, 1962), 128-140.

1044 __________. On Four Quartets of T. S. Eliot. Ilfracombe, Devon: Stockwell, 1966.

1045 __________. "T. S. Eliot's Four Quartets," Quest, 24 (January-March, 1960), 59-61.

1046 __________. Themes and Images in T. S. Eliot's Four Quartets. Diss. Arkansas: 1956.

1047 Smidt, Kristian. "Four Quartets," Poetry and Belief in the Work of T. S. Eliot. Revised ed. New York: Humanities Pr., 1961, pp. 213-221.

1048 Smith, Grover, Jr. "The Complete Consort: Four Quartets," T. S. Eliot's Poetry and Plays: A Study in Sources and Meaning. Chicago U. Pr., 1956, pp. 247-295.

1049 Spender, Stephen. "Rilke and the Angels, Eliot and the Shrines," SR, 61 (Autumn, 1953), 557-581. Contrasts Rilke's Duino Elegies and Eliot's Four Quartets.

1049a Srivastava, Narsingh. "The Ideas of the Bhagavad Gita in Four Quartets of T. S. Eliot: The Problem of Synthesis," VIndJ, 13, #2 (1975), 361-372. Cf., Narsingh Srivastava, CL, 19, #2 (Spring, 1977), 97-108.

1050 Symes, Gordon. "T. S. Eliot and Old Age," FnR, 169 (March, 1951), 192-193.

1051 Takaichi, Junichiro. "Itsumo naku Itsumo aru--Eliot Yottsu no Shijuso ni okeru Kotoba to Zai," Oberon, 14 (1973), 70-103. [Never and Always--Words and Existence in Eliot's Four Quartets.]

1052 Tello, Jaime. "El concepto del tiempo y del espacio en la poesía de Eliot," RNC, 18, #116 (1956), 113-122. Four Quartets according to Stephen Spender's theory of poetry.

1053 Thompson, Eric. T. S. Eliot's Four Quartets as a Philosophical Poem. Diss. Iowa: 1951.

1054 Thorlby, Anthony. "The Poetry of the Four Quartets," CamJ, 5, #5 (February, 1952), 280-299.

1055 Traversi, Derek. "Los Cuartetos de T. S. Eliot," FMod, 1 (October, 1960), 5-34.

1056 Verheul, K. "Music, Meaning and Poetry in Four Quartets by T. S. Eliot," Lingua, 16 (1966), 279-291.

1057 Villacañas Palomo, Beatriz. "Los cuatro cuartetos y T. S. Eliot," Estafeta Literaria, #553 (December 1, 1974), 16-17. The name of each Quartet is from a definite place.

1058 Virginia, Sister Marie. "Some Symbols of Death and Destiny in Four Quartets," Renascence, 10 (Summer, 1958), 187-191.

1059 Voskuil, Duane. "Some Philosophical Ideas in T. S. Eliot's Four Quartets," NDQ, 40, #3 (Summer, 1972), 5-12.

1060 Wagner, Robert D. "The Meaning of Eliot's Rose-Garden," PMLA, 69 (March, 1954), 22-23. "... We are ... prepared to learn ... that death itself, as a literal fact or as a fact in consciousness, may be the starting-point for the life of the spirit: 'In my end is my beginning.'"

1061 Watkins, Floyd C. "The Word without Flesh in the Four Quartets," The Flesh and the Word: Eliot, Hemingway, Faulkner. Nashville, Tenn.: Vanderbilt U. Pr., 1971, pp. 71-91.

1062 Watts, Harold H. Hound and Quarry. London: Routledge & Kegan Paul, 1953, pp. 226-238.

1063 Weatherhead, A. Kingsley. "Four Quartets: Setting Love in Order," WSCL, 3, #2 (Spring-Summer, 1962), 32-49. "The most significant strand in the evolution of the Quartets ... is the metamorphosis of love and the discovery of a proper context for it."

1063a Webb, Eugene. "The Way Up and the Way Down: The Redemption of Time in T. S. Eliot's Ash Wednesday and Four Quartets," The Dark Dove: The Sacred and Secular in Modern Literature. Seattle: U. of Washington Pr., 1975, pp. 194-236.

1064 Weinig, Mother Mary Anthony. Syntax and Rhetoric in T. S. Eliot's Four Quartets. Diss. Fordham: 1957.

1065 Weiss, Klaus. Das Bild des Weges: Ein Schlüssel zum Verständnis des Zeitlichen und Überzeitlichen in T. S. Eliots Four Quartets. (AKML, 28.) Bonn: Bouvier, 1965.

1066 ________. T. S. Eliots Four Quartets: Analyse und Interpretation. Diss. Freiburg: 1961.

1067 Weitz, Morris. "T. S. Eliot: Time as a Mode of Salvation," SR, 60 (Winter, 1952), 49-52, 55-64.

1068 West, Ray B., Jr. "Personal History and the Four Quartets," NMQR, 23 (Autumn, 1953), 269-282. Eliot's poem though mostly religious contains much personal history. "The philosophic concerns of our time, aesthetic and social, stand at its center."

1069 Wheelwright, Philip. "Pilgrim in the Wasteland," The Burning Fountain: A Study in the Language of Symbolism. Bloomington: Indiana U. Pr., 1954, pp. 330-364. A study of the Four Quartets.

1070 Whitfield, J. H. "T. S. Eliot's Four Quartets and Their Italian Version," EngMisc, 11 (March, 1960), 211-221.

1071 Williams, Charles. "A Dialogue on Mr. Eliot's Poem," DubR, 212 (1943), 114-122.

1072 Williams, Philip. "The Resurrection Lyric of Four Quartets," EigoS, 114 (1968), 590-592.

1073 Williamson, George. "Four Quartets and History," A Reader's Guide to T. S. Eliot: A Poem-by-poem Analysis. London; New York: Noonday Pr., 1953, pp. 205-236.

1074 Wilson, Frank. "The Four Quartets," Six Essays on the Development of T. S. Eliot. London: Fortune Pr., 1948, pp. 54-65.

1074a Woodward, Kathleen Middlekauff. "The Poetry of Old Age: The Late Poems of Eliot, Pound, Stevens, and Williams," DAI, 37 (San Diego, Calif.: 1976), 5821A.

(FOUR QUARTETS) BURNT NORTON

1075 Anthony, Mother Mary. "Verbal Pattern in Burnt Norton I," Criticism, 2, #1 (Winter, 1960), 81-89.

1076 Bergdahl, David L. "The Structure of Burnt Norton: An Exercise in Formal Stylistics," DAI, 32 (Syracuse: 1971), 1503A.

1077 Blamires, Harry. "Burnt Norton" and "Appendix I: Burnt Norton," Word Unheard: A Guide Through Eliot's Four Quartets. London: Methuen, 1969; New York: Barnes & Noble, 1970, pp. 7-40, 185-189.

1078 Bodelsen, C. A. "Two 'Difficult' Poems by T. S. Eliot," ES, 34 (February, 1953), 17-22.

1079 Carey, John, O.F.M. "T. S. Eliot's Wasteland," Cithara, 7, #1 (November, 1967), 3-38. The moment in the rose garden of Burnt-Norton is a moment of mystical illumination. The "still point" is God.

1080 Daiches, David, and William Charvat. Poems in English, 1530-1940. New York: Ronald Pr., 1950, pp. 738-742.

1081 De Laura, David J. "Echoes of Butler, Browning, Conrad, and Pater in the Poetry of T. S. Eliot," ELN, 3 (March, 1966), 211-221. Suggests Samuel Butler's Erewhon as a source for Burnt Norton.

1082 De Masirevich, Constance. "Burnt Norton," On the Four Quartets of T. S. Eliot. New York: Barnes & Noble, 1965, pp. 14-25.

1083 Deutsch, Babette. "The Auditory Imagination--Burnt Norton," Poetry in Our Time: A Critical Survey. 2nd ed. rev. & enlarged. Garden City, N. Y.: Doubleday, 1963, pp. 179-180.

1084 Drew, Elizabeth. T. S. Eliot: The Design of His Poetry. New York: Scribner's, 1950, pp. 151-162.

1085 ____________, and John L. Sweeney. Directions in Modern Poetry. New York: Norton & Co., 1940, pp. 138-140.

1086 "Eliot's Four Quartets: Burnt Norton, IV," Expl, 8, #2 (November, 1949), Item 9. Discussion of four levels of meaning.

1087 Erzgräber, Willi. "Die Gartenszene in T. S. Eliots Burnt Norton I," Archiv, 196 (July, 1959), 1-15.

1088 Everett, Barbara. "A Visit to Burnt Norton," CritQ, 16 (Autumn, 1974), 199-226.

1089 Friar, Kimon, and John M. Brinnin. Modern Poetry, American and British. New York: Appleton-Century-Crofts, 1951, pp. 461-465.

1090 Gardner, Colin O. "Some Reflections on the Opening of Burnt Norton," CritQ, 12, #4 (Winter, 1970), 326-335.

1091 Gerard, Sister Mary. "Eliot of the Circle and John of the Cross," Thought, 34, #132 (Spring, 1959), 107-127. Linkage of the thought in Burnt Norton with that of Saint John of the Cross not justified.

1092 Gross, Harvey. "Music and the Analogue of Feeling: Notes on Eliot and Beethoven," CentR, 3 (Summer, 1959), 272-274.

1093 Hahn, Paul D. "A Reformation of New Criticism: Burnt Norton Revisited," ESRS, 21, #1 (Summer, 1972), 5-64.

1094 Jordan, Roland Carroll, Jr. "Part 1: Time's Space (Encounters) for Small Mixed Chorus and [4-Channel] Pre-Recorded Tape. Original Composition by Author and Text from Burnt Norton by T. S. Eliot...." DAI, 34 (Washington: 1973), 7808A.

1095 Leavis, F. R. "Eliot's Later Poetry," Scrutiny, 11 (Summer, 1942), 65-67.

1096 Lewis, Arthur O. "Eliot's Four Quartets: Burnt Norton, IV," Expl, 8 (November, 1949), Item 9.

1097 Maccoby, H. Z. "A Commentary on Burnt Norton, I," N&Q, 15, #2 (February, 1968), 50-57.

1098 ______________. "A Commentary on Burnt Norton, II," N&Q, 17 (February, 1970), 53-59.

1099 ______________. "A Commentary on Burnt Norton, III, IV, and V," N&Q, 17 (December, 1970), 458-464.

1100 Mahulkar, D. D. "The Language of T. S. Eliot's Burnt Norton," JUB, 10 (April, 1961), 39-49.

1101 Marsh, T. N. "The Turning World: Eliot and the Detective Story," EngMisc, 8 (1957), 143-145.

1102 Martz, Louis L. "The Wheel and the Point," T. S. Eliot:

A Selected Critique. L. Unger, ed. New York: Rinehart, 1948, pp. 444-462.

1103 ___________. "The Wheel and the Point: Aspects of Imagery and Theme in Eliot's Later Poetry," SR, 55 (Winter, 1947), 126-147. A study of Eliot's "the still point."

1104 Masters, Charlie. "Analysis of Burnt Norton," American Prefaces, 6, #2 and 3 (1941), 99-112, 212-231.

1105 Matsuura, Kaichi. "An Appreciation of the Rose-garden Scene in Burnt Norton: Likeness Between T. S. Eliot and the Taoist Philosophers," E&S (T), 7 (Summer, 1959), 147-171. (In Japanese)

1106 Metcher, Thomas. "T. S. Eliots Burnt Norton: Eine Interpretation," Kleine Beiträge zur amerikanischen Literaturgeschichte: Arbeitsproben aus deutschen Seminaren und Instituten. Hans Galinsky, and Hans-Joachim Lang, eds. Heidelberg: Winter, 1961, pp. 75-91.

1107 Oden, Thomas C. "The Christology of T. S. Eliot: A Study of the Kerygma in Burnt Norton," Encounter, 21 (Winter, 1960), 93-101.

1108 Ong, Walter J. "Burnt Norton in St. Louis," AL, 33, #4 (January, 1962), 522-526. Eliot's memories of the Mary Institute near his boyhood home may have influenced the first forty-eight lines of Burnt Norton.

1109 Perkins, David. "Rose Garden to Midwinter Spring: Achieved Faith in the Four Quartets," MLQ, 23, #1 (March, 1962), 41-45. Comparison of the rose garden passage in Burnt Norton and Little Gidding.

1110 Reinsberg, Mark. "A Footnote to Four Quartets," AL, 21 (1949-50), 342-344.

1110a Robinson, David. "Eliot's Rose Garden: Illumination or Illusion?" CSR, 4 (1975), 201-210. Explanation of two passages in Burnt Norton.

1110b Salamon, Linda Bradley. "The Orchestration of Burnt Norton, II," UTQ, 45 (Fall, 1975), 50-66. Perhaps Sir Thomas Davies' Orchestra (1956) lay behind Burnt Norton.

1111 Schenk, W. "The Experience and the Meaning: A Note on T. S. Eliot's Burnt Norton," Humanitas (Manchester), I (1947), 23-27.

1112 Smith, Grover. "T. S. Eliot's Lady of the Rocks," N&Q, 194 (March, 1949), 123-125.

1113 Stenger, G. L. "Notes on Burnt Norton," N&Q, 19 (September, 1972), 340-341. Cf., L. Unger, SoR, 7 (1942), 667-689.

1114 Thompson, Eric. "Burnt Norton," and "Conclusion: View from Burnt Norton," T. S. Eliot: The Metaphysical Perspective. Carbondale: So. Ill. U. P., 1963, pp. 80-130, 131-142.

1115 Tschumi, Raymond. Thought in Twentieth-Century English Poetry. London: Routledge & Kegan Paul, 1951, pp. 149-154.

1116 Unger, Leonard. The Man in the Name: Essays on the Experience of Poetry. Minneapolis: Minnesota U. P., 1956, pp. 177-181.

1117 ________. "T. S. Eliot's Rose Garden: A Persistent Theme," SoR, 7 (Spring, 1942), 667-689.

1118 Watt, Donald. "Eliot, Huxley, and Burnt Norton, II," TSEN, 1 (Fall, 1974), 5-7.

1119 Weigand, Elsie. "Rilke and Eliot: The Articulation of the Mystic Experience," GR, 30 (October, 1955), 198-210. A discussion centering on the Eighth Duino Elegy and Burnt Norton.

1120 Wheelwright, Philip. "The Burnt Norton Trilogy," Chimera, I, #2 (Autumn, 1942), 7-18. Burnt Norton, East Coker, and The Dry Salvages explained as a "poeto-philosophical trilogy."

1121 White, Alison. "Tap-Roots into a Rose Garden," The Great Excluded: Critical Essays on Children's Literature. (Children's Literature, Vol. 1.) Including Essays Emanating from M. L. A. Seminar on Children's Literature. Estab. by Conn. U., 1969. Francelia Butler, ed. (Avail. from Conn. U. Bkstore, Storrs, Conn.) (See particularly as to Burnt Norton.)

1122 Worthington, Jane. "The Epigraphs to the Poetry of T. S. Eliot," AL, 21 (March, 1949), 16-17.

1123 Yasuda, Shoichiro. "'Naraba' to 'Totemo,'" EigoS, 115 (1969), 496-97.

(FOUR QUARTETS) EAST COKER

1124 "Battle with Words," [East Coker], TLS (February 22, 1941), 91.

1125 Blamires, Harry. "East Coker," Word Unheard: A Guide Through Eliot's Four Quartets. London: Methuen, 1969; New York: Barnes & Noble, 1970, pp. 41-78.

1126 Bradford, Curtis. "Footnotes to East Coker: A Reading," SR, 52 (Winter, 1944), 169-175.

1127 Brotman, D. Bosley. "T. S. Eliot: The Music of Ideas," UTQ, 18 (October, 1948), 22-29.

1127a Brown, Christopher. "Eliot on Yeats: 'East Coker, II,'" TSER, 3, #1-2 (1976), 22-24.

1128 Combecher, Hans. "Interpretation für den Englischunterricht: Langston Hughes, F. R. Scott, T. S. Eliot," NS, n. s., 17, #10 (October, 1968), 506-514. Suggests East Coker IV is a meditation on meaning of death.

1129 Cunningham, A. M. "Mr. Eliot's Poem East Coker," DownsideR, 59 (April, 1941), 196-204.

1130 De Masirevich, Constance. "East Coker," On the Four Quartets of T. S. Eliot. New York: Barnes & Noble, 1965, pp. 26-38.

1131 Gross, Harvey. "Music and the Analogue of Feeling: Notes on Eliot and Beethoven," CentR, 3 (Summer, 1959), 274-275.

1132 Häusermann, Hans W. "East Coker and The Family Reunion," L&LT, 47 (October, 1945), 32-38. Similarity of theme and structure in the poem and the play.

1133 ______. "East Coker by T. S. Eliot," ES, 23 (1941).

1134 Instone, Ralph. Review of East Coker. TLS (September 28, 1940), 500.

1135 Kennedy, Eileen. "Poet's Corner: Eliot's East Coker," CEA, 35, #2 (January, 1973), 30-32.

1136 Kligerman, Jack. "An Interpretation of T. S. Eliot's East Coker," ArQ, 18 (Summer, 1962), 101-112. "...the movement from Burnt Norton to East Coker is analogous to a birth, to a beginning...."

1137 "Last Trip to East Coker," ChrCen, 82 (January, 1965), 68.

1138 Leavis, F. R. Review of East Coker. TLS (September 21, 1940), 483.

1139 Lee, Jae Ho. "Alexander Pope in Eliot's East Coker," N&Q, 10, #10 (October, 1963), 381. The opening ten lines of East Coker parallel in phrasing and sequence of key words Pope's Essay on Man, Lines 143-6, Part II.

1140 Mellers, W. H. "East Coker," Scrutiny, 9, #3 (December, 1940), 298-300; repr., in The Importance of Scrutiny: Selections, 1932-1948. Eric Bentley, ed. New York: New York U. Pr., 1964, pp. 267-269.

1141 Moore, Dom Sebastian. "East Coker: The Place and the Poem," Focus Two. London: 1946, pp. 91-103.

1142 Schmidt, Gerd. "Späte Fahrt ins Unbekannte. Zur Interpretation von East Coker, V, 31-38," NS, 16, #4 (April, 1967), 153-157. In Lines V, 31-38, "Dante's negative evaluation [of Odysseus] appears turned by Eliot to the positive" indicating that "exploration of the unknown is justified, even demanded."

1143 Scott, Nathan A., Jr. Rehearsals of Discomposure. New York: King's Crown Pr., 1952, pp. 237-243.

1144 Smith, Francis J. "A Reading of East Coker," Thought, 21 (June, 1946), 272-286.

1145 Standop, Ewald. "Bemerkungen zu einer neuen Verslehre mit Analyse von East Coker, IV," Anglia, 76 (1958), 271-284.

1146 Stonier, G. W. "Mr. Eliot's New Poem," NS&N, 20 (September 14, 1940), 267-268. East Coker, Eliot's "best and most mature poem."

1147 Sweeney, James J. "East Coker: A Reading," SoR, 6, #4 (Spring, 1941), 771-791; excerpt repr., in T. S. Eliot: A Selected Critique. L. Unger, ed. New York: 1948, pp. 395-414.

1148 Tolhurst, Francesca. " 'In My Beginning Is My End,' " T. S. Eliot: A Symposium. Neville Braybrooke, ed. New York: Farrar, Straus, & Cudahy, 1958, pp. 106-108.

1149 Unger, Leonard. The Man in the Name: Essays on the Experience of Poetry. Minneapolis: Minnesota U. Pr., 1946, pp. 185-186.

1150 __________. "T. S. Eliot's Rose Garden: A Persistent Theme," SoR, 7 (Spring, 1942), 686-687.

1151 Wheelwright, Philip. "The Burnt Norton Trilogy," Chimera, I, #2 (Autumn, 1942), 7-18.

(FOUR QUARTETS) THE DRY SALVAGES

1152 Blamires, Harry. "The Dry Salvages," Word Unheard: A Guide Through Eliot's Four Quartets. New York: Barnes & Noble, 1970, pp. 79-122.

1153 Boyd, John D., S. J. "The Dry Salvages: Topography as Symbol," Renascence. 20 (Spring, 1968), 119-133. A reader should note "the strong intrinsic connection between the Cape Ann topography and the Eliot poem."

1154 Bugge, John. "Rhyme as Onomatopoeia in The Dry Salvages," PLL, 10 (Summer, 1974), 312-316. Eliot's use of "the figure of onomatopoeia to lend an unusual rhythmic accent to the work...."

1154a Cuddy, Lois A. "Eliot and Huck Finn: River and Sea in The Dry Salvages," TSER, 3, #1-2 (1976), 3-12.

1155 Davie, Donald. "T. S. Eliot: The End of an Era," TC, 159 (April, 1956), 350-362; repr., in T. S. Eliot: A Collection of Critical Essays. Hugh Kenner, ed. Englewood Cliffs: Prentice-Hall, 1962, pp. 192-205.

1156 Davis, Jack L. "Transcendental Vision in The Dry Salvages," ESQ, 62 (Winter, 1971), 38-44. The theme is the necessity "for modern men to change from spiritually dry salvages to fully living human beings who are in harmony with the life force."

1157 De Masirevich, Constance. "The Dry Salvages," On the Four Quartets of T. S. Eliot. New York: Barnes & Noble, 1965, pp. 39-49.

1158 Donoghue, Denis. "A Reading of Four Quartets--The Dry Salvages," The Ordinary Universe: Soundings in Modern Literature. New York: Macmillan, 1968, pp. 241-266.

1159 Drew, Elizabeth. Major British Poets. New York: Norton, 1959, p. 843.

1159a Dzwonkowski, F. Peter, Jr. "Time and the River, Time and the Sea: A Study of T. S. Eliot's Dry Salvages," CimR, 30 (1975), 48-57.

1160 "The Four Quartets--The Dry Salvages," NewEW, 26 (January 25, 1946), 112.

1161 Gross, Harvey. "Music and the Analogue of Feeling: Notes on Eliot and Beethoven," [The Dry Salvages], CentR, 3 (Summer, 1959), 277.

1161a Humphries, Rolfe. "Salvation from Sand in Salt," Poetry, 59 (March 9, 1942), 338-339.

1162 Kenner, Hugh. "Eliot's Moral Dialectic," HudR, 2 (Autumn, 1949), 421-449.

1163 Leavis, F. R. Education and the University: A Sketch for an "English School," London: Chatto & Windus, 1943; New York: Geo. W. Stewart, 1948, pp. 99-103.

1164 ________. "Eliot's Later Poetry: The Dry Salvages," Scrutiny, 11, #1 (Summer, 1942), 60-73.

1165 Lundstöl, John. "Öyeblikket i eksistensiell belysning," Vinduet, 17, #1 (Summer, 1942), 60-73. Lines 41-47, Part I, Dry Salvages, exemplify an existential experience of time as timelessness.

1166 Maxwell, J. C. "The Dry Salvages: A Possible Echo of Graham Greene," N&Q, 11, #10 (October, 1964), 387. Eliot's statement, Sec. V, about music is echoed in Chapter IV, of Greene's The Man Within.

1167 Morison, Samuel E. "The Dry Salvages and the Thatcher Shipwreck," AmNep, 25 (October, 1965), 233-247.

1168 Rodgers, Audrey T. "The Mythic Perspective of Eliot's The Dry Salvages," ArQ, 30 (Spring, 1974), 74-94. The poem as "a record of man's alienation from a life-giving source, here in the symbol of the water,...."

1169 Rosenthal, M. L. The Modern Poets: A Critical Introduction. New York: Oxford U. Pr., 1960, p. 99.

1170 Unger, Leonard. The Man in the Name: Essays on the Experience of Poetry. Minneapolis: Minnesota U. Pr., 1956, pp. 186-188.

1171 ________. "T. S. Eliot's Rose Garden: A Persistent Theme," SoR, 7 (Spring, 1942), 687-689.

1172 Waggoner, Hyatt. "The Dry Salvages," The Heel of Elohim: Science and Values in Modern American Poetry. Norman, Oklahoma: Oklahoma U. Pr., 1950, pp. 90-99.

1173 Wheelwright, Philip. "The Burnt Norton Trilogy--The Dry Salvages," Chimera, 1, #2 (Autumn, 1942), 7-18.

(FOUR QUARTETS) LITTLE GIDDING

1174 Bevington, Helen. "Little Gidding," NYTB (February 13, 1967), 2, 36.

1175 Blamires, Harry. "Little Gidding," Word Unheard: A Guide Through Eliot's Four Quartets. New York: Barnes & Noble, 1970, pp. 123-184.

1176 Chaning-Pearce, M. "Little Gidding," NineC, 133 (February, 1943), 74-78.

1177 Clark, Marden J. "Timeless Moments: The Incarnation Theme in Little Gidding," RMMLAB, 28, #1 (March, 1974), 10-17.

1177a Clausen, Christopher. "Tintern Abbey to Little Gidding: The Past Recaptured," SR, 84, #3 (July-September, 1976), 405-424.

1178 De Masirevich, Constance. "Little Gidding," On the Four Quartets of T. S. Eliot. New York: Barnes & Noble, 1965, pp. 50-64.

1179 Drew, Elizabeth. [Little Gidding], Poetry: A Modern Guide to Its Understanding and Enjoyment. New York: Norton, 1959, pp. 115-116.

1180 Harding, D. W. "We Have Not Reached Conclusion," Scrutiny, 11, #3 (Spring, 1943), 216-219; repr., in The Importance of Scrutiny. Eric Bentley, ed. New York U. Pr., 1964, pp. 269-273. Cf., R. N. Higinbotham. "Objections to a Review of Little Gidding," Scrutiny, 11 (1943), 259-261; F. R. Leavis. "Reflections on the Above," Scrutiny, 11 (1943), 261-267.

1181 Higinbotham, R. N. "Objections to a Review of Little Gidding," Scrutiny, 11, #4 (Summer, 1943), 259-261. Cf., F. R. Leavis. "Reflections on the Above," Scrutiny, 11 (1943), 261-267.

1182 Johnson, Maurice. "The Ghost of Swift in Four Quartets," MLN, 64 (April, 1949), 273. The ghost in Little Gidding identified with that of Dean Swift.

1183 Leavis, F. R. "Reflections on the Above," Scrutiny, 11, #4 (1943), 261-267. Cf., D. W. Harding. Scrutiny, 11, #3 (Spring, 1943), 216-219; R. N. Higinbotham. Scrutiny, 11, #4 (Summer, 1943), 259-261.

1184 Matthiessen, F. O. "Eliot's Quartets," KR, 5 (Spring, 1943), 173-175.

1185 Muir, Edwin. "Little Gidding," NS&N, n. s., 25 (February 20, 1943), 128; repr., in NewL (New York), (May 1, 1943).

1186 Perkins, David. "Rose Garden to Midwinter Spring: Achieved Faith in Four Quartets," MLQ, 23 (March, 1962), 41-45. Comparison of midwinter scene in Little Gidding with rose garden scene in Burnt Norton.

1187 Price, Fanny. "The Verse of Little Gidding," N&Q, 184 (April 10, 1943), 225.

1187a Ricks, Christopher. "A Note on Little Gidding," EIC, 25 (1975), 145-153.

1188 Rosenthal, M. Louis, and A. J. M. Smith. "Poetry in Its Frame of Reference," Exploring Poetry. New York: Macmillan, 3rd., 1959, 696-704.

1189 Schaar, Claes. "Palimpsest Technique in Little Gidding: The Second Movement and the Inferno, XV," OL, 14 (Spring, 1959), 33-37.

1190 Schmidt, G. "An Echo of Buddhism in T. S. Eliot's Little Gidding," N&Q, 20 (September, 1973), 330. Attitudes toward life expressed in third movement of Little Gidding are reminiscent of Añguttara-Nikāya.

1191 Shand, John. "Around Little Gidding," NineC, 136 (September, 1944), 120-132.

1192 Smith, Grover. "Lamb and Lear in Little Gidding," TSER, 2 (Spring, 1975), 2.

1193 ______. "Tourneur and Little Gidding; Corbière and East Coker," MLN, 65 (June, 1950), 418-421. Possible relationship between passage in The Atheist's Tragedy and passage in Little Gidding.

1194 Sweeney, James J. "Little Gidding: Introductory to a Reading," Poetry, 62 (July, 1943), 214-223.

1195 Weinig, Sister M. Anthony. "Verbal Pattern in Little Gidding, I," Greyfriar, 13 (1972), 25-33.

1196 Wrenn, C. L. "T. S. Eliot and the Language of Poetry," Thought, 32 (Summer, 1957), 239-254.

GERONTION

1197 Bailey, Ruth. [Gerontion], A Dialogue on Modern Poetry. London: Oxford U. Pr., 1939, passim.

1198 Blackmur, R. P. "T. S. Eliot--Gerontion," H&H, 1 (March, 1928), 201-203.

1199 Brown, Robert M., and Joseph B. Yokelson. 'Eliot's Gerontion, 56-61," Expl, 15 (February, 1957), Item 31. "...The only logic for the sequence as it stands seems to be the course of history, the change from Catholicism to Calvinism to secularism...."

1200 Clark, John A. "On First Looking into Benson's Fitzgerald," SAQ, 48 (April, 1949), 258-269. Comparison of Benson's description of Fitzgerald with Eliot's description of Gerontion.

1201 Culbert, Taylor. "Eliot's Gerontion, 13-14," Expl, 17, #3 (December, 1958), Item 20. Meaning of "...the woman sneezes while stirring the flickering fire in the stove...."

1202 Daiches, David, and William Charvat. [Gerontion], Poems in English. New York: Ronald, 1950, pp. 738-740.

1203 ________. "Some Aspects of T. S. Eliot," CE, 9 (December, 1947), 117-120.

1204 Daniels, Edgar F. "Eliot's Gerontion," Expl, 17 (May, 1959), Item 58. Allusion to Andrew Marvell, "A green thought in a green shade," The Garden, in Gerontion's line, "Thoughts of a dry brain in a dry season...."

1205 Dodsworth, Martin. "Gerontion and Christ," Rev (Oxford), #4 (November, 1962), 28-34. The poem's "dramatic centre" is "Gerontion's opposition to the Christian civilization responsible for the world of decay in which he lives."

1206 Douglas, Wallace, et al. The Critical Reader. New York: W. W. Norton, 1949, pp. 125-130.

1207 Drew, Elizabeth. "Gerontion," T. S. Eliot: The Design of His Poetry. New York: Scribner's, 1941, 1949, passim.

1208 ______, and John L. Sweeney. Directions in Modern Poetry. New York: Norton, 1940, pp. 42-44.

1209 Dye, F. "Eliot's Gerontion," Expl, 18 (April, 1960), Item 39. The relationship of Gerontion to God and to the natural world.

1210 "Eliot's Gerontion," Expl, 4 (June, 1946), Item 55.

1211 Eshelman, William R. "Eliot's Gerontion," Expl, 4, #6 (April, 1946), Item 44.

1212 Fairchild, Hoxie Neale. [Gerontion], Religious Trends in English Poetry. Vol. V. New York; London: Columbia U. Pr., 1962. pp. 566-568.

1213 Farrelly, James. "Gerontion: Time's Eunuch," UDR, 6, #2 (Fall, 1969), 27-34.

1214 Frank, Armin P. "Eliot's Gerontion," Expl, 30 (1972), Item 53.

1215 Frankenberg, Lloyd. Pleasure Dome: On Reading Modern Poetry. Boston: Houghton Mifflin, 1949, pp. 51-56.

1216 Friar, Kimon, and John M. Brinnin. Modern Poetry: American and British. New York: Appleton - Century - Crofts, 1951, pp. 497-498.

1217 Friedman, Alan Warren. "A 'Key' to Lawrence Durrell," WSCL, 8, #1 (Winter, 1967), 31-42.

1218 Gottfried, Leon. "Death's Other Kingdom: Dantesque and Theological Symbolism in Flowering Judas," PMLA, 84, #1 (January, 1969), 112-124. Says that Katherine Anne Porter's story Flowering Judas "owes its title and the use of the tree's blossoms as a substitute for the Host in a travesty of Christian communion directly to his [Eliot's] Gerontion. . . . "

1219 Griffith, Clark. "Eliot's Gerontion," Expl, 21 (February, 1963), Item 46. Interprets the image of the "boy" and the "Jew" in the first verse paragraph.

1220 Gross, Harvey. "Gerontion," The Contrived Corridor: History and Fatality in Modern Literature. Ann Arbor: Michigan U. Pr., 1971, pp. 32-44.

1221 ________. "Gerontion and the Meaning of History," PMLA, 73 (June, 1958), 299-304. In Gerontion, "historical knowledge is the unstable memory of man.... True history is enacted in the arena of moral choice.... History is a kind of exultant force ... known only by its effects."

1222 Halverson, John. "Prufrock, Freud, and Others," SR, 76, #4 (Autumn, 1968), 571-588. "If Freud's influence has distorted the reading of Prufrock, the same approach to Gerontion has produced plain bafflement....most critics, if willing to face Gerontion at all, have faced the unmistakable Christianity of the poem...."

1223 Hesse, Eva. "T. S. Eliot: Schwierigheiten beim Leben. Gerontion als Selbstinterpretation des Dichters," Merkur, 19 (Februar, März, 1965), 122-136, 246-257. Eliot has maintained his position as "Classisist, Monarchist, Anglican," but he has not radically changed the existentialist viewpoint present in Gerontion.

1224 Kaplan, Robert B., and Richard J. Wall. "Eliot's Gerontion," Expl, 19, #6 (March, 1961), Item 36. The influence of Joyce's A Portrait of the Artist as a Young Man.

1225 Kenner, Hugh. "Gerontion," Spectrum, 2 (Fall, 1958), 139-154. Gerontion's language "counteracts the characteristic 20th century development of American poetry,...."

1226 ________. "Gerontion," Invisible Poet: T. S. Eliot. New York: Obolensky, 1959, pp. 124-141.

1227 Kirk, Russell. "Gerontion and Servitude to Time," Eliot and His Age. New York: Random House, 1971, pp. 63-72.

1227a Leach, Elsie. "Gerontion and Marvell's The Garden," ELN, 13, #1 (September, 1975), 45-48.

1228 Leavis, F. R. New Bearings on English Poetry. London: Chatto & Windus, 1932, pp. 79-87.

1229 Maccoby, Hyam. "A Study of the 'Jew' in Gerontion," JewQ, 17, #2 (Summer, 1969), 19-22, 39-43. The Jew is associated with the Devil and stands outside "the House, which is Christendom," but Gerontion himself is a Jew.

1230 Major, John M. "Eliot's Gerontion and As You Like It," MLN, 74 (January, 1959), 28-31. "Among those plays by

Shakespeare uppermost in [Eliot's] thoughts at the time [of his writing Gerontion] was,... As You Like It, with its striking portraits and speeches of the dry-brained Touchstone and the melancholy Jacques."

1231 Mankowitz, Wolf. "Notes on Gerontion," Focus Three: T. S. Eliot. A Study of His Writings by Several Hands. B. Rajan, ed. London: Dennis Dobson, 1947, pp. 129-138.

1232 Marshall, W. H. "The Text of T. S. Eliot's Gerontion," SB, 4 (1951), 213-216.

1233 Mizener, Arthur. "To Meet Mr. Eliot," SR, 65 (Winter, 1957), 42-44.

1234 Monteiro, George. "Eliot's Gerontion, 65-75," Expl, 18, #5 (February, 1960), Item 30. The Education of Henry Adams echoed in Lines 65-75.

1235 O'Conner, William Van. "Gerontion and The Dream of Gerontius," Furioso, 3, #2 (Winter, 1947), 53-56. Comparison of Gerontion with Cardinal Newman's Dream of Gerontius: "In Eliot the borrowing and transforming of phrases and symbols is primarily a means of extending the Christian literary tradition."

1236 Pope, Myrtle P. "Eliot's Gerontion," Expl, 6, #7 (May, 1948), Item Q16.

1237 [Pottle, Frederick A.] [Eliot's Gerontion] Expl, 4, #8 (June, 1946), Item 55. Cf., Expl, 4 (April, 1946), Item 44.

1238 Ransom, John Crowe. "Gerontion," SR, 74, #2 (April-June, 1966), 389-414; repr., in T. S. Eliot: The Man and His Work. Allen Tate, ed. New York: Delacorte, 1966, pp. 133-158.

1238a Rezzano de Martini, Maria Clotilde. The Gerontion of T. S. Eliot: A Commentary. Buenos Aires: (Argentine Assn. of English Culture.) 1945.

1238b Rochat, Joyce Hamilton. "T. S. Eliot's Gerontion: Wisdom Literature of the Twentieth Century," Cresset (February, 1975), 3-11.

1239 Rosenthal, M. L., and A. J. M. Smith. Exploring Poetry. New York: Macmillan, 1955, pp. 638-644.

1240 Ryan, Marianna. "Retrieval of the Word in Gerontion and The Waste Land," AntigR, 20 (1974), 78-97.

1241 San Juan, E[pifanio], Jr. A Casebook on Gerontion. Columbus, Ohio: Charles E. Merrill, 1970.

1242 ____________. "Form and Meaning in Gerontion," Renascence, 22 (Spring, 1970), 115-126. "This essay hopes to fill up the lack of a thorough, detailed analysis of the poem, its argument, and its aesthetic realization."

1243 Schwarz, Daniel R. "The Unity of Eliot's Gerontion: The Failure of Meditation," BuR, 19, #1 (Spring, 1971), 55-76; repr., in T. S. Eliot: A Collection of Criticism. Linda Wagner, ed. New York: McGraw-Hill, 1974, pp. 49-63.

1244 Serpieri, Sandro. "Il significato di Gerontion nella poesia eliotiana," SA, 5 (1959), 219-232.

1245 Smith, Grover. "Eliot's Gerontion," Expl, 7, #4 (February, 1949), Item 26. Discussion of names of the characters.

1246 ____________. "The Word in the Whirlwind: Gerontion," T. S. Eliot's Poetry and Plays. Chicago U. Pr., 1956, pp. 57-66.

1247 Sveino, Per. "T. S. Eliot's Gerontion," Edda, 71 (1971), 219-228. Analysis of the speaker in the poem.

1248 Symes, Gordon. "T. S. Eliot and Old Age," FnR, 169 (March, 1951), 189-190.

1249 Unger, Leonard. The Man in the Name: Essays on the Experience of Poetry. Minneapolis: Minnesota U. Pr., 1956, pp. 172-173.

1250 ____________. "T. S. Eliot's Rose Garden: A Persistent Theme," SoR, 7 (Spring, 1942), 672-673.

1251 Vickery, John B. "Gerontion: The Nature of Death and Immortality," ArQ, 14, #2 (Summer, 1958), 101-115. "...Gerontion operates on four levels of subject and image--those of individual man, religion, nature, and history...."

1252 Vinograd, Sherna S. "The Accidental: A Clue to Structure in Eliot's Poetry," Accent, 9 (Summer, 1949), 233-235.

1253 Walker, Marshall. "Eliot's Little Symphony: A Note on Gerontion," ESA, 15, #2 (September, 1972), 99-104.

1254 Wheelwright, Philip. The Burning Fountain: A Study in the Language of Symbolism. Bloomington: Indiana U. Pr., 1954, pp. 336-338.

1255 Williamson, Mervyn W. "Gerontion and the Later Poetry of T. S. Eliot," UTSE, 36 (1957), 110-126. A study in thematic repetition and development.

1256 Wilson, Frank. "Poems, 1920," [Gerontion], Six Essays on the Development of T. S. Eliot. London: Fortune Pr., 1948, pp. 21-22.

1257 Worthington, Jane. "The Epigraphs to the Poetry of T. S. Eliot," AL, 21 (March, 1949), 5-6.

1258 Yamada, Akihiro. "Seneca--Chapman--Eliot," N&Q, 17, #12 (December, 1970), 457-458. Source of ending of Eliot's Gerontion may be found in Seneca's Hercules Furens which Eliot might have obtained from Chapman's Bussy d'Ambois.

THE HIPPOPOTAMUS

1259 McLuhan, Herbert M. "Eliot's The Hippopotamus," Expl. 2 (May, 1944), Item 50. "The inspiration, as well as the full explication of The Hippopotamus, is found in Bishop Lancelot Andrewes' 'Sermon preached before the King's Majesty at Whitehall, on the twenty-fourth of April, A. D. MDCXIV,.... '"

1260 Meyer, Christine. "Eliot's The Hippopotamus," Expl, 8 (October, 1949), Item 6. Discusses the symbolic meaning of the mango, the pomegranate and the peach.

1261 __________. "Some Unnoted Religious Allusions in T. S. Eliot's The Hippopotamus," MLN, 66 (April, 1951), 241-245.

1262 Sprich, Robert. "Theme and Structure in Eliot's The Hippopotamus," CEA, 31 (April, 1969), 8.

1263 Utley, Francis L. "Eliot's The Hippopotamus," Expl, 3, #2 (November, 1944), Item 10. Newman's A Letter Addressed to His Grace of Norfolk (1875) may be "another significant parallel."

1264 Worthington, Jane. "The Epigraphs to the Poetry of T. S. Eliot," AL, 21 (March, 1949), 10-11.

THE HOLLOW MEN

1265 ApIvor, Denis. "Setting The Hollow Men to Music," T. S.

Eliot: A Symposium for His Seventieth Birthday. Neville Braybrooke, ed. New York: Farrar, Straus & Cudahy, 1958, pp. 89-91.

1266 Benson, Donald R. "Eliot's and Conrad's Hollow Men," CEA, 29 (January, 1967), 10.

1267 Blackmur, R. P. "T. S. Eliot," H&H, 1 (March, 1928), 203-205.

1268 Boardman, G. R. "Restoring the Hollow Man," Rev, 4 (November, 1962), 35-45.

1269 Brooks, Harold F. "Between The Waste Land and the First Ariel Poems: The Hollow Men," English, 16, #93 (Autumn, 1966), 89-93. Finds The Hollow Men a study of the theme of the death requisite to rebirth, central to The Waste Land.

1270 Chiari, Joseph. "The Waste Land and The Hollow Men," T. S. Eliot: Poet and Dramatist. New York: Barnes & Noble, 1972, pp. 56-74.

1271 DeLaura, David J. "Echoes of Butler, Browning, Conrad, and Pater in the Poetry of T. S. Eliot," ELN, 3, #3 (March, 1966), 211-221. Samuel Butler's Erewhon suggested as source for Burnt Norton and The Hollow Men, Part II.

1272 Drew, Elizabeth, and John L. Sweeney. Directions in Modern Poetry. New York: Norton, 1940, pp. 134-136.

1273 Dzwonkowski, F. Peter, Jr. "The Hollow Men and Ash Wednesday: Two Dark Nights," ArQ, 30 (Spring, 1974), 16-42.

1274 Foster, Genevieve W. "Archetypal Imagery of T. S. Eliot," PMLA, 60 (June, 1945), 576-578.

1275 Fussell, Paul, Jr. "The Gestic Symbolism of T. S. Eliot," ELH, 22 (September, 1955), 198-201, 203.

1276 ________. "A Note on The Hollow Men," MLN, 65 (April, 1950), 254-255. An echo of Shakespeare's Julius Caesar, II, i, 63-69.

1277 Gillis, Everett A. "The Spiritual Status of T. S. Eliot's Hollow Men," TSLL, 2 (1961), 464-475.

1277a Keogh, J. G. "Eliot's Hollow Men as Graveyard Poetry," Renascence, 21 (Spring, 1969-70), 115-118.

1277b Kinsman, Robert S. "Eliot's The Hollow Men," Expl, 8,

#6 (April, 1950), Item 48. Comparison of Eliot's hollow men standing on the bank of the tumid river, and the predicament of the dead in Dante's Inferno, Canto III.

1278 McConnell, Daniel J. "The Heart of Darkness in T. S. Eliot's The Hollow Men," TSLL, 4, #2 (Summer, 1962), 141-153. The relationship of Conrad's work to Eliot's The Hollow Men and to The Waste Land.

1279 Richter, Dagny. "T. S. Eliot, Dante, and The Hollow Men," MSpr, 65 #3 (1971), 205-223. Allusions to the Divine Comedy in The Hollow Men.

1280 Romer, Karen T. "T. S. Eliot and the Language of Liturgy," Renascence, 24, (1972), 119-135.

1281 Sarang, Vilas. "A Source for The Hollow Men," N&Q, 15, #2 (February, 1968), 57-58. Conrad's An Outcast of the Islands suggested as source for the line "Life is very long," The Hollow Men, Part V.

1282 Schneider, Elisabeth. "The Hollow Men," T. S. Eliot: The Pattern in the Carpet. Berkeley; Los Angeles: California U. Pr., 1975, pp. 99-107.

1283 Smith, Grover, Jr. "Death's Dream Kingdom: The Hollow Men," T. S. Eliot's Poetry and Plays. Chicago U. Pr., 1956, pp. 99-109.

1284 Stanford, Donald L. "Two Notes on T. S. Eliot: The Ring Dance in The Hollow Men," TCL, 1 (October, 1955), 133-134. Considers implication of The Ring Dance in The Hollow Men and says: "... The modern ring dance is not around a fertility god or around a symbol which stands for fertility, but around the prickly pear, a fitting symbol of sterility...."

1285 Strothmann, Friedrich W., and Lawrence V. Ryan. "Hope for T. S. Eliot's 'Empty Men,'" PMLA, 73, #4, Pt. 1 (Septenber 1958), 426-432. The "empty men" of Section IV, The Hollow Men, "emptied by divine action of everything that is not God, have a legitimate hope of seeing him and becoming forever part of the Mystical Body,...."

1286 Symes, Gordon. "T. S. Eliot and Old Age," FnR, 169 (March, 1951), 191-192.

1287 Unger, Leonard. "The Hollow Men and Ash Wednesday," T. S. Eliot: Moments and Patterns. Minneapolis: Minnesota U. Pr., 1956, pp. 41-68.

1288 Vickery, John B. "Eliot's Poetry: The Quest and the Way," (Part I), Renascence, 10 (Autumn, 1957), 8-9.

1289 Waggoner, Hyatt Howe. "T. S. Eliot and The Hollow Men," AL, 15, #2 (1943-44), 101-126. "...Though the hollow men who people most of his poems are the product of a hostile observer, they are not distorted beyond recognition, for the intellectuals of the twenties saw in them a portrait of themselves....he [Eliot] reminded a generation of the meaning of its own culture--that is Eliot's poetic distinction."

1290 Wasser, Henry. "A Note on Eliot and Santayana," BUSE, 4, #2 (Summer, 1960), 125-126. Suggests George Santayana's comment on the world of Dante in Three Philosophical Poets (1910) as a source for the final lines of The Hollow Men.

1291 Williamson, George. "The Waste Land and The Hollow Men," A Reader's Guide to T. S. Eliot. London; New York: Noonday Pr., 1953, pp. 115-162.

1292 Wilson, Frank. "The Middle Period"--[The Hollow Men] Six Essays on the Development of T. S. Eliot. London: Fortune Pr., 1948, pp. 32-34.

1293 Worthington, Jane. "The Epigraphs to the Poetry of T. S. Eliot," AL, 21 (March, 1949), 14-15.

HYSTERIA

1294 Christian, Henry. "Thematic Development in T. S. Eliot's Hysteria," TCL, 6, #2 (July, 1960), 76-80. Hysteria "stands in the body of Eliot's work--an early observation of method and movement."

LINES TO RALPH HODGSON ESQRE

1295 Sykes, Robert H. "Eliot's Lines to Ralph Hodgson Esqre," Expl, 30 (1972), Item 79. Source suggested for the line referring to Hodgson's possession of "999 canaries."

MR. APOLLINAX

1296 Brown, Alec. "The Lyric Impulse in the Poetry of T. S. Eliot," Scrutinies. Edgell Rickword, ed. Vol. II. London: Wishart, 1931, pp. 29-31.

1296a Untermeyer, Louis. "T. S. Eliot," American Poetry Since 1900. New York: Henry Holt, 1923, p. 355. Mr. Apollinax may be Bertrand Russell.

1297 Watkins, Floyd C. "T. S. Eliot's Mysterious Mr. Apollinax," RSWSU, 38 (1970), 193-200.

1298 Worthington, Jane. "The Epigraphs to the Poetry of T. S. Eliot," AL, 21 (March, 1949), 3-4. Charles Whibley responsible for Eliot's use of the Zeuxis of Lucian.

MR. ELIOT'S SUNDAY MORNING SERVICE

1299 Atkins, Anselm. "Mr. Eliot's Sunday Morning Parody," Renascence, 21 (Autumn, 1968), 41-43, 54.

1300 Kahn, Sholom J. "Eliot's 'Polyphiloprogenitive': Another Whitman Link?" WWR, 5 (September, 1959), 52-54. A possible Whitman echo in the first line of the poem--the word "Polyphiloprogenitive" a 19th century phrenological term meaning love of mankind.

1300a Monteiro, George. "Christians and Jews in Mr. Eliot's Sunday Morning Service," TSER, 3, 1-2 (1976), 20-22.

1300b Orsini, Napoleone. "Nota in margine ad una poesia di T. S. Eliot," Let (Italy), 9 (March-April, 1947), 110-112. A comparison of Eliot's poem with Jules Laforgue's "La Rapsode foraine et le pardon de Ste Anne."

1301 Schanzer, Ernest. "Mr. Eliot's Sunday Morning Service," EIC, 5 (April, 1955), 153-158. Analysis and interpretation.

1302 Shulenberger, Arvid. "Mr. Eliot's Sunday Service," Expl, 10, #1 (October, 1951), Item 29. The poem's "dramatic oppositions" diagrammed in various terms.

1303 Watkins, Floyd C. "T. S. Eliot's Painter of the Umbrian School," AL, 36 (March, 1964), 72-75. Suggests that "...reading the poem with [Piero della] Francesca's painting [The Baptism of Christ] makes the imagery clear and the theme striking."

1304 Worthington, Jane. "The Epigraphs to the Poetry of T. S. Eliot," AL, 21 (March, 1949), 11-12.

NEW HAMPSHIRE

1305 Galvin, Brendan. "A Note on T. S. Eliot's New Hampshire as a Lyric Poem," MSE, 1, #2 (Fall, 1967), 44-45.

OLD POSSUM'S BOOK OF PRACTICAL CATS

1306 Clowder, Felix. "The Bestiary of T. S. Eliot," PrS, 34 (Spring, 1960), 30-37. Believes the book has definite religious or theological undertones.

1307 Fuller, John. "Five Finger Exercises," Rev (Oxford), #4 (November, 1962), 46-51. In Old Possum's Book of Practical Cats, the Five Finger Exercises give "some insight into basic structure and technique."

1307a Tinsley, Molly Best. "T. S. Eliot's Book of Practical Cats," SAmH, 2 (1975), 167-171.

"Macavity: The Mystery Cat" [Old Possum]

1308 Fleissner, Robert F. "'The Bafflement of Scotland Yard': T. S. Eliot's Mystery Cat and Dostoevsky's Raskolnikov," BSJ, 18 (September, 1968), 150-151.

1309 Loesch, Katherine. "A Dangerous Criminal Still at Large," N&Q, 6, #1 (January, 1959), 8-9. A source for Macavity in A. Conan Doyle's Professor Moriarty.

1310 Preston, Priscilla. "A Note on T. S. Eliot and Sherlock Holmes," MLR, 54 (October, 1959), 398-399.

1310a Webster, H. T., and H. W. Starr. "Macavity: An Attempt to Unravel His Mystery," BSJ, 4 (October, 1954), 205-210.

"Gus: The Theatre Cat" [Old Possum]

1311 Preston, Priscilla. "A Note on T. S. Eliot and Sherlock Holmes," MLR, 54 (October, 1959), 399. Suggestions concerning Eliot's indebtedness to Conan Doyle.

1312 Stonier, G. W. "The Gaiety of Mr. Eliot," NS&N, 19 (May, 1940), 627-628.

1313 Vaughn, F. H. "Smog: The Old Possum's Insidious Cat," LHR, 9 (1967), 37-41.

"Skimbleshanks: The Railway Cat" [Old Possum]

1314 Schmidt, G. "A Note on Skimbleshanks: The Railway Cat," N&Q, 17, #12 (December, 1970), 465. Thinks Eliot might have had Kipling's poem "The Long Trail" in mind when he wrote Skimbleshanks: The Railway Cat.

PORTRAIT OF A LADY

1315 Bartlett, Phyllis. "Other Countries, Other Wenches," MFS, 3, #4 (Winter, 1957-58), 345-349. Marlowe's The Jew of Malta as the ambiguous epigraph of Eliot's Portrait of a Lady.

1316 Clark, John Abbot. "On First Looking into Benson's Fitzgerald," SAQ, 48 (April, 1949), 258-269. Benson's Edward Fitzgerald as source of figures, moods, and ideas in Portrait of a Lady as well as in other poems of Eliot.

1317 Giannone, Richard J. "Eliot's Portrait of a Lady and Pound's Portrait d'une Femme," TCL, 5, #3 (October, 1959), 131-134. "...The early work of which 'Portrait d'une Femme' is representative nowhere reaches the level of Prufrock or Portrait in intensity because it is a preliminary purification of the artist as artist for the impersonal handling of things...."

1318 Laurentia, Sister M. "Structural Balance and Symbolism in T. S. Eliot's Portrait of a Lady," AL, 27 (November, 1955), 409-417. The poem "presents a precisely balanced structure paralleling the structure of meaning of the epigraph, and at the same time counterpointing this meaning at a secondary level."

1319 Shanahan, C. M. "Irony in Laforgue, Corbiére, and Eliot," MP, 53 (November, 1955), 123-124. "In both Légende [Laforgue's poem] and Portrait of a Lady we notice with what economy the bare essentials of the emotional relationships between the two characters are given to us...."

1320 Sinclair, May. "Prufrock: And Other Observations," LHR,

4 (December 1917), 8-14. Portrait of a Lady and Prufrock are masterpieces in the same sense as Browning's Romances and Men and Women.

1320a Turner, W. Arthur. "The Not So Coy Mistress of J. Alfred Prufrock," SAQ, 54 (Autumn, 1955), 517-518.

1321 Untermeyer, Louis. "T. S. Eliot," American Poetry Since 1900. New York: Henry Holt, 1923, pp. 351, 354.

1322 Worthington, Jane. "The Epigraphs to the Poetry of T. S. Eliot," AL, 21 (March, 1949), 2-3.

PRELUDES

1323 Aiken, Conrad. 'New Curiosity Shop--and a Poet," Dial, 64 (January 31, 1918), 112. "...Mr. Eliot's Preludes and Rhapsody [on a Windy Night] are, in a very minor way, masterpieces of black-and-white impressionism...."

1324 Mendilow, A. A. "T. S. Eliot's 'Long Unlovely Street,'" MLR, 63, #2 (April, 1968), 320-331. "The Preludes... raise the issue whether the end is a prelude to a new beginning on a higher level...."

1325 Montgomery, Marion. "Memory and Desire in Eliot's Preludes," SAB, 38, #2 (May, 1973), 61-65.

1325a Nicholson, John. "Musical Form and Preludes," T. S. Eliot: A Symposium. Neville Braybrooke, ed. New York: 1958, pp. 110-112.

1325b Short, M. H. "'Prelude I' to a Literary Linguistic Stylistics," Style, 6 (1972), 149-158.

1326 Smith, Grover, Jr. "Charles-Louis Philippe and T. S. Eliot," AL, 22 (November, 1950), 254-259. The influence of Charles-Louis Philippe on Preludes, and, as well, on other poems of Eliot.

1327 ________. T. S. Eliot's Poetry and Plays: A Study in Sources. Chicago: Chicago U. Pr., 1956, pp. 20-23, passim.

PRUFROCK AND OTHER OBSERVATIONS
[The Love Song of J. Alfred Prufrock]

1328 Abel, Darrel. "R. L. S. and Prufrock," N&Q, 198 (January, 1953), 37-38. "Resemblances in theme, treatment, and expression suggest that T. S. Eliot's Love Song of J. Alfred Prufrock contains reminiscences of Robert Louis Stevenson's Crabbed Age and Youth."

1329 Adams, Robert M. Strains of Discord: Studies in Literary Openness. Ithaca, New York: Cornell U. Pr., 1958, pp. 112-113.

1330 Ahearn, W. B. "A Possible Source for Prufrock," TSER, 2, 1 (Spring, 1975), 4.

1331 Aiken, Conrad. "Esoteric Catholicity," PoetryJ, (April, 1916), 127-129. Prufrock and Portrait of a Lady "subtle to the verge of insoluble idiosyncrasy, introspective, self-gnawing."

1332 ___________. "Homage to T. S. Eliot," HA, 125, #3 (December, 1938), 17. Eliot's efforts to publish Prufrock.

1333 Allen, Alexander. "A Note on the Tradition," STwenC, #3 (Spring, 1969), 15-18. "No poem could be more personal and impersonal than Prufrock." It is "the gap between the Eliot-self and the mask."

1334 Ames, Russell M. "Decadence in the Art of T. S. Eliot," S&S, 16 (Summer, 1952), 193-221.

1335 Anon. Prufrock and Other Observations. Review. TLS, 805 (June 21, 1917), 299. Says that the pieces "have no relation to poetry."

1336 Anon. "Prufrock and Other Poems: Is This Poetry?" Athenaeum, #4651 (June 20, 1919), 491.

1337 Anon. "Shorter Notices," NS&N, 9 (August 18, 1917), 477.

1338 Arden, Eugene. "The Echo of Hell in Prufrock," N&Q, 5, n. s., #8 (August, 1958), 363-364. Dantean allusions.

1339 ___________. "The 'Other' Lazarus in Prufrock," N&Q, 7, #1 (January, 1960), 33, 40. Suggests Lazarus, the beggar, in St. Luke, as the allusion.

1340 B. D. "Another Impressionist," NR, 14 (February 16, 1918), 89.

1341 Banerjee, Ron D. "The Dantean Overview: The Epigraph to Prufrock," MLN, 87 (1972), 962-966.

1342 Basler, Roy P. "Psychological Pattern in The Love Song of J. Alfred Prufrock," Twentieth Century English. W. S. Knickerbocker, ed. New York: Philosophical Lib., 1946, pp. 384-400.

1343 ________. Sex, Symbolism, and Psychology in Literature. New Brunswick, New Jersey: Rutgers U. Pr., 1948, pp. 203-221.

1344 Bedi, Jatinder. "The Love Song of J. Alfred Prufrock: An Explication," Variations on American Literature. Darshan Singh Maini, ed. New Delhi: U. S. Educ. Foundation in India, 1968, pp. 38-43.

1345 Bell, Vereen M. "A Reading of Prufrock," ES (Anglo-Amer. Supp.), 50 (1969), lxviii-lxxiv.

1346 Berland, Alwyn. "Some Techniques of Fiction in Poetry," EIC, 4 (October, 1954), 372-385. Comparison of Prufrock with Pope's Epistle to Dr. Arbuthnot and Dunciad.

1347 Blackmur, R. P. "T. S. Eliot," H&H, 1 (March, 1928), 209-212.

1348 Blum, Margaret Morton. "The Fool in The Love Song of J. Alfred Prufrock," MLN, 72 (June, 1957), 424-426. Thinks that Yorick is the fool that Eliot had in mind.

1349 Bracker, Jon. "Eliot's The Love Song of J. Alfred Prufrock, 89," Expl, 25, #3 (November, 1966), Item 21. Edward Fitzgerald's Rubaiyat of Omar Khayyam a possible source.

1350 Bratcher, James T. "Prufrock and the Mermaids Re-Viewed," Descant, 6, #3 (Spring, 1962), 13-17.

1351 Brooks, Cleanth, and Robert Penn Warren. Understanding Poetry. New York: Henry Holt, 1938, pp. 589-596; revised ed., pp. 433-444.

1352 Browning, Gordon. "Eliot's The Love Song of J. Alfred Prufrock, 55-61," Expl, 31, #6 (February, 1973), Item 49. Identification of the insect mentioned in the poem.

1353 Carson, Herbert L. "The Hollow Man: J. Alfred Prufrock," Cresset, 34, #9 (September, 1971), 9-12.

1354 Cauthen, Irby B., Jr. "Gross's 'Laurence Sterne and Eliot's Prufrock,'" CE, 19 (December, 1957), 132. Addendum to Gross's article, CE, 19 (1957), 72-73.

1355 Chiari, Joseph. "From Prufrock and Other Observations to Poems, 1920," T. S. Eliot: Poet and Dramatist. New York: Barnes & Noble, 1972, pp. 36-55.

1356 Clark, John A. "On First Looking into Benson's Fitzgerald," SAQ, 48 (April, 1949), 258-269. Benson's Edward Fitzgerald as a source of figures, moods, and ideas for Prufrock and other poems.

1357 Clendenning, John. "Time, Doubt and Vision: Notes on Emerson and T. S. Eliot," AmSch, 36, #1 (Winter, 1966-67), 125-132.

1358 Cohen, Savin. "Jargon, Prufrock, and the 'Cop Out,'" CC&C, 16 (February, 1965), 27-29.

1359 Collingwood, R. G. The Principles of Art. Oxford: Oxford U. Pr., 1938, pp. 310-311.

1360 Cook, Robert G. "Emerson's 'Self-Reliance,' Sweeney, and Prufrock," AL, 42, #2 (May, 1970), 221-226.

1361 Corder, Jim. "Prufrock and the Mermaids," Descant, 5, #3 (Winter, 1961), 36-38. Identification of the mermaids with women mentioned earlier in the poem.

1362 Cowley, Malcolm. "Laforgue in America: A Testimony," SR, 71, #1 (Winter, 1963), 62-74. The Love Song of J. Alfred Prufrock "the great example of a Laforgue poem in English."

1362a Day Lewis, C. A Hope for Poetry. 1st ed., 1934; repr., with postscript; 5th ed., Oxford: B. Blackwell, 1942, pp. 18-28.

1363 Deeney, John J. "The Love Song of J. Alfred Prufrock: A Study in Diction and Imagery," FJS, 2 (1969), 53-68.

1364 Dunn, Ian S. "Eliot's The Love Song of J. Alfred Prufrock," Expl, 22, #1 (September, 1963), Item 1. Allusion of the name "Prufrock" may be to the "proof-rock" (touchstone).

1365 Dwyer, Daniel N., S. J. "Eliot's The Love Song of J. Alfred Prufrock," Expl, 9 (March, 1951), Item 38. Discussion of Lazarus. Cf., Clifford J. Fish, Expl, 8 (1950), Item 62; Eugene Arden, N&Q, 5, #8 (1958), 363-364.

1366 Engle, Paul. "Why Modern Poetry," CE, 15 (October, 1953), 8.

1367 ______, and Warren Carrier. Reading Modern Poetry. Chicago: Scott, Foresman & Co., 1955, pp. 167-174.

1368 Everett, Barbara. "In Search of Prufrock," CritQ, 16 (Summer, 1974), 101-122. "Eliot's words imply that a poem like Prufrock will be a genuflection to literature as well as a transcript of experience, a 'Love Song' to certain sources as much as anything else."

1369 Faas, Egbert. "Formen der Bewusstseinsdarstellung in der dramatischen Lyrik Pounds und Eliots," GRM, 18, #2, n. s. (April, 1968), 172-191.

1370 Fish, Clifford J. "Eliot's The Love Song of J. Alfred Prufrock," Expl, 8 (June, 1950), Item 62. The allusion to Lazarus.

1371 Fleissner, Robert F. "The Browning of T. S. Eliot," 1, #1 (1974), 6-7. Comparison of Prufrock and My Last Duchess.

1371a __________. "Prufrock Not the Polonius Type," RSWSU, 43 (1975), 262-263.

1372 __________. "'Prufrock,' Pater, and Richard II: Retracing a Denial of Princeship," AL, 38 (March, 1966), 120-123. Walter Pater and Shakespeare as sources.

1373 __________. "Prufrock's 'Ragged Claws,'" ES, 53 (June, 1972), 247-248.

1374 Fortenberry, George. "Prufrock and the Fool Song," BSUF, 8, #1 (Winter, 1967), 51-54. Eliot's indebtedness to Jules Laforgue.

1375 Frankenberg, Lloyd. Pleasure Dome: On Reading Modern Poetry. Boston: Houghton Mifflin, 1949, pp. 40-42, 45-49.

1376 Fryxell, Donald R. "Understanding The Love Song of J. Alfred Prufrock," Mon/Aug, 1, #1 (November, 1969), 33-44. Themes of the poem.

1377 Gardner, Helen. "The Landscapes of Eliot's Poetry," CritQ, 10, #4, (Winter, 1968), 313-330. Visits to places associated with Eliot's poems--The Love Song of J. Alfred Prufrock, St. Louis.

1378 Giannone, Richard J. "Eliot's Portrait of a Lady and Pound's Portrait d'une Femme," TCL, 5, #3 (October, 1959), 131-134. Pound's Portrait d'une Femme "nowhere reaches the level of Prufrock or Portrait...."

1379 Gil, Kim Jong. "'You' in The Love Song of J. Alfred Prufrock," PhoenixK, 11 (1967), 41-51.

1380 Glaza, James F. "Transition," Wingover, [1] (Fall-Winter, 1958-59), 33-38.

1380a Gluck, Barbara. "Verbal Tension in T. S. Eliot's The Love Song of J. Alfred Prufrock," Descant, 19, #4 (Summer, 1975), 41-48.

1381 Greene, Edward J. H. T. S. Eliot et la France. Paris: 1951.

1382 Gross, Seymour L. "Laurence Sterne and Eliot's Prufrock: An Object Lesson in Explication," CE, 19, #2 (November, 1957), 72-73. Prufrock's reference to Hamlet and the Fool. Cf., I. B. Cauthen, Jr. CE, 19 (December, 1957), 132.

1383 Gwynn, Frederick L. "Faulkner's Prufrock--And Other Observations," JEGP, 52 (January, 1953), 63-70.

1384 Hakac, John. "The Yellow Fog of Prufrock," BRMMLA, 26, #2 (June, 1972), 52-54. The yellow-fog, 15-22, a possible symbol of happy and earthy love.

1385 Halverson, John. "Prufrock, Freud, and Others," SR, 76, #4 (Autumn, 1968), 571-588. "The overwhelming question about the universe is: What is it? What does it mean?"

1386 Harvey, Versa R. "T. S. Eliot's The Love Song of J. Alfred Prufrock," IEY, 6 (Fall, 1961), 29-31. "...perhaps if we regard the poem as an 'objective correlative' of our society, this tedium will give place to appreciation."

1387 Hirsch, David H. "T. S. Eliot and the Vexation of Time," SoR, n. s. 3 (July, 1967), 608-624. Analysis of "time and timelessness" in the poem.

1388 Hollahan, Eugene. "A Structural Dantean Parallel in Eliot's The Love Song of J. Alfred Prufrock," AL, 42, #1 (March, 1970), 91-93. Notes a parallel between Eliot's poem and Inferno, Canto 2, 1. 32.

1389 Holland, Robert. "Miss Glasgow's Prufrock," AmQ, 9, #4 (Winter, 1957), 435-440. Notes Parallel between Ellen Glasgow's novel They Stooped to Folly and Eliot's Prufrock.

1390 Iribarren Borges, Ignocio. "T. S. Eliot y las armas de la cultura," RNC, 27, #171 (September, 1965), 67-71. Eliot's poem as a picture of pre-war European society.

1391 Jackson, James L. "Eliot's The Love Song of J. Alfred Prufrock," Expl, 18, #8 (May, 1960), Item 48. The sea imagery implied in "the overwhelming question."

1392 Kenner, Hugh. "Prufrock," The Invisible Poet: T. S. Eliot. New York: Ivan Obolensky, 1959, pp. 3-12.

1393 __________. "Prufrock of St. Louis," PrS, 31 (Spring, 1957), 24-30. Analysis of sound and effect in the poem.

1394 Kim, Jong Gil. "'You' in The Love Song of J. Alfred Prufrock," Phoenix, 2 (Spring, 1967), 41-52.

1395 King, Bruce. "Prufrock and Marvell," TSEN, 1, #1 (Spring, 1974), 5-6.

1396 Kirk, Russell. "Prufrock and Tradition," Eliot and His Age: Eliot's Moral Imagination in the Twentieth Century. New York: Random House, 1972, pp. 57-63.

1397 Knapp, James F. "Eliot's Prufrock and the Form of Modern Poetry," ArQ, 30 (Spring, 1974), 5-14.

1398 Kreymborg, Alfred. "T. S. Eliot and The Waste Land," Our Singing Strength: An Outline of American Poetry. New York: Coward-McCann, 1929. Praises Prufrock.

1399 Kudo, Yoshimi. "Strether to Prufrock," EigoS, 114 (1968), 790-791. The influence of James on Eliot.

1400 Langbaum, Robert. The Poetry of Experience: The Dramatic Monologue in Modern Literary Experience. New York: Random House, 1957, pp. 189-192.

1401 LeClair, Thomas. "Prufrock and the Open Road," WWR, 17, #4 (December, 1971), 123-126. The striking parallel between the end of Whitman's Song of Myself and Prufrock is "the concept of the divided self."

1402 Lewis, Wyndham. "First Meeting with T. S. Eliot," Blasting and Bombardiering. Los Angeles: U. of Calif. Pr., 1967, pp. 282-283. Comparison of T. S. Eliot with his character Prufrock.

1403 Locke, Frederick W. "Dante and T. S. Eliot's Prufrock," MLN, 78 (January, 1963), 51-59.

1404 Locke, James. "Clough's Amours de Voyage: A Possible Source for The Love Song of J. Alfred Prufrock," WHR, 29 (Winter, 1975), 55-66.

1405 Lyman, Dean B., Jr. "Aiken and Eliot," MLN, 71 (May, 1956), 342-343. "Some striking parallels between several of Aiken's poems and Eliot's Prufrock, which preceded them."

1406 M. M. [Marianne Moore]. "A Note on T. S. Eliot's Book," Poetry, 12 (April, 1918), 36-37. Prufrock and Other Observations.

1407 Major, Minor W. "A St. Louisan's View of Prufrock," CEA, 23, (September, 1961), 5. St. Louis as the setting for the poem.

1408 Margolis, Joseph. "'Ljubavna Pjesma J. A. Prufrocka' T. S. Eliota," Republika, 17 (January, 1961), 18-20.

1409 __________. "T. S. Eliot: The Love Song of J. Alfred Prufrock," Interpretations: Essays on Twelve English Poems. John Wain, ed. London: Routledge and K. Paul, 1955, pp. 179-193.

1410 Marshall, William H. "A Note on Prufrock," N&Q, 6, #5 (May, 1959), 188-189. Cf., Eugene Arden. "The Echo of Hell in Prufrock," N&Q, 5 (August, 1958), 363-364.

1411 Martin, B. K. "Prufrock, Bleistein and Company," N&Q, 14, #7 (July, 1967), 257. Quotes Eliot as saying that if he had seen the name "Prufrock" in St. Louis "his appropriation of it in his poem must have been 'quite unconscious.'"

1412 Montgomerie, W. "Harry, Meet Mr. Prufrock (T. S. Eliot's Dilemma)," LL&T, 31 (1941), 115-128.

1413 Montgomery, Marion. ["Prufrock"] T. S. Eliot: An Essay on the American Magus. Athens, Ga.: Georgia U. Pr., 1970, p. 83f.

1414 Morgan, Roberta, and Albert Wohlstetter. "Observations on Prufrock," HA, 125, #3 (1938), 27-30, 33-38. "The form of T. S. Eliot's Love Song is an ironic union of two distinct traditions: the lovesong and the soliloquy...."

1415 Novak, Robert. "Prufrock and Arnold's Buried Life," WiOr, 12 (Winter, 1972-73), 23-26. Parallels between the two poems.

1415a Okenwa, Nnamdi. "A Leaf from T. S. Eliot's Tree: The Dilemma of the Modern Man," Muse, 7 (1974), 45-46.

1416 Owen, Guy. "Prufrock and Huxley's Crome Yellow," LaurelR, 10, 2 (1970), 30-35.

1417 Perrine, L., and J. Reid. 100 American Poems of the Twentieth Century. New York: Harcourt, Brace & World, 1966, pp. 110-112, 133-134.

1417a Peterson, R. G. "Concentric Structure and The Love Song of J. Alfred Prufrock," TSER, 3, 1-2 (1976), 25-28.

1418 Pietersma, H. "The Overwhelming Question," Folio, 21 (Summer, 1956), 19-32.

1419 Pope, John C. "Prufrock and Raskolnikov," AL, 17 (November, 1945), 213-230. Crime and Punishment as a source for Eliot's poem.

1420 ________. "Prufrock and Raskolnikov Again: A Letter from Eliot," AL, 18 (January, 1947), 319-321. Although Dostoevski was in Eliot's mind while he was writing Prufrock, he had not read Mrs. Garnett's translation of Crime and Punishment.

1421 Pound, Ezra. "Drunken Helots and Mr. Eliot," Egoist, 4, #5 (June, 1917), 72-74.

1422 ________. "T. S. Eliot," Poetry, 10, #5 (August, 1917), 264-271; repr., in Literary Essays of Ezra Pound. New York: New Directions, 1954.

1423 Powers, Lyall H. "Eliot's The Love Song of J. Alfred Prufrock," Expl, 14 (March, 1956), Item 39.

1424 Rajan, B. "The Overwhelming Question," SR, 74 (Winter, 1966), 358-375.

1425 ________. "The Overwhelming Question," T. S. Eliot: The Man and His Work. Allen Tate, ed. New York: Delacorte Pr., 1966, pp. 364-381.

1426 ________. The Overwhelming Question: A Study of the Poetry of T. S. Eliot. Ontario: Toronto U. Pr., 1975.

1427 Reed, Kenneth T. "Carl Sandburg and T. S. Eliot: Some Poetical Exchanges," Poet&C, 6, #1 (Fall, 1970), 45-46. Similarity between Sandburg's cat-fog image in Fog and the image in Prufrock.

1428 Reeves, Troy Dale. "Prufrock at the Roxy," IllQ, 33, #3 (February, 1971), 43-47.

1428a Rochat, Joyce Hamilton. "T. S. Eliot's 'Companion' Poems: Eternal Question, Temporal Response," ContempR, 227 (1975), 73-79.

1429 Rodgers, Audrey T. "Dance Imagery in the Poetry of T. S. Eliot," Criticism, 16, #1 (Winter, 1974), 23-38.

1430 Rosenthal, M. L., and A. J. M. Smith. Exploring Poetry. New York: Macmillan, 1955, pp. 376-377.

1431 Rosu, Anca. "T. S. Eliot's The Love Song of J. Alfred Prufrock: A Song of Experience," AUB-LG, 21 (1972), 99-105.

1432 Rumble, Thomas C. "Some Grail Motifs in Eliot's Prufrock," LSUSHS, #8 (1960), 95-103; repr., in Studies in American Literature. Waldo McNeir and Leo B. Levy, eds. Baton Rouge: Louisiana State U. Pr., 1960, pp. 95-103.

1433 Schneider, Elisabeth. "Prufrock," T. S. Eliot: The Pattern in the Carpet. Berkeley; Los Angeles: California U. Pr., 1975, pp. 22-33.

1434 ________. "Prufrock and After: The Theme of Change," PMLA, 87, #5 (October, 1972), 1103-1118. "Though scarcely touched upon in his prose writings, this process of inner change, individual not social, is a major unifying theme in Eliot's poetry."

1435 Seiler, Robert M. "Prufrock and Hamlet," English, 21, #110 (Summer, 1972), 41-43. Parallels between the two characters.

1436 Shanahan, C. M. "Irony in Laforgue, Corbière and Eliot," MP, 53 (November, 1955), 119.

1436a Simpson, Louis. "T. S. Eliot, or Religion: The Author of Prufrock," Three on the Tower. 1975, pp. 93-106.

1437 Sinclair, May. "'Prufrock: and Other Observations': A Criticism," LittleR, 4 (December, 1917), 8-14.

1438 Slack, Robert C. "Victorian Literature as It Appears to Contemporary Students," CE, 22 (February, 1961), 344-347. Comparison of Eliot's Prufrock and Tennyson's Maud.

1439 Smith, Gerald. "Eliot's The Love Song of J. Alfred Prufrock," Expl, 21, #2 (October, 1962), Item 17. Discussion of the image of the crab.

1440 Southam, B. C. A Guide to the Selected Poems of T. S. Eliot. New York: Harcourt, Brace & World, 1969, pp. 33-39.

1441 Spangler, George M. "The Education of Henry Adams as a Source for The Love Song of J. Alfred Prufrock," N&Q, 15, #8 (August, 1968), 295-296. Adams' discussion of the horseshoe crab, Chapter 30, of The Education of Henry Adams as a source for "pair of ragged claws."

1442 Stepanchev, Stephen. "The Origin of J. Alfred Prufrock," MLN, 66 (June, 1951), 400-401. Suggests the Prufrocks in St. Louis as source of the name.

1443 Stuckey, William J. "Eliot's The Love Song of J. Alfred Prufrock," Expl, 20, #1 (September, 1961), Item 10. Parallels between Prufrock and the Divine Comedy.

1444 Surette, P. L. "The Music of Prufrock," HAB, 25 (Winter, 1974), 11-21.

1445 Symes, Gordon. "T. S. Eliot and Old Age," FnR, 169 (March, 1951), 188-189.

1446 Thomas, Wright, and Stuart Gerry Brown. Reading Poems: An Introduction to Critical Study. New York: Oxford U. Pr., 1941, pp. 698-700.

1447 Tschumi, Raymond. "Prufrock," Thought in Twentieth-Century English Poetry. New York: Octagon Bks., 1972, pp. 127-132.

1448 Turner, W. Arthur. "The Not So Coy Mistress of J. Alfred Prufrock," SAQ, 54 (November, 1955), 516-522. The Love Song as a "companion piece" to The Portrait of a Lady and Marvell's To His Coy Mistress.

1449 Untermeyer, Louis. "T. S. Eliot," American Poetry Since 1900. New York: Henry Holt, 1923, pp. 354-355.

1450 Vaughan, Franklin H. "Smog: The Old Possum's Insidious Cat," LHR, 9 (1967), 37-41. Interpretation of the images of fog, smoke, and smog in Prufrock and Other Observations.

1450a Vig, Jill. "The Love Song of Sherlock Holmes," BSJ, 25, #1 (March, 1975), 18-21.

1451 Virtue, John. "Eliot's The Love Song of J. Alfred Prufrock," Expl, 13 (November, 1954), Item 10. The meaning of the rolled trouser-bottoms.

1452 Vondersmith, Bernard J. "My Last Duchess and The Love Song of J. Alfred Prufrock: A Method of Counterbalance," ContempE, 43 (1971), 106-110.

1453 Waggoner, Hyatt Howe. "T. S. Eliot: At the Still Point," The Heel of Elohim: Science and Values in Modern Poetry. Norman, Okla.: Oklahoma U. Pr., 1950, pp. 61-104.

1454 Walcutt, Charles Child. "Eliot's The Love Song of J. Alfred Prufrock," CE, 19 (October, 1957), 71-72. Prufrock's "overwhelming question" is a proposal of marriage to the lady with the shawl.

1454a Waldoff, Leon. "Prufrock's Defenses and Our Response," AI, 26 (Summer, 1969), 182-193.

1455 Walz, Rudolf. "T. S. Eliot: The Love Song of J. Alfred

Prufrock behandelt an einer Prima," NS, 15, #10 (October, 1966), 477-486. Use of the "overwhelming question" when one is teaching the poem to freshmen.

1456 Warren, Austin. "Continuity and Coherence in the Criticism of T. S. Eliot," Connections. Ann Arbor: Michigan U. Pr., 1970, pp. 152-183. "... the poet and the critic in Eliot began almost concurrently (Prufrock and Other Observations, 1917; The Sacred Wood, 1920), and have coexisted in close relation...."

1457 Waterman, Arthur E. "Eliot's The Love Song of J. Alfred Prufrock," Expl, 17 (June, 1959), Item 67.

1458 Weinstock, Donald J. "Tennysonian Echoes in The Love Song of J. Alfred Prufrock," ELN, 7 (1970), 213-214.

1459 Weitz, Morris. "A 'Reading' of Eliot's The Love Song of J. Alfred Prufrock," Philosophy of the Arts. Cambridge: Harvard U. Pr., 1950; reissued, New York: Russell & Russell, 1964, pp. 94-107.

1460 __________. "T. S. Eliot: Time as a Mode of Salvation," SR, 60 (Winter, 1952), 48-64.

1461 Wheeler, Charles B. "Metaphor," [Prufrock], The Design of Poetry. New York: W. W. Norton & Co., 1966, pp. 168-170.

1462 White, Robert. "Eliot's The Love Song of J. Alfred Prufrock," Expl, 20, #3 (November, 1961), Item 19. Prufrock compared with Guido de Montefeltro of Dante's Inferno.

1463 Wilson, Frank. "Prufrock and Other Observations," Six Essays on the Development of T. S. Eliot. London: Fortune Pr., 1948, pp. 7-14.

1464 Wimsatt, W. K. "Prufrock and Maud: From Plot to Symbol," YFS, 9 (Spring, 1952); repr., in Hateful Contraries: Studies in Literature and Criticism by W. K. Wimsatt. Kentucky U. Pr., 1965, pp. 201-212.

1465 Wormhoudt, Arthur. "A Psychoanalytical Interpretation of The Love Song of J. Alfred Prufrock," Perspective, 2 (Winter, 1949), 109-117.

1466 Worthington, Jame. "The Epigraphs to the Poetry of T. S. Eliot," AL, 21 (March, 1949), 1-2.

1467 Wycherley, H. Alan. "Levels of Recognition in Prufrock," Forum (Houston), 4, #3 (Winter, 1963), 33-36.

RHAPSODY ON A WINDY NIGHT

1468 Aiken, Conrad. "New Curiosity Shop--and a Poet," Dial, 64 (January 31, 1918), 112.

1469 Brooks, Cleanth, and Robert Penn Warren. "The Reading of Modern Poetry," AmR, 7 (February, 1937), 442-445.

1469a Brown, Calvin S., Jr. "T. S. Eliot and 'Die Droste,'" SR, 46 (October-December, 1938), 492-500. Eliot's indebtedness to Annette von Droste-Hulshoff's Durchwochte Nacht in relation to Eliot's poem.

1470 Smith, Grover C., Jr. "Charles-Louis Philippe and T. S. Eliot," AL, 22 (November, 1950), 254-259.

1471 ________. T. S. Eliot's Poetry and Plays: A Study in Sources. Chicago U. P., 1956, pp. 20-23.

SWEENEY AMONG THE NIGHTINGALES

1472 Basler, Roy P., and Kirschbaum, Leo. "Eliot's Sweeney Among the Nightingales," Expl, 2 (December, 1943), Item 18. Meaning of Line "And Sweeney guards the hornéd gate."

1473 Brown, Wallace Cable. "Mr. Eliot Without the Nightingales," UKCR, 14 (Autumn, 1947), 31-38.

1474 Buttle, Myra [pseudonym for Victor William Williams Saunders Purcell]. The Sweeniad. New York: Sagamore Press, 1957. Rev. by M. L. Rosenthal, Nation, 186 (1957-58), 211-212. Cf., Edmund Wilson. "Miss Buttle and Mr. Eliot," NY, 34 (May 24, 1958), 119-150.

1475 Davidson, James. "The End of Sweeney," CE, 27 (February, 1966), 400-403. "Sweeney is, in fact, already dead, one of the crowd flowing over London Bridge. He is devoid of the spiritual vitality which constitutes the only significant life...."

1476 Deutsch, Babette. Poetry in Our Time. New York: Henry Holt, 1952, pp. 168-170.

1477 Drew, Elizabeth. T. S. Eliot: The Design of His Poetry. New York: Scribner's Sons, 1949, pp. 44-46; abridged in The Case for Poetry. pp. 133-135.

1478 Gillis, Everett A. "Religion in a Sweeney World," ArQ, 20 (Spring, 1964), 55-63.

1479 Graves, Robert. "Sweeney Among the Nightingales," TQ, 1, #2 (Spring, 1958), 83-102.

1480 Grubb, Frederick. "T. S. Eliot, Alas?"--[Sweeney Among the Nightingales] A Vision of Reality. London: Chatto & Windus, 1965, pp. 54-55.

1481 Gwynn, Frederick L. "Correction to 'Sweeney Among the Epigraphs,'" MLN, 70 (1955), 490-491. Supplement to note in MLN, 69 (1954), 572-574.

1482 ________. "Eliot's Sweeney Among the Nightingales and The Song of Solomon," MLN, 68 (January, 1953), 25-27.

1483 ________. "Sweeney Among the Epigraphs," MLN, 69 (December, 1954), 572-574. Second epigraph from the anonymous The Reign of King Edward the Third and dropped from the 1920 Poems of Eliot, explains the obscure lines in Sweeney Among the Nightingales. Cf., MLN, 70 (1955), 490-491.

1484 Homann, Elizabeth R. "Eliot's Sweeney Among the Nightingales, 8," Expl, 17, #5 (February, 1959), Item 34. The fertility-rite symbols are "debased and attenuated for his [Eliot's] theme of degradation, betrayal and fertility in the contemporary world."

1485 Hyman, Stanley Edgar. "Poetry and Criticism: T. S. Eliot," AmSch, 30, #1 (Winter, 1960-61), 43-55.

1486 ________. "Poetry and Criticism: T. S. Eliot," Poetry and Criticism: Four Resolutions in Literary Taste. New York: 1961, pp. 159-178.

1487 Kaplan, Charles, "Eliot Among the Nightingales: Fair and Foul," NMQR, 24 (Summer, 1954), 228.

1488 Kirschbaum, Leo, and Roy P. Basler. "Eliot's Sweeney Among the Nightingales," Expl, 2, #3 (December, 1943), Item 18.

1489 Kunst, Herbert. "Sweeney Among the Birds and Brutes," Arcadia, 2, #2 (1967), 204-217. "Certain striking parallels...point toward a connection between the Irish king Sweeney and Eliot's Sweeney."

1490 Mudford, P. G. "Sweeney Among the Nightingales," EIC, 19, #3 (July, 1969), 285-291. The poem "makes concrete that area of the mind where the sacred and profane are uneasy companions of everyday affairs, and communicates how the appearance of the conflict is transformed by the social context into which it erupts."

1491 Ower, John B. "Pattern and Value in Sweeney Among the Nightingales," Renascence, 23 (1971), 151-158.

1492 Parkes, Henry B. "T. S. Eliot," H&H, 6, #2 (January, 1933), 350-356.

1493 Stauffer, Donald Alfred. The Nature of Poetry. New York: Norton, 1946, pp. 78-80.

1494 Tischler, Nancy M. "Sweeney, Absurdities, and Christians," C&L, 20, iii (1971), 8-10. Response to Wm. Spanos, "God and the Detective: The Christian Tradition and the Drama of the Absurd," C&L, 20, ii (1971), 16-22.

1495 Tribe, David. "Requiem for Sweeney," TC, 177, #1042 (1969), 26-31.

1496 Walcutt, Charles C. "Eliot's Sweeney Among the Nightingales," Expl, 2, #6 (April, 1944), Item 48. Sweeney's guard of the "horned gate."

1497 Williamson, George. A Reader's Guide to T. S. Eliot. New York: Noonday Press, 1953, pp. 97-98.

1498 Wilson, Edmund. "Miss Buttle and Mr. Eliot," NY, 34 (May 24, 1958), 119-150. Cf., Myra Buttle. The Sweeniad. New York: 1957.

1499 Worthington, Jane. "Sweeney Among the Nightingales--The Epigraphs to the Poetry of T. S. Eliot," AL, 21 (March, 1949, January, 1950), 13.

SWEENEY ERECT

1500 Casey, Thomas C. "An Analysis of T. S. Eliot's Sweeney Erect," DAI, 33 (St. John's: 1972), 2925A.

1501 Cook, Robert G. "Emerson's 'Self-Reliance,' Sweeney, and Prufrock," AL, 42, (May, 1970), 221-226. "It seems then that in both Sweeney Erect and The Love Song of J. Alfred Prufrock Eliot is giving the lie to Emerson's 'Self-Reliance.'"

1502 Mizener, Arthur. "To Meet Mr. Eliot," SR, 65 (Winter, 1957), 41-42.

1503 Peake, Charles. "Sweeney Erect and the Emersonian Hero," Neophil, 44, #1 (January, 1966), 54-61. Sweeney Erect "can be read as a conscious and ironic commentary on the matter and manner" of Emerson's Self-Reliance and History.

1504 Singer, Glen W. "Eliot's Sweeney Erect," Expl, 34, #1 (September, 1975), Item 7. The classical allusions in the poem.

1504a Walcutt, Charles Child. "Eliot's Sweeney Erect," Expl, 35, #2 (Winter, 1976), Item 31. Cf., G. W. Singer, Expl, 34, #1 (September, 1975), Item 7.

1505 Worthington, Jane. "The Epigraphs to the Poetry of T. S. Eliot," AL, 21 (March, 1949), 7-9.

TO THE INDIANS WHO DIED IN AFRICA

1506 Rao, G. Nageswara. "To the Indians Who Died in Africa," AryP, 39, #3 (March, 1968), 125-129. The poem shows that Eliot "assimilated the subtle intricacies of Indian philosophy [and] ... the very milieu and ethos of Indian life."

1506a Rao, K. S. Narayana. "Addendum on Eliot and the Bhagavad-Gita," AQ, 16 (1964), 102-103.

1507 ________. "T. S. Eliot and the Bhagavad-Gita," AQ, 15 (Winter, 1963), 572-578. The poem, To the Indians Who Died in Africa, which Eliot contributed to Queen Mary's Book of India (1943), "appears to have been almost wholly inspired by and permeated with Indian religious and philosophic thought."

THE WASTE LAND

1508 A. D. "Some Notes on The Waste Land," N&Q, 195 (August, 1950), 365-369.

1509 Adams, Richard P. "Sunrise Out of the Waste Land," TSE, 9 (1959), 119-131. Comparison of The Sun Also Rises and The Waste Land.

1510 Adams, Robert M. "Precipitating Eliot," Eliot in His Time: Essays on the Occasion of the Fiftieth Anniversary of The Waste Land. A. Walton Litz, ed. Princeton: Princeton U. P.; London: Oxford U. P., 1973, pp. 129-153.

1511 Aiken, Conrad. "An Anatomy of Melancholy," NR, 33 (February 7, 1923), 294-295; repr., in A Reviewer's ABC. New York: Meridian Bks., 1958, pp. 176-181; A Collection of Critical Essays. Jay Martin, ed. Englewood Cliffs,

N. J.: Prentice-Hall, 1968, pp. 52-58; SR, 74 (Winter, 1966), 188-196.

1512 Alvarez, Alfred. Stewards of Excellence: Studies in Modern English and American Poets. New York: Scribner's, 1958, pp. 11-32.

1513 Andreach, Robert J. "Paradise Lost and the Christian Configuration of The Waste Land," PLL, 5 (Summer, 1969), 296-309.

1514 Anon. "The Waste Land Forty Years On," TLS, 3161 (September 28, 1962), 760.

1515 Anon. "The Waste Land Revisited," TLS, 2691 (August 28, 1953), viii-ix.

1516 Bacon, Helen H. "The Sibyl in the Bottle," VQR, 34, #2 (Spring, 1958), 262-276. Eliot's possible use of the Satyricon by Petronius.

1517 Bailey, Bruce. "A Note on The Waste Land and Henry James's In the Cage," TSEN, 1, #2 (Fall, 1974), 2.

1518 __________. "A Note on The Waste Land and Hope Mirrlees' Paris," TSEN, 1, #2 (Fall, 1974), 3-4.

1518a __________. "A Note on The Waste Land and Joyce's Ulysses," TSER, 2, #2 (Fall, 1975), 10.

1519 Baker, John Ross. "Eliot's The Waste Land, 77-93," Expl, 14, (January, 1956), Item 27. The "sevenbranched candelabra" in a perverted setting.

1520 Baldi, Sergio. "L'organizzazione espressiva della Terra Desolata," SA, 4 (1958), 223-246.

1521 Balfour, Michael. "The Waste Land," TLS, 3644 (December 31, 1971), 1630.

1522 Barry, John. "The Waste Land: A Possible German Source," CLS, 9 (1972), 429-442. Oswald Spengler's Decline of the West (1918) a possible source.

1522a Barry, Peter. "Some Further Correspondences Between the 'Proteus' Section of James Joyce's Ulysses and The Waste Land," ES, 57 (June, 1976), 227-238.

1523 Bates, Ronald. "A Topic in The Waste Land: Traditional Rhetoric and Eliot's Individual Talent," WSCL, 5, #2 (Summer, 1964), 85-104. "In the description of his temple of Venus, his house of fame, his cave of Mammon... Eliot has chosen to be most consciously classical and traditional."

1524 Bateson, F. W. "Editorial Commentary," EIC, 19 (January, 1969), 1-5. Eliot's quarrel with Bateson. Cf., John Peter. "A New Interpretation of The Waste Land," EIC, 19 (April, 1969), 140-175.

1525 Beery, Judith A. "The Relevance of Baudelaire to T. S. Eliot's The Waste Land," SUS, 7 (1966), 283-302.

1526 Belgion, Montgomery. Reading for Profit. Chicago: Henry Regnery, 1950, pp. 258-286, passim.

1527 Bell, Clive. "How Pleasant to Know Mr. Eliot," T. S. Eliot: A Symposium. Richard March and Tambimuttu, comps. Freeport, N. Y.: Bks. for Libraries Pr., 1968, pp. 15-19.

1528 ________. "T. S. Eliot," Nation (London), 33 (September 22, 1923), 772-773; repr., as "The Elusive Art of T. S. Eliot," in Vanity Fair (September, 1923), 53.

1529 Benet, William Rose. "Poetry Ad Lib," YR, 13 (1923), 161.

1530 Bergonzi, Bernard. "Allusion in The Waste Land, II," EIC, 20 (1970), 382-385. Reply to John Lucas and William Myers. "II, The Waste Land Today," EIC, 19 (1969), 193-209.

1531 ________. "Maps of the Waste Land," Encounter, 38 (April, 1972), 80-83.

1532 Beringause, A. F. "Journey Through The Waste Land," SAQ, 56 (January, 1957), 79-90. Victorian antecedents of the poem.

1533 Berry, Francis. "Allusion in The Waste Land, I," EIC, 20 (1970), 380-382. Reply to William Myers, EIC, 20 (1970), 120-122.

1534 Birley, Robert. "The Waste Land," TLS, #3652 (February 25, 1972), 220.

1535 Blackmur, R. P. "T. S. Eliot," H&H, I, Nos. 3 & 4 (March, June, 1928), 187-213, 291-319.

1536 Bly, Robert. "Five Decades of Modern American Poetry," The Fifties, 1 (1958), 36-39.

1537 Bodkin, Maud. Archetypal Patterns in Poetry. London: Oxford U. P., 1934, pp. 310-315.

1537a Bogen, Donald Howard. "Composition and the Self in Three Modern Poets: W. B. Yeats, T. S. Eliot, and Theodore Roethke," DAI, 37 (Calif., Berkeley: 1976), 5813A.

1538 Bolgan, Anne C. Mr. Eliot's Philosophical Writings, or What the Thunder Said. Diss. Toronto: 1961.

1539 ________. What the Thunder Really Said: A Retrospective Essay on the Making of The Waste Land. Montreal & London: McGill-Queen's U. P., 1973.

1540 Bowra, E. M. "T. S. Eliot: The Waste Land," The Creative Experiment. London: Macmillan, 1949; New York: Grove Press, 1958, pp. 159-188. "... his [Eliot's] prepossessions with morality are more American than European, the product of New England and its Puritan tradition."

1541 Bradbrook, Muriel C. "Eliot's Critical Method," Focus Three: T. S. Eliot, A Study of His Writings by Several Hands. B. Rajan, ed. London: Dennis Dobson, 1947, 126.

1542 ________. "The Poet of The Waste Land," T. S. Eliot. London: Longmans Green, 1950, revised ed., 1965, pp. 9-20.

1543 ________. T. S. Eliot: The Making of The Waste Land. (WTW 226.) Harlow: Longman for the British Council, 1972.

1544 Bradley, Sculley, Richard Croom Beatty, and E. Hudson Long, eds. The American Tradition in Literature. New York: Norton, 1956, II, 917. Allusion to Line 128 of Waste Land.

1545 Brandabur, Edward. "Eliot and the Myth of Mute Speech," Renascence, 22 (1970), 141-150.

1546 Brooks, Cleanth. "Poetry Since The Waste Land," SoR, n. s., 1, #3 (Summer, 1965), 487-500. Since The Waste Land, poetry has generally moved away from Eliot's practices, that is, "... against overt analogy and overt logic...."

1547 ________. "T. S. Eliot: Discourse to the Gentiles," The Hidden God: Studies in Hemingway, Faulkner, Yeats, Eliot, and Warren. New Haven, Conn.: Yale U. P., 1963, pp. 68-69.

1548 ________. "The Waste Land: An Analysis," SoR, 3 (Summer, 1937), 106-136. "... an explicit account of the various symbols [in the poem] and a logical account of their relationship."

1549 ________. "The Waste Land: An Analysis," T. S. Eliot: A Study of His Writings by Several Hands. B. Rajan, ed. New York: Funk and Wagnalls, 1948, pp. 7-36.

1550 ________. "The Waste Land: Critique of the Myth," Modern Poetry and the Tradition. New York: Oxford U. P., 1965, pp. 136-172.

1551 ________, and Robert Penn Warren. Understanding Poetry. New York: Henry Holt, 1938, pp. 645-667.

1552 Brooks, Harold F. "Between The Waste Land and the First Ariel Poems: The Hollow Men," English, 16, #93 (Autumn, 1966), 89-93.

1553 Brown, Alec. "The Lyric Impulse in the Poetry of T. S. Eliot," Scrutinies, Vol. 2. E. Rickword, ed. London: Wishart, 1931, pp. 34-48.

1554 Brown, E. K. "Mr. Eliot and Some Enemies," UTQ, 8 (1938), 81.

1555 Buck, Gerhard. "Über die Anspielungen in T. S. Eliot's Waste Land," Anglia, 65 (November, 1940), 214-225.

1556 Burgess, Anthony. "The Waste Land Revisited," Horizon, 14, #1 (Winter, 1972), 104-109.

1557 Cajetan, Brother. "The Pendulum Starts Back," CathW, 140 (March, 1935), 654.

1558 Cambon, Glauco. "The Waste Land as Work in Progress," Mosaic, 6, #1 (Fall, 1972), 191-200.

1559 Cameron, H. D. "The Sibyl in the Satyricon," CJ, 65, #8 (May, 1970), 337-339. Finds the Satyricon of little help in interpretation of the epigraph about the Sibyl at Cumae.

1560 Carey, Sister M. Cecilia. "Baudelaire's Influence on The Waste Land," Renascence, 14 (Summer, 1962), 185-192, 198.

1561 Cargill, Oscar. "'Death in a Handful of Dust,'" Criticism, 11 (Summer, 1969), 275-296.

1562 ________. Intellectual America: Ideas on the March. New York: Macmillan, 1941, pp. 258-274, passim. "The Waste Land, coming at the culmination of Decadence, is the greatest poem thus far produced in the twentieth century...."

1563 Cauthen, I. B., Jr. "Another Webster Allusion in The Waste Land," MLN, 73, #7 (November, 1958), 498-499. "...the verbal echo [of Webster's The White Devil in Eliot's poem] is subtly used...."

1564 Chace, William M. "'Make It Not So New'--The Waste Land Manuscript," SoR, 9, #1 (January, 1973), 476-480. Suggests the reason for Pound's neglect of Part V.

1565 Chancellor, Paul. "The Music of The Waste Land," CLS, 6, #1 (March, 1969), 21-32. Notes that the symbols are arranged like "a tone poem."

1566 Charity, A. C. "T. S. Eliot: The Dantean Recognitions," The Waste Land in Different Voices. A. D. Moody, ed. New York: St. Martin's Press, 1974, pp. 117-162.

1567 Chase, Richard. "The Sense of the Present," KR, 7 (Spring, 1945), 225-231.

1568 Chew, Samuel C. "The Nineteenth Century and After (1789-1939)--The Waste Land," A Literary History of England. Albert C. Baugh, ed. New York: Appleton-Century-Crofts, 1948, p. 1586.

1569 Chiari, Joseph. "The Waste Land," TLS, #3644 (December 31, 1971), 1630.

1570 ______. "The Waste Land," TLS, #3652 (February 25, 1972), 220.

1571 ______. "The Waste Land and The Hollow Men," T. S. Eliot: Poet and Dramatist. London: Vision Press; New York: Barnes & Noble, 1972, pp. 56-74, passim.

1572 Claas, Dietmar. Erneuerung und Tradition im poetischen Wortschatz T. S. Eliots, dargestellt anhand von Motivreihen des Waste Land. Diss. Andernach: Selbstverl., 1971.

1573 Collingwood, R. G. [The Waste Land] The Principles of Art. Oxford: Clarendon Pr., 1938, pp. 310, 333-335; excerpt of pp. 334-336 in A Collection of Critical Essays. Jay Martin, ed. Englewood Cliffs, New Jersey: Prentice-Hall, 1968, pp. 50-51. The Waste Land illustrative of esthetic theories.

1574 Cook, Albert. "Eliot's Waste Land, III, 262-265," Expl, 6, #1 (October, 1947), Item 7.

1575 Cotton, Lyman A. "Eliot's The Waste Land, I, 43-46," Expl, 9 (October, 1950), Item 7. Origin of the name Sosostris. Cf., Lysander Kemp. Expl, 8 (1950), Item 27.

1576 Cowley, Malcolm. "Readings from the Lives of the Saints," Exile's Return. New York: Viking, 1951, pp. 110-115.

1577 Cox, C. B. "T. S. Eliot at the Cross-Roads," CritQ, 12, #4 (Winter, 1970), 307-320. The uncertainties and contradictions found in Eliot's preconversion poetry, particularly The Waste Land.

1578 __________, and Arnold P. Hinchliffe, eds. T. S. Eliot: The Waste Land: A Casebook. London: Macmillan, 1968.

1579 Craig, David. "The Defeatism of The Waste Land," CritQ, 2 (Autumn, 1960), 241-252. The poem "projects an almost defeatist personal depression in the guise of a full, impersonal picture of society...."

1579a __________. "The Defeatism of The Waste Land," Storm over The Waste Land. Robert E. Knoll, ed. Chicago: Scott, Foresman, 1964, pp. 122-135.

1580 Cross, Gustav. "A Note on The Waste Land," N&Q, 6 (July-August, 1959), 286-287.

1581 Cunningham, J. S. "Pope, Eliot, and 'The Mind of Europe,'" The Waste Land in Different Voices. A. D. Moody, ed. New York: St. Martin's Press, 1974, pp. 67-85.

1582 Curtius, Ernst Robert. "T. S. Eliot: Das Wueste Land," NRs, 3 (1950), 327-345.

1583 D., A. "More Notes on The Waste Land," N&Q, 196 (December 8, 1951), 538-540.

1584 __________. "Some Notes on The Waste Land," N&Q, 195 (August 19, 1950), 365-369.

1585 Dale, Peter. "The Waste Land," Agenda, 10 (Fall Winter, 1972-73), 155-157. Rev.-art., The Waste Land: A Facsimile and Transcript of the Drafts. Valerie Eliot, ed. London: Faber, 1971.

1586 Davidson, Arthur. The Eliot Enigma: A Critical Examination of "The Waste Land." London: 1941.

1587 Davie, Donald. "Eliot in One Poet's Life," The Waste Land in Different Voices. A. D. Moody, ed. New York: St. Martin's Press, 1974, pp. 221-237.

1588 Davis, R. G., et al. "The New Criticism," AmSch, 20 (Spring, 1951), 225-226.

1589 Davison, Richard. "Hart Crane, Louis Untermeyer, and T. S. Eliot: A New Crane Letter," AL, 44 (1972), 143-146. The "previously unpublished" letter by Hart Crane "adds more grist for the mill concerning T. S. Eliot's reputation and influence during the pivotal few months following the Dial publication of The Waste Land in November, 1922."

1590 Day, Robert A. "The 'City Man' in The Waste Land: The Geography of Reminiscence," PMLA, 80, #3 (June, 1965), 285-291. Discusses Eliot's use of actual scenes in London.

1591 __________. "Joyce's Waste Land and Eliot's Unknown God," Mon/LMWi, 4 (1971), 137-210. Indebtedness of Eliot's Waste Land to Ulysses.

1591a Day Lewis, C. A Hope for Poetry. Oxford: Basil Blackwell, 1934, passim.

1592 Deane, Paul. "Thematic Consistency in the Work of T. S. Eliot," RLV, 39 (November-December, 1973), 449-458.

1593 DeBiasio, Giordano. "Frammenti' della Ur-Waste Land di T. S. Eliot," AFF, 1 (1973), 331-346. "...offers a structural analysis of two short passages from those parts of The Waste Land that the poet discarded."

1594 DeLaura, David J. "Echoes of Butler, Browning, Conrad, and Pater in the Poetry of T. S. Eliot," ELN, 3, #3 (March, 1966), 211-221.

1595 DeMott, Benjamin. "Modeling a New Mind from a Brain-Breaking Vision," SatR, 54, #48 (November 27, 1971), 35-37, 61-62. Rev., -art., T. S. Eliot, The Waste Land: A Facsimile and Transcript of the Original Drafts. Valerie Eliot, ed. Harcourt, Brace Jovanovich, 1971.

1596 Deutsch, Babette. "The Auditory Imagination" [The Waste Land], Poetry in Our Time. 2nd ed., rev., and enl. Garden City, N. Y.: Doubleday & Co., 1963, pp. 173-178.

1597 __________. This Modern Poetry. New York: Norton, 1935, pp. 118-127.

1598 DeVoto, Bernard. "The Waste Land," The Literary Fallacy. Boston: Little, Brown, 1944, pp. 108-111.

1599 Dick, Bernard F. "A Marlovian Source for Belladonna's Beaudoir: The Waste Land, II, 77-100," TSEN, 1, #1 (Spring, 1974), 2-3.

1599a __________. "The Waste Land and the Descensus ad Inferos," CRCL, 2 (1975), 35-46.

1600 Dickerson, Mary Jane. "As I Lay Dying and The Waste Land: Some Relationships," MissQ, 17, #3 (Summer, 1964), 129-135. Use of The Golden Bough by Eliot and Faulkner.

1601 Diggle, Margaret. "The Ancient Mariner and The Waste Land," Poetry (London), 10 (December, 1944), 207.

1602 Dobree, Bonamy. "T. S. Eliot," The Lamp and the Lute. Oxford: Clarendon, 1929, pp. 107-133; New York: Barnes & Noble, 2nd ed., 1964, pp. 106-119.

1603 Donker, Marjorie. "The Waste Land and the Aeneid," PMLA, 89, #1 (January, 1974), 164-173.

1604 Donoghue, Denis. "The American Waste Land at Fifty," AInt, 16, #5 (May 20, 1972), 61-64, 67. The American characteristics of The Waste Land.

1605 ________. "'The Word Within a Word,'" The Waste Land in Different Voices. A. D. Moody, ed. New York: St. Martin's Press, 1974, pp. 185-201.

1606 Dorris, George E. "Two Allusions in the Poetry of T. S. Eliot," ELN, 2 (September, 1964), 54-57. Part III of The Waste Land has operatic allusions.

1607 Drain, Richard. "The Waste Land: The Prison and the Key," The Waste Land in Different Voices. A. D. Moody, ed. New York: St. Martin's Press, 1974, pp. 29-45.

1608 Drew, Elizabeth. T. S. Eliot: The Design of His Poetry. New York: Scribner's, 1949, pp. 58-90. A Jungian interpretation.

1609 ________. "The Waste Land," Direction in Modern Poetry. New York: Norton, 1940, pp. 37-55.

1610 Duffey, Bernard I. "The Experimental Lyric in Modern Poetry: Eliot, Pound, Williams," JML, 3 (1974), 1085-103. The Waste Land, The Cantos, and Paterson represent a kind of lyric that may be called "experimental."

1611 Dunn, Peter. "The Waste Land," TLS, #3650 (February 11, 1972), 156.

1612 Durham, Lorrayne. "The Death-Rebirth Motif in Eliot's Waste Land," Appalachian St. Teachers Col. Fac. Pub., (1959-60), 15-22.

1613 Du Sautoy, Peter. "The Waste Land," TLS, #3642 (December 17, 1971), 1580.

1614 Ehnmark, Anders. "Rebels in American Literature," WestR, 23, #1 (Autumn, 1958), 43-56.

1615 Eliot, Valerie. "T. S. Eliot and The Waste Land," TLS, #3714 (May 11, 1973), 529.

1616 ________, ed. The Waste Land: A Facsimile and Transcript of the Original Drafts Including the Annotations of Ezra Pound. Introduction by Valerie Eliot. New York: Harcourt, 1971, pp. ix-xxx.

1617 ___________, and Jayanta Padmanabha. "T. S. Eliot and The Waste Land," TLS (May 18, 1973), 556.

1618 Ellman, Richard. "The First Waste Land, I," NYBR, 17 (November 18, 1971), 10-16.

1619 ___________. "The First Waste Land," Eliot in His Time. A. Walton Litz, ed. Princeton, N. J.: Princeton U. P., 1973, pp. 51-66.

1620 Empson, William. "My God Man There's Bears on It," EIC, 22 (1972), 417-429. Review article, of Valerie Eliot's Facsimile Edition of The Waste Land.

1621 Everett, Barbara. "Eliot in and out of The Waste Land," CritQ, 17 (Spring, 1975), 7-30. "There is... a Waste Land Style, even a personality recognizable in the poem...."

1622 ___________. "The Waste Land," TLS, #3653 (March 3, 1972), 249.

1623 Every, Brother George. "Life, Life, Eternal Life," Student World, 31 (1938), 143.

1624 Farrell, William J. "The Waste Land as Rhetoric," Renascence, 22 (Spring, 1970), 127-140. Suggests that the poem should be read as rhetorical strategy. "The very genesis of The Waste Land implies strategy, and strategy in large amounts."

1625 Fasel, Ida. "A 'Conversation' Between Faulkner and Eliot," MissQ, 20, #4 (Autumn, 1967), 195-206. Contribution of The Waste Land to The Sound and the Fury.

1626 Fink, Ernst O. "Zur Waste Land--Ubertragung von Ernst Robert Curtius," NS, 19, #10 (October, 1970), 507-513. Influence of Curtius's German translation of Eliot's poem.

1627 Fisher, Ruth. "A Conversation with Robert Penn Warren," FQ, 21, #4 (May, 1972), 3-17. Describes influence of Eliot's The Waste Land in Warren's life.

1628 Forster, E. M. "T. S. Eliot," Abinger Harvest. New York: Harcourt Brace, 1936; Meridian Bks., 1955, pp. 84-91. "...The Waste Land is Mr. Eliot's greatest achievement...."

1629 Fortin, René E. "Eliot's The Waste Land, 207-214," Expl, 21, #4 (December, 1962), Item 32. "... radiation of meaning from the image 'the pocket full of currants.'"

1630 Foster, Genevieve W. "Archetypal Imagery of T. S. Eliot," PMLA, 60 (June, 1945), 571-576.

1631 Foster, Steven. "Relativity and The Waste Land: A Postulate," TSLL, 7 (Spring, 1965), 77-95; excerpt in Jay Martin's A Collection of Critical Essays. Englewood Cliffs, N. J.: 1968, pp. 17-19. "A poem in debt to modern physics, exhibiting the various states of subjective relativity, ... The Waste Land is something like Joyce's Ulysses... and rather opposite to Proust... in Remembrance of Things Past."

1631a Fowler, Rowena. "'Η Ἔρημη Χώρα: Seferis' Translation of The Waste Land," CLS, 9(1972), 443-454.

1632 Fowlie, Wallace. The Clown's Grail. London: Dennis Dobson, 1947, p. 148f.

1633 Frankenberg, Lloyd. Pleasure Dome: On Reading Modern Poetry. Boston: Houghton Mifflin, 1949, pp. 64-77.

1634 Franklin, Rosemary F. "Death or the Heat of Life in the Handful of Dust?" AL, 41, #2 (May, 1969), 277-279. Conrad's Youth as the source of Eliot's line.

1635 Freedman, Morris. "Jazz Rhythms and T. S. Eliot," SAQ, 51 (July, 1952), 423, 425, 427; repr., in A Collection of Critical Essays. Jay Martin, ed. Englewood Cliffs, N. J.: 1968, pp. 21-22.

1636 French, A. L. "Criticism and The Waste Land," SoR, (Adelaide), 1, #2 (1964), 69-81.

1637 ________. "Death by Allusion?" EIC, 20 (1970), 269-271. Cf., Juliet McLauchlan. "Allusion in The Waste Land," EIC, 19 (1969), 454-460.

1638 ________. "'Olympian Apathein': Pound's Hugh Selwyn Mauberley and Modern Poetry," EIC, 15, #4 (October, 1965), 428-445. Influence of The Waste Land.

1638a French, Warren. "The Age of Eliot: The Twenties as Waste Land," The Twenties: Fiction, Poetry, Drama. Deland, Florida: Everett/Edwards, 1975, pp. 1-26.

1639 Friar, Kimon, and John Malcolm Brinnin. Modern Poetry: American and British. New York: Appleton-Century-Crofts, 1951, pp. 425-426, 472-497.

1640 Fussell, Paul, Jr. "The Gestic Symbolism of T. S. Eliot," ELH, 22 (September 1955), 194-211, passim.

1641 Gallivan, Patricia. "'The Comic Spirit' and The Waste Land,"

UTQ, 45 (Fall, 1975), 35-49. Suggests that Eliot's original intention in The Waste Land was consistent with his conception of comedy revealed in his essays.

1642 Gallup, Donald. "T. S. Eliot and Ezra Pound: Collaborators in Letters," Atl, 225, #1 (January, 1970), 48-62.

1643 ________. "The Waste Land," T. S. Eliot: A Bibliography. New York: Harcourt, Brace & World, 1953, pp. 29-32, passim.

1644 Gardner, Helen. "Altered in Fulfillment," NSt, (November 12, 1971), 654-655. The various drafts of The Waste Land indicate its autobiographical quality.

1645 ________. "Four Quartets: A Commentary," Focus Three: T. S. Eliot, A Study of His Writings by Several Hands. B. Ragan, ed. London: Dennis Dobson, 1947, p. 60f. "...most people would agree today, in the light of Mr. Eliot's later work, that the original critics of The Waste Land misread it, not recognizing it as an Inferno which looked towards a Purgatorio."

1646 ________. "The Waste Land," TLS, #3649 (February 4, 1972), 128.

1647 ________. The Waste Land: The Adamson Lecture, 3rd May 1972, University of Manchester. Manchester: Manchester U. P., 1972.

1648 ________. "The Waste Land: Paris 1922," Eliot in His Time: Essays on the Fiftieth Anniversary of The Waste Land. Princeton: Princeton U. P., 1973, pp. 67-94.

1649 Gent, Margaret. "The Drowned Phoenician Sailor: T. S. Eliot and William Morris," N&Q, n. s., 17, #2 (February, 1970), 30-51. Morris's The Life and Death of Jason, Book 4, a possible source of Eliot's drowned Phoenician sailor, Phlebas.

1650 Germer, Rudolf. "Schwierigkeiten bei der Interpretation von T. S. Eliot's Waste Land," GRM, 8, #3 (July, 1958), 300-307. Three types of difficulties which account for diverging criticisms of The Waste Land.

1651 ________. T. S. Eliot's Waste Land. Die Geschichte seiner Wirkung und Beurteilung in den Jahren 1922-1956 unter besonderer Berücksichtigung der Rezeption in England, Amerika, Deutschland und Frankreich. Diss. Freiburg, 1957.

1652 Gerstenberger, Donna. "Steinbeck's American Waste Land," MFS, 11, #1 (Spring, 1965), 59-65. Parallels between The Waste Land and Steinbeck's The Winter of Our Discontent.

1653 ______. "The Waste Land in A Farewell to Arms," MLN, 76 (January, 1961), 24-25.

1654 Ghose, Sisirkumar. "The Waste Land Revisited," Literary Studies. K. P. K. Menon, et al, eds. St. Joseph's Press for the Dr. A. Sivaramasubramonia Aiyer Memorial Committee, pp. 4-7.

1655 Gibbons, Tom. "The Waste Land Tarot Identified," JML, 2 (1972), 560-565. Eliot probably familiar with the work of A. E. Waite.

1656 Gibson, William M. "Sonnets in T. S. Eliot's The Waste Land," AL, 32, #4 (January, 1961), 465-466; repr., in A Collection of Critical Essays. Jay Martin, ed. Englewood Cliffs, N. J., 1968, pp. 32-33.

1657 Giles, Richard F. "A Note on April," TSEN, 1, #1 (1974), 3. Comparison of Herrick's use of April in two poems and Eliot's use of April in the opening line of The Waste Land.

1658 Glazier, Lyle. "Eliot's The Waste Land, 1, 24-30," Expl, 8, #4 (February, 1950), Item 26. Cf., Eleanor M. Sickels, Expl, 9 (1950), Item 4.

1659 Göller, Karl Heinz. "T. S. Eliot: The Waste Land: From Ritual to Romance," NS, 14, #12 (December, 1965), 545-548. Eliot emphasizes "the necessity and possibility of salvation."

1659a Gordon, Lois. "Meaning and Myth in The Sound and the Fury and The Waste Land," The Twenties: Fiction, Poetry, Drama. Warren French, ed. DeLand, Florida: Everett/Edwards, 1975, pp. 269-302.

1660 Gordon, Lyndall. "The Waste Land Manuscript," AL, 45 (January, 1974), 557-570. The Waste Land "a kind of spiritual autobiography in an age that was not cordial to the genre...."

1661 Graham, Don B. "Lawd Today and the Example of The Waste Land," CLAJ, 17 (March, 1974), 327-332.

1662 Green, David Mason. The Waste Land: A Critical Commentary. New York: American Bk. Co., 1965.

1663 Grenander, M. E., and K. S. Narayana Rao. "The Waste Land and the Upanishads: What Does the Thunder Say?" IndL, 14, #1 (March, 1971), 85-98. Eliot's uses and departures from Hindu sources.

1664 Grennen, Joseph E. "Chaucer in a Chapel Perilous: The

Waste Land, 1-18, and 230-242," EngRec, 13, #2 (October, 1962), 42-44. Eliot's allusion to the Canterbury Tales at the beginning of the poem, and an analogy with Troilus in lines 230-242.

1665 Grigsby, Gordon Kay. "The Modern Long Poem: Studies in Thematic Form," DA, 21 (Wisconsin: 1960), 622-623. The Waste Land, one of the poems studied.

1666 Gross, Harvey. "'Métoikos' in London," Mosaic, 6, #1 (Fall, 1972), 143-155. "It is the fate of the modern artist to convey his feelings as the métoikos, Everywhere Everyman the Outsider."

1667 __________. "The Waste Land," The Contrived Corridor. Ann Arbor: Michigan U. P., 1971, pp. 44-58.

1668 Grubb, Frederick. [The Waste Land] A Vision of Reality. London: Chatto & Windus; New York: Barnes & Noble, 1965, pp. 55-59, passim.

1669 Grushow, Ira. "The 'Experience' of Poetry," CE, 31, #1 (October, 1969), 25-29.

1670 Guerin, Wilfred Louis. "Christian Myth and Naturalistic Deity: The Great Gatsby," Renascence, 14, #2 (Winter, 1961), 80-89. Has frequent echoes of The Waste Land.

1671 Hamilton, Ian. "The Waste Land," Eliot in Perspective: A Symposium. Graham Martin, ed. London: Macmillan; New York: Humanities, 1970, pp. 102-111.

1672 __________. "The Waste Land," A Poetry Chronicle: Essays and Reviews. New York: Barnes & Noble, 1973, pp. 19-29.

1673 Hamilton, K. M. "Wasteland To-Day: Recent Tendencies in the Arts in England," DalhousieR, 27 (April, 1947), 33-43.

1674 Harding, D. W. "What the Thunder Said," The Waste Land in Different Voices. A. D. Moody, ed. New York: St. Martin's, 1974, pp. 15-28.

1675 Harris, Bernard. "'This music crept by me': Shakespeare and Wagner," The Waste Land in Different Voices. A. D. Moody, ed. New York, 1974, pp. 105-116.

1675a Harter, Carol Clancy. "Strange Bedfellows: The Waste Land and An American Tragedy," The Twenties: Fiction, Poetry, Drama. Warren French, ed. De Land, Fla.: 1975, pp. 51-64.

1676 Hathaway, Richard D. "The Waste Land's Benediction," AN&Q, 2, #4 (December, 1963), 53-54. The last line of the poem "not only explicitly juxtaposes the benediction of 'the peace which passeth understanding' to the broken images and the Thunder, but suggests by its sound the swish of falling rain."

1677 Hays, Peter L. "Commerce in The Waste Land," ELN, 11 (1974), 292-294. Use and meaning of the word "commerce" in the poem.

1678 Headings, Philip R. "The Question of Exclusive Art: Tolstoy and T. S. Eliot's The Waste Land," RLV, 32 (January-February, 1966), 82-95.

1679 Helmcke, Hans. "Das wüste Land bei T. S. Eliot und Thomas Wolfe," Literatur und Sprache der Vereinigten Staaten: Aufsätze zu Ehren von Hans Galinsky. Heidelberg: Winter, 1969, pp. 190-205.

1680 Herdeck, Donald E. "A New Letter by Ezra Pound about T. S. Eliot," MassR, 12 (Spring, 1971), 287-292.

1681 Hesse, Eva. "The Waste Land," TLS, #3772 (June 21, 1974), 671.

1682 Hesse, Walter. "The Waste Land and the Duino Elegies," Lingua (Cape Town Univ.), 1 (1948), 37-41.

1683 Hewitt, Elizabeth K. "Structural Unity in The Waste Land," DAI, 30 (S. U. N. Y., Buffalo: 1969), 2513A.

1684 Hillyer, Robert. "Poetry's New Priesthood," SatR, 32 (June 18, 1949), 8.

1685 Hoffman, Frederick J. The Twenties: American Writing in the Postwar Decade. New York: Viking Pr., 1955, pp. 291-303. The Waste Land exemplified doubt in the Twenties.

1686 Holloway, John. "The Waste Land," Encounter, 31, #2 (August, 1968), 73-79.

1687 Hough, Graham. "Imagism and Its Consequences," Reflections on a Literary Revolution. Washington, D. C.: Catholic Univ. of America Pr., 1960, pp. 1-40.

1688 Howarth, Herbert. Notes on Some Figures Behind T. S. Eliot. Boston: Houghton Mifflin, 1964; excerpt of pp. 234-237 in A Collection of Critical Essays on The Waste Land. Jay Martin, ed. Englewood Cliffs, N. J.: 1968, pp. 20-21.

1689 Howell, John Michael. "The Waste Land Tradition in the American Novel," DA, 24 (Tulane: 1964), 3337. The

Waste Land's influence on Fitzgerald, Hemingway, Faulkner, and Salinger.

1690 Hunt, John Dixon. "'Broken Images': T. S. Eliot and Modern Painting," The Waste Land in Different Voices. A. D. Moody, ed. New York: St. Martin's Press, 1974, pp. 163-184.

1691 Isani, Mukhtar Ali. "The Wisdom of the Thunder in Eliot's The Waste Land," ELN, 10, #3 (March, 1973), 217-221. Paul Deussen's Sechzig Upanishad's des Veda as Eliot's source of the legend of the threefold message of the thunder.

1692 Izzo, Carlo. "Dall' 'Arnaldo da Brescia' di G. B. Niccolini a The Waste Land di T. S. Eliot per il tramite di W. D. Howells," Studi Lorenzo Bianchi. Bologna: Zanichelli, 1960, pp. 103-114.

1692a Johnson, Kenneth. "Eliot as Enemy: William Carlos Williams and The Waste Land," The Twenties: Fiction, Poetry, Drama. Warren French, ed. De Land, Fla.: Everett/Edwards, 1975, pp. 377-386.

1693 Jones, Florence. "T. S. Eliot Among the Prophets," AL, 38 (November, 1966), 285-302. Notes themes of the prophetic writings of the Old and New Testaments in The Waste Land.

1694 Jones, P. Mansell. "Laforgue's 'vers libre' and the Form of The Waste Land," The Assault on French Literature and Other Essays. Manchester: Manchester U. P., 1963, pp. 133-145. The possible influence on Eliot's The Waste Land of Jules Laforgue's "vers libre," and in particular, his L'Hiver qui vient.

1695 Judelevičius, Dovydas. "Nagailestingas poeto skalpelis," Pergale, 1 (1972), 104-111. Mostly on The Waste Land, with tr. by Tomas Venclova of the poem, pp. 91-103.

1695a Jungman, Robert E. "A Note on The Waste Land," TSER, 2, #2 (Fall, 1975), 9.

1696 Jury, C. R. T. S. Eliot's The Waste Land: Some Annotations. Adelaide, 1932.

1697 Kane, Patricia. "Place of Abomination: A Reading of Fitzgerald's 'Valley of Ashes,'" ELN, 1, #4 (June, 1964), 291-295. Notes that the dumping ground at beginning of the second chapter of The Great Gatsby suggests comparisons with Eliot's The Waste Land.

1698 Kemp, Lysander. "Eliot's The Waste Land, I, 49-50," Expl, 7, #8 (June, 1949), Item 60.

1699 __________. "Eliot's The Waste Land, I, 43-59," Expl, 8, #4 (February, 1950), Item 27. Origin of the name Sosostris.

1700 Kenner, Hugh. "Eliot and the Tradition of the Anonymous," CE, 28 (May, 1967), 558-564. "The poem [The Waste Land] is a grotesquerie, often nearly a parody; for only our assurance about intention will clearly distinguish parody from imitation or allusion."

1701 __________. "How the Poem Was Constructed," Storm over The Waste Land. Robert E. Knoll, ed. Chicago: Scott, Foresman, 1964, pp. 2-7.

1702 __________. "The Urban Apocalypse," Eliot in His Time. A. Walton Litz, ed. Princeton U. P., 1973, pp. 23-49; repr., in Literary Criticism. W. K. Wimsatt, ed. Los Angeles: California U. P., 1974, pp. 616-635.

1703 __________. "The Waste Land," The Invisible Poet: T. S. Eliot. New York: Ivan Obolensky, 1959; excerpt repr., "Notes to The Waste Land," A Collection of Critical Essays. Jay Martin ed. Englewood Cliffs, N. J.: 1968, pp. 36-38.

1703a __________. "Where the Penty [sic] Went," NR, 165 (November 13, 1971), 25-26. Rev.-art., The Waste Land by T. S. Eliot: A Facsimile and Transcript of the Original Drafts. Valerie Eliot, ed. New York: 1971.

1704 Keogh, J. G. "Eliot's Hollow Men as Graveyard Poetry," Renascence, 21 (Spring, 1969), 115-118. "T. S. Eliot's poem The Hollow Men may well be composed of some of the fragments from The Waste Land which he decided not to shore against the ruins of Christian society, but rather to dignify with separate burial."

1705 Kirk, Russell. "The Inner Waste Land and the Outer," Eliot and His Age. New York: Random House, 1971, pp. 73-91.

1706 __________. "The Waste Land Lies Unredeemed," SR, 80, #3 (Summer, 1972), 470-478. Rev.-art., The Waste Land: A Facsimile and Transcript of the Original Drafts. Valerie Eliot, ed. New York: 1971.

1707 Knight, G. W. "Thoughts on The Waste Land," UDQ, 7 (Summer, 1973), 1-13.

1708 __________. "The Waste Land," TLS, #3646 (January 14, 1972), 40; #3648 (January 28, 1972), 99; #3650 (February 11, 1972), 156.

1709 Knoll, Robert E., ed. Introduction. Storm over The Waste Land. Chicago: Scott, Foresman, 1964.

1710 Knust, Herbert. "The Artist, The King, and The Waste Land: Richard Wagner, Ludwig, II, and T. S. Eliot," DA, 22 (Penn. State: 1961), 2398.

1711 ________. "Eliot's The Waste Land, 74," Expl, 23 (May, 1965), Item 74. The "Dog" of line 74 suggested as a symbol of Eliot's cynicism. Cf., James D. Merritt. "The Waste Land, 74-75," Expl. 23 (1965), Item 31.

1712 ________. "Tristan and Sosostris," RLC, 40 (April-June, 1966), 235-245.

1713 ________. "Wagner, the King, and The Waste Land." (Penn. State Studies 22.) University Park: Penn State U. Comm. on Research, 1967.

1714 ________. "What's the Matter with One-Eyed Riley?" CL, 17 (Fall, 1965), 289-298. "...several figures in Madame Sosostris' Tarot pack resemble characters in Wagner's Ring, most notably the one-eyed merchant...."

1715 Korg, Jacob. "Modern Art Techniques in The Waste Land," JAAC, 18 (June, 1960), 456-463; repr., in A Collection of Critical Essays on The Waste Land. Jay Martin, ed. Englewood Cliffs, 1968, pp. 87-96. "The sensibility displayed by The Waste Land's stylistic innovations resembles that which animated the technical experiments of the Cubists, Futurists, Dadists, and Surrealists, Eliot's contemporaries in the graphic arts."

1716 ________. "T. S. Eliot," CLit, 13, #4 (Autumn, 1972), 535-540. Rev.-art., The Waste Land: A Facsimile and Transcript of the Original Drafts. Valerie Eliot, ed., 1971.

1717 Kramer, Dale. "Eliot's The Waste Land, 392-395," Expl, 24, #8 (April, 1966), Item 74. No image is more "relevant thematically" than the crowing weathercock.

1718 LaChance, Paul R. "The Function of Voice in The Waste Land," Style, 5 (1971), 101-118.

1719 Langbaum, Robert. "New Modes of Characterization in The Waste Land," Eliot in His Time. A. Walton Litz, ed. Princeton U. P., 1973, pp. 95-128.

1720 Lawlor, Nancy K. "Eliot's Use of Rhyming Quatrains in The Waste Land," Poet & C, 4 (1967), 29-37.

1721 Leavis, F. R. "The Poem's Unity"; "T. S. Eliot--The Waste

Land," New Bearings in English Poetry. London: Chatto & Windus, 1932; Ann Arbor: Michigan U. P., 1960, pp. 24-38; 93-115.

1722 Lees, Francis N. "Correspondence," CamQ, 6 (1973), 151. Reply to A. D. Moody. "Broken Images," CamQ, 6 (1972), 45-56.

1723 ________. "Mr. Eliot's Sunday Morning Satura: Petronius and The Waste Land," SR, 74 (Winter, 1966), 339-348. The Waste Land "is, as satura and (so to say) satira, a counterpart of the Satyricon...."

1724 ________. "T. S. Eliot and Nietzsche," N&Q, 11, #10 (October, 1964), 386-387. The Waste Land echoes Nietzsche's comments on Tristan und Isolde in The Birth of Tragedy.

1725 Lensing, George S. "Hart Crane's Tunnel from The Waste Land," ArielE, 6, #3 (1975), 20-35.

1725a Lento, Thomas Vincent. "The Epic Consciousness in Four Romantic and Modern Epics by Blake, Byron, Eliot, and Hart Crane," DAI, 35 (Iowa: 1975), 7911A.

1725b Levin, Harry. "La tierra baldia: De Ur a Echt," Plural, 13 (1972), 3-6.

1726 Lewis, Janet E. O. "The Wasteland Theme in James Joyce's Ulysses," DAI, 32 (Toronto: 1972), 5796A-97A.

1727 Litz, A. Walton, ed. Eliot in His Time: Essays on the Occasion of the Fiftieth Anniversary of The Waste Land. Princeton: Princeton U. P.; London: Oxford U. P., 1973.

1728 ________. "Pound and Eliot on Ulysses: The Critical Tradition," JJQ, 10 (1972), 5-18.

1728a ________. Pound and Eliot on Ulysses: The Critical Tradition," Germanistische Streifzuge. Gert Mellbourn, et al., eds. Stockholm: Almqvist & Wiksell, 1974, pp. 5-18.

1729 ________. "The Waste Land Fifty Years After," JML, 2 (1972), 455-471; repr., in Eliot in His Time. Princeton, N. J.: Princeton U. P.; London: Oxford U. P., 1973, pp. 3-22.

1730 Lorch, Thomas M. "The Relationship between Ulysses and The Waste Land," TSLL, 6 (Summer, 1964), 123-133.

1731 Lowry, E. D. "Manhattan Transfer: Dos Passos' Wasteland," UR, 30, #1 (October, 1963), 47-52.

1732 Lucas, F. L. "The Waste Land," NSt, 22 (November 3, 1923), 116, 118.

1733 Lucas, John. "The Waste Land Today," EIC, 20, #4 (1970), 497-500. Reply to Bernard Bergonzi, EIC, 20, #3 (1970), 382-385.

1734 __________, and William Myers. "The Waste Land Today," EIC, 19, #2 (April, 1969), 193-209. Cf., Bernard Bergonzi. EIC, 20, #3 (July, 1970), 382-385.

1735 Lucy, Seán. T. S. Eliot and the Idea of Tradition. London: Cohen & West; New York: Barnes & Noble, 1960, pp. 153-159, passim.

1736 Lund, Mary Graham. "Homesteading in the Waste Land: The Populous Legacy of T. S. Eliot," SWR, 51 (Spring, 1966), 101-109.

1737 __________. "Rebellion for Humanity's Sake," Trace, No. 57 (Summer, 1965), 124-127.

1738 MacCallum, H. Reid. "The Waste Land after Twenty-five Years," Here and Now, Vol. 1 (1947), 16-24. An interpretation of details.

1739 Maccoby, H. Z. "The Waste Land," TLS, #3642 (December 17, 1971), 1580-1581.

1740 __________. "The Waste Land," TLS, #3651 (February 18, 1972), 189.

1741 McCord, Howard. "The Wryneck in The Waste Land," CJ, 6 (March, 1965), 270-271. The song "Jug, Jug" in The Waste Land (11, 103 and 204) may have been that of the wryneck, a bird mythologically noted for its sexuality.

1742 McGreevy, Thomas. Thomas Stearns Eliot. London: Chatto & Windus, 1931, p. 57. Lines 233-234, The Waste Land, the only image in the poem which Thomas McGreevy disliked.

1743 MacGregor-Hastie, Roy. "Waste Land in Russell Square," Trace, #32 (June, July, 1959), 1-5.

1744 McKeever, Clare. "Man's Response to a Functional World Echoed in The Waste Land and Zorba the Greek," Humanities (Duquesne U.) 6 (1971), 325-350.

1745 McLauchlan, Juliet. "Allusion in The Waste Land," EIC, 19 (1969), 454-460. Cf., John Lucas and Wm. Myers. "The Waste Land Today," EIC, 19 (1969), 193-209. Cf., A. L. French. "Death by Allusion?" EIC, 20 (1970), 269-271.

1746 MacLeish, Archibald. "There Was Something About the Twenties," SatR, 49 (December 31, 1966), 10-13. It was "a generation whose patria,... was now no longer waiting for them anywhere. That realization produced ... The Waste Land and the forms in which the waste land was discovered.... "

1747 MacNeice, Louis. Modern Poetry: A Personal Essay. Oxford: At the Clarendon Pr., 1968, pp. 166-167, passim.

1748 Male, Roy R., Jr. "Toward The Wasteland: The Theme of The Blithedale Romance," CE, 16 (February, 1955), 277-283.

1749 Malekin, P. "The Waste Land," TLS, #3716 (May 25, 1973), 587. Cf., Craig Raine, TLS (May 4, 1973), 503-505.

1749a __________. "The Waste Land," TLS (June 29, 1973), 749. Cf., Craig Raine, TLS (June 15, 1973), 692.

1750 Marsh, Florence. "The Ocean-Desert: The Ancient Mariner and The Waste Land," EIC, 9 (April, 1959), 126-133.

1751 Marshall, William H. "Eliot's The Waste Land, 182," Expl, 17 (March, 1959), Item 42. Interpretation of line 183.

1752 Martin, Jay, "T. S. Eliot's The Waste Land," A Collection of Critical Essays on The Waste Land. Jay Martin, ed. Englewood Cliffs, N. J.: Prentice-Hall, 1968, pp. 1-14.

1753 Matthiessen, F. O. The Achievement of T. S. Eliot. New York: First Galaxy ed., Oxford U. P., 1959, pp. 49-50.

1754 __________. "Poetry," Literary History of the United States. Robert Spiller, ed. New York: Macmillan, 1948, II, 1343.

1755 Maxwell, D. E. S. "After The Waste Land," ISE, 1 (1969), 73-84.

1756 __________. "'He Do the Police in Different Voices,'" Mosaic, 6, #1 (1972), 167-180.

1757 __________. The Poetry of T. S. Eliot. New York: Barnes & Noble, 1961, pp. 100-117.

1758 Maxwell, J. C. "Flaubert in The Waste Land," ES, 44 (August, 1963), 279. Suggests that two references in The Waste Land, 1. 80, and 11. 124-126, could be traced to Madame Bovary, III, v.

1759 __________. "'Gareth and Lynette' and The Waste Land," N&Q, 17 (December, 1970), 458. Tennyson's poem a more probable source of lines 282-3 than the usually suggested "Child Roland to the Dark Tower Came."

1760 Melchiori, Giorgio. "Echoes in The Waste Land," ES, 32 (February, 1951), 1-11; repr., in The Tightrope Walkers. London: Routledge & Kegan Paul, 1957, pp. 53-88.

1761 ________. "Eliot and Apollinaire," N&Q, 11 (October, 1964), 385-386. Influence on Eliot of Apollinaire's Les mamelles de Tiresias.

1762 ________. "The Waste Land and Ulysses," ES, 35 (April, 1954), 56-68. Comparison of methods, imagery, symbolism, and vocabulary in the two works.

1763 Merritt, James D. "Eliot's The Waste Land, 74-75," Expl, 23, #4 (December, 1964), Item 31.

1764 Mesterton, Erik. The Waste Land, Some Commentaries. Chicago: Argus Bk. Shop, 1943.

1764a Miller, James E., Jr. "Sanctuary: Yoknapatawpha's Waste Land," The Twenties. Warren French, ed. De Land, Fla.: 1975, pp. 249-267.

1765 Miller, Milton. "What the Thunder Meant," ELH, 36 (June, 1969), 440-454.

1766 Millett, Fred B. Contemporary British Literature. New York: Harcourt, Brace, 1935, p. 82.

1767 Milward, Peter. "'In the End Is My Beginning': A Study of T. S. Eliot's The Elder Statesman in Comparison with The Waste Land," SELit, English No. (1967), 1-13.

1768 Mirsky, D. S. "T. S. Eliot et la fin de la poésie bourgeoise," Echanges, numéro 5 (December, 1931).

1769 Moakley, Gertrude. "The Waite-Smith 'Tarot': A Footnote to The Waste Land," BNYPL, 58 (October, 1954), 471-475. "It can be shown that [Eliot's] Tarot was actually a very modern one drawn by Pamela Coleman Smith under the direction of Arthur Waite," not "'the traditional pack' of Tarot cards."

1770 Monroe, Harriet. "A Contrast," Poetry, 21 (1923), 325-330. Contrasts The Waste Land and The Box of God by Lew Sarett.

1771 ________. "Eliot and Sarett: A Contrast," Poets and Their Art. New York: Macmillan, 1926; rev. and enl., Freeport, New York: Bks. for Libraries Pr., 1967, pp. 100-108.

1772 Montgomery, Marion. "The Awful Daring: The Self Surrendered in The Waste Land," ArQ, 30 (Spring, 1974), 43-52. The Waste Land "attempts to overcome that balance between memory and desire..." which impels a reliving of "desire and surrender."

1773 ________. "Beyond Pound's Quarrel with Eliot's Text," GaR, 26 (Winter, 1972), 415-425. Information as to Eliot's reactions to Pound's critique of The Waste Land.

1774 ________. "Eliot and 'Il Miglior fabbro,'" SCR, 6, #1 (November, 1973), 7-13. In the employment of Pound's adaptation of a phrase from Dante, Eliot acknowledges indebtedness to Pound but implies a limitation on that indebtedness.

1775 ________. "Lord Russell and Madame Sosostris," GaR, 28 (1974), 269-282. Discussion concerning Eliot and Huxley.

1776 Moody, A. D. "Broken Images/Voices Singing," CamQ, 6, #1 (1972), 45-58. Rev.-art., on The Waste Land: A Facsimile and Transcript of the Original Draft Including the Annotations of Ezra Pound. Valerie Eliot, ed. London: Faber, 1971.

1777 ________, ed. Preface. The Waste Land in Different Voices. New York: St. Martin's Press, 1974, pp. ix-xi.

1778 ________. "'To fill all the desert with inviolable voice,'" The Waste Land in Different Voices. New York: St. Martin's, 1974, pp. 47-66.

1779 Mooney, Stephen L. "Poe's Gothic Waste Land," SR, 70, #2 (Spring, 1962), 261-283. Influence of Eliot's The Waste Land.

1780 Moore, Merrill. "Homage to T. S. Eliot," HA, 125 (December, 1938), 45.

1781 Moorman, Charles. Arthurian Triptych: Mythic Materials in Charles Williams, C. S. Lewis, and T. S. Eliot. (Perspectives in Criticism 5.) Berkeley and Los Angeles: California U. Pr., 1960, pp. 127-148.

1782 ________. "Myth and Organic Unity in The Waste Land," SAQ, 57 (Spring, 1958), 194-203. Eliot's use of Weston's From Ritual to Romance.

1783 More, Paul Elmer. "The Cleft Eliot," SatR, 9 (November 12, 1932) 233.

1784 Morris, George L. K. "Marie, Marie, Hold on Tight,"

PartisanR, 21, #2 (March-April, 1954), 231-233; repr., in T. S. Eliot: A Collection of Critical Essays. Englewood Cliffs, N. J.: 1962, pp. 86-88. Similarity of names and places in Eliot's The Waste Land and Countess Marie Larisch's My Past (1916).

1784a Morse, J. I. "T. S. Eliot in 1921: Toward the Dissociation of Sensibility," WHR, 30 (Winter, 1976), 31-40. The Waste Land is "the final expression of all the disharmonies of [Matthew] Arnold's age."

1785 Motola, Gabriel. "The Mountains of The Waste Land," EIC, 19 (January, 1969), 67-69. "In the mountains, there you feel free," is a possible allusion to Turgenev's The Torrents of Spring.

1786 Moynihan, William T. "The Goal of the Waste Land Quest," Renascence, 13, #4 (Summer, 1961), 171-179. The three levels of man's search for eternal life.

1787 Munson, Gorham B. "The Esotericism of T. S. Eliot," 1924, No. 1 (July, 1924), 3-10. Prof. Munson felt The Waste Land was the poetic equivalent of Spengler's Der Untergang des Abendlandes, a "funeral keen for the nineteenth century," but in the present century "a subjective aberration from the facts."

1788 Murphy, George D. "Hemingway's Waste Land: The Controlling Water Symbolism of The Sun Also Rises," HemN, 1, #1 (Spring, 1971), 20-26. Comparison of Eliot's poem and Hemingway's novel.

1788a Murphy, Russell Elliott. "The Tragic Quandary: Hart Crane and the Poetry of T. S. Eliot," DAI, 36 (Mass.: 1975), 881A. Comparison of Crane's The Bridge and Eliot's The Waste Land.

1789 Musurillo, Herbert. "A Note on The Waste Land," CP, 51 (July, 1956), 174-175, n. 5. On the line "Consider Phlebas...."

1790 Myers, William. "Allusion in The Waste Land: A Reply," EIC, 20 (1970), 120-122. Reply to Juliet McLauchlan, EIC, 19 (1969), 454-460.

1791 Nagano, Yoshio. "The Stream of Consciousness in The Waste Land by T. S. Eliot: Its Linguistic and Technical Problem," SELL, 10 (1960), 35-44.

1792 Nageswara I, G. "The Upanisads and The Waste Land," Literary Studies. K. P. K. Menon, et al, eds. Trivandrum: St. Joseph's Pr. for the Dr. A. Sivaramasubramonia Aiyer Memorial Committee, 1973, pp. 195-200.

1793 Narasimhaiah, C. D. "An Indian Footnote to T. S. Eliot Scholarship on The Waste Land," LCrit, 10, #2 (1972), 75-91.

1794 Nath, Raj. "The Waste Land: The Facsimile Edition," LCrit, 10, #2 (1972), 69-74.

1795 Nathan, Norman. "Eliot's Incorrect Note on 'C. i. f. London,'" N&Q, 5, #6 (June, 1958), 262. The Waste Land, 211.

1796 Nelson, Armour H. "The Critics and The Waste Land, 1922-1949," ES, 36 (February, 1955), 1-15. A survey of "what specific problems the critics were considering, and what ... conclusions they reached."

1797 Nelson, F. William. "The Waste Land Manuscript," Mon/WSUBUS, 47, #86 (February, 1971), 1-9. Provides a complete history of the manuscript.

1798 Neto, Maria A. "Os cinquenta anos de The Waste Land," Colóquio, 15 (1973), 65-69.

1799 Nevo, Ruth. "The Vanished Mind: or, The Waste Land Revisited," Studies in English Language and Literature. Alice Shalvi, et al, eds. (Scripta Hierosolymitana, Pubs. of the Hebrew U., 17.) Jerusalem: Hebrew U. [Avail. from Oxford U. Pr.], 1966, pp. 226-242.

1800 Nicholson, Norman. "T. S. Eliot," Writers of Today. Denys V. Baker, ed. London: Sidgwick & Jackson, 1946, p. 140f.

1801 Niikura, Shunichi. "Pound to Eliot--Arechi-teki naru mono," EigoS, 119 (1973), 9-10.

1802 Nitchie, George W. "Eliot's Borrowing: A Note," MassR, 6 (Spring, 1965), 403-406. "If we consider the footnotes to The Waste Land ... as a part of ... self-exploration, we can make more coherent something that too often appears to be an affectation, an aberration, or a deceit."

1803 Nitze, William A. "The Waste Land: A Celtic Arthurian Theme," MP, 43 (August, 1945), 58-62.

1804 Nott, Kathleen. "Ideology and Poetry," The Waste Land in Different Voices. A. D. Moody, ed. New York: St. Martin's Pr., 1974, pp. 203-220.

1805 Nuhn, Ferner, "Orpheus in Hell: T. S. Eliot," The Wind Blew from the East. New York: Harper & Bros., 1942, pp. 249-258.

1806 Ohashi, Isamu. "Arechi no Kaishaku ni tsuite," EigoS, 115

(1969), 687-689, 776-778. Interpretation of The Waste Land.

1807 Olson, Elder. "A Defense of Poetry," Poetry, 50 (April, 1937), 56.

1808 Osotsi, W. "Short-sighted Fascism in T. S. Eliot's The Waste Land," Busara, 5, #2 (1973), 61-68.

1808a Owen, Guy. "Robert Frost and The Waste Land," The Twenties: Fiction, Poetry, Drama. Warren French, ed. De Land, Florida: Everett/Edwards, 1975, pp. 351-363.

1809 Padmanabha, Jayanta. "The Waste Land," TLS, #3655 (March 17, 1972), 308; TLS (May 18, 1973), 556. Cf. Craig Raine. "Met Him Pikehoses: The Waste Land as a Buddhist Poem," TLS 3713 (May 4, 1973), 488.

1810 Palmer, H. E. "The Hoax and Earnest of The Waste Land," DubM, 8 (April, 1933), 11-19.

1811 Paris, Jerome Marvin. "Poetry and the Uses of Stoicism: Motives of Consolation in Matthew Arnold and T. S. Eliot," DAI, 33 (Cornell: 1972), 5742A.

1812 Patrides, Constantinos A. "The Renascence of the Renaissance: T. S. Eliot and the Pattern of Time," MQR, 12, #2 (Spring, 1973), 172-196.

1813 Patterson, Gertrude. "The Waste Land," T. S. Eliot: Poems in the Making. New York: Barnes & Noble, 1971, pp. 134-168. "The Waste Land is Eliot's Divine Comedy...."

1814 __________. "The Waste Land in the Making," CritQ, 14, #3 (Autumn, 1972), 269-283. Finds that the original drafts of The Waste Land reveal Pound's role in the shaping of the poem.

1815 Patteson, Richard F. "An Additional Source for The Waste Land," N&Q, 23, #7 (July, 1976), 300-301. Madison Cawein's Waste Land suggested as a possible source. Cawein's poem appears in Poetry, 1, #4 (January, 1913), 104-105.

1816 Paul, Leslie. "A Conversation with T. S. Eliot," KR, 27, #1 (Winter, 1965), 11-21. Eliot discussed (among other things) the disappearance of the original Waste Land manuscript.

1817 Pearce, Roy Harvey. "Eliot: The Poetics of Myth," The Continuity of American Poetry. Princeton: Princeton U. P., 1961, pp. 306-309; repr., in A Collection of Critical Essays on The Waste Land. Jay Martin, ed. Englewood Cliffs, N. J.: 1968, pp. 23-26.

1818 Perret, Marion. "Eliot, the Naked Lady, and the Missing Link," AL, 46, #3 (November, 1974), 289-303.

1819 Peter, John. "A New Interpretation of The Waste Land," EIC, 2 (July, 1952), 242-266. Cf., F. W. Bateson. "Editorial Commentary," EIC, 19 (January, 1969), 1-5.

1819a ________. "A New Interpretation of The Waste Land (1952). With Postscript (1969)," EIC, 19, #2 (April, 1969), 140-175. Sees the poem as a monologue, a meditation on a lost love, the object of the love being a young man who has met his death by drowning.

1820 Pinto, Vivian de Sola. Crisis in English Poetry, 1880-1940. New York: 4th ed., Hutchinson's Univ. Libr., 1961, pp. 170-174.

1821 Poirier, Richard. "A Literature of Law and Order," PartisanR, 36, #2 (1969), 189-204.

1822 ________. "T. S. Eliot and the Literature of Waste," NR, 156 (May 20, 1967), 19-25.

1823 Pound, Ezra, and T. S. Eliot. "An Exchange of Letters on The Wasteland," Nine, 4 (Summer, 1950), 176-179.

1824 Pratt, Linda R. "The Holy Grail: Subversion and Revival of a Tradition in Tennyson and T. S. Eliot," VP, 11, #4 (Winter, 1973), 307-321. Similarities in Idylls of the King and The Waste Land.

1825 Praz, Mario. "Eliot e Montale," Fle (November 14, 1948). Similarities in Ossi di Seppia and The Waste Land.

1826 ________. Mnemosyne, The Parallel Between Literature and the Visual Arts. Princeton, N. J.: Princeton U. P., 1970, pp. 201-207, passim. "Desolate landscapes of a kind which surrealist paintings have vulgarized are a salient feature of Eliot's The Waste Land..."

1827 ________, tr. La Terra Desolata. Frammento di un Agone. Marcia Trionfala. Turin: Einaudi, [1965?].

1828 Press, John. "The Waste Land," EA, 26 (1971), 80-85. Rev.-art., on T. S. Eliot: The Waste Land. London: 1971, Valerie Eliot, ed.

1829 Prince, F. T. "T. S. Eliot and The Waste Land," TLS, #3714 (May 11, 1973), 529.

1830 Pritchard, William H. "I. Reading The Waste Land Today," EIC, 19, #2 (April, 1969), 176-192. Eliot's criticism of Jonson in The Sacred Wood might be applied to The Waste Land.

1831 Prosky, Murray. "Lamb, Palgrave, and the Elizabethans in T. S. Eliot's The Waste Land," Studies in the Humanities. 2: i. William F. Grayburn, ed. Indiana: Indiana U. P., 1971, pp. 11-16.

1832 Puhvel, Martin. "Reminiscent Bells in The Waste Land," ELN, 2 (June, 1965), 286-287. The Waste Land, V, 382-383, "strikingly parallel in phrasing and ideas to Browning's Child Roland to the Dark Tower Came, 193-198." Cf., J. C. Maxwell. "'Gareth and Lynette' and The Waste Land," N&Q, 17 (1970), 458.

1833 Quinn, Sister M. Bernetta. The Metamorphic Tradition in Modern Poetry. New Brunswick, N. J.: Rutgers U. P., 1955, pp. 130-142.

1834 Raffel, Burton. "The Waste Land: A Common Sense Exegesis," Yes, No. 13 (December, 1964), 11 pp. Notes that the poem concerns spiritual squalor, but in Section V Eliot is committed to the path toward faith.

1835 Rai, Vikramaditya. The Waste Land: A Critical Study. Varanasi, India: 1965; Gordon Pr., 1974.

1836 Raine, Craig. "Met Him Pikehoses: The Waste Land as a Buddhist Poem," TLS, #3713 (May 4, 1973), 503-505. Sees the central theme as reincarnation, thus Buddhist. Cf., Jayanta Padmanabha. TLS (May 18, 1973), 556.

1837 __________. "The Waste Land," TLS, #3719 (June 15, 1973), 692. Cf., P. Malekin, TLS (June 29, 1973), 749.

1838 Raine, Kathleen. "The Poet of Our Time," T. S. Eliot: A Symposium. Richard March and M. J. Tambimuttu, comps. Chicago: Henry Regnery, 1949, p. 79f.

1839 Rainer, M. L. "T. S. Eliot's The Waste Land: Some Early Responses," LCrit, 10, #2 (1972), 57-68.

1840 Rajan, Balachandra. "The Dialect of the Tribe," The Waste Land in Different Voices. A. D. Martin, ed. New York: St. Martin's Pr., 1974, pp. 1-14.

1841 __________. "The Overwhelming Question," SR, 74 (Winter, 1966), 358-375; excerpt of pp. 367-368 in A Collection of Critical Essays. Jay Martin, ed. Englewood Cliffs, N. J.: Prentice-Hall, 1968, pp. 48-49.

1842 __________, ed. T. S. Eliot: A Study of His Writings by Several Hands. London: D. Dobson, 1947; New York: Russell & Russell, 1947.

1843 Ramsey, Jarold. "The Waste Land and Shackleton on South

Georgia," ELN, 8 (1970), 42-45. [The Antarctic explorer, Sir Ernest Shackleton.]

1844 Randall, Dale B. J. "The 'Seer' and 'Seen' Themes in Gatsby and Some of Their Parallels in Eliot and Wright," TCL, 10, #2 (July, 1964), 51-63. "...In The Waste Land Eliot suggests the nightmare fragmentation of life, and the possibility that a seer--even a degenerate modern one--may glimpse the need for spirituality...."

1845 Ransom, John Crowe. "The Inorganic Muses," KR, 5 (Spring, 1943), 298-300.

1846 ________. "Waste Lands," LiteraryR, 3 (July 14, 1923), 826.

1847 ________. "Waste Lands," Modern Essays. Christopher Morley, ed. New York: Harcourt, Brace, 1924, pp. 345-359.

1848 Rauber, D. F. "The Notes on The Waste Land," ELN, 7 (1970), 287-294.

1849 Raybould, Edith. "'The Man with Three Staves' in the Structure of The Waste Land," Anglistische Studien: Festschrift zum 70. Geburstag von Professor Friedrich Wild. (WBEP, Vol. 66.) Karl Brunner, et al, eds. Wien: W. Braumüller, 1958, pp. 170-178.

1850 Read, Herbert, and Edward Dahlberg. "Robert Graves and T. S. Eliot," TC, 166, #990 (August, 1959), 54-62. Sees The Waste Land as central to all modern poetry, for in it a new "fusion takes place, a new symbolic imagery is created, the unknown becomes known."

1851 Rebmann, David R. "The Waste Land," TLS, #3650 (February 11, 1972), 156.

1852 Reeves, Gareth. "The Obstetrics of The Waste Land," CritQ, 17 (Spring, 1975), 33-53. Differences between views of Eliot and Pound as to The Waste Land.

1853 Reid, B. L. The Man from New York: John Quinn and His Friends. New York: Oxford U. Pr., 1968, p. 540, passim.

1854 Rice, Philip Blair. "Out of The Waste Land," Symposium, 3, #4 (October, 1932), 422-442.

1855 Richards, I. A. Poetries and Sciences. London: Routledge and K. Paul, 1970, p. 64, n3. [A re-issue of Science and Poetry (1926).]

1856 ________. "The Poetry of T. S. Eliot," The Principles

of Literary Criticism. New York: Harcourt, Brace, 1934, pp. 290-292.

1857 ________. "The Waste Land," TLS, #3646 (January 14, 1972), 40. Eliot's dislike of literary biography.

1858 Richardson, Joanna. "T. S. Eliot," LHY, 3, #1 (January, 1962), 9-12. Now when The Waste Land has become a classic, finds it interesting to recall when Eliot was avant-garde.

1859 Richmond, Lee J. "Eliot's The Waste Land, 380-395," Expl, 30, #3 (November, 1971), Item 23. Sees the lines as an allusion to Bram Stoker's 1897 novel, Dracula.

1860 Rickword, Edgell. "The Modern Poet," Towards Standards of Criticism. F. R. Leavis, ed. London: Wishart, 1933, pp. 100-106.

1860a Riding, Laura, and Robert Graves. A Survey of Modernist Poetry. New York: Doubleday, Doran, 1928, pp. 50-58, passim.

1861 Ridler, Anne. "A Question of Speech," Focus Three: T. S. Eliot, A Study of His Writings by Several Hands. B. Rajan, ed. London: Dennis Dobson, 1947, p. 109f.

1862 ________. "The Waste Land," TLS, #3647 (January 21, 1972), 69.

1863 ________. "The Waste Land," TLS, 3651 (February 18, 1972), 189.

1864 Rodgers, Audrey T. "'He Do the Police in Different Voices': The Design of The Waste Land," CollL, 1 (1974), 48-63. The structure of The Waste Land is mythic because it takes form from the perspective of the poet as seer.

1864a Rogers, William N., II. "'Laquearia' in The Waste Land," AN&Q, 13 (1975), 105-106.

1865 Rosenthal, M. L. "The Waste Land and Four Quarters," The Modern Poets: A Critical Introduction. New York: Oxford U. P., 1960, pp. 88-94.

1866 ________. "The Waste Land as an Open Structure," Mosaic, 6, #1 (Fall, 1972), 181-189; repr., in T. S. Eliot: A Collection of Criticism. Linda W. Wagner, ed. New York: McGraw Hill, 1974, pp. 37-47.

1867 Ross-Williamson, Hugh. "Commentary on T. S. Eliot's The Waste Land," Bookman, 82 (July, 1932), 193-195; (August, 1932), 244-248; September, 1932), 289-291.

1867a ______. The Poetry of T. S. Eliot. London: 1932; New York: Putnam, 1933.

1868 Rothwell, Kenneth S. "Grammar, History, and Criticism," CE, 27, #1 (October, 1965), 27-32. The analogy between the development of language and the development of plot.

1869 Ryan, Marianna. "Retrieval of the Word in Gerontion and The Waste Land," AntigR, 20 (1974), 78-97.

1870 Sampley, Arthur M. "The Woman Who Wasn't There: Lacuna in T. S. Eliot," SAQ, 67, #4 (Autumn, 1968), 603-610. The undesirable women characters in the body of Eliot's work.

1871 Sanesi, Roberto. "Con Eliot sui banchi di Terranova," Aut Aut, 4 (March, 1954), 127-134.

1872 ______. "Un'immagine di The Waste Land," OPL, 7 (1961), 66-70.

1873 Santoy, Peter Du. "The Waste Land," TLS (December 17, 1971), 1580.

1874 Schmidt, A. V. C. "Eliot, Swinburne, and Dante: A Note on The Waste Land," N&Q, 23 (January, 1976), 17-18. Lines 215-248; the sources of Eliot's character Tiresias.

1875 Schneider, Elisabeth. "The Waste Land," T. S. Eliot: The Pattern in the Carpet. Berkeley, Los Angeles: California U. P., 1975, pp. 59-91. "...at its most abstract level, The Waste Land again asks the question: ... is change possible?"

1876 Schnetzer, Dean. "The Man with Three Staves in The Waste Land," BNYPL, 78 (Spring, 1975), 347-350.

1877 Schwartz, Delmore. "Speaking of Books," NYTBR (July 17, 1955), 2. Observation that April ("the cruelest month") is the month of the highest suicide rate.

1878 ______. "T. S. Eliot as the International Hero," PartisanR, 12, #2 (Spring, 1945), 199-206; repr., in A Collection of Critical Essays on The Waste Land. Jay Martin, ed. Englewood Cliffs, N. J.: 1968, pp. 97-104.

1879 Scott, Nathan A., Jr. Rehearsals of Discomposure: Alienation and Reconciliation in Modern Literature. New York: King's Crown Press, 1952, pp. 203-225.

1880 Seelye, John. "The Waste Land," TLS, #3484 (December 5, 1968), 1392.

1881 Sen, Mihir K. "A Psychological Interpretation of The Waste Land," LCrit, 3 (Summer, 1957), 29-44.

1882 ___________. "The Waste Land: An Attempt at a Commentary," ModRev (July, 1950), 64-67.

1883 Sencourt, Robert. "The Waste Land," T. S. Eliot: A Memoir. Donald Adamson, ed. London: Garnstone Pr.; New York: Dodd, Mead, 1971, pp. 98-115.

1884 Serpieri, Alessandra. ["The Waste Land"], Hopkins-Eliot-Auden: saggi sul parallelismo poetico. Bologna: R. Pàtron, 1969.

1885 ___________. "L'incubo della mutilazione in Eliot: Da Rhapsody on a Windy Night a The Waste Land," Paragone, 266 (1972), 101-119.

1886 ___________. "La poesia di T. S. Eliot: Dalla Terra Desolata alla Terra Promessa," Il Ponte, 15 (July-August, 1950), 935-948.

1887 Shanahan, C. M. "Irony in Laforgue, Corbière, and Eliot," MP, 53 (November, 1955), 125-127.

1888 Shapiro, Karl. "T. S. Eliot: The Death of Literary Judgment," In Defense of Ignorance. New York: Random House, 1960, pp. 35-60; repr., in Storm over The Waste Land. Robert E. Knoll, ed. Chicago: Scott, Foresman, 1964, pp. 136-153.

1889 Sheppard, Richard. "Cultivating The Waste Land," JES, 2 (1972), 183-189.

1890 Shulman, Robert. "Myth, Mr. Eliot, and the Comic Novel," MFS, 12, #4 (Winter, 1966-67), 395-403. The Waste Land provides "both a target and a point of departure" for comic novels such as Fitzgerald's The Great Gatsby and Malamud's The Natural.

1891 Sickels, Eleanor M. "Eliot's The Waste Land, I, 24-30, and Ash Wednesday, IV-VI," Expl, 9, #1 (October, 1950), Item 4.

1892 Silverstein, Norman. "Movie-going for Lovers of The Waste Land and Ulysses," Salmagundi, I, i (1965), 37-55.

1893 Simon, Irène. "Echoes in The Waste Land," ES, 34 (April, 1953), 64-72.

1894 Simons, John W. "Eliot and His Critics," Cw, 57 (February 27, 1953), 515-516.

1894a Smailes, T. A. "The Music of Ideas in The Waste Land," UES, 11, #1 (1973), 25-29.

1895 Smidt, Kristian. "The Waste Land," Poetry and Belief in the Work of T. S. Eliot. Rev. ed., New York: Humanities Press, 1961, pp. 147-151.

1896 Smith, Grover. "The Fortuneteller in Eliot's Waste Land," AL, 25 (January, 1954), 490-492. The immediate source of "Madame Sostris" is an incident in Huxley's Crome Yellow, first published in November, 1921, at about the time Eliot was working on the poem.

1897 __________. "The Making of The Waste Land," Mosaic, 6, #1 (Fall, 1972), 127-141. "Since the publication of the facsimilies, there can be no doubt that The Waste Land was controlled by Eliot's architectonic skill at every stage of composition...."

1898 __________. "Memory and Desire: The Waste Land," T. S. Eliot's Poetry and Plays. Chicago: Chicago U. P., 1956, pp. 72-98.

1899 __________. "T. S. Eliot's Lady of the Rocks," N&Q, 194 (March 19, 1949), 123-125.

1900 Smith, James. "A Note on the Text of The Waste Land," TCBS, 6 (1973), 131-133.

1901 Smith, Ray. "Eliot's The Waste Land, I, 74-75," Expl, 9 (October, 1950), Item 8.

1902 Sorescu, Marin. "T. S. Eliot: Tara pustie. Unghiuri drepte si unghiuri ascutite in poezie," Luceafarul, 10, #21 (May 27, 1967), 6; 10, #22 (June 3, 1967), 6.

1903 Southam, B. C. "The Waste Land," A Guide to the Selected Poems of T. S. Eliot. New York: Harcourt, Brace & World, 1969, pp. 72-93.

1904 Spangler, George M. "Eliot's 'Red Rock' and Norris's McTeague," N&Q, 20, #9 (September, 1973), 330-331. Eliot's image of a "red rock" in the Waste Land may derive from Norris's McTeague, and not from Isaiah 32:2.

1905 Spencer, Theodore. "The Poetry of T. S. Eliot," Atl 151 (January, 1933), 64-65.

1906 Spender, Stephen. The Destructive Element. Boston and New York: Houghton, Mifflin, 1936, pp. 144-147.

1907 __________. "Remembering Eliot," SR, 74 (Winter, 1966), 66-67; repr., in A Collection of Critical Essays on The

Waste Land. Jay Martin, ed. Englewood Cliffs, New Jersey: Prentice-Hall, 1968, p. 16.

1908 ______. T. S. Eliot. Frank Kermode, ed. New York: Viking, 1975, passim.

1909 Squire, J. C. "Poetry," LonMerc, 8 (October, 1923), 655-656. Thought a "grunt would serve equally well" as the poem.

1910 Stauffer, Donald. The Nature of Poetry. New York: W. W. Norton, 1946. Says The Waste Land is "a narrative of betrayal by the brute lust of the world."

1911 ______. "Poetry as Symbolic Thinking," SatR 30 (March 22, 1947), 10.

1912 Steiner, George. "The Cruellest Months," NY, 48 (April 22, 1972), 134-142.

1913 Stephenson, E. M. "The Waste Land," T. S. Eliot and the Lay Reader. London: Fortune Press, 1944, pp. 18-36.

1914 Stonier, G. W. "Eliot and the Plain Reader," FnR, 138 (November, 1932), 627.

1915 Sugiyama, Yoko. "The Waste Land and Contemporary Japanese Poetry," CL, 13 (Summer, 1961), 254-262.

1916 Sutton, Walter. "Mauberley, The Waste Land, and the Problem of Unified Form," WSCL, 9 (Winter, 1968), 15-35. Comparison of Pound's Hugh Selwyn Mauberley and The Waste Land.

1917 Takayanagi, Shunichi. "T. S. Eliot to Ezra Pound--The Waste Land no Seiritsu wo megutte," ELLS, 9 (1972), 100-144. The genesis of The Waste Land.

1918 ______. "The Waste Land: Manuscript and the Poem," ELLS, 10 (1973), 109-131.

1919 Tamplin, Ronald. "The Tempest and The Waste Land," AL, 39 (November, 1967), 352-372. Colin Still's book Shakespeare's Mystery Play: A Study of The Tempest is proposed as a major, not a minor, source for The Waste Land.

1920 Taranath, Rejeev. "Coriolanus, The Waste Land and the Coriolan Poems," LCritM, 6 (Winter, 1963), 111-120.

1921 Tate, Allen. "Irony and Humility," H&H, 4 (1931), 294.

1922 ______. "T. S. Eliot," On the Limits of Poetry. New York: The Swallow Press & Morrow, 1948, pp. 341-349.

1923 Thomas, Wright, and Stuart Gerry Brown. Reading Poems: An Introduction to Critical Study. New York: Oxford U. P., 1941, pp. 716-731, 749-751.

1924 Thompson, Eric. "Appendix: The Waste Land," T. S. Eliot: The Metaphysical Perspective. Carbondale: Southern Illinois U. P., 1963, pp. 143-160. An excerpt, "Technique," repr., in A Collection of Critical Essays on The Waste Land. Jay Martin, ed. Englewood Cliffs, N. J.: 1968, pp. 39-41.

1925 Thompson, T. H. "The Bloody Wood," LonMerc, 29 (January, 1934), 238.

1926 Tillotson, Geoffrey. "The Critic and the Dated Text," SR, 68 (Autumn, 1960), 595-602. Comments on an authorial note to The Waste Land.

1927 Torrens, James. "Charles Maurras and Eliot's 'New Life,'" PMLA, 89, # 2 (March, 1974), 312-322. Maurras's influence on T. S. Eliot.

1928 Toth, Susan Allen. "Henderson The Rain King, Eliot, and Browning," NConL, 1, # 5 (November, 1971), 6-8. Possible sources and influences on Saul Bellow's work.

1928a Traversi, Derek. "The Waste Land: Introduction," T. S. Eliot: The Longer Poems. New York: Harcourt, Brace, Jovanovich, 1976, pp. 57-83.

1929 ________. "The Waste Land Revisited: A Critical Analysis of Mr. Eliot's Work," DubR, 443 (1948), 106-123. The poem studied in relation to Eliot's later work.

1930 Trigona, Prospero. Saggio su "The Waste Land." Napoli: Guida, 1973.

1931 Tschumi, Raymond. Thought in Twentieth-Century English Poetry. Chicago: Chicago U. P., 1947, pp. 132-144.

1932 Unger, Leonard. "T. S. E. on The Waste Land," Mosaic, 6, i (Fall, 1972), 157-165. In various lectures, Eliot made statements which reveal his preoccupation with ideas expressed in The Waste Land.

1933 ________. T. S. Eliot: Moments and Patterns. Minneapolis: Minnesota U. P., 1967, pp. 104-114, passim.

1934 ________. "T. S. Eliot's Rose Garden: A Persistent Theme," SoR, 7 (Spring, 1942), 667-689.

1935 Untermeyer, Louis. "T. S. Eliot," American Poetry Since 1900. New York: Henry Holt, 1923, pp. 350-362. Called The Waste Land "a piece of literary carpentry."

1936 Verma, Rajendra. "The Web of The Waste Land," Royalists in Politics: T. S. Eliot and Political Philosophy. London: Asia Pub. House, 1968, pp. 1-46.

1937 Vickery, John B. "Eliot's Poetry: The Quest and the Way," (Part I), Renascence, 10 (Autumn, 1957), 5-8.

1938 ________. "A Note on The Waste Land," L&P, 10 (Winter, 1960), 3-4. Comment on two phrases which Eliot borrowed from Freud's Totem and Taboo: April's "memory and desire" and "Those are pearls that were his eyes."

1939 Wain, John. "A Walk in the Sacred Wood," LonMerc, 5, i (1958), 45-53.

1940 Waldron, Philip. "T. S. Eliot, Mr. Whiteside and 'The Psychobiographical Approach,'" SoRA, 6, #2 (June, 1973), 138-147.

1941 ________, and George Whiteside. "Eliot and Psychobiography," SoRA, 6 (September, 1973), 253-256.

1942 Walton, James. "Joyce's Waste Land and Eliot's Unknown God," Literary Monographs, 4 (n. d.), 137-213.

1943 Ward, David E. T. S. Eliot: Between Two Worlds. A Reading of T. S. Eliot's Poetry and Plays. London and Boston: Routledge and Kegan Paul, 1973.

1944 Ward, Nicole. "'Fourmillante Cité': Baudelaire and The Waste Land," The Waste Land in Different Voices. A. D. Moody, ed. New York: St. Martin's Press, 1974, pp. 87-104.

1945 Wasserstrom, William. "T. S. Eliot and the Dial," SR, 70, #1 (Winter, 1962), 81-92; repr., in Storm over the Waste Land. Robert E. Knoll, ed. Chicago: Scott, Foresman, 1964, pp. 13-22.

1946 Watkins, Floyd C. "The Waste Land--Enjoyment of the Poetry," The Flesh and the Word: Eliot, Hemingway and Faulkner. Nashville, Tenn.: Vanderbilt U. P., 1971, pp. 41-52.

1946a Watson-Williams, Helen. "The Blackened Wall: Notes on Blake's London and Eliot's The Waste Land," English, 10 (Summer, 1955), 181-184.

1947 Weathers, Willie T. "Eliot's The Waste Land, I, 24-30," Expl, 9, #4 (February, 1951), Item 31.

1948 Wecter, Dixon. "The Harvard Exiles," VQR, 10 (1934), 251.

1949 Weirick, Margaret C. "Myth and Water Symbolism in T. S. Eliot's The Waste Land," TQ, 10, #1 (Spring, 1967), 97-104. The three myths indicate man's development in which water participates, first as a life-sustaining force, next as a means of symbolic cleansing, and third, as indication of man's fate as he loses touch with his environment.

1950 Wetzel, Heinz. Banale Vitalität und Lähmendes Erkennen: Drei vergleichende Studien zu T. S. Eliots The Waste Land. Bern und Frankfurt: Herbert Lang, 1974.

1951 ________. "The Seer in the Spring: On Tonio Kroger and The Waste Land," RLC, 174, #3 (July-September, 1970), 322-332. Considers man's reaction to the "banalities" of life in Thomas Mann's novella and Eliot's poem.

1952 ________. "Spuren des Ulysses in The Waste Land," GRM, 20, n. s., (1970), 442-466.

1953 Wheelwright, Philip Ellis. "Pilgrim in the Wasteland," The Burning Fountain: A Study in the Language of Symbolism. Bloomington: Indiana U. P., 1954, pp. 330-338.

1954 ________. "Two Ways of Metaphor," Metaphor and Reality. Bloomington: Indiana U. P., 1962, pp. 60-62.

1955 White, Georgiana Donase. "The Theme of Guilt in the Poetry and Plays of T. S. Eliot," DAI, 37 (Fordham: 1976), 2906A.

1956 Whiteside, George. "T. S. Eliot: The Psychobiographical Approach," SoRA, 6, #1 (March, 1973), 3-26. The biographical character of The Waste Land.

1957 ________. "T. S. Eliot's Character and Work up to The Waste Land," DA, 31 (Columbia: 1969), 1820A.

1958 Widmer, Kingsley. "The Waste Land and the American Breakdown," The Twenties: Fiction, Poetry, Drama. Warren French, ed. De Land, Florida: Everett/Edwards, 1975, pp. 475-496.

1959 Wilks, A. John. A Critical Commentary on T. S. Eliot's The Waste Land. London: Macmillan, 1971.

1960 Williams, Haydn Moore. T. S. Eliot: The Waste Land and Other Poems. 1st ed. Calcutta: Mukhopadhyay, 1965.

1961 Williams, Helen. T. S. Eliot: The Waste Land. London: Arnold, 1968; Woodbury, New York: Barron's Educ. Series, 1968.

1962 Williams, William Carlos. "The Waste Land," Autobiography. New York: New Directions, 1967, pp. 146-156.

1963 __________. "The Structure of The Waste Land," MP, 47 (February, 1950), 191-206. A study of the materials involved in the genesis of the poem, as well as an evaluation of the structure.

1964 __________. "The Talent of T. S. Eliot," SR, 35 (July, 1927), 284-295.

1965 __________. The Talent of T. S. Eliot. (Chapbook, No. 32). Seattle: Washington Univ. Bk. Store, 1929, p. 33.

1966 __________. "The Waste Land," A Reader's Guide to T. S. Eliot. New York: Noonday Press, 1953, pp. 115-162.

1967 Wilson, Edmund. Axel's Castle. New York: Scribner's Sons, 1931, pp. 104-111.

1967a __________. "The First Waste Land," NYRB, 17 (November 18, 1971), 16-17. The early version of the poem submitted to Ezra Pound subsequently altered in accordance with Pound's suggestions. Cf., Valerie Eliot, ed. The Waste Land: A Facsimile and Transcript of the Original Drafts Including the Annotations of Ezra Pound. New York: Harcourt, 1971.

1968 __________. "The Poetry of Drouth," Dial, 73 (December, 1922), 611-616.

1968a __________. "The Waste Land in Deshabile," The Devils and Canon Barkam: Ten Essays on Poets, Novelists and Monsters. New York: Farrar, Straus & Giroux, 1973, pp. 112-117.

1969 Wilson, Frank. "The Waste Land," Six Essays on the Development of T. S. Eliot. London: Fortune Press, 1948, pp. 23-31.

1970 Wilson, Timothy. "The Wife of the Father of The Waste Land," Esquire, 77, #5 (May, 1972), 44, 46, 50. (Interview).

1971 Winters, Yvor. "Some Later Critics," The Anatomy of Nonsense. Norfolk: 1943, p. 167; repr., in Storm over the Waste Land. Robert E. Knoll, ed. Chicago: Scott, Foresman, 1964, p. 97.

1972 Woodward, Daniel H. "Notes on the Publishing History and Text of The Waste Land," PBSA, 58 (July-September, 1964), 252-269.

1973 Wool, Sandra. "Weston Revisited," Accent, 10, #4 (Autumn, 1950), 207-212.

1974 Worthen, John. "The Waste Land," TLS, #3768 (May 24, 1974), 559.

1975 Worthington, Jane. "The Epigraphs to the Poetry of T. S. Eliot," AL, 21 (March, 1949-January, 1950), 13-14.

1976 Wright, George. The Poet in the Poem. (Perspectives in Criticism, 4) Berkeley and Los Angeles: California U. P., 1960, pp. 60-76.

1977 Wylie, Elinor. "Mr. Eliot's Slug Horn," LiteraryR (January 20, 1923), 396.

1978 Yasuda, Shoichiro. "Arechi no Sokoban wo yomu Towaku kara Ifu e," EigoS, 117 (1972), 745-747. On reading The Waste Land.

1979 __________. "Arechi Saiko," EigoS, 119 (1974), 684-685. The Waste Land reconsidered.

1980 Yerbury, Grace D. "Of a City Beside a River: Whitman, Eliot, Thomas, Miller, WWR, 10 (September, 1964), 67-73. Whitman's "Crossing Brooklyn Ferry" anticipated certain qualities in The Waste Land.

1981 Zabel, Morton D. "T. S. Eliot in Mid-Career," Poetry, 36 (September, 1930), 330-336. "... The Waste Land cut cleanest to the core of its inner meaning when it found symbolical instruments of unqualified accuracy...."

1982 Zasurskii, Ya. Foreword. Russian Translation of The Waste Land and Selected Poems. Moscow: Progress, 1971.

1983 Zimmerman, Lester F. "Shifted Values in the Later Nineteenth Century," Mon/TuMS, #7 (1969), 23-31. Eliot in The Waste Land a spokesman for the 30's.

(THE WASTE LAND) I. "THE BURIAL OF THE DEAD"

1984 Barry, John B. "Eliot's 'Burial of the Dead': A Note on the Morphology of Culture," XUS, 11, #3 (Winter, 1972), 18-26.

1985 __________. "Eliot's 'Burial of the Dead': A Note on the Morphology of Culture," ArQ, 30 (Spring, 1974), 63-73. The significance of the dissolution of culture depicted in 'The Burial of the Dead.'

1986 Cotten, Lyman A. "Eliot's The Waste Land," Expl, 9 (October, 1950), Item 7. Source of the name Sosostris.

1987 Cross, Gustav. "A Note on The Waste Land," N&Q, 6 (July-August, 1959), 286-287. The "red rock" may represent Christ or His Church. Cf., Geo. M. Spangler, N&Q, 20 (September, 1973), 330-331.

1988 Glazier, Lyle. "Eliot's The Waste Land, I, 24-30," Expl. 8, #4 (February, 1950), Item 26. "...the passage can be read as an extension of the Limbo imagery with which 'The Burial of the Dead' is saturated...."

1988a Hyams, C. Barry, and Karl H. Reichert. "The Month of April in English Poetry (with Special Reference to Geoffrey Chaucer and T. S. Eliot)," NS (November, 1957), 522-528.

1989 Janoff, Ronald W. "Eliot and Horace: Aspects of the Intrinsic Classicist," Cithara, 5, #1 (November, 1965), 31-44. Comparison of Horace's "Ode to Pyrrha" and Eliot's "The Burial of the Dead."

1990 Kemp, Lysander. "The Waste Land," Expl, 7 (June, 1949), Item 60.

1991 ________. "The Waste Land," Expl, 8 (February, 1950), Item 27. Source of the name Sosostris.

1992 Montgomery, Marion. "Eliot's Hyacinth Girl and the Times Literary Supplement," Renascence, 25 (Winter, 1973), 67-73. As to the Hyacinth Girl of "The Burial of the Dead," Eliot's point of view often ignored.

1993 Moynihan, William T. "The Goal of the Waste Land Quest," ["The Burial of the Dead"], Renascence, 13, #1 (Autumn, 1960), 175-176.

1994 Sickels, Eleanor M. "Eliot's The Waste Land, I, 24-30, and Ash Wednesday, iv-vi," Expl, 9 (October, 1950), Item 4.

1995 Smith, Ray. "Eliot's The Waste Land, I, 74-75," Expl, 9 (October, 1950), Item 8. Discussion of substitution of "Dog" for John Webster's "Wolf" in the line "Oh keep the Dog far hence...."

1996 Vickery, John B. "Two Sources of 'The Burial of the Dead,'" L&P, 10 (Winter, 1960), 3-4.

1997 Weathers, Willie T. "Eliot's The Waste Land, I, 24-30," Expl, 9 (February, 1951), Item 31. Significance of the "red rock."

(THE WASTE LAND) II. "A GAME OF CHESS"

1998 Auffret, Helene. "Etude comparée de deux poèmes-conversation: Apollinaire, 'Les femmes,' Eliot, 'A Game of Chess,'" RLC, 43 (July-September, 1969), 415-426.

1999 Bates, Ronald. "A Topic in The Waste Land: Traditional Rhetoric and Eliot's Individual Talent," WSCL, 5 (Summer, 1964), 85-104.

2000 Drew, Elizabeth. Discovering Poetry. New York: Norton, 1935, pp. 119-120.

2001 Empson, William. Seven Types of Ambiguity. London: Chatto & Windus, 1930; rev. ed., New York: New Directions, 1947, pp. 77-78.

2002 Hager, Philip E. "T. S. Eliot's 'A Game of Chess': Another 'Source' of the Dressing Room Scene," AntigR, 1, #2 (Summer, 1970), 91-93. There are parallels in idea and words between Beardsley's Under the Hill and Eliot's scene.

2003 L. L. S. "Eliot's Wasteland," Expl, 5, #5 (March, 1947), Item 17. Asks if the line "Hurry up please It's Time," Section 2, "A Game of Chess," is intended to suggest the closing of the London pub. Cf., Eleanor Sickels, Expl, 7 (December, 1948), Item 20.

2004 McElderry, B. R. "Eliot's 'Shakespeherian Rag,'" AQ, 9 (Summer, 1957), 185-186. Identification of the song alluded to in The Waste Land, 1. 128.

2005 Morris, Robert L. "Eliot's 'Game of Chess' and Conrad's The Return," MLN, 65 (June, 1950), 422-423.

2006 Schwalb, Harry M. "Eliot's 'A Game of Chess,'" Expl, 11, #6 (April, 1953), Item 46. The Relationship to Shakespeare's Antony and Cleopatra. Cf., George Williamson, MP, 47 (February, 1950), 191-206.

2007 Sickels, Eleanor M. "Eliot's Wasteland," Expl, 7, #3 (December, 1948), Item 20. Cf., L. L. S. Expl, 5 (March, 1947), Item 17.

(THE WASTE LAND) III. "THE FIRE SERMON"

2008 Cook, Albert. "Eliot's Waste Land, III (Fire Sermon, 262-265)," Expl, 6 (October, 1947), Item 7.

2009 Empson, William. "Mr. Empson and the Fire Sermon," EIC, 6 (October, 1956), 481-482.

2010 Gibson, William M. "The Fire Sermon--Sonnets in T. S. Eliot's The Waste Land," AL, 32, #4 (January, 1961), 465-466.

2011 Kemp, Lysander. "Eliot's Waste Land, I, 49-50," Expl, 7 (June, 1949), Item 60. Madame Sosostris as the typist in the Fire Sermon.

2012 Perret, Marion. "Eliot, the Naked Lady, and the Missing Link," AL, 46 (November, 1974), 289-303. Sweeney's coming to Mrs. Porter is comparable to the "analogous encounter of Tiresias and Athene."

2012a Tate, Allen. "T. S. Eliot - The Fire Sermon," Reactionary Essays. New York: Scribner's, 1936, pp. 214-216.

(THE WASTE LAND) IV. "DEATH BY WATER"

2013 Smith, Grover. "Observations on Eliot's 'Death by Water,'" Accent, 6 (Summer, 1946), 257-263. "It would be a mistake to suppose that 'Death by Water' was a passage of triumphant life: it is a passage of spiritual death."

(THE WASTE LAND) V. "WHAT THE THUNDER SAID"

2014 Blackmur, R. P. "T. S. Eliot," H&H, 1 (March, 1928), 197-201.

2015 Bolgan, Anne C. Mr. Eliot's Philosophical Writings, or What the Thunder Said. Diss. Toronto, 1961.

2016 ________. What the Thunder Really Said: A Retrospective Essay on the Making of The Waste Land. Montreal and London: McGill-Queen's U. P., 1973.

2017 Fowler, D. C. "The Waste Land: Mr. Eliot's 'Fragments,'" CE, 14 (January, 1953), 234-235. Suggests that quotations at the end of the poem are used to break the evil spell of the waste land.

2018 Motola, Gabriel. "The Waste Land: Symbolism and Structure," L&P, 18, #4 (1968), 205-212. In "What the Thunder Said," Part V, through the questor in the poem, Eliot expresses his reaction to carnality that threatens to destroy him; he concludes with repudiation of such feelings.

WHISPERS OF IMMORTALITY

2019 Blackmur, R. P. "T. S. Eliot," H&H, 1 (March, 1928), 207-208.

2020 Cleophas, Sister M., R. S. M. "Eliot's 'Whispers of Immortality,'" Expl, 8 (December, 1949), Item 22.

2021 Strandberg, Victor. "Eliot's 'Whispers of Immortality,'" Expl, 17 (May, 1959), Item 53.

2022 Walcutt, Charles C. "Eliot's 'Whispers of Immortality,'" Expl, 7 (November, 1948), Item 11.

COLLECTED POEMS, 1909-1935; 1909-1962

2023 B. M. K. "Collected Poems, 1909-1935 by T. S. Eliot," Cw, 145 (May, 1937), 245-247.

2024 Blackmur, R. P. "Collected Poems, 1909-1935 by T. S. Eliot," Poetry, 50 (April, 1937), 48-51.

2025 Boie M. "Collected Poems by T. S. Eliot," NAR, 242 (Autumn, 1936), 189-192.

2026 Cowley, M. "Collected Poems by T. S. Eliot," NR, 87 (May 20, 1936), 49.

2027 Harding, D. W. "Collected Poems, 1909-1935 by T. S. Eliot," Scrutiny, 5, # 2 (September, 1936), 171-176; repr., in T. S. Eliot: A Collection of Critical Essays. Englewood Cliffs, N. J.: 1962, pp. 104-109.

2028 Holmes, J. H. "Collected Poems by T. S. Eliot," Unity, 117 (August, 1936), 218.

2029 Jack, P. M. "T. S. Eliot," NYTBR (June, 1936), 1, 14.

2030 Kenner, Hugh. "The Seven-Year Shaman," NatlR, 16, # 6 (February 11, 1964), 113-114.

2031 Kermode, Frank. "Reading Eliot Today," Nation, 197, # 13 (October 26, 1963), 263-264. Eliot's work an effort "to give a whole mind to poetry."

2032 Moore, Marianne. "T. S. Eliot--It's Not Forbidden to Think," Nation, 142 (May 27, 1936), 680-681.

2033 Muir, Edwin. "Collected Poems," Spectator, 156 (April 3, 1936), 622.

2034 Rubin, Larry. "T. S. Eliot: A Revaluation," ModA, 8 (Spring, 1964), 221-223.

2035 Untermeyer, Louis. "Collected Poems by T. S. Eliot," YR, 26 (Autumn, 1936), 165-168.

CRITICISM

AFTER STRANGE GODS (1934)

2036 Aiken, Conrad. "After Ash Wednesday," Poetry, 45 (December, 1934), 161-165.

2037 Anon. "After Strange Gods," Review, L&L, 10 (April, 1934), 111-113.

2038 Anon. "After Strange Gods," TLS, 1681 (April 19, 1934), 278.

2039 Barber, C. L. "T. S. Eliot: After Strange Gods," SoR, 6 (Autumn, 1940), 387-416.

2040 Belgion, W. R. "Some Recent Books," DubR, 194 (April, 1934), 320-324.

2041 Benét, William Rose. "T. S. Eliot and Original Sin," SatRL, 10 (May 5, 1934), 673, 678.

2042 Blackmur, R. P. "The Dangers of Authorship," H&H, 7, #4 (July, 1934), 719-726.

2043 ________. "The Dangers of Authorship," The Double Agent. New York: Arrow Editions, 1935, pp. 172-183.

2044 Calverton, V. F. "T. S. Eliot, An Inverted Marxism," ModM, 8, #6 (July, 1934), 372-373.

2045 Chace, William M. "T. S. Eliot: The Plea Against Consciousness," Mosaic, 5, #1 (Fall, 1971), 133-143. Eliot's political theories as shaped around "consciousness."

2046 Common, Jack. "After Strange Gods," Review, Adelphi, 8 (April, 1934), 68-69.

2047 Gregory, Horace. "The Man of Feeling," NR, 79 (May 16, 1934), 23-24.

2048 Hayakawa, S. Ichiye. "Mr. Eliot's Auto da Fé," SR, 42 (July-September, 1934), 365-371.

2049 John, K. (Mrs.) "The Grand Inquisitor," NSt, 7 (February 24, 1934), 274.

2050 Knights, L. C. "Shakespeare and Shakespearians," Scrutiny, 3 (December, 1934), 306.

2051 Leavis, F. R. "Mr. Eliot, Mr. Wyndham Lewis, and Lawrence: After Strange Gods: A Primer of Modern Heresy by T. S. Eliot," Scrutiny, 3, #2 (September, 1934), 184-191; repr., in The Importance of Scrutiny. Eric Bentley, ed. New York: New York U. P., 1964, pp. 276-283.

2052 Margolis, John D. ["After Strange Gods"], T. S. Eliot's Intellectual Development: 1922-1939. Chicago: Chicago U. P., 1972, pp. 171-174.

2053 Muir, Edwin. "Mr. Eliot on Evil," Spectator, 152, #5515 (March 9, 1934), 378-379.

2054 Oras, Ants. The Critical Ideas of T. S. Eliot. (Acta et Commentationes, Universitatis Tartuensis, Ülihool, B. Humaniora, XXVIII, 3.) Tartu, Estonia: K. Mattieson, 1932.

2055 Pound, Ezra. "Mr. Eliot's Mare's Nest," New EW, 4, #21 (March, 1934), 307-309.

2056 Troy, William. "T. S. Eliot: Grand Inquisitor," Nation, 138, #3590 (April 25, 1934), 478.

DANTE (1929)

2057 Bergonzi, Bernard. ["Dante"], T. S. Eliot. New York: Macmillan, 1972, pp. 118, 120, 138.

2058 Gary, Franklin. "Review of Dante and Animula," Symposium, 1 (April, 1930), 268-271.

2059 Headings, Philip R. T. S. Eliot. New York: Twayne, 1964.

2060 Kermode, Frank, ed. Introduction. The Selected Prose of T. S. Eliot. New York: Harcourt, Brace, 1975, pp. 20-21.

2061 Kojecky, Roger. T. S. Eliot's Social Criticism. New York: Farrar, Straus and Giroux, 1972, p. 62, passim.

2062 Leighton, Lawrence. "Eliot on Dante," H&H, 3 (April, 1930), 442-444.

2063 Margolis, John D. T. S. Eliot's Intellectual Development, 1922-1939. Chicago and London: Chicago U. P., 1972, pp. 128-132, 143, 168-169.

2064 Roberts, R. Ellis. "Two Poets," Bookman (English), 77 (March, 1930), 359-360.

2065 Unger, Leonard. T. S. Eliot: Moments and Patterns. Minneapolis: Minnesota U. P., 1966, 69-71.

ESSAYS ANCIENT AND MODERN (1936)

2066 Aiken, Conrad. "Mr. Eliot in the Wilderness," NR, 88, #1142 (October 21, 1936), 326-327.

2067 Anon. "Mr. Eliot's New Essays," TLS, 1779 (March 7, 1936), 192.

2067a Arns, Karl. "Essays Ancient and Modern by T. S. Eliot," EStudien, 71 (1936), 291-292.

2068 Colum, Mary M. "Life and Literature: Studies of the American Mind," Forum, 96 (October, 1936), 175.

2069 Beutsch, Babette. "The Orthodox Mr. Eliot," NYHTB (September 13, 1936), 14.

2070 Farmer, A. J. "Essays Ancient and Modern," EA, 3 (1939), 153.

2071 Fieling, Keith. "Set in Authority: Mr. Eliot's Essays," Observer (May 3, 1936), 9.

2072 Humphries, Rolfe. "Anima Naturaliter Marxiana?" New Masses, 20 (September 8, 1936), 24-26.

2073 Jack, Peter Monroe. "The World of T. S. Eliot," NYTBR (September 13, 1936), 5, 26.

2074 Jones, Howard Mumford. "The Legend of T. S. Eliot," SatRL, 14 (September 19, 1936), 13-14.

2075 Leavis, F. R. "Mr. Eliot and Education," Scrutiny, 5, 1 (June, 1936), 84-89; repr., in The Importance of Scrutiny. Eric Bentley, ed. New York: New York U. P., 1964, pp. 283-287.

2076 Meter, W. J. "Eliot, Morals, and Censorship," SatRL, 14 (October 3, 1936), 9.

2077 Munson, Gorham B. "Book Reviews," NAR, 242 (Winter, 1936), 394-400.

2078 Rice, Philip Blair. "The Critic as Prophet," Poetry, 50, #1 (April, 1937), 51-54.

2079 Van Doren, Mark. "Mr. Eliot Glances Up," Nation, 143 (September 19, 1936), 340-342.

2080 ________. "Mr. Eliot Glances Up," The Private Reader. New York: Henry Holt, 1942, 212-216.

EZRA POUND: HIS METRIC AND POETRY (1917)

2081 "Ezra Pound: His Metric and Poetry," Bookman, 47 (March, 1918), 106, "A little essay of critical appreciation."

2082 Orage, A[lfred] R[ichard]. "Mr. Ezra Pound as Metricist," The New Age. London: New Age Press, 1918; repr., in Readers and Writers (1917-1921). London: Allen & Unwin, 1922, pp. 57-60.

2083 Woodward, Daniel H. "John Quinn and T. S. Eliot's First Book of Criticism," PBSA, 56 (2nd Quarter, 1962), 259-265. Eliot stated: "I remember that it was through Pound himself that I was commissioned to write the book. I believe that as my name was almost unknown at that time it was considered that the little essay might be more impressive without being signed by the author."

FOR LANCELOT ANDREWES (1928)

2084 Aiken, Conrad. "For Lancelot Andrewes," Dial, 86, #7 (July, 1929), 628.

2085 Anon. "For Mr. T. S. Eliot," NSt, 32 (December 29, 1928), 387-388.

2085a Anon. "Mr. Eliot's New Essays," [For Lancelot Andrewes.] TLS, #1401 (December 6, 1928), 953.

2086 Bergonzi, Bernard. T. S. Eliot. New York: Macmillan, 1972, pp. 114, 116, 117.

2087 Fergusson, Francis. "Golden Candlesticks, H&H, 2, #3 (April, 1929), 297-299.

2088 Kermode, Frank, ed. Introduction. Selected Prose of T. S. Eliot. New York: Harcourt, Brace, Jovanovich, 1975, p. 19.

2089 Leavis, F. R. "T. S. Eliot--A Reply to the Condescending," CamR, 50 (February 8, 1929), 254-256.

2090 Margolis, John D. "Second Thoughts," T. S. Eliot's Intellectual Development, 1922-1939. Chicago: Chicago U. P., 1972, pp. 103-115, 141.

2091 Murry, John Middleton. "The Return of the 'Mayflower,'" New Adelphi, 2, #3 (March, 1929), 195-198.

2092 Spender, Stephen. T. S. Eliot. Frank Kermode, ed. New York: Viking, 1976, pp. 144-150.

2093 Takayanagi, Shunichi. "About the Center of the Silent Word: T. S. Eliot and Lancelot Andrewes," ELLS, 7 (1970), 37-81.

HAMLET AND HIS PROBLEMS (1919)
(Revised and reprinted as Hamlet, 1919-1920)

2094 Anon. "Justifying Hamlet," Outlook (London), 50 (September 2, 1922), 196. Approves Clutton-Brock for his criticism of Eliot as to Hamlet.

2095 Anon. "The Razor of Croce," TLS, #1014 (June 23, 1921), 393.

2096 Bergonzi, Bernard. T. S. Eliot. New York: Macmillan, 1967, pp. 55, 67.

2097 Clutton-Brock, Arthur. "The Case Against Hamlet," Shakespeare's "Hamlet." London: Methuen & Co., 1922, pp. 14-32. Objects to Eliot's view of Hamlet as "an artistic failure."

2098 Fergusson, Francis. "Hamlet as Artistic Failure," HudR, 2 (Summer, 1949), 166-170.

2099 H. J. M. "The World of Books," Nation and Athenaeum, 31 (May 27, 1922), 309. Cites Eliot's criticism of Hamlet as "flimsy."

2100 Heller, Eric. "From Hegel to Hamlet: The Prince of Romantic Inwardness," List, 73, #1868 (January 14, 1965), 53-55. Disagrees with Eliot's judgment of Hamlet.

2101 Jamil, Maya. "Hamlet and The Family Reunion," Venture,

5, #1 (June, 1968), 21-29. Finds the two works essentially similar in concept, theme, and structure.

2102 Lynd, Robert. "Buried Alive," Nation (English), 18 (December 4, 1920), 359-360. In response to Eliot's essay on Hamlet says that "Mr. Eliot fails as a critic because he brings the reader neither light nor delight."

2103 Pal, R. M. "Hamlet: The Culmination of a Tradition," Quest, 44, (Winter, 1965), 60-66.

2104 Quillian, William Howell. "Prince Hamlet in the Age of Modernism: James Joyce and T. S. Eliot," DAI, 37 (Princeton: 1976), 1543A-44A. "...Eliot's Hamlet was an important first step toward a unique interpretation of Shakespeare...."

2105 Robertson, J. M. Review: "Hamlet and His Problems," Athenaeum, 4665 (September 26, 1919), 940-941.

2106 Stallings, Laurence. "Enter Robert Lynd with Flare of Critical Brass," New Word World (March 25, 1923), Sec. E. 9. Praises Lynd for his attack on Eliot's essay on Hamlet.

2107 Stevenson, David L. "An Objective Correlative for T. S. Eliot's Hamlet," JAAC, 13 (September, 1954), 69-79. Eliot's conviction that the play is an artistic failure "...forces from us a consciousness of the startling originality of the dramatic structure from which emerges the play's artistic success."

2108 Thompson, Eric. T. S. Eliot: The Metaphysical Perspective. Carbondale: Southern Illinois U. P., 1965, pp. 73-75.

2109 Unger, Leonard. T. S. Eliot: Moments and Patterns. Minneapolis: Minnesota U. P., 1967, pp. 36-37.

2109a Zulli, Floyd, Jr. "T. S. Eliot and Paul Bourget," N&Q, 13 (1966), 415-416. Paul Bourget may have given Eliot the idea of the latter's description of Hamlet as 'the Mona Lisa' of literature."

HOMAGE TO JOHN DRYDEN (1924)

2110 Anon. "Comment," Dial, 80 (February, 1926), 178.

2111 Austin, Allen. T. S. Eliot: The Literary and Social Criticism. Bloomington: Indiana U. P., 1971, p. 109.

2112 Bergonzi, Bernard. T. S. Eliot. New York: Macmillan, 1964, pp. 86-89, 177.

2113 Bradbrook, M. C. "The Critic and the Man of Letters," T. S. Eliot. London: Longmans, Green, rev. ed., 1965, p. 52f.

2114 Freeman, John. "Literary History and Criticism--II," LonMerc, 11 (April, 1925), 662-664.

2115 Lucy, Sean. T. S. Eliot and the Idea of Tradition. New York: Barnes & Noble, 1960, p. 61.

2116 Margolis, John D. T. S. Eliot's Intellectual Development, 1922-1939. Chicago and London: Chicago U. P., 1972, pp. 68, 103.

2117 Mortimer, Raymond. "New Books from the Morning Room Table," Vogue (British) (January, 1925). Sees Eliot as "always serious, always clear-headed...."

2118 Muir, Edwin. "Recent Criticism," Nation and Athenaeum, 36 (December 6, 1924), 370-372.

2119 Van Doren, Mark. "First Glance," Nation, 119 (December 31, 1924), 732-733; repr., in The Private Reader. New York: Henry Holt, 1942, pp. 131-133.

2120 Wilson, Edmund. "T. S. Eliot and the Seventeenth Century," NR, 41 (January 7, 1925), 177-178.

THE IDEA OF A CHRISTIAN SOCIETY (1939)

2121 Anon. "A Christian Society. Mr. Eliot on Ideals and Methods: Democracy's Spiritual Problem," TLS (November 4, 1939), 640, 642.

2122 Anon. "The Idea of a Christian Society," CJR, 3 (March-April, 1940), 217.

2123 Anon. "The Idea of a Christian Society," Tablet, 174 (November 18, 1939), 576-577. Says Eliot's essay is written from Roman Catholic viewpoint.

2124 Anon. "The Idea of a Christian Society," List, 22 (November 30, 1939), 1086.

2125 Anon. "Recent and Readable," Time, 25 Pt. 1 (January 15, 1940), 67.

2126 Anon. "Shorter Notices," Nation, 150 (March 16, 1940), 370-371.

2127 Anon. "The Spirit and the Crisis," TLS, 1970 (November 4, 1939), 641.

2128 Austin, Allen. "Eliot's Ideal Society," T. S. Eliot: The Literary and Social Criticism. Bloomington: Indiana U. P., 1971, pp. 71-72, passim.

2129 Bell, Bernard I. "T. S. Eliot examines the State of Society Today," NYTBR (January 7, 1940), 3, 19.

2130 Bergonzi, Bernard. T. S. Eliot. New York: Macmillan, 1972, pp. 127-130, passim.

2131 Binsse, Harry L. "About a Possible Future," Cw, 31 (January 19, 1940), 288. Eliot's analyses called "brilliant."

2132 Bishop, Virginia C. "Letters to the Editor: Humble Rebuttal," SatR, 21 (March 2, 1940), 9. A defense of Eliot. Cf., J. Ratner, SatRL, 21 (Jan. 6, 1940), 7.

2133 Blackmur, R. P. "It Is Later Than He Thinks," The Expense of Greatness. New York: Arrow Editions, 1940, pp. 239-244.

2134 Chace, William M. "T. S. Eliot: The Plea Against Consciousness," Mosaic, 5, i (1971), 133-143.

2135 Cowley, Malcolm. "Tract for the Times," NR, 102 (June 17, 1940), 829-830.

2136 D. W. H. "The Idea of a Christian Society," Review, Scrutiny, 8, #3 (December, 1939), 309-313.

2137 Gallup, Donald C. "Our Society Is a Negative One, T. S. Eliot Declares in Essay," Dallas Morning News (January 14, 1940), Sec. 5, 4. Notes similarity of Eliot's thesis with that of Matthew Arnold.

2138 Harding, D. W. "Christian or Liberal," Scrutiny, 8, #3 (December, 1939), 309-313. "... Mr. Eliot believes that we must now choose between working for a new Christian culture and accepting a pagan one, whether fascist or communist;...."

2139 Holmes, John Haynes. "The World and the Faith," NYHTB (February 18, 1940), 16.

2140 Howarth, Herbert. Notes on Some Figures Behind T. S. Eliot. Boston: Houghton Mifflin, 1964, p. 270.

2141 Jones, Howard Mumford. "Shadow Boxing," Boston Evening Transcript (January 20, 1940), Sec. 6, 1. Asserts that Eliot has not defined term "Christian."

2142 Kayden, Eugene M. "Mr. Eliot's Idea of the Christian Elite," SR, 48 (1940), 282-284.

2143 Kirk, Russell. Eliot and His Age. New York: Random House, 1971, pp. 276-282, passim.

2144 Kojecky, Roger. "A Christian Elite," T. S. Eliot's Social Criticism. New York: Farrar, Straus and Giroux, 1972 passim.

2145 Margolis, John D. T. S. Eliot's Intellectual Development, 1922-1939. Chicago: Chicago U. P., 1973, pp. xvii, 209-215.

2146 Marks, Emerson R. "T. S. Eliot and the Ghost of S. T. C.," SR, 72 (Spring, 1964), 262-280.

2147 Oldham, J. H. "The Idea of a Christian Society," Review ChrNL, 18, Supp (February 28, 1940).

2148 Ratner, Joseph. "Letters to the Editor: Mr. Ratner Replies," SatRL, 21 (March 2, 1940), 9, 18. Cf., Virginia C. Bishop. SatR, 21 (March 2, 1940), 9.

2149 __________. "T. S. Eliot and Totalitarianism," SatR, 21, #11 (January 6, 1940), 7. A strong attack.

2150 Reckitt, Maurice. "A Sub-Christian Society," NewEW, 16, #8 (December 7, 1939), 115-116. Does not think Eliot's "society" religious enough to be termed Christian.

2151 Spender, Stephen. "How Shall We Be Saved?" Horizon, 1 (January, 1940), 51-56.

2152 __________. "Politics," T. S. Eliot. Frank Kermode, ed. New York: Viking, 1975, pp. 239-241, 248-249, passim.

2153 Sperry, W. L. "Pagan and Neutral Societies," YR, 29 (1940), 624-626.

2154 Thompson, Eric. T. S. Eliot: The Metaphysical Perspective. Carbondale: Southern Illinois U. P., 1965, p. 133.

2155 Thompson, Ralph. "Books of the Times," NYT (January 8, 1940), 13.

2156 Trilling, Lionel. "Elements That Are Wanted," PartisanR, 7 (September-October, 1940), 367-369.

2157 Weinstein, Jacob J. "Religion and the Wasteland," JF, 7, #3 (March, 1940), 25-26.

2158 Williams, Raymond. "Second Thoughts: T. S. Eliot on Culture," EIC, 6 (July, 1956), 302-318.

2159 __________. "T. S. Eliot," Culture and Society, 1780-1950. New York: Columbia U. P., 1958, pp. 227-243, passim.

2160 Wiseman, James. "Of loneliness and Communion," DramaCrit, 5, #1 (February, 1962), 14-21.

KNOWLEDGE AND EXPERIENCE IN THE PHILOSOPHY OF F. H. BRADLEY (1964)

2161 Austin, Allen. T. S. Eliot: The Literary and Social Criticism. Bloomington: Indiana U. P., 1971, p. 121.

2162 Carruth, Hayden. "Upon Which to Rejoice," Poetry, 106 (June, 1965), 239-241.

2163 Lees, F. N. Review. TLS (May 21, 1964), 440.

2164 Review. "Knowledge and Experience...," TLS (May 7, 1964), 394.

2165 Schneewind, J. B. "Knowledge and Experience...," Victorian Studies, 8, #2 (December, 1964), 198.

2166 Wolheim, Richard. "Eliot and F. H. Bradley: An Account," Eliot in Perspective. Graham Martin, ed. New York: Humanities, 1970, pp. 169-193.

2167 __________. "Eliot, Bradley, and Immediate Experience," NS&N, 67 (March 13, 1964), 401-402.

2168 Yamada, Yoichi. "T. S. Eliot no Ninshiki to Keiken no Shuppan," Oberon, 29 (1968), 2-12.

THE METAPHYSICAL POETS (1921)

2169 Crewe, J. V. "T. S. Eliot: A Metaphysical Problem," ESA, 15, #2 (September, 1972), 105-114.

2170 Duncan, Joseph Ellis. "Eliot and the Twentieth Century Revival," The Revival of Metaphysical Poetry. Minneapolis:

Minnesota U. P., 1959, pp. 143-164. "... For Eliot's numerous disciples these essays [The Metaphysical Poets] became a new critical gospel, often not clearly understood but seldom doubted."

2171 Kuna, F. M. "T. S. Eliot's Dissociation of Sensibility and the Critics of Metaphysical Poetry," EIC, 13 (1963), 241-252.

2172 Lees, F. N. "The Dissociation of Sensibility: Arthur Hallam and T. S. Eliot," N&Q, 14, #8 (August, 1967), 308-309. Comparison of Arthur Hallam's statement on the metaphysical poets with Eliot's views as expressed in The Metaphysical Poets.

2173 Orgel, Stephen. "Affecting the Metaphysics," Mon/HES, #2 (1971), 225-245.

2174 Ransom, John Crowe. "Eliot and the Metaphysicals," Accent, 1 (Spring, 1941), 148-156; partially repr., in New Criticism. Norfolk, Conn.: 1941.

2175 __________. "T. S. Eliot: The Historical Critic," New Criticism. Norfolk, Conn.: New Directions, 1941, pp. 135-158, 192-208.

2176 Spender, Stephen. T. S. Eliot. Frank Kermode, ed. New York: Viking, 1976, p. 74.

2177 Thale, Mary. "T. S. Eliot and Mrs. Browning on the Metaphysical Poets," CLAJ, 11 (March, 1968), 255-258.

2178 Thompson, Eric. T. S. Eliot: The Metaphysical Perspective. Carbondale: Southern Illinois U. P., 1965, p. 51.

2179 Unger, Leonard. "T. S. Eliot," Donne's Poetry and Modern Criticism. New York: Russell & Russell, 1962, pp. 6-7.

2180 Van Doren, Mark. "Seventeenth-Century Poetry and Twentieth-Century Critics," Studies in Metaphysical Poetry. New York: Columbia U. P., 1939, 1964, pp. 21-29.

NOTES TOWARD THE DEFINITION OF CULTURE (1948)

2181 Acton, H. B. "Religion, Culture, and Class," Ethics, 60 (January, 1950), 120-130.

2182 Anon. "Back to the Waste Land," Time, 53 (March 21, 1949), 104ff.

2183 Anon. "Leisure and Culture," TLS, #2445 (December 11, 1948), 697.

2184 Anon. "A Vision of Humanity," TLS, #2445 (December 11, 1948), 691.

2185 Astre, Georges-Albert. "T. S. Eliot et la nostalgie de la 'culture,'" Critique, 5 (September, 1949), 774-811.

2186 Auden, W. H. "Port and Nuts with the Eliots," NY, 25 (April 23, 1949), 92-97.

2187 Austin, Allen. T. S. Eliot: The Literary and Social Criticism. Bloomington: Indiana U. P., 1971, passim.

2188 Bantock, G. H. "Mr. Eliot and Education," Scrutiny, 16, #1 (March, 1949), 64-70.

2189 Barrett, William. "Aristocracy and/or Christianity," KR, 11 (Summer, 1949), 489-496.

2190 Blackmur, R. P. "Mr. Eliot and Notions of Culture: A Discussion," PartisanR, 11, #3 (Summer, 1944), 302-312.

2191 ________. "T. S. Eliot on Culture," Nation, 168 (April 23, 1949), 475-476.

2192 Brooks, Cleanth. "The Crisis in Culture," HAB, 52, #18 (1950), 768-772.

2193 Bush, Douglas. "No Small Program," VQR, 25 (Spring, 1949), 287-290.

2194 Catlin, George. "T. S. Eliot and the Moral Issue," SatR, 32 (July 2, 1949), 7-8, 36-38.

2195 Chace, William M. "T. S. Eliot: The Plea Against Consciousness," Mosaic, 5, #1 (Fall, 1971), 133-143.

2196 Cormican, L. A. "Mr. Eliot and Social Biology," Scrutiny (England), 17 (Spring, 1950), 2-13.

2197 Czamanske, Palmer, and Karl Hertz. "The Beginning of T. S. Eliot's Theory of Culture," Cresset, 15, #9 (July, 1952), 9-21.

2198 Davis, Robert Gorham. "Culture, Religion, and Mr. Eliot," PartisanR, 16 (July, 1949), 750-753.

2199 Edman, Irwin. "T. S. Eliot's Sociology," NYTBR (March 6, 1949), 3, 22.

2200 Falck, Colin. "Hurry Up Please! It's Time," Rev, #4 (November, 1962), 59-64.

2201 Forster, E. M. "The Three T. S. Eliots," List, 41 (January 20, 1949), 111.

2202 Greenberg, Clement. "Mr. Eliot and Notions of Culture," PartisanR, 11, # 3 (Summer, 1944), 305-307.

2203 Hook, Sidney. "The Dilemma of T. S. Eliot," Nation, 160, # 3 (January 20, 1945), 69-71.

2204 Howarth, Herbert. Notes on Some Figures Behind T. S. Eliot. Boston: Houghton Mifflin, 1964, p. 270.

2205 Kenner, Hugh. "Notes Towards the Definition of Culture," HudR, 2, # 2 (Summer, 1949), 289-294.

2206 Kirk, Russell. "Culture and Class," Eliot and His Age. New York: Random House, 1971, pp. 321ff.

2207 Lerner, Max. "Toward a Definition of T. S. Eliot," NR, 120 (May 9, 1949), 22-23.

2208 Marks, Emerson R. "T. S. Eliot and the Ghost of S. T. C." SR, 72 (Spring, 1964), 262-280.

2209 Orwell, George. "Culture and Classes," Obs (London), (November 28, 1948), 4.

2210 Phillips, William. "Mr. Eliot and Notions of Culture: A Discussion," PartisanR, 11, # 3 (Summer, 1944), 307-309.

2211 Pocock, D. F. "Symposium on Mr. Eliot's 'Notes,'" Scrutiny, 17, # 3 (December, 1950), 273-276.

2212 Poore, Charles. "Books of the Times," NYT (March 3, 1949), 23.

2213 Rago, Henry. "T. S. Eliot on Culture," Cw, 50, # 5 (May 13, 1949), 122-125.

2214 Read, Herbert. "Mr. Eliot's New Book," HudR, 2, # 2 (Summer, 1949), 285-289.

2215 Rees, Goronwy. "Modest Proposal," Spectator, 181, # 6282 (November 19, 1948), 660.

2216 Rees, Richard. "T. S. Eliot on Culture and Progress," JCHist, 2, # 2 (1967), 103-112; adapted from HistA, 16, # 1 (March, 1970), 65.

2217 Richards, I. A. "Mr. Eliot and Notions of Culture: A Discussion," PartisanR, 11 (Summer, 1944), 310-312.

2218 Sisson, C. H. "What Is Culture?" NewEW, 34, # 8 (December, 1948), 91-92.

2219 Spender, Stephen. T. S. Eliot. Frank Kermode, ed. New York: Viking, 1976, pp. 242-243, passim.

2220 Verma, Rajendra. Royalist in Politics: T. S. Eliot and Political Philosophy. London: Asia Pub. House, 1968, pp. 64-67, passim.

2221 Weaver, Richard M. "Culture and Construction," SR, 57 (Autumn, 1949), 714-718.

2222 Williams, Raymond. "Second Thoughts: T. S. Eliot on Culture," EIC, 6 (July, 1956), 302-318.

2223 __________. "T. S. Eliot," Culture and Society, 1780-1950. New York: Columbia U. P., 1958, pp. 230-243.

ON POETRY AND POETS (1957)

2224 Anon. "Poet's Shoptalk," Time, 70, #12 (September 16, 1957), 125-126.

2225 Cunningham, J. V. "T. S. Eliot on Poetry and Poets," VQR, 34, #1 (Winter, 1958), 126-129.

2226 Farmer, A. J. "On Poetry and Poets," EA, 12 (1959), 77-78.

2227 Good, Thomas. "T. S. Eliot et la tradition anglaise," CdS, #352 (October-November, 1959), 427-443.

2228 Gregory, Horace. "The Authority of T. S. Eliot," Cw, 67, #6 (November 8, 1957), 148-150.

2229 Kenner, Hugh. "On Poetry and Poets," Poetry, 92, #2 (May, 1958), 121-126.

2230 Kermode, Frank. "T. S. Eliot on Poetry," ILA, 1 (1958), 131-134.

2231 Leavis, F. R. "T. S. Eliot's Status as Critic: A Revaluation," Commentary, 26 (November, 1958), 399-410.

2232 Lucy, Seán. "Critical Work and Influence," T. S. Eliot and the Idea of Tradition. New York: Barnes & Noble, 1960, p. 60f.

2233 Pritchett, V. S. "On Poetry and Poets," NYTB (September, 1957), 4.

2234 Raditsa, Leo F. "The View from Parnassus," Griffin, 6 (October, 1957), 11-17.

2235 Robson, W. W. "Eliot's Later Criticism," Rev, 1, #4 (November, 1962), 51-57.

2236 Rodman, Selden. "The Moral Value of Verse," SatR, 40 (November 9, 1957), 14.

2237 Schneider, Elisabeth. T. S. Eliot: The Pattern in the Carpet. Berkeley, Los Angeles: California U. P., 1975, passim.

2238 Smith, Carol H. T. S. Eliot's Dramatic Theory and Practice. Princeton: Princeton U. P., 1963, pp. 27, 28.

2239 Sutherland, James R. Review: "On Poetry and Poets," RES, 10, #38 (May, 1959), 211-213.

2240 Wain, John. "A Walk in the Sacred Wood," LonMag, 5 (January, 1958), 45-53.

THE SACRED WOOD (1920)

2241 Aiken, Conrad. "The Scientific Critic," Freeman, 2, #51 (March 2, 1921), 593-594.

2242 Aldington, Richard. "A Critic of Poetry," Poetry, 17 (March, 1921), 345-348.

2243 Anon. "Comment," Dial, 73 (December, 1922), 685-687.

2244 Anon. "The Sacred Wood," NS&N, 16 (March 26, 1921), 733-734.

2245 Anon. "A Wooden Rod," Obs, (November 28, 1920).

2246 Austin, Allen. T. S. Eliot: The Literary and Social Criticism. Bloomington: Indiana U. P., 1971, pp. 41-42, 107-108, passim.

2247 Barfoot, Gabriele. "Dante in T. S. Eliot's Criticism," EM, 23 (1972), 231-246. In The Sacred Wood Eliot showed "some insights" into Dante.

2248 Bergonzi, Bernard. "The Sacred Wood after Fifty Years," CritS, 4 (1970), 164-171.

2249 ______. T. S. Eliot. New York: Macmillan, 1967, passim.

2249a Birrell, Augustine. "The Reader," Bookman (English), 61 (November, 1921), 80.

2250 Blum, Walter C. "Journalist Critics," Dial, 76 (June, 1924), 557-558.

2251 Bollier, Ernest Philip. "T. S. Eliot and The Sacred Wood," ColQ, 8 (Spring, 1960), 308-317. Finds that the "greatness" of The Sacred Wood "lies less in ... particular judgments than in what Eliot had to say in general about the nature of poetry and criticism."

2252 Bradbrook, M. C. "The Critic and Man of Letters," T. S. Eliot. London: Longmans, Green & Co., 1965, p. 49, passim.

2253 Brown, Wallace C. "Mr. Eliot Without the Nightingales," UKCR, 14, #1 (Autumn, 1947), 31-38.

2254 E. S. "Literary History, Criticism," LonMerc, 3 (February, 1921), 447-450.

2255 Kirk, Russell. Eliot and His Age. New York: Random House, 1971, pp. 62-63.

2256 L. W. "Back to Aristotle," Athenaeum, #4729 (December 17, 1920), 834-835.

2257 Leavis, F. R. "Approaches to T. S. Eliot," Scrutiny, 15, #1 (December, 1947), 56-67.

2258 ______. "T. S. Eliot: A Reply to the Condescending," CamR, 50 (February 8, 1929), 254-256.

2259 LeMaster, J. R. "Stevens and Eliot on the Mind of the Poet," ForumH, 10, #3 (Winter, 1972), 27-30.

2260 Lovell, Ernest J., Jr. "The Heretic in the Sacred Wood; or, the Naked Man, the Tired Man, and the Romantic Aristocrat: William Blake, T. S. Eliot, and George Wyndham," Romantic and Victorian: Studies in Memory of William H. Marshall. W. P. Elledge and R. L. Hoffman, eds. Rutherford, N. J.: Fairleigh Dickinson U. P., 1971, pp. 75-94.

2261 Lucy, Seán. T. S. Eliot and the Idea of Tradition. New York: Barnes & Noble, 1960, p. 65, passim.

2262 Lynd, Robert. "Buried Alive," Nation (English), 18 (December 4, 1920), 359-360.

2263 Margolis, John D. T. S. Eliot's Intellectual Development, 1922-1939. Chicago: Chicago U. P., 1973, pp. 21-30, 103-104, passim.

2264 Martin, Graham, ed. Eliot in Perspective: A Symposium. London: Macmillan, 1970, passim.

2265 Meckier, Jerome. "T. S. Eliot in 1920: The Quatrain Poems and The Sacred Wood," FMLS, 5 (October, 1969), 350-376.

2266 Moore, Marianne. "The Sacred Wood," Dial, 70, #3 (March, 1921), 336-339.

2267 Murry, John Middleton. "The Sacred Wood," NR, 26, #332 (April 13, 1921), 194-195.

2268 Peterson, Sven. "Mr. Eliot in The Sacred Wood," Greyfriar, 8 (1965), 33-43.

2269 Preston, Keith. "Respecting the Handy Man," Chicago Daily News (February 9, 1921), 12.

2270 Seldes, Gilbert. "T. S. Eliot," Nation, 115 (December 6, 1922), 614-616.

2271 Thompson, Eric. T. S. Eliot: The Metaphysical Perspective. Carbondale: Southern Ill. U. P., 1965, p. 57.

2272 Van Doren, Mark. "England's Critical Compass," Nation, 112 (May 4, 1921), 669.

2273 Wain, John. "A Walk in the Sacred Wood," LonMerc, 5 (January, 1958), 45-53.

2274 W[oolf], L. "Back to Aristotle," Athenaeum, #4729 (December, 1920), 834.

SELECTED ESSAYS, 1917-1932

2275 Anon. "Mr. T. S. Eliot," TLS, #1602 (October 13, 1932), 728.

2276 Bantock, G. H. T. S. Eliot and Education. New York: Random House, 1969, pp. 38-39, 77-78.

2277 Bergonzi, Bernard. T. S. Eliot. New York: Macmillan, 1972, passim.

2278 Blackmur, R. P. "T. S. Eliot in Prose," Poetry, 42, #1 (April, 1933), 44-49.

2279 Breit, Harvey. "Repeat Performances," NYTBR (November 5, 1950), 36.

2280 Burke, Sister Margaret J., S. S. I. Dryden and Eliot: A Study in Literary Criticism. Diss. Niagara, 1945.

2281 Chew, Samuel C. "Essays in Criticism, 1917-1932," YR, 22, #2 (December, 1932), 386-390.

2282 Dobree, Bonamy. "A Major Critic," List, 8 (October 5, 1932), Sup, xi.

2283 Frank, Waldo. "The Universe of T. S. Eliot," NR, 72, #934 (October, 1932), 294-295.

2284 ________. "The Universe of T. S. Eliot," In the American Jungle. New York: Farrar & Rinehart, 1937.

2285 Hazlitt, Henry. "The Mind of T. S. Eliot," Nation, 135, #3509 (October 5, 1932), 312-313.

2286 Hillyer, Robert. "Selected Essays by T. S. Eliot," NEQ, 6 (June, 1933), 402-404.

2287 Hošek, Chaviva and Viiu Menning. An Index to References in T. S. Eliot's "Selected Essays." Montreal. (Avail. from C. Hosek, 6225 Wilderton, Apt. 101, Montreal 26, Quebec.) 196[8].

2288 Jack, Peter Monroe. "The Cream of T. S. Eliot's Literary Criticism," NYTBR (January 29, 1933), 2.

2289 Lucy, Seán. T. S. Eliot and the Idea of Tradition. New York: Barnes & Noble, 1960, p. 60, passim.

2290 Martin, Graham, ed. Eliot in Perspective. London: Macmillan, 1970, passim.

2291 More, Paul Elmer. "The Cleft Eliot: Selected Essays by T. S. Eliot," SatR, 9, #17 (November 12, 1932), 233, 235.

2292 Parsons, I. M. "Miss West, Mr. Eliot, and Mr. Parsons," Spectator, 149, #5443 (October 22, 1932), 534.

2293 ________. "Mr. Eliot's Authority," Spectator, 149, #5441 (October 8, 1932), 450-452.

2294 Pound, Ezra. "Praefatio aut tumulus cimicium," Active Anthology. London: Faber & Faber, 1933, pp. 9-27.

2295 Quennell, Peter. "T. S. Eliot the Critic," NS&N, 4, n. s. (October 1, 1932), 377-378.

2296 Redman, Ben Ray. "New Editions," SatR, 34 (February 17, 1951), 27.

2297 Rickword, Edgell. "Selected Essays by T. S. Eliot," Scrutiny, 1, #4 (March, 1933), 390-393; repr., in The

Importance of Scrutiny. Eric Bentley, ed. New York: Geo. W. Stewart, 1964, pp. 273-376.

2298 Roberts, Michael. Review: Selected Essays, 1917-1932. Adelphi, 5, n. s. (November, 1932), 141-144.

2299 Sackville-West, V. "Books of the Week," List, 8 (September 28, 1932), 461.

2300 Schappes, Morris U. "T. S. Eliot Moves Right," ModM, 7 (August, 1933), 403-408.

2301 Schneider, Elisabeth. T. S. Eliot: The Pattern in the Carpet. Berkeley: California U. P., 1975, passim.

2302 Shuster, George N. "Mr. Eliot Returns," Cw, 16 (October 19, 1932), 581-583.

2303 Spender, Stephen. T. S. Eliot. Frank Kermode, ed. New York: Viking, 1976, pp. 70-88, 150-151, passim.

2304 Thompson, Eric. T. S. Eliot: The Metaphysical Perspective. Carbondale: Southern Ill. U. P., 1965, p. 54.

2305 Watson, C. B. "T. S. Eliot and the Interpretation of Shakespearian Tragedy in Our Time," EA, 17, #4 (October-December, 1964), 502-521.

2306 West, Rebecca. "Miss West, Mr. Eliot, and Mr. Persons," Spectator, 149, #5442 (October 15, 1932), 480. Attacks Eliot's criticism as dull.

THREE VOICES OF POETRY (1953)

2307 "Three-Stringed Lyre," TLS (November 27, 1953).

2308 Bergonzi, Bernard. T. S. Eliot. New York: Macmillan, 1972, pp. 92-93, passim.

2309 Donoghue, Denis. The Third Voice: Modern British and American Verse Drama. Princeton, New Jersey: Princeton U. P., 1959, passim.

2310 Eliot, T. S. "The Three Voices of Poetry," Atl, 193 (April, 1954), 38-44. A slightly condensed version of the essay.

2311 Poore, Charles. "Books of the Times," NYT (April 8, 1954), 25. A summary of the essay.

2312 "Three Voices of Poetry," (Review) List, 51 (1954), 107.

2313 Weedon, William S. "Mr. Eliot's Voices," VQR, 20 (Autumn, 1954), 610-613.

TO CRITICIZE THE CRITIC AND OTHER WRITINGS (1965)

2314 Anon. "Critic Criticized," TLS (December 16, 1965), 1177.

2315 Bantock, G. H. T. S. Eliot and Education. New York: Random House, 1969, pp. 5, 7, 9.

2316 Bergonzi, Bernard. T. S. Eliot. New York: Macmillan, 1972, passim.

2317 Frank, Joseph. "To Criticize the Critic and Other Writings," Commentary, 42 (September, 1966), 87-91.

2318 Furbank, P. N. "To Criticize the Critic," List, 75 (1966), 142.

2319 Hoffman, Frederick J. "T. S. Eliot: The Poet as Critic," Nation, 203, #10 (October 3, 1966), 324-325.

2320 Kazin, Alfred. "To Criticize the Critic," Book Week (February 13, 1966), 1, 20.

2321 Kenner, Hugh. "To Criticize the Critic," NatlR, 18, (May 3, 1966), 420-421.

2322 Kirk, Russell. Eliot and His Age. New York: Random House, 1971, pp. 395ff.

2323 Langbaum, Robert. "To Criticize the Critic and Other Writings": Review, PartisanR, 33, #2 (Spring, 1966), 300-302.

2324 Litz, A. Walton. "To Criticize the Critic," Shenandoah, 17 (Spring, 1966), 100-104.

2325 Martin, Graham, ed. Eliot in Perspective. London: Macmillan, 1970, p. 237.

2326 Ong, Walter J. "Only Through Time," Poetry, 108, #4 (July, 1966), 265-268.

2327 Rahv, Philip. "To Criticize the Critic and Other Writings," NYRB (March 3, 1966), 7-9.

2328 Ray, Paul G. "To Criticize the Critic," JA, 24 (1966), 606-607.

2329 Ricks, Christopher. "To Criticize the Critic," NSt, (November 26, 1965), 832-834.

2330 Schneider, Elisabeth. T. S. Eliot: The Pattern in the Carpet. Berkeley: California U. P., 1975, passim.

2331 Seymour-Smith, Martin. "Out into the Open," Spectator, 215 (November 12, 1965), 621.

2332 Spender, Stephen. T. S. Eliot. Frank Kermode, ed. New York: Viking, 1975, pp. 69-70, 145, 152-153.

2333 ______. "To Criticize the Critic and Other Writings," NYTBR, (January 16, 1966), 6.

2334 Tate, Allen, ed. "American Literature and the American Language," SR, 74, #1, (Special T. S. Eliot issue), (January-March, 1966), 1-20; repr., from To Criticize the Critic (1965) by T. S. Eliot.

2335 Watson, George. "To Criticize the Critic and Other Writings," RES, 18 (February, 1967), 96-99.

2336 Wimsatt, W. K. "To Criticize the Critic and Other Writings," MassR, 7 (1966), 584-590.

TRADITION AND THE INDIVIDUAL TALENT (1920)

2337 Anon. "Poetry and Criticism," TLS, #985 (December 2, 1920), 795.

2338 Anon. "The Writer's Personality," Everyman, 8 (September 15, 1932), 240.

2339 Austin, Allen. T. S. Eliot: The Literary and Social Criticism. Bloomington: Indiana U. P., 1971, pp. 17-18, passim.

2340 Bantock, G. H. T. S. Eliot and Education. New York: Random House, 1969, pp. 38-40, 78-79, 80.

2341 Bergonzi, Bernard. T. S. Eliot. New York: Macmillan, 1972, pp. 61-67, passim.

2342 Blackmur, R. P. "In the Hope of Straightening Things Out," KR, 13 (Spring, 1951-52), 303-314.

2343 Bollier, E. P. "Mr. Eliot's 'Tradition and the Individual Talent' Reconsidered," UCSLL, No. 6 (January, 1957), 103-118.

2344 Ellis, P. G. "The Development of T. S. Eliot's Historical Sense," RES, 23, #91 (August, 1972), 291-301.

2345 Hentz, Ann Louis. "Language in Hopkins' Carrion Comfort," VP, 9, #3 (Autumn, 1971), 343-347. Provides a gloss on Eliot's Tradition and the Individual Talent.

2346 Hopwood, V. G. "Acid Without Hydrogen," N&Q, 14, #1 (January, 1967), 26-27.

2347 Hyman, Stanley Edgar. "Poetry and Criticism: T. S. Eliot," AmSch, 30 (Winter, 1961), 43-55.

2348 Kirk, Russell. Eliot and His Age. New York: Random House, 1971, pp. 74-75, passim.

2349 Margolis, John D. "Tradition and the Individual Talent," T. S. Eliot's Intellectual Development, 1922-1939. Chicago: U. P., 1972, pp. 25-26, passim.

2350 Martin, Graham, ed. Eliot in Perspective. London: Macmillan, 1970, pp. 197-199, passim.

2351 Montgomery, Marion. "Eliot, Wordsworth, and the Problem of Personal Emotion in the Poet," SHR, 2, #2 (Spring, 1968), 185-197.

2351a Pinkerton, Jan. "A Source for Tradition and the Individual Talent," TSER, 2, #2 (Fall, 1975), 11. Influence of Stuart P. Sherman.

2352 Ransom, John Crowe. "The Inorganic Muses," KR, 5 (1943), n2.

2353 __________. The New Criticism. Norfolk, Conn.: New Directions (1941), 136.

2354 Scarfe, Francis. "Notes on the Individual Talent," STwenC, #3 (Spring, 1969), 1-14.

2355 Schneider, Elisabeth. T. S. Eliot: The Pattern in the Carpet. Berkeley: California U. P., 1975, pp. 2-4, 56-57, passim.

2356 Vivas, Eliseo. "The Objective Correlative of T. S. Eliot," AmBk, 1, #1 (Winter, 1944), 7-18; repr., in Critiques and Essays in Criticism: 1920-1948. Robert W. Stallman, ed. New York: Ronald, 1949, pp. 389-400.

THE USE OF POETRY AND THE USE OF CRITICISM (1933)

2357 Aiken, Conrad. "The Use of Poetry," YR, 23 (March, 1934), 643-646.

2358 Anon. "Poetry and Criticism," Independent, 1 (November 25, 1933), 21-22.

2359 Anon. "The Use of Poetry," TLS, #1663 (December 14, 1933), 892.

2360 Austin, Allen. T. S. Eliot: The Literary and Social Criticism. Bloomington: Indiana U. P., 1971, pp. 17-18, passim.

2361 Belgion, Montgomery. "The Use of Poetry," DubR, 194, #388 (January, 1934), 151-153.

2362 Bennett, Joan. "The Use of Poetry and the Use of Criticism," CamR, 55 (November 24, 1933), 132-133.

2363 Bergonzi, Bernard. T. S. Eliot. New York: Macmillan, 1967, pp. 120-121, passim.

2364 Brooks, Cleanth. "Eliot's Harvard Lectures," SWR, 19, Supp. 1-2, (January, 1934), 1-2.

2365 Davies, Hugh Sykes. "Criticism and Controversy," List, (November 29, 1933).

2366 Dodds, A. E. "The Use of Poetry and the Use of Criticism," MLN, 51 (January, 1936), 49-52.

2367 Fergusson, Francis. "Eliot's Norton Lectures," H&H, 7, #2 (January, March, 1934), 356-358. Cf., Waldo Frank, NR, 72 (Oct. 26, 1932), 294-295.

2368 G. R. B. R. "T. S. Eliot Discourses on the Use and Function of Poetry," Boston Evening Trans. (December 9, 1933), Bk. Sec, 1.

2369 Gohdes, Clarence. "Poetry and Criticism," SAQ, 33 (April, 1934), 205-207.

2370 Gregory, Horace. "The Man of Feeling," NR, 79, #1015 (May 16, 1934), 23-24.

2371 Harding, D. W. "Mr. Eliot at Harvard," Scrutiny, 2, #3 (December, 1933), 289-292.

2372 Hawkins, Desmond. "Mr. Eliot's Criticism," Week-End Rev, 8 (December 9, 1933), 636. Calls Eliot's criticism "the finest ... of the century."

2373 Jack, Peter Monroe. "Mr. Eliot's New Essays in the Field of Poetry," NYTBR (December 3, 1933), 2.

2374 Kirk, Russell. Eliot and His Age. New York: Random House, 1971, pp. 199-207.

2375 Krutch, Joseph Wood. "A Poem Is a Poem," Nation, 137, #3571 (December 13, 1933), 679-680.

2376 Lattimore, Richmond. "The Use of Poetry and the Use of Criticism," JEGP, 33 (July, 1934), 482-484.

2377 Leavis, F. R. "Approaches to T. S. Eliot," Scrutiny, 15, #1 (December, 1947), 57-67.

2378 Lucy, Seán. T. S. Eliot and the Idea of Tradition. New York: Barnes & Noble, 1960, pp. 99-101, passim.

2379 Lunn, Hugh Kingsmill. "Goethe, Wordsworth, and Mr. Eliot," EngRev, 57, #12 (December, 1933), 667-670.

2380 Lynd, Robert. "The Explorations of Mr. Eliot," News Chronicle (London), (December 8, 1933), 4.

2381 Margolis, John D. T. S. Eliot's Intellectual Development, 1922-1939. Chicago: Chicago U. P., 1973, pp. 171, 184.

2382 Martin, Graham, ed. Eliot in Perspective. London: Macmillan, 1970, pp. 201-202, 208-209, passim.

2383 Muir, Edwin. "The Use of Poetry," Spectator, 151, #5499 (November 17, 1933), 703.

2384 Pound, Ezra. "What Price the Muses Now?" NewEW, 5, #6 (May, 1934), 130-133.

2385 Ransom, John Crowe. "T. S. Eliot on Criticism," SatR 10, #36 (March, 1934), 574.

2386 Reed, Henry. "'If and Perhaps and But' ... on the Prose Writings of T. S. Eliot," List, 49 (June 18, 1953), 1017-1018.

2387 Salmon, Christopher. "Critics and Criticism, Nineteenth Century and After," 115, #685 (March, 1934), 359-369.

2388 Sampson, Ashley. "In Pursuit of Psyche," SatR, 157 (February 17, 1934), 190.

2389 Schneider, Elisabeth. T. S. Eliot: The Pattern in the Carpet. Berkeley: California U. P., 1975, passim.

2390 Smith, Grover, Jr. T. S. Eliot's Poetry and Plays. Chicago: Chicago U. P., 1956, passim.

2391 Spender, Stephen. "The Use of Poetry and the Use of Criticism," NSt, 6 (November 18, 1933), 637-638.

2392 Van Doren, Mark. "Shall We Be Saved by Poetry?" NYHTB (December 17, 1933), 5.

2393 Warren, Austin. "Eliot's Literary Criticism," SR, 74, #1 Special T. S. Eliot Issue, (Winter, 1966), 272-292.

2394 Wilson, James Southall. "The Faculty of Poets," VQR, 10 (July, 1934), 477-478.

2395 Zabel, M. D. "The Use of the Poet," Poetry, 44 (April, 1934), 32-37.

INTERVIEWS
(and Conversations and Meetings)

2396 Alt, Helmut. "Thomas Stearns Eliot in Deutschland: Interview mit dem englischen Dichter-Philosophen," Neue Zeitung (October 31, 1949).

2397 Bordwell, Harold. "Remembering Mr. Eliot," ChiR, 17 (1964), 33-36. Account of an interview with Eliot five years previously.

2398 Breit, Harvey. "An Interview with T. S. Eliot," NYTBR (November 11, 1948), 3.

2399 Desternes, Jean. "T. S. Eliot: Interview par Jean Desternes Combat de la Résistance à la Revolution, 7° année 1, 182 (vendredi, 23 avril, 1948).

2400 Fasel, Ida. "A 'Conversation' Between Faulkner and Eliot," MissQ, 20 (Fall, 1967), 195-206.

2401 Fleisher, Frederick, and Boel Fleisher. "En eftermiddag med T. S. Eliot," Göteborgs Handels-och Sjöfarts-Tidning, 130, # 3 (October 18, 1961). An interview with T. S. Eliot in London.

2402 Gardner, Helen. "The 'Aged Eagle' Spreads His Wings. A 70th-Birthday Talk with T. S. Eliot," Sun Times (September 21, 1958), 8.

2403 Greenwell, Tom, ed. "The Function of Art," Books and Bookmen, 8 (January, 1963), 44-46. An interview.

2404 Hailey, Foster. "An Interview with T. S. Eliot," NYT, (April 16, 1950), Sec. 2, p. 1, col. 5.

2405 Hall, Donald. "The Art of Poetry: T. S. Eliot," ParisR, # 21 (Winter, 1959), 47-70. An interview.

2406 Hamilton, Ian. "[Eliot's] Reflections on The Cocktail Party," WorldRev, n. s. # 9 (November, 1949), 19-22.

2407 Hewes, Henry. "Eliot on Eliot: Interview," SatR, 41 (September 13, 1958), 32.

2408 __________. "T. S. Eliot at Seventy," SatR, 41 (September 13, 1958), 30-32.

2409 __________. "T. S. Eliot: Confidential Playwright," SatR, 36 (August, 1953), 26-28.

2410 Hodin, J. P. "T. S. Eliot on the Condition of Man Today: An Interview with T. S. Eliot," Horizon, 12, #68 (August, 1945), 82-89.

2411 Koch, Werner. "Ein Gespräch mit T. S. Eliot," Der Monat, 16 Heft, 185 (1964), 84-87.

2412 Lehmann, John. "Conversazioni con T. S. Eliot," Veltro, 9 (1965), 283-288.

2413 __________. "T. S. Eliot Talks About Himself and the Drive to Create," NYTBR, 58, #48 (November 29, 1953), 5, 44.

2414 MacGregor-Hastie, Roy. "Waste Land in Russell Square," Trace, #32 (June-July, 1959), 1-5. An interview with Eliot on Contemporary poetry.

2415 Mackworth, Cecily. "Visite à T. S. Eliot," Paru, #44 (July, 1948), 11-13.

2416 "Mr. Eliot and Notes on Culture: A Discussion," PartisanR, 11 (1944), 302-312.

2417 Paul, Leslie. "A Conversation with T. S. Eliot," KR, 27 (Winter, 1965), 11-21.

2418 __________. "A Conversation with T. S. Eliot in 1958," List, 82 (1969), 334-336.

2419 Pellegrini, Alessandro. "A London Conversation with T. S. Eliot," SR, 57, #2 (June, 1949), 287-292.

2420 Pfeffer, Franz. "Gespräch mit T. S. Eliot," Rheinischer Merkur, 4, #46 (1949), 7.

2421 Plimpton, George, ed. "T. S. Eliot," Writers at Work: The Paris Review Interviews. 2nd Series. New York: Viking, 1963, pp. 91-110.

2422 Pons, Christian. "Conférences: Eliot et Sartre," CdS, (Aout-sept-oct, 1965).

2423 Reeves, George M. "Mr. Eliot and Thomas Wolfe," SAB, 32, #4 (November, 1967), 7-8.

2424 Russell, Francis. "Some Non-encounters with Mr. Eliot," Horizon, 7 (Autumn, 1965), 37-41.

2425 Seferis, George. (Edmund and Mary Keeley, trs.) "T. S. E. (Pages from a Diary)," QRL, Nos. 1/2, (1967).

2426 Shahani, Ranjee. "T. S. Eliot: Answers and Questions," JO'LW, 58, #1369 (August, 1949), 497-498.

2427 "T. S. Eliot ... An Interview," Grantite Rev, 24, #3 (1962), 16-20.

2428 "T. S. Eliot Talks About His Poetry [With Introductory Note by Lionel Trilling]," Columbia Univ Forum, 2 (Fall, 1958), 11-14.

LECTURES

2429 Anon. "Poetry and Criticism: Mr. Eliot's Harvard Lectures," Scotsman (November 23, 1933), 2. A summary of the lectures.

2430 Brooks, Cleanth. "Eliot's Harvard Lectures," SWR, 19 (January, 1934), Supp. 1-2.

2431 Eden, Anthony. "Foreword [to] 'The Literature of Politics,'" TLS (September 20, 1955), 573.

2432 Fausset, Hugh I'Anson. "T. S. Eliot's Harvard Lectures on Poetry," Yorkshire Post (November 22, 1933), 6.

2433 Fergusson, Francis. "Eliot's Norton Lectures," H&H, 7, #2 (March, 1934), 356-358.

2434 "The Influence of Landscape upon the Poet," Daedalus, 89 (Spring, 1960), 420-428. Eliot's address upon acceptance of the Emerson-Thoreau medal from American Academy of Arts and Sciences, October 21, 1959.

2435 "Rudyard Kipling," MdF, 335, #1145 (janvier, 1959), 5-15.

2436 Sansom, Clive. "The Poetry of T. S. Eliot: Text of a lecture to the Speech Fellowship (May 18, 1946). London: Speech Fellowship, 1947.

2437 Schuchard, Ronald. "T. S. Eliot as an Extension Lecturer, 1916-1919, Part I," RES, 25 (May, 1974), 163-172.

2438 ___________. "T. S. Eliot as an Extension Lecturer, 1916-1919, Part II," RES, 25 (August, 1974), 292-304.

2439 Shapiro, Karl. "The Three Hockey Games of T. S. Eliot," AR, 22 #3 (Fall, 1962), 284-286. Cf., Richard Foster. "Frankly, I Like Criticism," AR, 22 (1962), 273-283. Foster reported that Eliot's Minneapolis lecture in 1956 drew a crowd equal in size to three hockey games.

2440 "Speech to the BBC Governors," LonM, 4 (September, 1957), 54-56.

LETTERS

2441 Chatterji, Nimai. "A Letter from Eliot," NSt (March 5, 1965), 361.

2442 "A Letter from T. S. Eliot," Poetry, 76 (May, 1950), 88.

2443 "A Letter to the Editors," PartisanR, 9 (March, 1942), 117-118.

2444 Levy, William T., and Victor Scherle. Affectionately, T. S. Eliot: The Story of a Friendship, 1947-1965. Philadelphia: Lippincott, 1968. Based on many letters.

2445 Marder, Louis. "Shakespeare's Bones, Birthplace and Burial," Shakespeare Newsletter, 12, #4 (September, 1962), 28-29. Eliot among those protesting exhumation of Shakespeare.

2446 Pound, Ezra. "An Exchange of Letters on The Waste Land," Nine, 4 (Summer, 1950), 176-179.

2447 Rose, W. K. "Wyndham Lewis in His Letters," Ramparts, 2, #1 (May, 1963), 85-89. Correspondence with Eliot, among others.

2448 Wagner, Robert D. "Correspondence: Lawrence and Eliot," Scrutiny, 18, #2 (Autumn, 1951), 136-143.

2449 Weber, Alfred. "Ein Briefwechsel mit T. S. Eliot," JA, 16 (1971), 204-212. Seven letters from Eliot to Weber (1949 to 1958) are quoted.

GENERAL CRITICISM

2450 Abel, Richard O. "The Relationship Between the Poetry of T. S. Eliot and Saint-John Perse," DAI, 31 (Southern Calif.: 1971), 6041A.

2450a ________. "Saint-John Perse Encounters T. S. Eliot," RLC, 49 (1975), 423-437.

2451 Adams, J. Donald. "Speaking of Books," NYTBR, 61 (December 16, 1956), 3.

2452 Adams, Robert M. "Donne and Eliot: Metaphysicals," KR, 16 (Spring, 1954), 278-291.

2453 Adell, Alberto. "Releyendo a Eliot," Insula, 24 (December, 1969), 12.

2454 ________. "Thomas Stearns Eliot," Insula, #220 (March, 1965), 13. Eliot's influence on Spanish poets resident in England.

2455 Aguilar, A. Eliot: El Hombre no el viejo gato. Santiago, 1962.

2456 Aiken, Conrad. "An Anatomy of Melancholy," SR, 74 (Winter, 1966), 188-196.

2457 ________. "The Poetic Dilemma," Dial, 87, #5 (May, 1927), 420-423.

2458 ________. "A Portrait of T. S. Eliot," LugR, 1, #2 (1965), 115-116.

2459 ________. "T. S. Eliot," Life, 58 (January 15, 1965), 92-93.

2460 ________. "T. S. Eliot (1916, 1921, 1923, 1927, 1929, 1934, 1935, 1936, 1949," Collected Criticism [Formerly A Reviewer's ABC] New York: Oxford U. P., 1968, pp. 171-197.

2461 ________. "Varieties of Realism: Wilfrid Williamson Gibson, William Aspenwall Bradley, T. S. Eliot," Scepticisms: Notes on Contemporary Poetry. New York: Knopf, 1919, pp. 199-205.

2462 Aldington, Richard. Ezra Pound and T. S. Eliot: A Lecture. Reading: Peacocks Press, 1954.

2463 ________. "The Poetry of T. S. Eliot," Outlook (London), 49 (January 7, 1922), 12-13; repr., in Literary Studies and Reviews. New York: Dial Press, 1924, pp. 181-191.

2464 Allan D. Mowbray. Some Basic Concepts in T. S. Eliot's Criticism. Diss. Harvard: 1972.

2465 ________. T. S. Eliot's Impersonal Theory of Poetry. Lewisburg, Pa.: Bucknell U. P., 1973; Cranbury, N.J.: Bucknell U. P., 1974.

2466 Allen, Walter. "The Time and Place of T. S. Eliot," NYTBR (April 9, 1961), 1, 40-41.

2467 Alpers, Paul J. "The Milton Controversy," Mon/HES, #2 (1971), 269-298. Eliot's "A Note on the Verse of John Milton" one of the works considered.

2468 Alvarez, Alfred. "Eliot and Yeats: Orthodoxy and Tradition," TC, 162 (August, 1957), 149-163; (September, 1957), 224-234.

2469 ________. "Lawrence, Leavis, and Eliot," KR, 18 (Summer, 1956), 478-484.

2470 ________. "Playing Possum," NS&N, 59 (April 9, 1960), 531. Rev. art., Hugh Kenner's Invisible Poet: T. S. Eliot. New York: 1959.

2471 ________. The Shaping Spirit: Studies in Modern English and American Poets. London: Chatto & Windus, 1958; American ed., Scribner, 1958; repr., by Gordian Press, 1971.

2472 "Ambassador for Books," TLS (June 26, 1943), 307.

2473 Amery, Carl. "Der gelehrte Revolutionär: T. S. Eliots Beitrag zur Weltliteratur," Frankfurter Hefte, 15 (1960), 345-352.

2474 Ames, Russell M. "Decadence in the Art of T. S. Eliot," S&S, 16 (Summer, 1952), 193-198.

2475 Amis, Kingsley. "Laughter's to Be Taken Seriously," NYTBR, 62, #27 (July 7, 1957), 1.

2476 Ana, Masahito. An Introduction to T. S. Eliot. Tokyo: Nanundo, 1961.

2477 Anand, Mulk Raj. "Mr. Eliot's Kipling," L&LT, 32, #55 (March, 1942), 165-170.

2478 Anant, Victor. "'Pop' Fiction," LibJ, 14 (February, 1958), 197-198.

2479 Anceschi, Li. "Eliot e la poesia," FLe (November 14, 1948), 34.

2480 Anceschi, Luciano. "Eliot, la poesia, l'Europa," Humanitas, 4 (February, 1949), 193-203.

2481 __________. "T. S. Eliot and Philosophical Poetry," T. S. Eliot: A Symposium. Richard March and Tambimuttu, comps. Freeport, N. Y.: Books for Libraries Press, 1968, pp. 154-166.

2482 __________. "T. S. Eliot o delle difficoltà del mondo!" La Rassegna d'Italia, #3 (March 1949), 285-293.

2483 Anderson, Chester G. "On the Sublime and Its Anal-Urethral Sources in Pope, Eliot, and Joyce," Modern Irish Literature: Essays in Honor of William York Tindall. Raymond J. Porter and James D. Brophy, eds. New York: Iona Coll. Pr., and Twayne Pubs, 1972, pp. 235-249.

2484 Anderson, Paul Victor. "T. S. Eliot's Changing Dispositions of Thought," DAI, 37, #2 (Washington: 1975), 977A-978A.

2485 Andreach, Robert Joseph. "The Spiritual Life in Hopkins, Joyce, Eliot, and Hart Crane," DA, 25 (NYU: 1964), 467.

2486 __________. Studies in Structure: The Stages of the Spiritual Life of Four Modern Authors. London: Burns & Oates; New York: Fordham U. P., 1964. T. S. Eliot one of the authors studied.

2487 Andrews, J. R. "Bacon and the 'Dissociation of Sensibility,'" N&Q, n. s., 1 (November, 1954), 484-486. Eliot's "the unification of sensibility" anticipated by Hazlitt.

2488 Anér, Kerstin. "Rudyard Kipling and T. S. Eliot," Samtid och Framtid, 5 (1948), 400-406.

2489 Angioletti, G. B. (G. S. Fraser, tr.) "Encounters with Mr. Eliot," T. S. Eliot: A Symposium. Richard March and Tambimuttu, comps. Freeport, New York: Bks. for Libraries Pr., 1968, pp. 138-140.

2490 Anon. "Author Against Critics," TLS (May 6, 1955), 237.

2491 Anon. "The Church and the World: Problems of Common Social Action," The Times (London), #47,739 (July 17, 1947), 18.

2492 Anon. "Eliot and an Age of Fiction," NSt (January 8, 1965), 47.

2493 Anon. "A Great Man Gone," TLS (January 7, 1965), 21-35.

2494 Anon. "An Individual Talent," TLS, #3080 (March 10, 1961), 152.

2495 Anon. "Milton Lost and Regained," TLS (March 29, 1947), 140. Eliot's criticism of Milton.

2496 Anon. "T. S. Eliot and the 'Out There,'" TLS (December, 1971), 1551-52.

2497 Anon. "T. S. Eliot and the TLS," TLS, #3480 (November 7, 1968), 1251.

2498 Anon. "T. S. Eliot Goes Home," LivAge, 342 (May, 1932), 234-236.

2499 Anon. "T. S. Eliot Receives British Order of Merit," PubW, 153 (January 31, 1948), 632.

2500 Antrim, Harry T. T. S. Eliot's Concept of Language: A Study of Its Development. (Fla. U. Humanities Monographs, #35.) Gainesville: Florida U. P., 1971. Rev., by Stephen Stepanchev, AL, 44 (1972), 505-507.

2501 __________. T. S. Eliot's 'Raid on the Inarticulate': A Study in His Concept of Language. Diss. Florida: 1968.

2502 Appleman, Philip. "The Dread Factor: Eliot, Tennyson, and the Shaping of Science," ColuF, 3, #4 (Fall, 1974), 32-38.

2503 Arakawa, T. "T. S. Eliot's Interpretation of Arnold and Pater," SEL, 13 (1933), 161-181.

2504 Arbasino, Alberto. Sessanta Posizioni. Milano: Feltrinelli, 1971. T. S. Eliot and others.

2504a Arrowsmith, William. "Daedal Harmonics: A Dialogue on Eliot and the Classics," SoR, 13 (Winter, 1977), 1-47.

2505 __________. "Eliot and Euripides," Arion, 4, #1 (1965), 21-35.

2506 __________. "Transfiguration in Eliot and Euripides," SR, 63 (Summer, 1955), 421-442.

2507 Ashraf, A. S. "Eliot's Poetry from the Point of View of Islamic Mysticism," Venture, 5, #1 (June, 1968), 63-74.

2508 __________. T. S. Eliot Through Pakistani Eyes. Karachi: Dept. of English, U. of Karachi, 1968.

2509 Astre, Georges-Albert. "T. S. Eliot," LetF, # 1062 (January 7-13, 1965), 7.

2510 __________. "T. S. Eliot et la nostalgie de la 'culture,'" Critique (Paris), 5 (Summer, 1949), 804-811.

2511 __________. "T. S. Eliot, poète spirituel," Critique (Paris), Nos. 23, 24 (April, May, 1948), 307-314, 408-421.

2512 Auden, Wystan Hugh. "For T. S. Eliot [a poem], T. S. Eliot: A Symposium. Richard March and Tambimuttu, comps. Freeport, N. Y.: Bks. for Libraries Press, 1968, 43.

2513 __________. "Port and Nuts with the Eliots," NY, 25, # 9 (April, 1949), 85-87.

2514 __________. Secondary Worlds: The T. S. Eliot Memorial Lectures Delivered at Eliot College in the University of Kent at Canterbury, October, 1967. London: Faber, 1968.

2515 __________. "T. S. Eliot, O. M.: A Tribute," List, 73, # 1867 (January 7, 1965), 5.

2516 Austin, Allen. T. S. Eliot: The Literary and Social Criticism. Bloomington: Indiana U. P., 1971.

2517 __________. "T. S. Eliot as a Literary Critic," DA, 19 (NYU: 1959), 3301-3302.

2518 __________. "T. S. Eliot's Objective Correlative," UKCR, 26, # 2 (Winter, 1959), 133-140.

2519 __________. "T. S. Eliot's Quandary," UKCR, 27, # 2 (December, 1960), 143-148.

2520 __________. "T. S. Eliot's Theory of Dissociation," CE, 23, # 4 (January, 1962), 309-312.

2521 __________. "T. S. Eliot's Theory of Personal Expression," PMLA, 81, # 3 (June, 1966), 303-307.

2522 __________, and Ronald Schuchard. "Eliot and Hulme [an exchange]," PMLA, 89 (1974), 582-585.

2523 Avădănei, Stefan. "T. S. Eliot, cititor, poet, critic" [T. S. Eliot, reader, poet, critic], Cronica, 5, # 49 (December 1970), 9.

2524 __________. "T. S. Eliot: Savoarea culturii" [The Culture's Flavour], ASUI, 17 (1971), 91-95.

2525 __________. "Trei capodopere" [Three Masterpieces], Cronica, 5, #20 (May, 1970), 9.

2526 "Awarded $2,800--T. S. Eliot," PubW, 158, #23 (December 9, 1950), 2445. London Sunday Times Literary Award to T. S. Eliot.

2527 Aylen, Leo. Greek Tragedy and the Modern World. London: Methuen, 1964.

2528 Bacon, Helen H. "The Sibyl in the Bottle," VQR, 34 (Spring, 1958), 262-276.

2529 Baeröe, Per Richard. "T. S. Eliot's Eksistensielle Holdning," KogK, 64, #6 (June, 1959), 409-419.

2530 Bagg, Robert. "The Electromagnet and the Shred of Platinum," Arion, 8, #3 (Autumn, 1969), 407-429.

2531 __________. "The Rise of Lady Lazarus," Mosaic, 2, #4 (1969), 9-36.

2532 Baker, Carlos. "Speaking of Books," NYTBR (July 6, 1952), 2.

2533 Baker, Howard. "Homage to T. S. Eliot," HA, 125, #3 (1938), 46-47.

2534 Baker, James V. "T. S. Eliot. American Winners of the Nobel Literary Prize. Warren G. French and Walter E. Kidd, eds. Norman: Oklahoma U. P., 1968, pp. 111-137.

2535 Balakanian, Nona. "Affirmation and Love in Eliot," NewL, 42 (May, 1959), 20-21.

2536 Baldi, Sergio. "La Poesia di T. S. Eliot," Conv (Torino), 2 (1938).

2537 Baldini, Gabriele. "Il poeta sui trampoli," Mondo, 17, #3 (1965), 9.

2538 __________. "T. S. Eliot ha parlato a Roma," FLe (December 18, 1947), n. 51.

2539 Baldridge, Marie. "Some Psychological Patterns in the Poetry of T. S. Eliot," Psychoanalysis, 3 (Fall, 1954), 19-47.

2540 Balotă, Nicolae. "Criticul Eliot si ideea de ordine" [Eliot, the Critic and the Order Idea]. Euphorion. Bucureşti: Editura pentru literatură, 1969, pp. 592-608.

2541 Banerjee, Ron D. Kumar. "Dante Through the Looking Glass: Rossetti, Pound, and Eliot," CL, 24 (1972), 136-149.

2542 __________. T. S. Eliot and Dante. Diss. Harvard: 1971.

2543 Bantock, G. H. "Mr. Eliot and Education," Scrutiny, 16, #1 (March, 1949), 64-70.

2544 __________. T. S. Eliot and Education. New York: Random House, 1969; London: Faber, 1970.

2545 __________. "T. S. Eliot's View of Society," CritQ, 15 (Spring, 1973), 37-46.

2546 Barber, C. L. "The Power of Development ... in a Different World," the final chapter in The Achievement of T. S. Eliot by F. O. Matthiessen. 3rd ed. revised. New York: Oxford U. P., 1958, pp. 198-243.

2547 Barfoot, Gabrielle. "Dante in T. S. Eliot's Criticism," EM, 23 (1972), 231-246.

2548 Barilli, Renato. Poetica e retorica. Milano: Mursia, 1969.

2549 Barker, George. "Verses for the Sixtieth Birthday of Thomas Stearns Eliot" [a poem]. T. S. Eliot: A Symposium. Richard March and Tambimuttu, comps. Freeport, New York: Bks. for Libraries Press, 1968, pp. 136-137.

2550 Barnett, Gail Z. "The Endless Journey: An Ontogenetic Study of Three Poets," DAI, 33 (Maryland: 1972), 2314A.

2551 Barnhill, Viron Leonard. "Poetic Context in the Collected Poems (1909-1935) of T. S. Eliot: A Linguistic Investigation of Poetic Context," DA, 21 (Michigan: 1961), 2284.

2552 Baron, C. E. "Lawrence's Influence on Eliot," CamQ, 5 (1971), 235-248.

2553 Barry, Iris. "The Ezra Pound Period," Bookman, 74, #2 (October, 1931), 159-171.

2554 Barry, Sister Mary Martin. The Prosodic Structure in Selected Poems of T. S. Eliot. Diss. Catholic Univ of America, 1948; rev. ed., Washington, D. C.: Catholic U. of Amer. Pr., 1969.

2555 Barth, J. Robert. "T. S. Eliot's Image of Man," Renascence, 14, #3 (Spring, 1962), 126-138.

2556 Bartlett, Phyllis. "Other Countries, Other Wenches," MFS, 3 (Winter, 1957-58), 345-349.

2557 Barucca, Primo. "Tutto Eliot," FLe, 5 (March 11, 1962), 12-16.

2558 Basu, N. K. "T. S. Eliot and Literary Criticism," BDEC, 4, #1 and 2 (1963), 26-37.

2559 Bates, Ernest Sutherland. "T. S. Eliot: Leisure Class Laureate," ModM, 7, #1 (February, 1933), 17-24.

2560 Bates, R. "Donner un sens plus pur aux mots de la tribu," N&Q, 198 (November, 1953), 493-494.

2561 Bateson, F. W. "Dissociation of Sensibility," EIC, 1, #3 (July, 1951), 302-312.

2562 ________. "Editorial Commentary," EIC, 19 (1969), 1-5. Concerns Eliot's quarrel with Bateson.

2563 ________. "The Poetry of Learning," Eliot in Perspective: A Symposium. Graham Martin, ed. New York: Humanities, 1970. pp. 31-44.

2564 ________. "T. S. Eliot: 'Impersonality' Fifty Years After," SoR, 5, n. s. (July, 1969), 630-639.

2565 ________. "T. S. Eliot: The Poetry of Pseudo-Learning," JGE, 20, #1 (April, 1968), 13-27.

2566 Battenhouse, Henry M. Poets of Christian Thought. New York: Ronald Press, 1947, passim.

2567 Baumgaertel, Gerhard. "The Concept of the Pattern in the Carpet: Conclusions from T. S. Eliot," RLV, 25 (July-August, 1959), 300-306.

2568 Bayley, John. "The Collected Plays," Rev (Oxford), #4, T. S. Eliot Issue (November, 1962), 3-64.

2569 ________. "T. S. Eliot, Poet and Portent," NaR, 131 (November, 1947), 481-482.

2570 Beach, Joseph Warren. "Conrad Aiken and T. S. Eliot: Echoes and Overtones," PMLA, 69 (September, 1954), 753-762.

2571 ________. Obsessive Images: Symbolism in Poetry of the 1930's and 1940's. Minneapolis: Minnesota U. P., 1960, passim.

2572 ________. "T. S. Eliot," The Concept of Nature in Nineteenth-Century English Poetry. New York: Macmillan, 1936; Pageant Bks., 1956, pp. 554-555.

2573 Beare, Robert L. "Notes on the Text of T. S. Eliot: Variants from Russell Square," SB, 9 (1957), 21-49. Textual variations discussed.

2574 __________. "T. S. Eliot and Goethe," GR, 28 (December, 1953), 243-253.

2575 Becker, Mary L. "The Reader's Guide," SatR, 9 (January 14, 1933), 382. "The latest attention that T. S. Eliot has received in print is in H. G. Wells's new novel The Bulpington of Blup. . . ."

2576 Beer, Ernst. Thomas Stearns Eliot und der Antiliberalismus des XX, Jahrhunderts. Wien: W. Bräumüller, 1953.

2577 Beer, J. B. "Ezra Pound," TLS, 13 (April, 1973), 421. On Pound's editing of Eliot's work.

2578 Beharriell, Frederick J. "Freud and Literature," QQ, 65 (1958), 118-125.

2578a Behrmann, Alfred. "Focus on the Critic," TSER, 2, #1 (1975), 7-10.

2579 Bejenaru, Cornelia. "Rainer Maria Rilke, Thomas Stearns Eliot, Jorge Guillén şi Ion Pillat, discipoli şi exegeţi ai lui Paul Valéry," AUB-LUC, 20, #1 (1971), 15-20.

2580 Beker, Miroslav. "Eliotov kritički opus u perspektivi" [Eliot's critical opus in perspective], Forum (Zagreb), 11 (1968), 7-8, 171-220.

2581 __________. "T. S. Eliot's Theory of Impersonality and Henry James: A Note," SRAZ, 27-28 (July-December, 1969), 163-167.

2582 Belgion, Montgomery. "Irving Babbitt and the Continent," T. S. Eliot. Richard March and Tambimuttu, comps. Freeport, New York: Bks. for Libraries Press, 1968, pp. 51-59.

2583 Bellis, William Ward. "Thomas Becket: An Emerging Myth," DA, 25 (Indiana: 1964), 2976-77. Study of T. S. Eliot, Jean Anouilh, and Christopher Fry.

2584 Benét, William Rose. "The Phoenix Nest," SatR, 26 (October 9, 1943), 20.

2585 __________. "T. S. Eliot Again," SatR, 9 (January 21, 1933), 393.

2586 Bennett, Mitchell Bruce. "In Altera Persona": The Dramatic Monologue in the Poetry of Pound, Eliot and Frost. Diss. Harvard: 1967.

2587 Bentley, Eric. The Importance of "Scrutiny": Selections from "Scrutiny," 1932-1948. New York: New York U. P., 1964, passim.

2588 Benziger, James. Images of Eternity: Studies in the Poetry of Religious Vision from Wordsworth to T. S. Eliot. Carbondale: So. Ill. U. P., 1962, passim.

2589 __________. "The Romantic Tradition: Wordsworth and T. S. Eliot," BuR, 8, #4 (December, 1959), 277-286.

2590 Bergel, Lienhard. "La fase piu recente del pensiero critico di T. S. Eliot," SPe, 4 (December, 1951), 316-324.

2591 Bergonzi, Bernard. "Eliot on Culture," New Blackfriars, 52 (1971), 109-114.

2592 __________. T. S. Eliot. (Masters of World Lit. Ser.) New York: Macmillan, 1972.

2593 __________. "T. S. Eliot: The Early Poems," T. S. Eliot: A Collection of Criticism. Linda W. Wagner, ed. New York: McGraw Hill, 1972, pp. 27-36.

2594 Bergsten, Staffan. "Eliotforskningen idag: en liten krönika," [Eliot research today: a brief chronicle.] Samlaren, 91 (1971), 130-135.

2595 __________. "Illusive Allusions. Some Reflections on the Critical Approach to the Poetry of T. S. Eliot," Orbis Litterarum (Copenhagen), 14 (1959), 9-18.

2596 Beringause, Arthur. "T. S. Eliot--Christian Intellectual?" Cresset, 25, #10 (October, 1962), 8-12.

2597 Bernadette, Jose A. "Eliot's Water Imagery: An Adventure in Symbolism," Adam (London) 18 (May-June, 1950), 25-29.

2598 Berti, Luigi. "Intorno alle note aliotane sulla cultura," Inventario (Spring, 1946).

2599 __________. "Traduzione e prefazione di Luigi Berti," Poesie di T. S. Eliot con testo a fronte. (Collezione Fenice diretta da Attilio Bertolucci. Edizione fuori serie, n. 4) Modena: Guanda, 1949.

2600 Betjeman, John. "T. S. Eliot the Londoner," T. S. Eliot: A Symposium. Neville Braybrooke, ed. New York: Farrar, Straus, & Cudahy, 1958, pp. 193-195.

2601 __________. "The Usher of Highgate Junior School," T. S. Eliot: A Symposium. Richard March and Tambimuttu, comps. Freeport, N. Y.: Bks. for Libraries Pr., 1968, pp. 89-92.

2602 Bewley, Marius. "Eliot, Pound, and History," Masks and Mirrors: Essays in Criticism. New York; London: Chatto & Windus, 1970, pp. 302-323.

2603 Bhattacharyya, Debiprasad. "T. S. Eliot: A Great Critic," ModRev, 118 (September, 1965), 201-212.

2604 ________. "T. S. Eliot on Shakespeare," Quest, 50 (July-September, 1966), 45-54.

2605 Blackburn, Thomas. "T. S. Eliot," The Price of an Eye. New York: Wm. Morrow, 1961, pp. 50-65.

2606 Blackmur, R. P. The Expense of Greatness. New York: Arrow Editions, 1940, passim.

2607 ________. "In the Hope of Straightening Things Out," KR, 13, #2 (Spring, 1951), 303-314; repr., in The Lion and Honeycomb. New York: Harcourt, Brace, 1955.

2608 ________. "Irregular Metaphysics," Anni Mirabiles, 1921-1925. Washington, D. C.: Library of Congress, 1956, pp. 26-32; repr., in T. S. Eliot: A Collection of Essays. Hugh Kenner, ed. Englewood Cliffs, N. J.: Prentice-Hall, 1962, pp. 58-64.

2609 ________. "T. S. Eliot," H&H, 1, #3 and 4 (March-June, 1928), 187-213, 291-319.

2610 ________. "T. S. Eliot: From Ash-Wednesday to Murder in the Cathedral," Form and Value in Modern Poetry. Garden City, New York: Doubleday, 1957, pp. 121-151. Also in The Double Agent. New York: Arrow Editions, 1935, pp. 184-218; Language as Gesture. New York: Harcourt, Brace, 1952, pp. 163-191.

2611 ________. "The Whole Poet," Poetry, 50 (April, 1937), 48-51.

2612 ________, et al. "Mr. Eliot and Notions of Culture," PartisanR, 11, #3 (Summer, 1944), 302-304.

2613 Blau, Herbert. "W. B. Yeats and T. S. Eliot: Poetic Drama and Modern Poetry," DA, 14 (Stanford: 1954), 523-524.

2614 Blissett, William. "Pater and Eliot," UTQ, 22, #3 (April, 1953), 261-268.

2615 ________. "T. S. Eliot," CanF, 28 (July, 1948), 86-87.

2616 Bloom, Harold. "Lawrence, Blackmur, Eliot, and the Tortoise," A "D. H. Lawrence" Miscellany. Harry T. Moore, ed. Carbondale: So. Ill. U. P., 1959, pp. 360-369; repr., in The Ringers in the Tower. Chicago U. P., 1971, pp. 197-204.

2617 Bloomberg, Lawrence. "Eliot and His Problems," Pylon, 12 (1951), 18-23.

2618 Bluestein, Gene. "Emerson's Epiphanies," NEQ, 39, #4 (December, 1966), 447-460.

2619 Boardman, Gwenn R. "T. S. Eliot and the Mystery of Fanny Marlow," MFS, 7, #2 (Summer, 1961), 95-105. On a possible pseudonym of Eliot.

2620 Bogan, Louise. Achievement in American Poetry, 1900-1950. Chicago: Henry Regnery, 1951, passim.

2621 Bohnsack, Fritz. Zeit und Ewigkeit im Spatwerk T. S. Eliots. Diss. Hamburg: 1951.

2622 Bolgan, Anne C. "The Philosophy of F. H. Bradley and the Mind and Art of T. S. Eliot: An Introduction," English Literature and British Philosophy: A Collection of Essays. S. P. Rosenbaum, ed. Chicago, London: Chicago U. P., 1971, pp. 251-277.

2623 Bollier, E. P. "From Scepticism to Poetry: A Note on Conrad Aiken and T. S. Eliot," TSE, 13 (1963), 59-69.

2624 __________. "Mr. Eliot's 'Tradition and the Individual Talent' Reconsidered," UCSLL, #6 (January, 1957), 103-118.

2625 __________. "La Poésie Pure: The Ghostly Dialogue between T. S. Eliot and Paul Valéry," ForumH, 8, #1 (Spring, 1970), 54-59.

2626 __________. "T. S. Eliot and F. H. Bradley: A Question of Influence," TSE, 12 (1962), 87-111. Believes Eliot was influenced by the scepticism of Bradley.

2627 __________. "T. S. Eliot and John Donne: A Problem in Criticism," TSE, 9 (1959), 103-118.

2628 __________. "T. S. Eliot and John Milton: A Problem in Criticism," TSE, 8 (1958), 165-192.

2629 __________. "T. S. Eliot and the Idea of Literary Tradition," DA, 20 (Columbia: 1959), 1023.

2630 __________. "T. S. Eliot's 'Lost' Ode of Dejection," BuR, 16, #1 (March, 1968), 1-17.

2631 Boonstra, Harry. "T. S. Eliot and the Netherlands: The Critical Reception, A Dutch Parallel, and the Translations," DAI, 34 (Loyola, Chicago: 1973), 1893A.

2632 Bordwell, Harold. "Remembering Mr. Eliot," ChiR, 17 (1964), 33-36.

2633 Bornstein, George. "Beyond Modernism," MQR, 12, #3 (Summer, 1973), 278-284.

2634 Boschere, Jean de. "T. S. Eliot," L'Age Nouveau (Paris), #33 (January, 1949), 18-23.

2635 Bose, Amalendu. "T. S. Eliot and Bengali Poetry," T. S. Eliot: A Symposium. Richard March and Tambimuttu, comps. Freeport, N. Y.: Bks. for Libraries Press, 1968, pp. 225-230.

2636 Bottomore, T. B. Elites and Society. New York: Basic Bks., 1965, p. 118.

2637 Bottorff, William K. "Hindu and Buddhist Usages in the Poetry of T. S. Eliot," From Irving to Steinbeck: Studies of American Literature in Honor of Harry R. Warfel. Motley Deakin and Peter Lisca, eds. Gainesville: Florida U. P., 1972, pp. 111-124.

2638 Bottrall, Ronald. "Dead Ends" [poem], T. S. Eliot: A Symposium. Richard March and Tambimuttu, comps. Freeport, N. Y.: Bks. for Libraries Press, 1968, pp. 71-72.

2639 Bovey, J. A. "The Literary Criticism of T. S. Eliot," American Prefaces, 1, #4 (January, 1936), 67-71.

2640 Bowers, Frederick. "Arthur Hugh Clough: The Modern Mind," SEL, 6 (1967), 709-716.

2641 Boyd, Ernest A. "Hyphenated Poets" [T. S. Eliot], Studies from Ten Literatures. New York: Scribner's, 1925, pp. 315-317. Eliot's poems in French.

2642 Boyd, John D. "T. S. Eliot as Critic and Rhetorician: The Essay on Jonson," Criticism, 11 (1969), 167-182.

2643 Boynton, Grace M. "Without a Parable: An Encounter with the Poetry of T. S. Eliot," WindsorQt, 1, #2 (1933), 102-310.

2644 Brace, Marjorie. "Dying Into Life," SatR, 31, #25 (June 19, 1948), 17.

2645 Bradbrook, M. C. "Eliot's Critical Method," Focus Three:

T. S. Eliot, A Study of His Writings by Several Hands. B. Rajan, ed. London: Dennis Dobson, 1947, pp. 119-128.

2646 ________. T. S. Eliot. Rev. ed. (Writers and Their Work, No. 8.) London: Longmans, Green & Co. for The British Council, 1955.

2647 Bradbury, Malcolm. "The Criterion: A Literary Review in Retrospect," LonMag, 5, #2 (February, 1958), 41-54.

2648 Bradford, Curtis B. "Journeys to Byzantium," VQR, 25, #2 (Spring, 1949), 205-225.

2649 Bradley, Francis Herbert. Appearance and Reality. A Metaphysical Essay. London: 1893. The Philosopher said to have influenced T. S. Eliot.

2650 Brandabur, Edward. "Eliot and the Myth of Mute Speech," Renascence, 22 (1970), 141-150.

2651 Brandell, Gunnar. "Quarter Century of Scandinavian Literature," BA, 28 (Autumn, 1954), 407-422.

2652 Braun, Elisabeth. T. S. Eliot als Kritiker, Diss. Freiburg: 1963.

2653 Braybrooke, Neville. "Les écrits de jeunesse de T. S. Eliot: Un Apercu de ses Poèmes et Contes écrits à l'Age de 16 Ans," Syntheses, 20, #232 (Septembre, 1965), 321-326.

2654 ________. "Eliot y los niños," Arbor, 313 (1972), 5-12. [Tr., Francisco de A. Caballero.]

2655 ________. "Eliot's Search for a Lost Eden," CathW, 190, (December, 1959), 151-156.

2656 ________. "Los primeros escritos de T. S. Eliot," Arbor #65 (1966), 357-363.

2657 ________. T. S. Eliot: A Critical Essay. Roderick Jellema, ed. (Contemporary Writers in Christian Perspective Ser.) Grand Rapids, Michigan: Wm. B. Eerdmans, 1967.

2658 ________, ed. T. S. Eliot: A Symposium for His Seventieth Birthday. New York: Farrar, Straus and Cudahy, 1958.

2659 ________. "T. S. Eliot and Children," DR, 39, #1 (Spring, 1959), 43-49.

2660 ________. "T. S. Eliot in Pursuit of the Whale," CeyJH, 2, #1 (January, 1971), 98-103.

2661 __________. "T. S. Eliot in the Pursuit of the Whale--His Teenage Poems and Stories," Comment, 9, #2 (March-April, 1969), 33-35.

2662 __________. "T. S. Eliot in the South Seas," T. S. Eliot: The Man and His Work. Allen Tate, ed. New York: Delacorte Pr., 1966, pp. 382-388.

2663 __________. "T. S. Eliot in the South Seas: A Look at the Poems and Short Stories That He Wrote When He Was Sixteen in St. Louis," SR, 74, #1 (Winter, 1966), 376-382.

2664 __________. "T. S. Eliot und die Kinder, DRs, 85, #11 (November, 1959), 999-1004.

2665 __________. "T. S. Eliot's Earliest Writings," TC (Australia), 19 (1965), 317-323.

2666 __________. "Thomas Stearns Eliot," ConR, #1113 (September, 1958), 123-126.

2667 Bredin, Hugh. "T. S. Eliot and Thomistic Scholasticism," JHI, 33, #2 (April-June, 1972), 299-306.

2668 Bredvold, Louis I. "Eliot's Issue with His Age," IntercollegiateRev, 8, #3 (1972), 123-126.

2669 Breit, Harvey. "An Unconfidential Close-up of T. S. Eliot," NYTMS, (February 7, 1954), 16, 24-25.

2670 Brenner, Rica. "Thomas Stearns Eliot," Poets of Our Time. New York: Harcourt, Brace, 1941, pp. 159-206.

2671 Breslin, James E. "Too Far and Not Far Enough," VQR, 50 (Autumn, 1974), 632-637.

2672 Breslin, Paul Robert. "Eliot's Shadow: The Struggle Against Cultural Determinism," DAI, 36 (Virginia: 1975), 6080A.

2673 Brett, R. L. "Ambiguity and Mr. Eliot," English, 8 (Autumn, 1951), 284-287.

2674 Bridges, G. A. "Presentazione d'Eliot," (trad. di P. Jahier). Conv, 1 (January, 1947), 54-64.

2675 Brombert, Victor H. The Criticism of T. S. Eliot: Problems of an "Impersonal Theory" of Poetry. New Haven: Yale U. P., 1949.

2676 __________. "T. S. Eliot and the Romantic Heresy," YFS, 13 (Spring, 1954), 3-16.

2677 Brooks, Cleanth. "Dionysus and the City," SR, 80, #2 (Spring, 1972), 361-376.

2678 __________. "T. S. Eliot as a 'Modernist' Poet," Literary Theory and Structure: Essays in Honor of William K. Wimsatt. Frank Brady, et al, eds. New Haven: Yale U. P., 1973, pp. 353-377.

2679 __________. "T. S. Eliot: Discourse to the Gentiles," The Hidden God: Studies in Hemingway, Faulkner, Yeats, Eliot, and Warren. New Haven, Conn.: Yale U. P., 1963, pp. 68-97.

2680 __________. "T. S. Eliot: Thinker and Artist," SR, 74, #1 (Special Eliot Issue) (Winter, 1966), 310-326.

2681 __________. "T. S. Eliot: Thinker and Artist," A Shaping Joy: Studies in the Writer's Craft. New York: Harcourt, Brace, 1971, pp. 37-51.

2682 __________. "T. S. Eliot: Thinker and Artist," T. S. Eliot: The Man and His Work. Allen Tate, ed. New York: Delacorte, 1966, pp. 316-332.

2683 __________. "Three Revolutions in Poetry. III. Metaphysical Poetry and the Ivory Tower," SoR, 1 (Winter, 1936), 568-583.

2684 __________. The Well-Wrought Urn. Studies in the Structure of Poetry. New York: Harcourt, Brace & World, 1947, passim.

2685 Brooks, Van Wyck. "What Is Primary Literature?" Opinions of Oliver Allston. New York: Dutton, 1941, pp. 218-227.

2686 Brophy, Robert J. "T. S. Eliot and Robinson Jeffers: A Note," Robinson Jeffers Newsl, 38 (1974), 4-5.

2687 Brotman, D. Brosley. "T. S. Eliot, the Music of Ideas," UTQ, 18 (October, 1948), 20-29.

2688 Brown, Alec. "The Lyric Impulse in the Poetry of T. S. Eliot," Scrutinies, 2 (E. Rickword, ed.). London: Wishart, 1931, pp. 34-48.

2689 Brown, Calvin S., Jr. "T. S. Eliot and 'Die Droste,'" SR, 46 (October-December, 1938), 492-500.

2690 Brown, E. K. "Mr. Eliot and Some Enemies," UTQ, 8 (October, 1938), 69-84.

2691 __________. "T. S. Eliot: Poet and Critic," CanF, 10, #120 (September, 1930), 448.

2691a Brown, J. M. "Honorable Intentions," SatR, 33 (February 4, 1950), 28-30.

2692 Brown, Lloyd W. "The Historical Sense: T. S. Eliot and Two African Writers," Conch, 3, #1 (1971), 59-70.

2693 Brown, Wallace C. "T. S. Eliot and the Demon of the Ego," New Humanist, 8, #3 (Summer, 1935), 81-85.

2694 Bruno, Francesco. "Definizione della cultura secondo Thomas Stearns Eliot," FLe, #40 (October 5, 1952), 3.

2695 Buck, Philo M., Jr. "Faith of Our Fathers: T. S. Eliot," Directions in Contemporary Literature. New York: Oxford U. P., 1942, pp. 261-291.

2696 Buckley, Vincent. "The Persistence of God," CR, 10 (1967), 74-87.

2697 ________. "T. S. Eliot: Impersonal Order," and "T. S. Eliot: The Question of Orthodoxy," Poetry and Morality: Studies on the Criticism of Matthew Arnold, T. S. Eliot, and F. R. Leavis. London: Chatto & Windus, 1959, pp. 87-128, 129-157.

2698 Büdel, Maria. Der Essay Theodor Haeckers und T. S. Eliots als Beitrag zur abendländischen Literatur-und Kulturkritik. Diss. Marburg, 1949.

2699 Bullaro, John Joseph. "The Dante of T. S. Eliot," A Dante Profile, 1265-1965: Dante Lectures, Seventh Centennial of His Birth. Franca Schettino, ed. Trs. by David H. Malone and Franca Shettino. Los Angeles: So. Calif. U. P., 1967, pp. 27-37.

2699a ________. "The Dantean Image of Ezra Pound, T. S. Eliot, and Hart Crane," DA, 22 (Wisconsin: 1962), 4012.

2700 Bullough, Geoffrey. "Christopher Fry and the 'Revolt' against Eliot," Experimental Drama. William A. Armstrong, ed. London: G. Bell, 1963, pp. 56-78.

2700a ________. The Trend of Modern Poetry. Edinburgh: Oliver and Boyd, 1934, pp. 133-152.

2701 Burch, Francis F. Tristan Corbière: L'originalité des 'Amours jaunes' et leur influence sur T. S. Eliot. Paris: Nizet, 1970.

2702 Burgess, Anthony. "Lament for a Maker," Spectator (January 8, 1965), 37.

2703 Burke, Kenneth. "Acceptance and Rejection," SoR, 2, #3 (1937), 600-632.

2704 ________. "The Allies of Humanism Abroad," The

Critique of Humanism. C. Hartley Grattan, ed. New York: Brewer & Warren, 1930, pp. 169-192.

2705 Burne, Glenn S. "T. S. Eliot and Rémy de Gourmont," BuR, 8 (February, 1959), 113-126.

2706 Burney, S. M. H. "The Poetry of T. S. Eliot," ModRev (Calcutta), (May, 1949), 393-394.

2707 Bush, Douglas. "American Poets," Mythology and the Romantic Tradition in English Poetry. Cambridge: Harvard U. P., 1937, pp. 506-518.

2708 Butz, Hazel E. "The Relation of T. S. Eliot to the Christian Tradition," DA, 14 (Indiana: 1955), 1213-1214.

2709 Caffi, Andrea. "Stato, nazione e cultura: Note su T. S. Eliot e Simone Weil," TPr, 6 (1961), 5-16.

2710 Cahill, Audrey F. T. S. Eliot and the Human Predicament. Pietermaritzburg, South Africa: Natal U. P., 1967.

2711 Cahill, Daniel Joseph. "A Comparative Study of the Criticism of Arnold and Eliot," DA, 27 (Iowa: 1966), 452A-453A.

2712 Cajetan, Brother. "Pendulum Starts Back," CathW, 140 (March, 1935), 650-656.

2713 Calder, Angus. "T. S. Eliot: The Governor," B&B, 17, #4 (January, 1972), 22-26.

2714 Călinescu, Matei. "Poetica lui T. S. Eliot. Tradiţie şi modernitate." [The Poetics of T. S. Eliot. Tradition and Modern Vision.] Tribuna, 14, #29 (July, 1970), 16; #30 (July, 1970), 10.

2715 Calliebe, Gisela. Das Werk T. S. Eliots und die Tradition der Mystik. Diss. Berlin, 1955.

2716 Calverton, V. F. "T. S. Eliot: An Inverted Marxian," ModernM, 8 (July, 1934), 372-373.

2717 Cameron, J. M. "Eliot and Fascism," NSt (October 7, 1966), 516.

2718 ________. "T. S. Eliot as a Political Writer," T. S. Eliot: A Symposium. Neville Braybrooke, ed. New York: Farrar, Straus & Cudahy, 1958, pp. 138-151.

2719 Campbell, Harry M. "An Examination of Modern Critics: T. S. Eliot," RockyMR, 8, #3 (Spring, 1944), 128-137.

2720 Campbell, Roy. "Contemporary Poetry," Scrutinies. Edgell Rickword, ed. London: Wishart, 1928, pp. 162-179.

2721 Cantwell, Robert. "Mr. Eliot's Sunday Afternoon," NR, 72, #928 (September 14, 1932), 132-133. Concerns Eliot's Introduction to Bubu of Montparnasse by Charles-Louis Philippe.

2722 Caprariu, Al. "Puncte de reper. Despre T. S. Eliot," Tribuna, 11, #36 (September 7, 1967), 8.

2723 Caretti, Laura. "A Case of Resemblance: Eugenio Montale," T. S. Eliot in Italia: saggio e bibliografia (1923-1965). Bari: Adriatica Editrice, 1968. Revs.: TLS (January 8, 1970), 26; by G. Singh, N&Q, 19 (1972), 68-69.

2724 __________. "Eliot come Pécuchet," SA, 14 (1968), 247-264.

2725 Carew, Rivers. "Georges Rouault and T. S. Eliot: A Note," HJ, 60 (April, 1962), 230-235.

2726 Cargill, Oscar. "American Decadence," Intellectual America: Ideas on the March. New York: Macmillan, 1941, pp. 258-274.

2727 __________. "Mr. Eliot Regrets....," Nation, 184 (February 23, 1957), 170-172.

2728 __________. "Techniques for Survival II. Consensus in Literature," CEA, 34, #2 (January, 1972), 2-6.

2729 Carnell, Corbin S. "Creation's Lonely Flesh: T. S. Eliot and Christopher Fry on the Life of the Senses," MD, 6, #2 (September, 1963), 141-149.

2730 Carne-Ross, D. S. "T. S. Eliot: Tropheia," Arion, 4, #1 (Spring, 1965), 5-20.

2731 Carson, Herbert L. "The Wasting Away of Europe," Cresset, 31, (1968), 6-12.

2732 Carter, Barbara B. "Modern English Poetry," CathW, 143 (1936), 292-300.

2733 Catlin, George. "T. S. Eliot and the Moral Issue," SatR, 32, #2 (July 2, 1949), 7-8, 36-38.

2734 Cattaui, Georges. "Lettres anglaises: T. S. Eliot, prix Nobel 1948," RN (January 15, 1949), 91-95.

2735 __________. "Notes sur T. S. Eliot," Le Journal des Poètes (November 15, 1951).

2736 __________. "La Poésie d'Eliot," Le Journal des Poètes (January, 1954), 5-6.

2737 __________. "T. S. Eliot," RdP, 72 (February, 1965), 139-140.

2738 __________. T. S. Eliot. London: Merlin Pr., 1966; Tr. by Claire Pace and Jean Stewart. New York: Funk & Wagnalls [1st Amer. ed.], 1968.

2739 __________. "T. S. Eliot, poète symboliste et chrétien," Vie Intellectuelle (December 10, 1937), 284-301.

2740 __________. "Thomas Stearns Eliot; ou le retour du 'Mayflower,'" Trois Poëtes: Hopkins, Yeats, Eliot. Paris: Egloff, 1947. Enlarged: T. S. Eliot. Paris: Ed. universitaires, 1957.

2741 Causley, Charles. "Down by the Riverside" [poem], T. S. Eliot: A Symposium. Neville Braybrooke, ed. New York: Farrar, Straus, & Cudahy, 1958, p. 28.

2742 Cecchi, Emilio. "A Meeting with Eliot," T. S. Eliot: A Symposium. Richard March and Tambimuttu, comps. Freeport, N.Y.: Bks. for Libraries Pr., 1968, pp. 73-76.

2743 Ceechin, Giovanni. "Echi de T. S. Eliot nei Romanzi di Evelyn Waugh," EM, #9 (1963), 237-275.

2744 Chace, William M. "The Political Affinities of T. S. Eliot and Ezra Pound," DAI, 29 (Berkeley: 1968), 4479.

2745 __________. The Political Identities of Ezra Pound and T. S. Eliot. Stanford, Calif.: Stanford U. P., 1973.

2746 Chalker, John. "Aspects of Rhythm and Rhyme in Eliot's Early Poems," English, 16, #93 (Autumn, 1966), 84-88.

2747 __________. "Authority and Personality in Eliot's Criticism," Eliot in Perspective: A Symposium. Graham Martin, ed. London: Macmillan; New York: Humanities, 1970, pp. 194-210.

2748 Chapin, Katherine Garrison. "T. S. Eliot at the National Gallery," Poetry, 70 (September, 1947), 328-329. Description of Eliot's public reading at the National Gallery, Washington, D. C.

2749 Charity, A. C. "T. S. Eliot: The Dantean Recognitions," The Waste Land in Different Voices. A. D. Moody, ed. New York: St. Martin's Press, 1974, pp. 117-162.

2750 Chase, Richard. "The Sense of the Present," KR, 7, #2 (Spring, 1945), 218-231.

2751 ________. "T. S. Eliot in Concord," AmSch, 16, #4 (Autumn, 1947), 438-443.

2752 Chaturvedi, B. N. "The Indian Background of Eliot's Poetry," English, 15 (Autumn, 1965), 220-223.

2753 Chew, S. C. "Appraisal," CSMM (November 6, 1935), 14.

2754 Chiari, Joseph. T. S. Eliot: Poet and Dramatist. New York: Barnes & Noble, 1972.

2755 Chiereghin, Salvino. "T. S. Eliot e l'ultima opera del Pizzetti," Conv, 26 (July-August, 1958), 501-502.

2756 Child, Ruth C. "The Early Critical Work of T. S. Eliot: An Assessment," CE, 12 (February, 1951), 269-275.

2757 Chinol, Elio. "Lawrence al tribunale di Eliot," FLe, 12 (March 16, 1952), 4.

2758 ________. "La poesia di T. S. Eliot," SA, 3 (1957), 221-238.

2759 ________. "Poesia e tradizione nel pensiero critico di T. S. Eliot," Studi in onore di Vittorio Lugli e Diego Valeri. Venezia: Neri Possa. 2 vols. 1962, pp. 243-260.

2760 Chmielewski, Inge. Die Bedeutung der Göttlichen Komödie für die Lyrik T. S. Eliots. Neumünster: 1969.

2761 Christopher, J. R. "Two More Notes on Edward Lear," Unicorn (Brooklyn), 2, #3 (1972), 12-14. T. S. Eliot, Auden, and the "Lear Tradition."

2762 Church, R. W. "Eliot on Bradley's Metaphysics," HA, 125, #3 (December, 1938), 24-26.

2763 Church, Richard. "T. S. Eliot: A Search for Foundations," FnR, 155 (n. s. 149), (Fall, 1941), 163-170.

2764 ________. "T. S. Eliot: A Search for Foundations," Eight for Immortality. London: Dent, 1941; Freeport, New York: Bks. for Libraries Press, 1969, pp. 83-97.

2765 Ciardi, John. "Thomas Stearns Eliot: 1888-1965," SatR, 48 (January 23, 1965), 35-36.

2766 Cimatti, Pietro. "Saggi di Eliot sulla poesia, FLe, 15 (March 27, 1960), 5.

2767 Clark, John A. "On First Looking into Benson's Fitzgerald," SAQ, 48 (April, 1949), 258-269. Benson's Edward Fitzgerald as a source for ideas and figures in various poems of Eliot's.

2768 Clark, Richard C. "George Steiner on the 'Christian Barbarism' of Claudel and Eliot," RNL, 4, #2 (Fall, 1973), 119-125.

2769 Clemen, Wolfgang. "Kurze bibliographische: T. S. Eliot," Deutsche Beiträge. München, II (Heft 6, 1948), 483-499.

2770 Clendenning, John. "Time, Doubt and Vision: Notes on Emerson and T. S. Eliot," AmSch, 36 (Winter, 1966-67), 125-132.

2771 Cleophas, Sister M. Costello. Between Fixity and Flux: A Study in the Concept of Poetry and the Criticism of T. S. Eliot. Diss. Catholic U. of America: 1947; pub. by Catholic U. P., 1947.

2772 ___________. "Eliot's Whispers of Immortality," Expl. 8 (December, 1949), Item 22.

2773 Closs, August. "Formprobleme und Möglichkeiten zur Gestaltung der Tragödie in der Gegenwart," Stil-und Formprobleme in der Literatur. Paul Böckmann, ed. Vortäge des VII. Kongresses der Internationalen Vereinigung fur moderne Sprachen und Literaturen in Heidelberg. Heidelberg: Carl Winter, 1959, pp. 483-491.

2774 Clowder, Felix. "The Bestiary of T. S. Eliot," PrS, 34 (Spring, 1960), 30-37.

2775 Clutton-Brock, Alan. "Letters to the Editor: T. S. Eliot and Conan Doyle," TLS, #2555 (January 19, 1951), 37.

2776 Coblentz, Stanton A. "Must We End in the Wasteland?" The Poetry Circus. New York: Hawthorn Bks., 1967, pp. 205-222, passim.

2777 Coffman, Stanley K. Imagism: A Chapter for the History of Modern Poetry. Norman, Okla.: Oklahoma U. P., 1951, pp. 42-43, 216-221.

2778 Cohen, J. M. "In the Waste Land," Poetry of This Age, 1908-1958. Philadelphia: Dufour Editions, 1962, pp. 117-149.

2779 Coleman, Antony. "T. S. Eliot and Keith Douglas," TLS, #3566 (July 2, 1970), 731. Cf., Harold Jenkins, TLS, 3568 (July 16, 1970), 775; Antony Coleman, #3570 (July 31, 1970), 854; Desmond Graham, #3573 (August 21, 1970), 928.

2780 Collin, W. E. "T. S. Eliot," SR, 39 (January-March, 1931), 13-24.

2781 ________. "T. S. Eliot the Critic," SR, 39 (October-December, 1931), 419-424.

2782 Colum, Padraic. "A Commemorative Book," SatR, 41, #37 (September 13, 1958), 31. Essay-rev., T. S. Eliot: A Symposium for His Seventieth Birthday. Neville Braybrooke, New York: 1958.

2783 Combecker, Hans. "Interpretationen für den Englischunterricht: Langston Hughes, F. R. Scott, T. S. Eliot," NS, 17 (1968), 506-514.

2784 Congress for Cultural Freedom: T. S. Eliot. Bombay: Manaktalas, 1965.

2785 Connolly, Cyril. "The Break-Through in Modern Verse," LonMerc, n. s. 1, (June, 1961), 27-40.

2786 Coomaraswamy, Ananda K. "Primordial Images," PMLA, 61 (June, 1946), 601-602. Cf., Genevieve W. Foster. "The Archetypal Imagery of T. S. Eliot," PMLA, 60 (1945), 567-585; and PMLA, 61 (1946), 602-603.

2787 Cornwell, Ethel F. "Eliot's Concept of the 'Still Point,'" in The "Still Point": Theme and Variations in the Writings of T. S. Eliot, Coleridge, Yeats, Henry James, Virginia Woolf, and D. H. Lawrence. New Brunswick, N. J.: Rutgers U. P., 1962, pp. 17-63.

2788 Corrigan, Matthew. "The Poet's Intuition of Prose Fiction: Pound and Eliot on the Novel," UWR, 2, #1 (Fall, 1966), 33-51.

2789 Cossu, Nunzio. "Dantismo Politicoreligioso di T. S. Eliot," NA, 495 (1965), 181-191.

2790 ________. "Eliot e Dante," FLe, 13, #23 (June 8, 1958), 1-2.

2790a Coulon, H. J. "T. S. Eliot and Anglo-Catholicism," SatR, 35 (April 5, 1952), 23.

2791 Cowley, Malcolm. "Afterthoughts on T. S. Eliot," NR, 87 (May 20, 1936), 49.

2792 ________. "The Battle over Ezra Pound," NR, 121 (October 3, 1949), 18. A defense of T. S. Eliot. Cf., Robert Hillyer. SatR, 32 (June 11, 1949), 9-11; (June 18, 1949), 7-9, 38.

2793 ________. "Laforgue in America: A Testimony," SR, 71 (January-March, 1963), 62-74.

2794 ________. The Literary Situation. New York: Viking Press, 1947, passim.

2795 ________. "Readings from the Lives of the Saints," Exile's Return: A Literary Odyssey of the 1920's. New York: Norton, 1934; new ed., Viking, 1963, pp. 123-128.

2796 ________. "The Religion of Art," NR, 77, #996 (January 3, 1934), 216-220.

2797 ________. "T. S. Eliot's Ardent Critics and Mr. Eliot," NYHTB, 25 (March 13, 1949), 1-2.

2798 ________. "Tract for the Times," NR, 102 (June 17, 1940), 829-830.

2798a Cowley, V. J. E. "A Source for T. S. Eliot's Objective Correlative," RES, 26 (1975), 320-321.

2799 Cox, Charles B. "Eliot's Criterion," Spectator, #7261 (August 25, 1967), 216-217.

2800 ________. "T. S. Eliot at the Cross-Roads," CritQ, 12 (Winter, 1970), 307-320.

2801 Coxe, Louis O. "Winters on Eliot," KR, 3 (Autumn, 1941), 498-500.

2802 Crane, R. S. "Two Essays in Practical Criticism: Prefatory Note," UKCR, 8 (Spring, 1942), 199-202.

2803 Creaser, John. "Marvell's Effortless Superiority," EIC, 20, #4 (October, 1970), 403-423. Influence of Eliot's critical views of Andrew Marvell.

2803a Crick, Bernard. "Poets and Partisans," TLS, 30 (May, 1975), 586. Rev.-art., on W. M. Chace. The Political Identities of Ezra Pound and T. S. Eliot. Stanford, Calif.: Stanford U. P., 1973.

2804 Cronin, Anthony. "A Question of Modernity," XR, 1 (1960), 283-292. The "literary revolution" of the past fifty years.

2805 Cronin, Francis C. "T. S. Eliot's Theory of Literary Creation," DA, 28 (Pittsburgh: 1967), 1391A.

2806 Cronin, Vincent. "T. S. Eliot as a Translator," T. S. Eliot: A Symposium for His Seventieth Birthday. Neville Braybrooke, ed. New York: Farrar, Straus & Cudahy, 1958, pp. 129-137.

2807 Cruttwell, Patrick. "One Reader's Beginning," OL, 14 (1959), 1-8.

2808 Cruz, Juan M. de la. "Alcance de la 'via negativa' en la poesia de T. S. Eliot como contraposición a la 'utopia' de W. Whitman," FMod, 42 (1971), 273-295.

2809 Cummings, E. E. "T. S. Eliot," Dial, 68 (June, 1920), 781-784. Praised Eliot's vocabulary, orchestration, and technique.

2810 Cunliffe, John W. English Literature in the Twentieth Century. New York: Macmillan, 1933, pp. 323-329.

2811 Cunliffe, Marcus. "Poetry and Criticism Since World War I," The Literature of the United States. Baltimore: Penguin Bks., 1955, pp. 321-326, passim.

2812 Cunningham, Adrian. "Continuity and Coherence in Eliot's Religious Thought," Eliot in Perspective: A Symposium. Graham Martin, ed. New York: Humanities, 1970, pp. 211-231.

2813 Cunningsworth, A. J. "T. S. Eliot, Francis Vielé-Griffin, and the 'Objective Correlative,'" ELN, 8 (1971), 208-211.

2814 Curtis, Anthony. "Social Improvements and Literary Disasters," List, 89, #2290 (February 15, 1973), 211-213.

2815 Curtius, Ernst-Robert. Kritische Essays zur Europäischen Literatur. Bern: 1950; Tr. by Michael Kowal: Essays on European Literature. Princeton, N. J.: Princeton U. P., 1973, pp. 355-371, 371-399.

2816 __________. "T. S. Eliot," Paragone (Italy), #14 (February, 1951), 3-15.

2817 __________. "T. S. Eliot," Merkur (Baden-Baden), 3, #1 (1949), 1-23.

2818 __________. "T. S. Eliot als Dichter," Neue Schweizer Rundschau, 32 (1927), 349-361.

2819 __________. T. S. Eliot als Kritiker," Die Literatur, (October, 1929), 11-15.

2820 __________. "T. S. Eliot and Germany," T. S. Eliot: A Symposium. Richard March and Tambimuttu, comps. Freeport, N. Y.: Bks. for Libraries Pr., 1968, pp. 119-125.

2821 Czamanske, Palmer, and Karl Hertz. "The Beginning of T. S. Eliot's Theory of Culture," Cresset, 15 (July, 1952), 9-21.

2822 Czerniawski, Adam. "Eliot jako krytyk [Eliot as a Critic], Kultura, #228 (October, 1966), 135-137. (In Polish).

2823 D., J. "De Essayist Eliot," De Spectator (December 9, 1949), 9.

2824 D'Agostino, Nemi. "Gli anni di tirocinio di Thomas Stearns Eliot," Belfagor, 8 (January, 1953), 16-50.

2824a ________. "La fin de siècle francese e la poesia di Pound e Eliot," Galleria (Italy), 4 (December, 1954), 327-339.

2825 Dahlberg, Edward, and Herbert Read. "On T. S. Eliot and Ezra Pound," Truth Is More Sacred: A Critical Exchange on Modern Literature. New York: Horizon Press, [1961?], pp. 169-222.

2826 ________ and ________. "Robert Graves and T. S. Eliot," TC, 166 (August, 1959), 54-62.

2827 Daiches, David. Critical Approaches to Literature. Englewood Cliffs, N.J.: Prentice-Hall, 1956, passim.

2828 ________. Literary Essays. Chicago: Chicago U. P., 1956, passim.

2829 ________. "Literature and Belief," A Study of Literature. New York: Norton, 1964, pp. 212-226.

2830 ________. The Place of Meaning in Poetry. Edinburgh and London: Oliver & Boyd, 1935, pp. 49-55.

2831 ________. "Some Aspects of T. S. Eliot," CE, 9 (December, 1947), 115-122.

2832 ________. "T. E. Hulme and T. S. Eliot" and "T. S. Eliot," Poetry and the Modern World. Chicago: Chicago U. P., 1940, pp. 90-105, 106-127.

2833 ________. "T. S. Eliot," YR, 38, #3 (March, 1949), 460-470.

2833a Daley, A. Stuart. "Eliot's English 26, Harvard University, Spring Term, 1933," TSER, 2, #2 (Fall, 1975), 5-7.

2834 Daniels, J. R. "T. S. Eliot and His Relation to T. E. Hulme," UTQ, 2, #3 (April, 1933), 380-396.

2835 Daniels, Roy. "The Christian Drama of T. S. Eliot," Canadian Forum, 16, #187 (1936), 20-21.

2836 Darby, James M. An Approach to T. S. Eliot's Religious Imagery. Diss. Harvard: 1957.

2837 D'Arcy, M. C. "The Thomistic Synthesis and Intelligence," Criterion, 6, #3 (September, 1927), 210-228.

2838 Daus, H. J. "T. S. Eliot, The Boston Evening Transcript," Anglia, 74 (Heft 3, 1956), 364-368.

2839 Davie, Donald. "Eliot in One Poet's Life," Mosaic, 6, #1 (Fall, 1972), 229-241.

2840 __________. "Mr. Eliot," NSt, 66 (October 11, 1963), 496-497.

2841 __________. "Pound and Eliot: A Distinction," Eliot in Perspective: A Symposium. Graham Martin, ed. New York: Humanities, 1970, pp. 62-82.

2842 __________. "T. S. Eliot: The End of an Era," TC, 159, #950 (April, 1956), 350-362.

2843 Davies, M. B. "Correspondence: Mr. Bottrall and Mr. Eliot," Scrutiny, 15, #2 (Spring, 1948), 136.

2844 Davis, Robert Gorham. "Culture, Religion and Mr. Eliot," PR, 16, #7 (July, 1949), 750-753.

2845 __________. "The New Criticism and the Democratic Tradition," AmSch, 19, #1 (Winter, 1949), 9-15.

2846 Davison, Richard Allan. "Hart Crane, Louis Untermeyer, and T. S. Eliot: A New Crane Letter," AL, 44, #1 (March, 1972), 143-146. Crane in letter to Untermeyer praises Untermeyer for his criticism of Eliot.

2847 Dawson, Christopher. "Mr. T. S. Eliot on the Meaning of Culture," Month, 1, n. s. (March, 1949), 151-157.

2848 Dawson, N. P. "Enjoying Poor Literature," Forum, 69 (1923), 1371-1379.

2849 Day, Douglas. "The Background of the New Criticism," Journal of Aesthetics and Art Criticism, 24, #3 (Spring, 1966), 429-440.

2850 Day, Robert A. "Joyce's Waste Land and Eliot's Unknown God," Festskrift til Søren Holm på 70-årsdagen den 4. Peter Kemp, ed. marts 1971. Copenhagen: Nyt Nordist Forlag, 1971, pp. 139-210.

2850a Day Lewis, C. A Hope for Poetry. Oxford: Basil Blackwell, 1934, passim.

2851 De Arment, Warren Earl. "Irving Babbitt and T. S. Eliot: The New Humanist--New Critical Nexus," DAI, 36 (Pittsburgh: 1974), 877A.

2852 Delasanta, Rodney. "The Bartenders in Eliot and Chaucer," NM, 72 (1971), 60-61.

2853 DeLaura, David J. "Echoes of Butler, Browning, Conrad and Pater in the Poetry of T. S. Eliot," ELN, 3 (March, 1966), 211-221.

2854 ___________. "Pater and Eliot: The Origin of the 'Objective Correlative,'" MLQ, 26, #3 (September, 1965), 426-431.

2855 ___________. "The Place of the Classics in T. S. Eliot's Christian Humanism," Hereditas: Seven Essays on the Modern Experience of the Classical. Frederic Will, ed. Austin: Texas U. P., 1964, pp. 153-197.

2856 Delpech, Jeanine. "Le poète dans le cité," NL, 31 (1951), 1, 5.

2857 Dembo, L. S. Conceptions of Reality in Modern American Poetry. Berkeley: California U. P., 1966, pp. 183-207.

2858 Demers, Pierre E. Spiritual Progress in the Poetry of T. S. Eliot. Diss. Harvard: 1963.

2859 De Stasio, Marina. "Il mondo classico nella poesia di T. S. Eliot," SA, 15 (1969), 201-244.

2860 Deutsch, Babette. Poetry in Our Time: A Critical Survey of Poetry in the English-speaking World, 1900-1960. Garden City, N. Y.: 1963, pp. 173-178, passim.

2861 ___________. "T. S. Eliot and the Laodiceans," AmSch, 9, #1 (Winter, 1939), 19-30.

2862 ___________. This Modern Poetry. London: Faber & Faber, 1936, passim; New York: Norton, 1935, passim.

2863 Dey, Bishnu. "Mr. Eliot Among the Arjunas," T. S. Eliot: A Symposium. Richard March and Tambimuttu, comps. Freeport, N. Y.: Bks for Libraries Press, 1968, pp. 96-102.

2864 Dickinson, D. H. "Mr. Eliot's Hotel Universe," DramaCrit, 1 (February, 1958), 33-44.

2865 Dickinson, Hugh. "Eliot's Dramatic Use of Myth," DramaCrit, 5, #2 (May, 1962), 50-58.

2866 Dierickx, J. "Eliot, de Griekse toneelschrijvers en Ibsen," TVUB, 5 (1963), 145-157.

2867 Dijkhuis, Dirk W. "Nijhoff en Eliot/Eliot en Nijhoff," Merlyn, 2 (1964), 1-24.

2868 Dillon, George. "Correspondence from Paris," Poetry, 67, #1 (October, 1945), 50-51. Describes Eliot's lecture in Paris.

2869 Dinwiddy, Hugh. "Reading T. S. Eliot with Schoolboys," T. S. Eliot: A Symposium. Neville Braybrooke, ed. New York: Farrar, Straus & Cudahy, 1958, pp. 92-97.

2870 DiPasquale, Pasquale, Jr. "Coleridge's Framework of Objectivity and Eliot's Objective Correlative," JAAC, 26, #4 (Summer, 1968), 489-500.

2871 Dobrée, Bonamy. "T. S. Eliot," The Lamp and the Lute: Studies in Seven Authors. New York: Barnes & Noble, 1929, 1964, pp. 99-121.

2872 Dobson, Charles A. "Three of Mr. Eliot's Poems," New Review (Calcutta), 12 (1940), 361-372.

2873 Dodsworth, Martin. "The Pound Era," NSt, 84 (July 28, 1972), 129. Rev. art., The Pound Era by Hugh Kenner. Faber, 1972.

2874 Dolan, Paul Joseph. "Tradition in Modern Literary Criticism," DA, 27 (New York University: 1966), 768A-769A.

2875 Donoghue, Denis. "Criteria Omnia," CamR, 89A, #2164 (February 9, 1968), 257-260. Rev.-art., The Criterion, 18 vols. T. S. Eliot, ed.

2876 ________. "Eliot in the Sibyl's Leaves," SR, 68 (1960), 138-143.

2877 ________. "Eliot's Verse Line," The Third Voice: Modern British and American Verse Drama. Princeton: Princeton U. P., 1959, pp. 169-179.

2878 ________. "An Interview with Richard Eberhart," Shenandoah, 15, #4 (Summer, 1964), 7-29.

2879 ________. "La parola nella parola," Paragone, 280 (1973), 5-24. (Giovanna Morsiani, tr.)

2880 ________. "Saint Langage," Art International, 14, #2 (1970), 18-20, 27.

2881 Dorris, George E. "Two Allusions in the Poetry of T. S. Eliot," ELN, 2 (Summer, 1964), 54-57.

2882 Drew, Elizabeth. Discovering Poetry. London: Milford; New York: Norton, 1933, passim.

2883 ________. Major British Poets. New York: Norton, 1959, passim.

2884 ________. Poetry: A Modern Guide to Its Understanding and Enjoyment. New York: Norton, 1959, passim.

2885 ________. "T. S. Eliot," Directions in Modern Poetry. New York: Norton, 1940, 37-55, 133-147.

2886 ________. T. S. Eliot: The Design of His Poetry. New York: Scribner's, 1949. Revs.: N. Foerster, AL, 21, 496-7; Albert F. Gegenheimer, AQ, 7, 186-92; Alfred Neumeyer, JA, 8, 196-8; Curtis B. Bradford, VQR, 26, 157-60; J. G. Ritz, EA, 5, 180-1; Donald A. Stauffer, NYTB, Mar. 27, p. 27; Geo. Williamson, Poetry, 75, 112-13; L. A. Fiedler, Nat, 169, 42; B. Duffey, WR, 14, 71-2.

2887 Driver, Tom F. "T. S. Eliot: 1888-1965," Christianity and Crisis, 25 (February 8, 1965), 2-3.

2888 Drumm, Sister Robert Mary, O. P. "Johnson, Arnold, and Eliot as Literary Humanists," DA, 27 (Western Reserve: 1966), 745A.

2889 Drummond, Mary. "On Thomas Stearns Eliot," T. S. Eliot: A Symposium. Neville Braybrooke, ed. New York: Farrar, Straus & Cudahy, 1958, pp. 105-106.

2890 Duffey, Bernard I. "The Experimental Lyric in Modern Poetry: Eliot, Pound, Williams," JML, 3 (July, 1974), 1085-1103.

2891 Duffy, John J. "T. S. Eliot's Objective Correlative: A New England Commonplace," NEQ, 42 (March, 1969), 108-115.

2892 Dunkel, W. D. "An Exchange of Notes on T. S. Eliot: A Rejoinder," Theology Today, 7 (January, 1951), 507-508.

2893 ________. "T. S. Eliot's Quest for Certitude," Theology Today, 7, #2 (July, 1950), 228-236.

2894 Duparc, Jean. "T. S. Eliot et le sens de la réalité," NCRMM, No. 168 (July-August, 1965), 27-35.

2895 Dupee, F. W. "Difficulty as Style," AmSch, 14, #3 (Spring, 1945), 355-357.

2896 Durrell, Lawrence. "Anniversary" [poem], T. S. Eliot: A Symposium. Richard March and Tambimuttu, comps. Freeport, N.Y., Bks. for Libraries Press, 1968, p. 88.

2897 ________. "The Other T. S. Eliot," Atl, 215 (May, 1965), 60-64.

2898 ________. "T. S. Eliot," A Key to Modern British

Poetry. London: 1952; Norman, Okla.: Oklahoma U. P., 1952, pp. 143-163.

2899 ______. "Tse-lio-t," Preuves, No. 170 (1965), 3-8.

2900 Dwivedi, A. N. "The Indian Temper in Eliot's Poetry," BP, 19 (1972; pub. 1974), 48-53.

2901 Dyson, A. E., ed. English Poetry: Select Bibliographical Guides. London; New York: Oxford U. P., 1971, passim.

2902 Dzwonkoski, Felix P., Jr. "T. S. Eliot: Time and the Human Will," DAI, 31 (Indiana: 1971), 1766A.

2903 Eagleton, Terry. "Eliot and a Common Culture," Eliot in Perspective: A Symposium. Graham Martin, ed. New York: Humanities, 1970, pp. 279-295.

2904 Eastman, Max. "The Swan Song of Human Letters," Scribner's, 88 #6 (December, 1930), 598-607.

2905 Eberhart, Richard. "Homage to T. S. Eliot," HA, 125, #3 (1938), 18-19.

2905a Eder, Doris L. "Louis Unmasked: T. S. Eliot in The Waves," VWQ, 2, #1-2 (1975), 13-27.

2906 Edfelt, Johannes. "T. S. Eliot Obtains Nobel Prize," NYT (November 5, 1948), 22.

2907 Edman, Irwin. "Incantations by Eliot," SatR, 33 (June 24, 1950), 56-57.

2908 ______. "Notes Towards the Definition of Culture," NYTBR (March 6, 1949).

2909 Edmonds, Dorothy. "T. S. Eliot: Toward the 'Still Point,'" BSTCF, 5, #2 (Spring, 1964), 49-54.

2910 Egawa, Toru. "T. S. Eliot ni okeru 'Muku'--Shall We Follow the Deception of the Thrush?" EigoS, 118 (1972), 322-324.

2911 Eglinton, John. "Mr. T. S. Eliot's Mission," DubM, 30 (October-December, 1954), 35-39. Finds Eliot "extraordinarily indifferent to melody in verse,..."

2912 Egri, Déter. "T. S. Eliot's Aesthetics," HSE, 8 (1974), 5-34.

2913 ______. "Thomas Stearns Eliot," Az angol irodalom a huszadik században. [English literature in the twentieth century.] Lásló Báti and Istvan Kristo-Nagy, eds. Budapest: Gondalot, Vol. 1, 1970, pp. 283-322.

2914 El-Azma, Nazeer. "The Tammūzi Movement and the Influence of T. S. Eliot on Badr Shākir al-Sayyāb," JAOS, 88 (1968), 671-678.

2915 Elbaz, Shlomo. "Auteur et traducteur face à face (A propos de la traduction par T. S. Eliot d'Anabase de St. J. Perse)," FMLS, 9 (1973), 269-292.

2915a ________. "Le Pari de la traduction poétique: Analyse comparée de quatre traductions anglaises d'un passage d'Anabase de St. J. Perse," HUSL, 3 (1975), 47-65.

2916 ________. "Traduction littérale ou littéraire," CLS, 11, #1 (March, 1974), 48-68.

2917 Eleanor, Mother Mary. "The Debate of the Body and the Soul," Renascence, 12 (Summer, 1960), 192-197. Includes comment on Eliot.

2918 "Eliot: Chronicler of the Lost Generation," Kans. City Times (July 10, 1969), 16E. "He [Eliot] once said of William Wordsworth that 'his name marks an epoch.' The same can be said of T. S. Eliot."

2919 "Eliot and an Age of Fiction," NSt (January 8, 1965), 47.

2920 "Eliot and Faith: The Demon of Doubt and the Joy of Belief," TLS, #3585 (November 13, 1970), 1313-1315.

2921 Elliott, George Roy. "T. S. Eliot and Irving Babbitt," AmR, 7, #4 (September, 1936), 442-454.

2922 Ellis, P. G. "The Development of T. S. Eliot's Historical Sense," RES, 23 (1972), 291-301.

2923 Ellmann, Richard. Eminent Domain: Yeats among Wilde, Joyce, Pound, Eliot and Auden. London and New York: Oxford U. P., 1967, passim.

2924 ________. "Yeats and Eliot," Encounter, 25, #1 (July, 1965), 53-55.

2925 Embler, Weller. "Simone Weil and T. S. Eliot," Costerus, 4 (1972), 49-67.

2926 Emerson, D. "Poetry Corner," Scholastic, 24 (February 17, 1934), 12.

2926a ________. "Poetry Corner," Scholastic, 30 (February 13, 1937), 15f.

2927 Emery, Sarah Watson. "Saints and Mr. Eliot," EUQ, 7 (October, 1951), 129-142.

2927a Empson, William. "Eliot and Politics," TSER, 2, #2 (1975), 3-4.

2928 __________. "The Style of the Master," T. S. Eliot: A Symposium. Richard March and Tambimuttu, eds. Chicago: Regnery, 1949; Freeport, N.Y.: Bks. for Libraries Press, 1968, pp. 35-37.

2929 Enebjelm, Helen. "T. S. Eliots ökenkansla--En anglosachsisk företeelse," Literatur, Kunst, Teater (Stockholm, 1945), pp. 11-15.

2930 Engel, Claire-Eliane. "Essais de T. S. Eliot," Esquisses anglaises. Paris: Editions "Je sers," 1949 (Collection: Les Essayestes), pp. 99-171.

2931 English, Isobel. "'Rose of Memory,'" T. S. Eliot: A Symposium for His Seventieth Birthday. Neville Braybrooke, ed. New York: Farrar, Straus & Cudahy, 1958, pp. 185-186.

2932 Esch, Arno. "T. S. Eliot als Literaturkritiker," Sprache und Literatur Englands und Amerikas: Lehrgangsvortrage der Akademie Comburg, II. Carl August Weber, ed. Tübingen: M. Niemeyer, 1956, pp. 103-120.

2933 Espmark, Kjell. "Edelof och Eliot: En studie kring Farjesang," BLM, 28 (October, 1959), 683-690. Eliot's influence on Gunnar Ekelof.

2934 Etienne, Fernard. Thomas Stearns Eliot. Studie met bibliografie. Bruges: Desclee De Brouwer, 1961, pp. 55.

2935 Evans, B. Ifor. "T. S. Eliot," English Literature Between the Wars. London: Methuen & Co., 1948, 3rd ed., 1951, pp. 91-101.

2936 __________. "Towards the Twentieth Century: Gerard Manley Hopkins and T. S. Eliot," Tradition and Romanticism: Studies in English Poetry from Chaucer to W. B. Yeats. London: Methuen, 1940; repr., Hamden, Conn.: Archon Bks., 1964, pp. 185-200.

2937 Evans, David W. "The Case Book of T. S. Eliot," MLN, 71 (November, 1956), 501.

2938 __________. "The Domesticity of T. S. Eliot," UTQ, 23 (July, 1954), 380-385.

2939 __________. "The Penny World of T. S. Eliot," Renascence, 10 (Spring, 1958), 121-128.

2940 __________. "T. S. Eliot, Charles Williams, and the Sense of the Occult," Accent, 14, #2 (Spring, 1954), 148-155.

2941 Every, George. "Christian Polity," Purpose, 12, #1 (January, 1940), 31-37.

2942 ________. "Mr. Eliot and the Classics," NewEW, 26, #22 (March, 1945), 191.

2943 ________. "The Way of Rejections," T. S. Eliot: A Symposium. Richard March and Tambimuttu, comps. Freeport, N. Y.: Bks. for Libraries Press, 1968, pp. 181-188.

2944 Ewen, D. R. "Eliot, Bantock, and Education," TSEN, 1, #1 (1974), 7-9. Rev.-art., G. H. Bantock's T. S. Eliot and Education. N. Y.: Random House, 1969.

2945 An Exhibition of Manuscripts and First Editions of T. S. Eliot. Austin: University of Texas Humanities Research Center, 1961.

2946 Faas, Egbert. "Formen der Bewusstseinsdarstellung in der dramatischen Lyrik Pounds und Eliots," GRM, 18 (1968), 172-191.

2947 Fabricius, Johannes. The Unconscious and Mr. Eliot: A Study in Expressionism. Copenhagen: Nyt Nordisk Forlag, 1967.

2948 Fain, John T., and Thomas D. Young, eds. "The Agrarian Symposium," SoR, 8 (1972), 845-882. Includes a record of Tate's impressions of Eliot.

2949 Fairchild, Hoxie Neale. Religious Trends in English Poetry: 1920-1965. Vol. VI. New York and London: Columbia U. P., 1968, pp. 489-497.

2950 Falck, Colin. "Hurry Up Please It's Time," Rev, No. 4 (November, 1962), 59-64.

2951 Falconieri, John V. "Il Saggio di T. S. Eliot su Dante," Ital, 34 (June, 1957), 75-80.

2952 Faraque, Muhammad. "The Impact of Eliot on Bengali Criticism," Venture, 5, #1 (June, 1968), 51-55.

2953 Farber, Marjorie. "A Choice of Kipling's Verse: Made by T. S. Eliot," NYTBR (September 26, 1943), Sec. 7, pp. 1, 22. Cf., W. R. Benét. "The Phoenix Nest," SatR, 26 (October 9, 1943), 20.

2954 Farooqui, M. A. "The Technique of T. S. Eliot's Poetry," Hindusthan Rev. (Lucknow), 1947.

2955 Fasel, Ida. "A 'Conversation' Between Faulkner and Eliot," MissQ, 20 (Fall, 1967), 195-206.

2955a Feder, Lillian. "Narcissus as Saint and Dancer," TSER, 3, 1-2 (1976) 13-19. Meaning of Narcissus figure in Eliot.

2956 ___________. "T. S. Eliot: The Retreat from Myth," "T. S. Eliot: Fulfillment through Sacrifice," and "T. S. Eliot: '... Timeless Moments,'" Ancient Myth in Modern Poetry. Princeton, New Jersey: Princeton U. P., 1971, pp. 121-136, 219-242, 307-316.

2957 Fergusson, Francis. "T. S. Eliot and His Impersonal Theory of Art," The American Caravan. Van Wyck Brooks, et al., eds. New York: Macauley, 1927, pp. 446-453.

2958 ___________. "Three Allegorists: Brecht, Wilder, and Eliot," SR, 64 (October-December, 1956), 544-573.

2959 Fernandez, Ramon. "The Classicism of T. S. Eliot," Message. Trans., by Montgomery Belgion. New York: Harcourt, Brace, 1927, pp. 295-304.

2960 Ferris, Bob. "T. S. Eliot, the Poet," CEJ, 1, #3 (Fall, 1965), 54-60.

2961 Ferry, David. "The Diction of American Poetry," American Poetry. John Russell Brown, Irvin Ehrenpreis, and Bernard Harris, eds. (Stratford-upon-Avon Studies, No. 7.) London: Edward Arnold, 1965, pp. 135-153. Emphasis on Williams, Cummings, and Eliot.

2962 Ficimi, Fausto. "T. S. Eliot: La figlia che piange," SA, 15 (1969), 245-280.

2963 Fields, Kenneth W. "The Rhetoric of Artifice: Ezra Pound, T. S. Eliot, Wallace Stevens, Walter Conrad Arensberg, Donald Evans, Mina Loy, and Yvor Winters," DA, 28 (Stanford: 1967), 4627A.

2964 Findlater, Richard. "The Camouflaged Dream," TC, 94 (October, 1953), 311-316.

2965 ___________. The Unholy Trade. London: Gollancz, 1952, passim.

2966 Finn, H. Seth. "Cummings' Memorabilia," Expl, 29 (1971), Item 42.

2967 Fishbein, Michael. "The Influence of the Idealism of F. H. Bradley on the Thought and Poetry of T. S. Eliot," DAI, 32 (Yale: 1971), 2684A.

2968 Fitz, Reginald. "The Meaning of Impotence in Hemingway and Eliot," ConnR, 4, #2 (1971), 16-22.

2969 Fitzgerald, Robert. "Generations of Leaves: The Poet in the Classical Tradition," Perspectives USA, No. 8 (1954), 68-85. Discusses Homer, Virgil, Dante, Hopkins, Eliot.

2970 Fiumi, Annamaria B. "G. Benn e T. S. Eliot: Poetiche a confronto," SA, 16 (1970), 301-351.

2971 Fiumi, Fausto. "Virgilio e il classicismo di T. S. Eliot," SA, 17 (1971 [1973]), 121-166. Vol. 17 was dated 1971, but appeared in 1973.

2972 Fleisher, Frederic and Boel. "En eftermiddag med T. S. Eliot," Göteborgs Handelsoch Sjöfarts-Tidning, 130, (October 18, 1961), 3; Aarhuus Stiftstidende, 169 (January 11, 1962), 23-24.

2973 Fleissner, Robert F. "The Browning of T. S. Eliot," TSEN, 1, #1 (Spring, 1974), 6-7.

2974 __________. "Reacting to The Reactionaries: Libertarian Views," JHR, 17 (1969), 138-145. Rev.,-art.

2975 __________. "'Scarecrow Men,'" AN&Q, 7 (June, 1969), 151; 8 (1970), 89-90.

2976 Fletcher, J. G. "Poems in Counterpoint," Poetry, 63 (October, 1943), 44-48.

2977 Fluchère, Henri. "L'Attitude Critique de T. S. Eliot," CdSud, 35, #292 (2nd Half, 1948), 499-511.

2978 __________. "Défense de la Lucidité," T. S. Eliot: A Symposium. Richard March and Tambimuttu, comps. Freeport, N. Y.: Bks. for Libraries Press, 1968, pp. 141-145.

2979 __________. "Le dolce stil nuovo de T. S. Eliot," LetF, #1066 (February 4-10, 1965), 1, 6.

2980 __________. "Un Européen," Adam (London), 16 (May, 1948), 5-6. The "Europeanization" of Eliot.

2981 __________. "Un grand poète anglais, T. S. Eliot," CdSud, 19 (May, 1940), 304-318.

2982 __________. "T. S. Eliot ou l'intelligence faite homme," NL (Jan. 14, 1965), 1, 7.

2983 Foltinek, Herbert. "The Mythical Method in the Early Poems of T. S. Eliot," Anglistische Studien. Karl Brunner, Herbert Koziol and Siegfried Korninger, eds. Friedrich Wild zum 70. Begurtstag. (Wiener Beiträge zur englischen Philologie, LXVI.) Wien: Braumüller, 1957-58, pp. 27-38.

2984 Forster, E. M. "T. S. Eliot," Abinger Harvest. New York: Meridian Bks., Harcourt, Brace, 1936; 1955, pp. 89-90; repr., in T. S. Eliot: A Selected Critique. Leonard Unger, New York: Rinehart, 1948, pp. 11-17.

2985 ________. "T. S. Eliot and His Difficulties," L&L, 2, #13 (June, 1929), 417.

2986 ________. Two Cheers for Democracy. New York: Harcourt, Brace & World, 1951, pp. 259-260, 261-262.

2987 Foster, Genevieve W. "The Archetypal Imagery of T. S. Eliot," PMLA, 60 (June, 1945), 567-585. Cf., A. K. Coomaraswamy. "Primordial Images," PMLA, 61 (1946), 601-602.

2988 ________. "Reply," [to A. K. Coomaraswamy] PMLA, 61 (June, 1946), 602-603.

2989 Fowler, Helen. "The Eliot of Yvor Winters," Approach, 10 (Winter, 1953-54), 2-8.

2990 Fowlie, Wallace. "Baudelaire and Eliot: Interpreters of Their Age," SR, 74, #1 (Special T. S. Eliot Issue), (Winter, 1966), 293-309; repr., in T. S. Eliot: The Man and His Work. Allen Tate, ed. New York: Delacorte Press, 1966, pp. 299-315.

2991 ________. "Eliot and Tchelitchew," Accent, 5 (Spring, 1945), 166-170.

2992 ________. "Jorge Guillén, Marianne Moore, T. S. Eliot: Some Recollections," Poetry, 90 (May, 1957), 103-109.

2993 ________. "Le Mythe de l'Enfance--T. S. Eliot et Tchelitchew," Arts et Lettres (Paris), (March, 1946), 53-59. Eliot's symbolism of children and trees.

2994 ________. "T. S. Eliot, la poésie comme un jeu du temps," La pureté dans l'art. Montreal: Editions de l'arbre, [1941], pp. 69-88.

2995 Foxall, Edgar. "T. S. Eliot and Keith Douglas," TLS, #3570 (July 31, 1970), 854.

2996 Franciosa, M. "Significato di un premio," FLe (November 14, 1948), 34.

2997 Franck, Jacques. "T. S. Eliot: De la poésie et de quelques poètes," RGB, #2 (1965), 112-117.

2998 Frank, Armin Paul. "Eliot and Babbitt: A Note on Influence," TSEN, 1, #2 (Fall, 1974), 7-9.

2999 ________. "Eliot on Milton: Tone as Criticism," Ansichten zu Faust: Karl Theens zum 70. Günther Mahal, ed. Geburtstag. Stuttgart: Kohlhammer, 1973, pp. 184-201.

3000 ________. Die Sehnsucht nach dem unteilbaren Sein: Motive und Motivationen in der Literaturkritik T. S. Eliots. München: Fink, 1973.

3001 ________. "T. S. Eliot's Concept of Tradition and the American Background," JA, 16 (1971), 151-161.

3002 ________. "T. S. Eliot's Objective Correlative and the Philosophy of F. H. Bradley," JAAC, 30, #3 (Spring, 1972), 311-318.

3003 Frank, Waldo. "The 'Universe' of T. S. Eliot," NR, 72, #934 (October 26, 1932), 294-295.

3004 ________. "The 'Universe' of T. S. Eliot," Adelphi, 5 (February, 1933), 321-325.

3005 ________. "The 'Universe' of T. S. Eliot," In the American Jungle. Freeport, N. Y.: Bks. for Libraries Press, 1st ed., 1937; repr., 1968, pp. 220-227.

3006 Frankenberg, L. "Eliot Re-estimated," SatR, 30 (December 6, 1947), 48.

3007 Franzen, Erich. "T. S. Eliot und die Masken Ezra Pounds," Die Wandlung, 4 (August, 1949), 593-604.

3008 Fraser, G. S. "A Language by Itself," T. S. Eliot: A Symposium. Richard March and Tambimuttu, comps. Freeport, N. Y.: Bks. for Libraries Press, 1968, pp. 167-177.

3009 ________. "Mr. Eliot and the Great Cats," Adam (London), 16 (May, 1948), 10-14. Eliot's symbolism of tigers and the destructive nature of human instincts.

3010 ________. The Modern Writer and His World. Baltimore: Penguin Bks., 1964, passim.

3010a ________. "Poetic Politics," TSER, 2, #1 (1975), 4-7.

3011 ________. "T. S. Eliot: A Re-appraisal," RLV, 34 (November-December, 1968), 551-566.

3012 ________. "W. B. Yeats and T. S. Eliot," T. S. Eliot: A Symposium for His Seventieth Birthday. Neville Braybrooke, ed. New York: Farrar, Straus & Cudahy, 1958, pp. 196-216.

3013 Frattini, Alberto. "Eliot critico della poesia," HumB, 15 (1960), 718-720.

3014 Freddi, Giovanni. Idea Di Religione in T. S. Eliot. Brescia: Antigianelli, 1953.

3014a Freed, Lewis. "Eliot and Bradley: A Review," TSER, 3, #1-2 (1976), 29-58.

3015 __________. T. S. Eliot: Aesthetics and History. La Salle, Ill.: Open Court Pub. Co., 1962.

3016 Freedman, Morris. "Jazz Rhythms and T. S. Eliot," SAQ, 51 (July, 1952), 419-435.

3017 __________. "The Meaning of T. S. Eliot's Jew," SAQ, 55 (April, 1956), 198-206.

3018 __________. "The Tagging of Paradise Lost: Rhyme in Dryden's The State of Innocence." MiltonQ, 5, #1 (March, 1971), 18-22.

3018a French, Warren. "The Age of Eliot: The Twenties as Waste Land," The Twenties: Fiction, Poetry, Drama. Warren French, ed. De Land, Florida: Everett/Edwards, 1975, pp. 1-26.

3019 __________. "The Thirties: Poetry," The Thirties: Fiction, Poetry, Drama. Warren French, ed. De Land, Florida: Everett/Edwards, 1967, pp. 116-117, 126-127, 137-138.

3020 Friar, Kimon. "Politics and Some Poets," NR, 127 (July 7, 1952), 17-18.

3021 __________, and John Malcolm Brinnin. "T. S. Eliot," Modern Poetry: American and British. New York: Appleton-Century-Crofts, 1951, pp. 425-426, 459-498.

3022 Friend, A. C. "T. S. Eliot: An Appreciation," St. LouisR, 2 (1932), 6-8.

3023 Frise, Adolf. "Begegnung mit T. S. Eliot in Hamburg," Wirtschafts-Zeitung (Stuttgart), 4, #89 (1949), 15.

3024 Frohock, W. M. "The Morals of T. S. Eliot," SWR, 37, #8, x-xi (Spring, 1962), 163-166.

3025 Fry, William A. "The Poetry of Personal Quest: Images in the Religious Verse of Six Christian Poets," DAI, 34 (Columbia: 1974), 7704A.

3026 Frye, Northrop. Anatomy of Criticism. Princeton: Princeton U. P., 1957, passim.

3027 ________. "The Road of Excess," Myth and Symbol: Critical Approaches and Applications. Bernice Slote, ed. Lincoln: Nebraska U. P., 1963, pp. 3-20.

3028 ________. T. S. Eliot. (Writers and Critics Ser.) London and Edinburgh: Oliver & Boyd, 1963; New York: Barnes & Noble, 1966.

3029 ________. The Well Tempered Critic. Bloomington: Indiana U. P., 1963, passim.

3030 Fukase, Kikan. A Study of T. S. Eliot. Tokyo: Eihosha, 1956.

3031 Fukase, Motohiro. T. S. Eliot's Poetics. Tokyo: Sogensha, 1952.

3032 ________. T. S. Eliot's Theory of Arts. Hieishobo, 1949.

3033 Fuller, John. "Five Finger Exercises," Rev, #4 (November, 1962), 46-51.

3034 Fuller, Roy. Owls and Artificers: Oxford Lectures on Poetry. New York: Library Pr., 1971, passim.

3035 ________. "Poetic Memories of the Thirties," MQR, 12, #3 (Summer, 1973), 217-231.

3036 ________. "Poetry of My Time," EDH, 35 (1969), 67-84.

3037 Funato, Hideo. "T. S. Eliot's Idea of Time," RRAL, (Tokyo), #16 (1955), 19-51.

3038 Fussell, Edwin S. "What the Thunder Said," Lucifer in Harness: American Meter, Metaphor, and Diction. Princeton: Princeton U. P., 1973.

3039 Fussell, Paul, Jr. "The Gestic Symbolism of T. S. Eliot," ELH, 22 (1955), 194-211.

3040 Galinsky, Hans. "Deutschland in der Sicht von D. H. Lawrence und T. S. Eliot: Eine Studie zum anglo-amerikanischen Deutschland des 20. Jahrhunderts," Abhandlungen der Akademie der Wissenschaften zu Berlin. Geistes- und Sozialwissenschaftlichen Klassen, No. 1, (1956). Mainz: Verlag der Akademie der Wissenschaften und der Litteratur, 1956, pp. 1-46.

3041 ________. "The Expatriate Poet's Style with Reference to T. S. Eliot and W. H. Auden," English Studies Today, Third Series: Lectures and Papers Read at the Fifth

Conference of the International Association of Professors of English Held at Edinburgh and Glasgow, August, 1962. G. I. Duthie, ed. Edinburgh: Edinburgh U. P., 1964, pp. 215-226.

3042 __________. "G. B. Shaw als Gegenstand der Kritik und Quelle dramatischer Anregung für T. S. Eliot," GRM, n. s., 7 (April, 1957), 146-164.

3043 __________. Sprache und Sprachkunstwerk in Amerika: Studien und Interpretationen. Heidelberg: Quelle and Meyer, 1961, passim. Essays on T. S. Eliot and others.

3044 Gállego, Cándido Pérez. "Notas a los Occasional Verses de T. S. Eliot," FMod, 4, xvii-xviii (1965), 75-81.

3045 Gallup, Donald. "The 'Lost' Manuscripts of T. S. Eliot," BNYPL, 72 (December, 1968), 641-652; TLS (November 7, 1968), 1238-1240.

3046 __________. "T. S. Eliot and Ezra Pound: Collaborators in Letters," Atl, 225 (January, 1970), 48-62; repr., in Poetry Australia, 32 (February, 1970), 58-80.

3047 Gamberini, Sparto. La Poesia di T. S. Eliot con Prefazione di A. Obertello. Genova: Pubblicazioni dell'Instituto Universitario di Magistero, 1954.

3048 García Lara, José. "T. S. Eliot y la curvatura del tiempo," Insula, 8 (June 15, 1953), 3-10.

3049 Garcon, Maurice. "Compliment à T. S. Eliot," MdF, 335 (January, 1959), 16-25.

3050 Gardner, Helen. The Art of T. S. Eliot. London: Cresset, 1949; Faber & Faber, 1968; New York: Dutton, 1950. Revs., Babette Deutsch, NYHTB (December 6, 1959), 10; (Oct. 1, 1950), 21; R. W. Flint, Poetry, 77 (1949), 41-47; Albert Frank Gegenheimer, AQ, 7 (1950-52), 186-92; D. Krook, CamJ, 3 (1950-52), 632-6.

3051 __________. "Explorer of Moral Distress," NSt, 78 (November 28, 1969), 760-762.

3052 __________. "The Landscapes of Eliot's Poetry," CritQ, 10 (Winter, 1968), 313-330.

3053 __________. Religion and Literature: The T. S. Eliot Memorial Lectures. New York: Oxford U. P., 1971, pp. 113-118.

3054 __________. "T. S. Eliot," HES, 2 (1971), 27-44.

3055 __________. "T. S. Eliot," Twentieth-Century Literature in Retrospect. (Harvard Eng. Studies, 2.) Reuben A. Brower, ed. Cambridge: Harvard U. P., 1971, pp. 27-44; repr., in T. S. Eliot: A Collection of Criticism. Linda W. Wagner, ed. New York: McGraw-Hill, 1974, pp. 125-139.

3056 __________. T. S. Eliot and the English Poetic Tradition. (Byron Foundation Lecture, 1965,) Nottingham, England: Nottingham U. P., 1966.

3057 Garelick, Judith Spritzer. Marianne Moore, Modern Poet: A Study of Miss Moore's Relationships with William Carlos Williams, E. E. Cummings, T. S. Eliot, Wallace Stevens, and Ezra Pound. Diss. Harvard: 1972.

3058 Garetti, Laura. T. S. Eliot in Italia. Saggio e bibliografia. Bari: Adriatica, 1968.

3059 Gary, F. "Dante," Symposium, 1, #2 (April, 1920), 268-271.

3060 Geier, Norbert Joseph. "The Problem of Aesthetic Judgment and Moral Judgment of Literary Value in the Critical Theories of Irving Babbitt, Paul Elmer More, Yvor Winters, and T. S. Eliot," DA, 24 (Wisconsin: 1964), 4188.

3061 George, Arapura G. T. S. Eliot: His Mind and Art. London: Asia Pub. House, 1962; 2nd rev. ed., 1969.

3062 Gerard, Martin. "It Means What It Says," QRL, 2, #2 (August, 1961), 100-107.

3063 Gerard, Sister Mary. "Eliot of the Circle and John of the Cross," Thought, 34 (Spring, 1959), 107-127.

3064 Germer, Rudolf. "Die Bedeutung Shakespeares für T. S. Eliot," SJ, 95 (1959), 112-132.

3065 __________. T. S. Eliots Anfänge als Lyriker, 1905-1915. (Beihefte zum JA 17.) Heidelberg: Winter, 1966.

3066 __________. "T. S. Eliots Bedeutung als Dichter und Kritiker," NS, 7 (December, 1958), 545-552.

3067 Gerster, M. "T. S. Eliot," Weltstimmen (Stuttgart), 18, #4 (1949), 24-30.

3068 Gervais, Terence White. "T. S. Eliot and Asian Culture," Aryan 36, #10 (October, 1965), 453-455.

3069 Ghosh, Damayanti B. "The Concept of Karma in T. S. Eliot," JJCL, 12 (1974), 14-21.

3070 __________. "Indian Thought in T. S. Eliot," DAI, 32 (Indiana: 1972), 5182A.

3070a __________. "Karma as a Mode of Salvation in T. S. Eliot," JJCL (1974), 125-135.

3071 Gibbs, A. M., Kevin Margarey and A. L. French, "Critical Exchange: Mr. French's Mr. Eliot," SoR, 1, #2 (1964), 82-88.

3072 Gil, Kim Jong. "T. S. Eliot's Influence on Modern Korean Poetry," LE&W, 13 (1969), 359-376.

3073 Gilbertson, Philip N. "Time and the Timelessness in the Poetry of T. S. Eliot, Dylan Thomas, and Edwin Muir," DAI, 33 (Kentucky: 1971), 752A.

3074 Giles, Richard F. "A Note on 'April,'" TSEN, 1 (Spring, 1975), 3.

3075 Gillet, Louis. "T. S. Eliot et les Faux Dieux," RdM (July 1, 1934), 199-211.

3076 Gillis, Everett A. "The Scurrilous Parody in T. S. Eliot's Early Religious Verse," Descant, 16, #3 (Spring, 1972), 43-48.

3077 Gish, Nancy Kathryn Dunkle. "Time in the Poetry of T. S. Eliot," DAI, 34 (Michigan: 1973), 1909A.

3078 Giudici, Giovanni. "La via della saggezza," FLe, 9 (May, 1954), 1.

3079 Glaser, Michael S. "T. S. Eliot and F. H. Bradley: A Study of Bradley's Influence on Eliot's Major Poems," DAI, 32 (Kent State: 1971), 1510A.

3080 Glass, Malcolm S. "T. S. Eliot: Christian Poetry Through Liturgical Allusion," The Twenties, Poetry and Prose. Richard E. Langford and William E. Taylor, eds. De Land, Florida: Everett/Edwards, 1966, pp. 42-45.

3081 Glaza, J. F. "Transition," Wingover, 1 (Fall-Winter, 1958-59), 33-38.

3082 Glicksberg, Charles I. "T. S. Eliot as Critic," ArQ, 4 (Autumn, 1948), 225-236.

3083 __________. "Thomas Stearns Eliot," American Literary Criticism, 1900-1950. Charles I. Glicksberg, ed. New York: Hendricks House, 1951, pp. 129-133.

3084 Golden, William F. "...II. A Study of Transcendent Moments in the Poetry of Eliot and Yeats....," DAI, 35 (Rutgers: 1974), 402A.

3085 Goldfarb, Russell M. "R. P. Warren's Tollivers and Eliot's Tullivers," (II), UR, 36 (Summer, 1970), 275-279.

3086 Golffing, Francis, and Barbara Gibbs. "The Public Voice: Remarks on Poetry Today," Commentary, 28, #1 (July, 1959), 63-69.

3087 Gomme, Andor. "Appendix B: Winters and Eliot," Attitudes to Criticism. Carbondale & Edwardsville: Southern Ill. U. P., 1966, pp. 145-152.

3088 Good, Thomas. "T. S. Eliot et la Tradition Anglaise," CdSud, 48, 352 (October-November, 1959), 427-443.

3089 Goodwin, K. L. "Pound and Eliot," The Influence of Ezra Pound. New York: Oxford U. P., 1967, pp. 106-142.

3090 Gordon, Elizabeth. "The Voice of T. S. Eliot," T. S. Eliot: A Symposium. Neville Braybrooke, ed. New York: Farrar, Straus & Cudahy, 1958, pp. 112-114.

3091 Gordon, George S. Poetry and the Moderns. Oxford: Clarendon Press, 1935.

3092 Gordon, Lyndall Felicity. "T. S. Eliot's Early Years," DAI, 37 (Columbia: 1973), 331A.

3093 Gottfried, Leon. "Death's Other Kingdom: Dantesque and Theological Symbolism in Flowering Judas," PMLA, 84, #1 (January, 1969), 112-124. Notes allusions drawn from Eliot's poetry.

3094 Graham, Desmond. "T. S. Eliot and Keith Douglas," TLS, 3573 (August 21, 1970), 928. Cf., Antony Coleman. TLS, #3568 (July 16, 1970), 775; TLS, #3570 (July 31, 1970), 854.

3095 Graham, James C. The Critical Theories of T. S. Eliot and I. A. Richards. Diss. Wisconsin: 1941.

3096 Grasmuck, Gloria. "'A Second Look at T. S. Eliot,'" Gys, 2, #1 (1974), 47-51.

3097 Graves, Robert. The Common Asphodel. London: H. Hamilton, 1949, passim.

3098/9 ____________. "These Be Thy Gods, O Israel," NR, 134 (February 27, 1956), 16-18.

3100 Greenbaum, Leonard. "The Hound & Horn Archive," YULG, 39, #3 (January, 1965), 137-146.

3101 Greenberg, Clement. "Mr. Eliot and Notions of Culture: A Discussion," PR, 11, #3 (Summer, 1944), 305-307.

3102 ________. "T. S. Eliot: The Criticism, the Poetry," Nation, 171, #24 (December 9, 1950), 531-533.

3103 Greene, Edward J. H. "Jules Laforgue et T. S. Eliot," RLC, (Paris), 22 (July-September, 1948), 363-397.

3104 ________. T. S. Eliot et la France. Diss. Paris: 1948.

3105 ________. T. S. Eliot et la France. Paris: Boivin, 1951.

3106 Greenhut, Morris. "Sources of Obscurity in Modern Poetry: The Examples of Eliot, Stevens, and Tate," CRAS, 7, #2 (Spring, 1963), 171-190.

3107 Greenwell, Tom. "The Function of Art," B&B, (January, 1963), 44-46.

3108 Greenwood, E. B. "On Poetry and Poets," EIC, 3, #3 (July, 1958), 319-324.

3109 Gregor, Ian. "Eliot and Matthew Arnold," Eliot in Perspective: A Symposium. Graham Martin, ed. New York: Humanities, 1970. pp. 267-278.

3110 Gregory, Horace. "The Man of Feeling," NR, 79, #1015 (May 16, 1934), 23-24.

3111 ________, and Marya Zaturenska. "T. S. Eliot, the Twentieth-Century 'Man of Feeling' in American Poetry," A History of American Poetry. New York: Harcourt, Brace, 1946, pp. 413-428.

3112 Grierson, H. J. C., and J. C. Smith. "Twentieth Century Poetry between the Wars, 1919-1939," A Critical History of English Poetry. London: Chatto and Windus, 1944, 548-569.

3113 Grigsby, Gordon Kay. "The Modern Long Poem: Studies in Thematic Form," DA, 21 (Wisconsin: 1960), 622-623.

3114 Grigson, Geoffrey. "Leavis against Eliot," Encounter, 12, #4 (April, 1959), 68-69.

3115 Grochowiak, Stanislaw. "Eliotowa propozycja," Więź, #3 (1959), 75-79.

3116 Gross, Harvey S. The Contrived Corridor: A Study in Modern Poetry and the Meaning of History. Diss. Michigan: 1955.

3117 ___________. "Music and the Analogue of Feeling: Notes on Eliot and Beethoven," CentR, 3 (Summer, 1959), 269-288.

3118 ___________. "T. S. Eliot," The Contrived Corridor: History and Fatality in Modern Literature. Ann Arbor: Michigan U. P., 1971, pp. 32-73.

3119 Grubb, Frederick. "Reply," PoetryR, 59 (1968), 123-125. Cf., Paul Roche. "Since Eliot: Some Notes toward a Reassessment," PoetryR, 59 (Spring, 1968), 37-46.

3120 ___________. "T. S. Eliot, Alas?" A Vision of Reality: A Study of Liberalism in Twentieth-Century Verse. London: Chatto & Windus, 1965; New York: Barnes & Noble, 1965, pp. 46-69.

3121 Grudin, Louis. Mr. Eliot among the Nightingales. London: Joiner & Steele; Paris: L. Drake, 1932; repr., 1969. Concerns Eliot's criticism.

3122 Guidi, Augusto. "Il classicismo di T. S. Eliot," Veltro, 4, #1-2 (1960), 51-58.

3123 ___________. "Il classicismo di T. S. Eliot," Studi in onore di Vittorio Lugli e Diego Valeri. 2 vols. Venezia: Neri Pozza, 1962, pp. 507-517.

3124 ___________. Occasioni americane: Saggi di Letteratura Americana. Rome: Edizioni Moderne, 1958.

3125 ___________. "Omaggio a Eliot," FLe (Italy) (November 14, 1949).

3126 ___________. "Prose di T. S. Eliot," Idea, 5 (September 13, 1953), 2.

3127 Guidubaldi, Egidio. "Eliot contro Croce a proposito di Dante," FLe, #41 (October 15, 1950), 2.

3128 ___________. "Riempire gli uomini vuoti," FLe, #50 (December 30, 1951), 1-2.

3129 ___________. "T. S. Eliot e B. Croce. Due opposti atteggiamenti critici di fronte a Dante," Aevum, 31 (March-April, 1957), 147-185.

3130 Gunter, J. Bradley Hunt. "T. S. Eliot and Anglicanism: The Man of Letters as Religious and Social Critic," DAI, 30 (Virginia: 1970), 4450A.

3131 Gupta, N. D. Plato to Eliot. London: Probsthain, 1965.

3131a Gustafsson, Barbro. "Framtidens öde land: Oswald Spengler, T. S. Eliot och Karin Boye," SLT, 38, #3 (1975), 30-35.

3132 Guttmann, Allen. "From Brownson to Eliot: The Conservative Theory of Church and State," AmQ, 17 (Fall, 1965), 483-500.

3133 Haas, Rudolf. "Der frühe T. S. Eliot," NS, 9, #12 (December, 1960), 561-572.

3133a Habedank, Klaus. Kultur-und Sozialkritik bei T. S. Eliot: Eine Untersuchung der Werke Eliots 1909-39. Hamburg: Ludke, 1974.

3134 Hacikyan, A. "Art of T. S. Eliot's Imagery," La Revue de l'Universite de Sherbrooke, 5 (February, 1965), 155-160.

3135 Hagger, Nicholas. "Reflections on T. S. Eliot's Poetry," EigoS, 111 (May, 1965), 314-316.

3136 Hall, Donald. "The Art of Poetry," ParisR, 7, #28 (Summer-Fall, 1962), 22-51.

3136a ________. Remembering Poets: Reminiscences of Ezra Pound, Dylan Thomas, Robert Frost and T. S. Eliot. New York: Harper & Row, 1978.

3137 Hall, Ian Roger. "Murdering the Time: A Study of Temporal Order in Selected Works of Henry Thoreau, Nathaniel Hawthorne, T. S. Eliot and Ezra Pound," DAI, 36 (Kent State: 1975), 6099A.

3138 Halper, Nathan. "Joyce and Eliot: A Tale of Shem and Shaun," Nation, 200, #22 (May 31, 1965), 590-595.

3139 Hamalian, Leo. "Mr. Eliot's Saturday Evening Service," Accent, 10 (Autumn, 1950), 195-206.

3140 ________. "Wishwood Revisited," Renascence, 12 (Summer, 1960), 167-173.

3141 Hamburger, Michael. "T. S. Eliot," [poem], T. S. Eliot: A Symposium. Richard March and Tambimuttu, comps. Freeport, N.Y.: Bks. for Libraries Pr., 1968, p. 178.

3142 ________. "The Unity of Eliot's Poetry," Review (Oxford), #4 (November, 1962), 16-27.

3143 Hamilton, George Rostrevor. "Tradition and the Sense of Man's Greatness: The Work of T. S. Eliot," The Tell-Tale Article: A Critical Approach to Modern Poetry. London: Heinemann, 1949; Freeport, N.Y.: Bks. for Libraries Pr., 1972, pp. 63-94.

3144 Hancock, C. M. "A Dry Season," EA&A, 2 (1964), 53-65.

3145 Hansen, Erik Arne. "T. S. Eliot's 'Landscapes,'" ES, 50 (August, 1969), 363-379.

3146 Hanshell, Deryck. "L'Ascesa di T. S. Eliot," Letture, 20 (1965), 755-768.

3147 Hara, Ichiro. "Poetry and Belief: Richards vs. Eliot," SEL, 15 (1935), 221-244.

3148 Hardenbrook, Don. "T. S. Eliot and the Great Grimpen Mire by Gaston Huret III," BSJ, n. s., 6 (April, 1956), 88-93.

3149 Harding, D. W. "Christian or Liberal?" Scrutiny, 8, #3 (December, 1939), 309-313; repr., in The Importance of "Scrutiny" Eric Bentley, ed. New York: Geo. W. Stewart, 1948, pp. 287-290.

3150 ________. "T. S. Eliot, 1925-1935," Scrutiny, 5 (September, 1936), 171-176; repr., in T. S. Eliot: A Collection of Critical Essays. Hugh Kenner, ed. Englewood Cliffs, N. J.: Prentice-Hall, 1962, pp. 104-109.

3151 ________. "Words and Meanings: A Note on Eliot's Poetry," and "The Changed Outlook in Eliot's Later Poems," Experience into Words. New York: Horizon, 1963, pp. 104-111, 112-131.

3152 Hardy, J. E. "An Antic Disposition," SR, 65 (Winter, 1957), 50-60.

3153 Hargrove, Nancy D. "Landscape as Symbol in the Poetry of T. S. Eliot," DAI, 31 (South Carolina: 1971), 3548A.

3154 ________. "Symbolism in T. S. Eliot's 'Landscapes,'" SHR, 6, #3 (Summer, 1972), 273-282.

3155 Harmon, William. "Braybrooke Refuted," T. S. Eliot Review, 2 (Spring, 1975), 3.

3155a ________. "Eliot, Russell, and The Hibbert Journal," TSER, 2, #2 (Fall, 1975), 8-9.

3156 ________. "T. S. Eliot's Raids on the Inarticulate," PMLA, 91, #3 (May, 1976), 450-459.

3156a Harrex, S. C. "Dancing in the Dark: Balachandra Rajan and T. S. Eliot," WLWE, 14 (1975), 310-321.

3157 Harris, Wendell V. "English Short Fiction in the Nineteenth Century," SSF, 6, #1 (Fall, 1965), 1-93.

3158 Harrison, John. The Reactionaries: Yeats, Lewis, Pound, Eliot, Lawrence: A Study of the Anti-Democratic Intelligentsia. New York: Schocken Bks., 1967, passim.

3159 Hart, Jeffrey. "Christ and Apollo: The Modern Debate," Renascence, 16 (Winter, 1964), 95-102.

3160 ______. "Frost and Eliot," SR, 84 (Summer, 1976), 425-447.

3161 ______. "T. S. Eliot: His Use of Wycherley and Pope," N&Q, n. s., 4 (September, 1957), 389-390.

3162 Hartley, Anthony. "The Age of Eliot," EigoS, 111 (March, 1965), 168-171.

3163 Hartley, L. P. "A Garland from the Young: Introduction," T. S. Eliot: A Symposium for His Seventieth Birthday. Neville Braybrooke, ed. New York: Farrar, Straus & Cudahy, 1958, pp. 102-103.

3164 Hartman, Geoffrey H. Beyond Formalism: Literary Essays, 1958-1970. Yale U. P., 1970, passim.

3165 Harvey, C. J. D. "T. S. Eliot: Poet and Critic," Standpunte, 18, #5 (1965), 5-10.

3166 Harvey-Jellie, W. "T. S. Eliot among the Prophets?" DR, 18 (1938), 83-90.

3167 Hasegawa, Mitsuaki. "Poet's Communication of Meaning: An Approach to T. S. Eliot," HSELL, 9, #1-2 (June, 1963), 66-74.

3168 Hassan, Ihab H. "Baudelaire's 'Correspondances': The Dialectic of a Poetic Affinity," FR, 27 (May, 1954), 437-445.

3169 ______. "French Symbolism and Modern British Poetry with Yeats, Eliot and Edith Sitwell as Indices," DA, 13 (Pennsylvania: 1953), 539.

3170 Häusermann, Hans W. "T. S. Eliot's Conception of Poetry," Etudes de Lettres, 16, #4 (October, 1942), 165-178.

3171 ______. "T. S. Eliots religiose Entwicklung," EStudien, 69 (1935), 373-391, 8-9.

3172 Hawkins, Desmond. "Hamlet and T. S. Eliot," NewEW, 15, #25 (October, 1939), 312-313.

3173 Hays, Peter L. "Two Landscapes: Frost's and Eliot's," Max Reinhardt, 1873-1973: A Centennial Festschrift of Memorial Essays. George E. Wellwarth, and Alfred G.

Brooks, eds. Binghamton, New York: Max Reinhardt Archive, S. U. N. Y. at Binghamton, 1974, pp. 256-264.

3174 Hayward, John. "Den okände T. S. Eliot," BLM (Stockholm), 17 (December, 1949), 736-741.

3175 __________. Prose Literature Since 1939. London: Longmans Green, 1947, passim.

3175a Headings, Philip Ray. "Among Three Worlds: Ward, Eliot and Dante," TSER, 2, #2 (Fall, 1975), 11-14.

3176 __________. T. S. Eliot. New York: Twayne, 1964; New Haven, Connecticut: College and U. P., 1964.

3177 __________. "T. S. Eliot," ConL, 9 (Spring, 1968), 265-274.

3178 __________. "The Tiresias Tradition in Western Literature," DA, 19 (Indiana: 1959), 2337-38.

3179 Heath-Stubbs, John. "We Have Heard the Key Turn," T. S. Eliot: A Symposium. Richard March and M. J. Tambimuttu, eds. Chicago: Henry Regnery, 1949, pp. 236-242.

3180 Heller, Erich. "Glaube, Weisheit und Dichtung: zu T. S. Eliots Rede über Goethe," Merkur, 10 (1956), 234-444.

3181 __________. "T. S. Eliot: Die Tradition und das Moderne," GuG, 11 (1966), 98-137.

3182 Henderson, Philip. "The Agony of Mr. Eliot," The Poet and Society. London: Secker & Warburg, 1939, pp. 154-171.

3183 Hennecke, Hans. "T. S. Eliot: Der Dichter als Kritiker," Europäische Revue, 12, #9 (September, 1936), 721-735.

3184 Herdeck, Donald E. "A New Letter by Ezra Pound about T. S. Eliot," MassR, 12 (1971), 287-292.

3185 Hewes, Henry. "Eliot on Eliot: 'I feel younger than I did at 60,'" SatR, 41 (September 13, 1958), 32.

3186 __________. "Journey to Simplicity," SatR, 48 (January 23, 1965), 53-54.

3187 Hicks, Granville. "T. S. Eliot, Humanism, and Thornton Wilder," The Great Tradition: An Interpretation of American Literature Since the Civil War. New York: Macmillan, 1935, pp. 268-272.

3188 Hidden, Norman. "Studying T. S. Eliot in the Sixth Form," English, 14 (Summer, 1962), 53-56.

3189 Higgins, Bertram. "The Critical Method of T. S. Eliot," Scrutinies II. Edgell Rickwood, ed. London: Wishart, 1931, pp. 54-71.

3190 Higgins, David. "The Power of the Master: Eliot's Relation to Dante," DSARDS, 88 (1970), 129-148.

3191 Hildebrand, K. G. "Eliot," Svensk Tidskrift (Stockholm), 26 (1949), 59-66.

3191a Hildesheimer, Wolfgang. "Die Wirklichkeit der Reaktionäre: Uber [The Reality of the Reactionary: About] T. S. Eliot und Ezra Pound," Merkur, 28 314 (July, 1974), 630-647.

3192 Hill, Brennan. "The Literary Criticism of T. S. Eliot: Its Source and Tenets," AylR, 7 (1965), 95-101, 126.

3193 Hillyer, Robert. "The Crisis in American Poetry," AmMerc, 70 (January, 1950), 65-71.

3194 __________. "Poetry's New Priesthood," SatR, 32, #25 (June 18, 1949), 7-9, 38.

3195 __________. "Treason's Strange Fruit: The Case of Ezra Pound and the Bollingen Award," SatR, 32, #24 (June 11, 1949), 9-11, 28. Includes an attack on T. S. Eliot.

3196 Hilton, Charles. "The Poetry of T. S. Eliot," EJ, 20 (November, 1931), 749-761.

3197 Hirai, Masao. "The Problems of Human Nature in T. S. Eliot," SELit, 25, #3, (1948), 4.

3198 __________. "T. S. Eliot, the Poet," Fushicho, 2 (1949).

3199 __________, and E. W. F. Tomlin, eds. T. S. Eliot: A Tribute from Japan. Tokyo: Kenkyusha, 1966.

3200 Hirsch, David H. "T. S. Eliot and the Vexation of Time," SoR, n. s. 3 (July, 1967), 608-624.

3201 Hobsbaum, Philip. "Eliot, Whitman, and the American Tradition," JAmS, 3 (December, 1969), 239-264.

3202 Hodgson, R. A. "Tradition and Mr. Eliot," NewEW, 19, #23 (September, 1941), 221.

3203 Hodin, J. P. "Bertrand Russell og T. S. Eliot om menneskehetens fremtid," Samtiden (Oslo), 56 (1947), 78-89.

3204 __________. "T. S. Eliot on the Condition of Man Today," Horizon, 12, #68 (August, 1945), 83-89.

3205 Hoffman, Frederick J. The Imagination's New Beginning: Theology and Modern Literature. Notre Dame, Indiana: Notre Dame U. P., 1967, passim.

3206 __________. The Twenties: American Writing in the Postwar Decade. New York: Viking, 1955; Collier Bks., 1962, passim.

3207 Hogan, J. P. "Eliot's Later Verse," Adelphi, 28 (January-March, 1942), 54-58.

3208 Holbrook, David. "Mr. Eliot's Chinese Wall," EIC, 5 (October, 1955), 418-426.

3209 Holden, Alan. "Three Voyagers in Search of Europe: A Study of Henry James, Ezra Pound, and T. S. Eliot," DA, 26 (Columbia: 1965), 1646-47.

3210 __________. Three Voyagers in Search of Europe: A Study of Henry James, Ezra Pound, and T. S. Eliot. Philadelphia: Pennsylvania U. P., 1966, passim.

3211 __________. "T. S. Eliot on Henry James," PMLA, 79, #4 (September, 1964), 490-497.

3212 Holland, Norman N. "Realism and the Psychological Critic; or, How Many Complexes Had Lady Macbeth?" L&P, 10 (1960), 5-8.

3213 Holliday, Howard J. "The Rhetorical Development of T. S. Eliot's Criticism," DAI, 31 (Texas Christian: 1971), 5405A.

3214 Holroyd, Stuart. Emergence from Chaos. New York: Houghton Mifflin, 1957, passim.

3215 Holthusen, Hans Egon. "Das Schöne und das Wahre in der Poesie: Zur Theorie des Dichterischen bei Eliot und Benn," Merkur, 11 (April, 1957), 305-330.

3216 Hook, Sidney. "The Dilemma of T. S. Eliot," Nation, 160, #3 (January 20, 1945), 69-71.

3216a Hoover, Judith Myers. "Hindu and Buddhist Mysticism: The Still Point in the Turning Worlds of T. S. Eliot and Octavio Paz," DAI, 37 (Urbana, Ill.: 1976), 6464A.

3217 Hoskot, S. S. T. S. Eliot: His Mind and Personality. Bombay: University of Bombay Press, 1961.

3218 Hough, Graham. "Dante and Eliot," CritQ, 16 (Winter, 1974), 293-305.

3219 House, Humphrey. "Mr. Eliot as a Critic," New Oxford Outlook, 1, #1 (May, 1933), 95-105.

3220 Howarth, Herbert. "Eliot and Hofmannsthal," SAQ, 59 (Autumn, 1960), 500-509.

3221 __________. "Eliot and Milton: The American Aspect," UTQ, 30 (January, 1961), 150-162.

3222 __________. "Eliot, Beethoven, and J. W. N. Sullivan," CL, 9 (Fall, 1957), 322-332.

3223 __________. "Eliot: The Expatriate as Fugitive," GaR, 13 (Spring, 1959), 5-17.

3224 __________. Notes on Some Figures Behind T. S. Eliot. Boston: Houghton Mifflin, 1964.

3225 __________. "T. S. Eliot and the 'Little Preacher,'" AQ, 13 (Summer, 1961), 179-187.

3226 __________. "T. S. Eliot's Criterion: The Editor and His Contributors," CL, 11 (Spring, 1959), 97-110.

3227 Howarth, R. G. "T. S. Eliot's Literary Reminiscences," N&Q, 176 (June 24, 1939), 436-437.

3228 Hubbell, Jay B. "T. S. Eliot," Who Are the Major American Writers? Durham, North Carolina: Duke U. P., 1972, pp. 195-200, passim.

3228a Huffman, Claire. "T. S. Eliot, Eugenio Montale, and the Vagaries of Influence," CL, 27 (1975), 193-207.

3229 Huisman, David Arthur. "'An Extra-Human Measure': T. S. Eliot and the Theological Evaluation of Literature," DA, 28 (Michigan: 1967), 5056A-57A.

3230 Hungiville, Maurice. "A Choice of Critics: T. S. Eliot's Editions of Kipling's Poetry," DR, 52 (1972-73), 572-587.

3231 Hunter, George K. "T. S. Eliot and the Creation of a Symbolist Shakespeare," HES, 2 (1971), 191-204.

3232 __________. "T. S. Eliot and the Creation of a Symbolist Shakespeare," Twentieth-Century Literature in Retrospect. Reuben A. Brower, ed. (Harvard Eng. Studies 2.). Cambridge: Harvard U. P., 1971, pp. 191-204.

3233 Husain, S. M. "T. S. Eliot as a Critic of Dickens," Venture 5, #1 (June, 1968), 30-37.

3234 Husain, Syed Sajjad. "Eliot and My Generation," Venture, 5, #1 (June, 1968), 7-11.

3235 Hutchins, Robert M. "T. S. Eliot on Education," Measure, 1, #1 (Winter, 1950), 1-8.

3236 Huxley, Aldous. Letters of Aldous Huxley. Grover Smith, ed. New York: Harper & Row, 1970, passim.

3237 Hyman, Stanley E. "Poetry and Criticism: T. S. Eliot," AmSch, 30 (Winter, 1960-61), 43-55.

3238 __________. "Poetry and Criticism: T. S. Eliot," Poetry and Criticism: Four Revolutions in Literary Taste. New York: Atheneum, 1961, pp. 159-178.

3239 __________. "T. S. Eliot and Tradition in Criticism," The Armed Vision: A Study in the Methods of Modern Literary Criticism. New York: Vintage Books, 1955, pp. 54-91.

3240 __________. "T. S. Eliot, 1888-1965," NewL, 48 (February 1, 1965), 21-22.

3241 Inserillo, Charles R. "Wish and Desire: Two Poles of the Imagination in the Drama of Arthur Miller and T. S. Eliot," XUS, 1 (1962), 248-258.

3242 Irvine, Lyn. "Mr. T. S. Eliot Among the Critics," Monologue, 1, #4 (March 15, 1934), 1-8.

3243 Isaacs, J. "Eliot's Friends," Obs (June 18, 1967), 19.

3244 Iser, Wolfgang. "Walter Pater und T. S. Eliot: Der Übergang zur Modernität," GRM, 9, #4 (October, 1959), 391-408.

3245 Ishak, Fayek M. The Mystical Philosophy of T. S. Eliot. New Haven, Conn.: College & Univ. Press, 1970.

3246 __________. The Philosophical Bearing of Eastern and Western Mysticism on the Poetry of T. S. Eliot. Diss. Liverpool, 1961-62.

3247 Iwasaki, Soji. "Eliot no Borei--Hitotsu no Bungaku Fudo ni tsuite," EigoS, 120 (1974), 265-267.

3248 Jain, Sushil Kumar. "Indian Elements in the Poetry of T. S. Eliot, with Special Reference to the Influence of the Bhagavad-Gita," AryP, 40, #2 (February, 1969), 66-72.

3249 Jameson, R. D. "Poetry and Plain Sense: A Note on the Poetic Method of T. S. Eliot," Tsing Hua Review (November, 1931); repr., in Poetry and Plain Sense. Peiping: Natl. Tsing Hua Univ.: 1931.

3250 Jankowsky, Kurt R. Die Versauffassung bei Gerard Manley Hopkins, den Imagisten und T. S. Eliot: Renaissance altgermanischen Formgestaltens in der Dichtung des 20 Jahrhunderts. Diss. Münster, 1956.

3251 ______. Die Versauffassung bei Gerard Manley Hopkins, den Imagisten und T. S. Eliot.... München: Hueber, 1967.

3252 Janoff, Ronald W. "Eliot and Horace: Aspects of the Intrinsic Classicist," Cithara, 5, #1 (1965), 31-44.

3253 Janssens, G. A. M. The American Literary Review: A Critical History 1920-1950. Paris: Hague-Mouton, 1968, passim.

3254 Jarrell, Randall. "Fifty Years of American Poetry," PrS, 37, #1 (Spring, 1963), 1-27.

3255 Jarrett-Kerr, Martin. "'Not Much About Gods,'" T. S. Eliot: A Symposium. Neville Braybrooke, ed. New York: Farrar, Straus & Cudahy, 1958, pp. 176-180.

3256 ______. "'Of Clerical Cut': Retrospective Reflections on Eliot's Churchmanship," Eliot in Perspective: A Symposium. Graham Martin, ed. New York: Humanities, 1970, pp. 232-251.

3257 Jarv, Harry. "Kritik av den nya kritiken," [Criticism of the new criticism], Läsarmekanismer: Essäer och utblickar. [Reader mechanisms: essays and outlooks]. Staffanstorp: Cavefors, 1971, pp. 71-126.

3258 Jay, Douglas. "Mr. T. S. Eliot: After Lambeth," Oxford Outlook, 11 (June, 1931), 78-85.

3259 Jenkins, Harold. "T. S. Eliot and Keith Douglas," TLS, #3568 (July 16, 1970), 775. Cf., Antony Coleman, TLS, 3566 (July 2, 1970), 731; Foxall, Edgar, TLS, 3570 (July 31, 1970), 854; Gent, Margaret, N&Q, n. s., 17 (February, 1970), 50-51.

3260 Jenkins, William D. "The Sherlockian Eliot," BSJ, 12 (June, 1962), 81-84, 128.

3261 Jennings, Paul. "'O City City,'" T. S. Eliot: A Symposium. Neville Braybrooke, ed. New York: 1958, pp. 45-48.

3262 Jha, Akhileshwar. "T. S. Eliot and Christopher Fry: A Note on Possible Influence and Counter-Influence," LCritM, 8, #2 (1967), 46-54.

3262a Johnson, A. E. "T. S. Eliot and Posterity," SatR, 32

(April 16, 1949), 31. Cf., Ben Ray Redman. SatR, 32 (March 14, 1949), 9-11, 30-31.

3263 Johnson, Geoffrey. "English Poetry Today," LHY, 6, #1 (January, 1965), 30-35.

3264 Johnson, L. Eric. "T. S. Eliot's 'Objective Correlative' and Emotion in Art," AP&P, 1, #1 (1974), 20-33.

3265 Johnson, Maurice. "T. S. Eliot on Satire, Swift, and Disgust," PLL, 5 (Summer, 1969), 310-315.

3266 Jones, Dan L. "The Poetics of Ezra Pound and T. S. Eliot," DAI, 34 (Utah: 1973), 777A.

3267 Jones, Florence, "T. S. Eliot among the Prophets," AL, 38 (November, 1966), 285-302.

3268 Jones, Genesius. _Approach to the Purpose: A Study of the Poetry of T. S. Eliot._ New York: Barnes & Noble, 1964.

3269 Jones, Joyce Maria Meeks. "Jungian Concepts in the Poetry of T. S. Eliot," DAI, 36 (East Texas State: 1975), 6084A.

3270 Joost, Nicholas. "Some Primitives in _The Dial_ of the Twenties, Part I," ForumH, 10, #3 (Winter, 1972), 34-44.

3271 __________. "Some Primitives in _The Dial_ of the Twenties, Part II," ForumH, 11, #1 (Spring, 1973), 12-18.

3272 __________. "The Use of a Review," Re: A&L, 1, #1 (Spring, 1968), 1-4.

3272a __________. _Years of Transition: The Dial, 1912-1920._ Barre, Mass.: Barre Pubs., 1967, passim.

3273 Joseph, Brother, F.S.C. "The Concept of 'Poetic Sensibility' in the Criticism of T. S. Eliot," Fresco, 8, #1 (1957), 40-47.

3274 Joshi, B. N. "Hopkins and T. S. Eliot: A Study in Linguistic Innovation," OJES, 1, #1 (1961), 13-16.

3275 Jouve, Pierre Jean. "Gravitation" [poem], _T. S. Eliot: A Symposium._ Richard March, et al, eds. Freeport, N.Y.: 1968, pp. 93-95.

3276 Juhasz, Suzanne H. "Patterns of Metaphor: Their Function in Some Modern Long Poems: Studies in Williams, Pound, Stevens, and Eliot," DAI, 32 (Calif., Berkeley: 1971), 920A-21A.

3277 Julian, Constance. "T. S. Eliot and the Anglo-Catholics," Fireside, 12, #8 (1946), 11-14.

3278 Kagiya, Yukinobu, ed. Eliot no Shi to Geijutsu. Tokyo: Shimizu Kobundo, 1972. [The Poetry and Art of Eliot.]

3279 Kahn, Sholom J. "Eliot's 'Polyphiloprogenitive': Another Whitman Link?" WWR, 5 (Summer, 1959), 52-54.

3280 Kameyama, Masako. "An Essay on T. S. Eliot: His Idea of Tradition," CEKWJC, No. 6 (December, 1962), 72-88.

3281 ________. "An Essay on T. S. Eliot: On the Function of Poetry," CEKWJC, No. 9 (December, 1965), 117-131.

3282 Karanikas, Alexander. Tillers of a Myth: Southern Agrarians as Social and Literary Critics. Madison: Wisconsin U. P., 1966, passim.

3283 Karlin, Ken. "Critical Notes," ChiR, 7 (1953), 52-54.

3284 Kashfi, Abdul Khair. "Eliot's Impact on Urdu Literature and Thought," Venture, 5, #1 (June, 1968), 56-62.

3285 Kaul, R. K. "The Poetry of T. S. Eliot," BP, 9 (1967), 10-25.

3286 ________. "Rhyme and Blank Verse in Drama: A Note on Eliot," English, 15, #87 (Autumn, 1964), 96-99.

3287 Kazin, Alfred. "About T. S. Eliot," NR, 85 (January 15, 1936), 290-291.

3288 Keeley, Edmund. "Seferis and the 'Mythical Method,'" CLS, 6 (1969), 109-125.

3289 ________. "T. S. Eliot and the Poetry of George Seferis," CL, 8 (Summer, 1956), 214-226.

3290 Kelly, Gerald. "Literary Portraits: III. T. S. Eliot," LCUT, No. 3 (May, 1971), 50-51. Reproduction of Sir Gerald Kelly's oil portrait of Eliot.

3291 Kelly, Robert G. The Premises of Disorganization: A Study of Literary Form in Ezra Pound, T. S. Eliot, James Joyce, and Dorothy Richardson. Diss. Stanford: 1952.

3292 Kelly, Thomas, and Brian Kelly. "He Do the Police in Different Voices," TLS, (January 9, 1969), 38. Cf., TLS (January 23, 1969), 86; (January 30, 1969), 110; (February 13, 1969), 158; (March 6, 1969), 242; (March 20, 1969), 299.

3293 Kenner, Hugh. "Art in a Closed Field," VQR, 38 (1962), 597-613.

3294 ________. "Dante tra Pound ed Eliot," Verri, #18 (1964), 35-40.

3295 ________. "Eliot and the Tradition of the Anonymous," CE, 28 (May, 1967), 558-564.

3296 ________. "Eliot's Moral Dialectic," HudR, 2 (Autumn, 1949), 421-448.

3297 ________. "For Other Voices," Poetry, 94 (September, 1959), 36-40.

3298 ________. The Invisible Poet: T. S. Eliot. New York: McDowell, Obolensky, 1959; London: Methuen, 1965.

3299 ________. "Poetry and Such: A Stilton Catechized upon a Table," NatlR, 10, #15 (April 22, 1961), 250, 263.

3300 ________. The Pound Era. Berkeley: Calif. U. P., 1971, passim.

3300a ________. "Sweeney Among the Puppets," The Invisible Poet: T. S. Eliot. New York: Obolensky, Inc., 1959, pp. 195-235.

3301 ________. T. S. Eliot: A Collection of Critical Essays. New Jersey: Prentice-Hall, 1962.

3302 ________. "The Tone of a Terrible Century," NatlR, 20, #5 (February 6, 1968), 147-149. Rev.-art., T. S. Eliot: The Man and His Work. Allen Tate, ed. Delacorte Pr., 1966.

3303 Kereaski, Rodica. "The Idea of Impersonality in the Poetry of T. S. Eliot," AUB-LG, 21 (1972), 89-98.

3304 Kermode, Frank. "A Babylonish Dialect," SR, 74, #1 (Special T. S. Eliot Issue), (Winter, 1966), 225-237; repr., in T. S. Eliot: The Man and His Work. Allen Tate, ed. 1966, pp. 231-243.

3305 ________. "The Classic," UDQ, 9 (1974), 1-33.

3306 ________. "Dissociation of Sensibility," KR, 19 (Spring, 1957), 169-194.

3307 ________. "Eliot's Dream," NS&N, 69 (February 19, 1965), 280-281.

3308 ________. Romantic Image. New York: Vintage Bks., 1964, passim.

3309 Kerr, Walter F. "T. S. Eliot Strolls the Same Garden," NYHT (February 21, 1954), 1.

3310 Kilgallin, Anthony R. "Eliot, Joyce and Lowry," CanA&B, 41 (Winter, 1965), 3-4, 6.

3311 Kim, Jong Gil. "T. S. Eliot's Influence on Modern Korean Poetry," LitEW, 13 (December, 1969), 359-376.

3312 Kincaid, Arthur N. "The Dramatic Monologue: Eliot's Debt to Browning," BSNotes, 2, #2 (1972), 4-11.

3313 King, S. K. "Eliot, Yeats and Shakespeare," Theoria, 5 (1953), 113-119.

3314 Kirk, Russell. *Eliot and His Age: T. S. Eliot's Moral Imagination in the Twentieth Century.* New York: Random House, 1971.

3315 __________. "Following Eliot's Antique Drum," NatlR, 22 (January 13, 1970), 34.

3316 __________. "Personality and Medium in Eliot and Pound," SR, 82 (1974), 698-705.

3317 __________. "T. S. Eliot's Permanent Things," *Enemies of the Permanent Things.* New York: Arlington House, 1969, pp. 51-62.

3318 Kirkup, James. "Notes Towards the Definition of Eliot," EigoS, 111 (May, 1965), 308-311.

3319 Kitamura, Tsuneo. "Shijin T. S. Eliot no Hyoka," EigoS, 116 (1971), 812-814.

3320 Kittredge, Selwyn. "Mr. Tambimuttu's Birthday Books," PBSA, 67, #2 (2nd Qt., 1973), 188-192.

3321 __________. "Richard Aldington's Challenge to T. S. Eliot: The Background of Their James Joyce Controversy," JJQ, 10 (1973), 339-341.

3322 Kline, George L., tr., and Introduction. "Joseph Brodsky's 'Verses on the Death of T. S. Eliot,'" RusR, 27 (April, 1968), 195-198.

3323 Klingopulos, G. D. "Eliot's Heir," Scrutiny, 14, #2 (December, 1946), 141-145.

3324 Knickerbocker, William S. "Bellwether: An Exercise in *Dissimulatio*," SR, 41, #1 (January, 1933), 64-79.

3325 Knight, G. Wilson. *The Christian Renaissance. With Interpretations of Dante, Shakespeare, and Goethe, and a Note on T. S. Eliot.* London: Macmillan, 1933; rev. and repr., London: Methuen, 1962, passim.

3326 __________. "T. S. Eliot: Some Literary Impressions," SR, 74, #1 (Winter, 1966), 239-255; repr., in T. S. Eliot: The Man and His Work. Allen Tate, ed. New York: 1966, pp. 245-261.

3327 Knight, W. F. Jackson. "T. S. Eliot as a Classical Scholar," T. S. Eliot: A Symposium for His Seventieth Birthday. Neville Braybrooke, ed. New York: 1958, pp. 119-128.

3328 Knights, L. C. "Shakespeare and Shakespeareans," Scrutiny, 3, #3 (December, 1934), 306-314.

3329 Knoll, Robert E. "The Style of Contemporary Poetry," PrS, 29 (Summer, 1955), 118-125. Analyzes the metaphors of Eliot.

3329a Koch, Richard Earl. "Walt Whitman, T. S. Eliot, and the Dilemma of Modern Consciousness," DAI, 36 (Michigan State: 1974), 319A.

3330 Kochetkova, I. K. "Poeziya T. S. Eliot," ["The Poetry of T. S. Eliot"], VMU, 4 (1967), 15-28.

3331 Kogan, P[auline]. "The Bourgeois Line on Culture and Anarchy in Matthew Arnold and T. S. Eliot," L&I, 8 (1971), 1-14.

3332 Kohli, Devindra. "Yeats and Eliot: The Magnitude of Contrast?" Quest, 58 (July-September, 1968), 42-46.

3333 Kojecky, Roger. "Eliot the European," SELit (Eng. No.), (1974), 63-73.

3334 __________. T. S. Eliot's Social Criticism. New York: Farrar, Straus & Giroux, 1972.

3335 Kornbluth, Martin L. "A Twentieth-Century Everyman," CE, 21 (October, 1959), 26-29.

3336 Kraemer, Konrad W. "Thomas Stearns Eliot," Begegnung, 20, #1 (January, 1965), 29.

3337 Kramer, Hilton. "T. S. Eliot in New York," WR, 14 (Summer, 1950), 303-305.

3338 Krasavcenko, T. "Eliot-kritik v sovremennyx tolkovanijax," VLit, 17, #7 (1973), 280-287.

3339 Krieger, Murray. The New Apologists for Poetry. Minneapolis: Minnesota U. P., 1956, passim.

3340 Krishnamurti, S. "Indian Poetics and T. S. Eliot's Three Voices of Poetry," Half-yearly Jour., n. s., 15 (September, 1954), Sec. A, 15-18.

3341 Kronenberger, Louis. "T. S. Eliot as Critic," Nation, 140, #3641 (April, 1935), 452-453.

3342 Krutch, J. W. "A Poem Is a Poem," Nation, 137 (December 13, 1933), 679.

3343 Kuhn, Ortwin. Mythos--Neuplatonismus--Mystik: Studien zur Gestaltung des Alkestisstoffes bei Hugo von Hofmannsthal, T. S. Eliot und Thornton Wilder. München: Goldmann, 1972.

3344 Kühnelt, Harro H. "T. S. Eliot als Poe-Kritiker," NS, n. s., (Heft 3, 1956), 105-112.

3345 Kuin, J. "De Engelse Beatrice op de Aswoensdag van het Christelijk Leven: In Memoriam T. S. Eliot," Raam, #15 (1965), 46-55.

3346 Kumar, Jitendra. "Consciousness and Its Correlatives: Eliot and Husserl," PPR, 28, #3 (March, 1968), 332-352.

3347 ________. "La coscienza e i suoi correlati: Eliot e Husserl," Verri, 31 (1969), 37-59.

3348 ________. "Poesia e percezione: Eliot e Merleau Ponty," Verri, 31 (1969), 60-82.

3349 Kumashiro, Sobu. Ezra Pound to T. S. Eliot. Tokyo: Hokuseido, 1970.

3350 Kuna, F. M. "T. S. Eliot's Dissociation of Sensibility and the Critics of Metaphysical Poetry," EIC, 13, #3 (July, 1963), 241-252.

3351 Kunst, Herbert. "What's the Matter with One-Eyed Riley?" CL, 17 (Fall, 1965), 289-298.

3352 Kytohonka, Arto. "Kirjallisuuskritiikin pälevyys. Näkökanta T. S. Eliot in metakritiikkiin [Validité de la critique littéraire]." KSV, 24 (1969), 35-67.

3353 Laboulle, M. J. J. "T. S. Eliot and Some French Poets," RLC, 16 (April, 1936), 389-399.

3354 Lair, Robert L. Barron's Simplified Approach to T. S. Eliot. Woodbury, N. Y.: Barron's, 1968.

3355 Lake, D. J. "T. S. Eliot's 'Vita Nuova' and 'Mi-Chemin': 'The Sensus Historicus,'" ArielE, 2, #1 (January, 1971), 43-57.

3356 Lal, P., ed. T. S. Eliot: Homage from India. Lake Gardens, Calcutta: 1965.

3357 Lalou, René. "T. S. Eliot: Prix Nobel," NL (Paris), 1006 (November 11, 1948), 1.

3358 Lancaster, Serena. "A Listing of the Materials in the T. S. Eliot Collection of the Colgate University Library," Philobiblon (Colgate U. Lib.), 9 (1972), 18-31.

3359 Langbaum, Robert W. The Dramatic Monologue and the Poetry of Experience: A Study of Romantic Form [Browning, Tennyson, T. S. Eliot]. Diss. Columbia: 1954.

3360 __________. The Modern Spirit: Essays on the Continuity of Nineteenth and Twentieth Century Literature. New York: Oxford U. P., 1970, passim.

3361 __________. The Poetry of Experience: The Dramatic Monologue in Modern Literary Tradition. New York: Norton, 1963, passim.

3362 Langslet, Lars R. "Tre dikteres møste med helgenen," KogK, 63 (September, 1958), 406-415.

3363 Larrabee, Ankey. "Three Studies in Modern Poetry," Accent, 3 (Winter, 1943), 115-121.

3364 Laski, Harold J. Faith, Reason and Civilization. New York: Viking, 1944, pp. 96-100, 180-182.

3365 Lasser, Michael L. "Discordia Concors: A Humanistic Reconciliation," Discourse, 5 (Autumn, 1962), 436-443.

3366 Lawler, James R. "T. S. Eliot et Paul Valéry," MdF, #341, 1169 (January, 1961), 76-97.

3367 Leach, Elsie. "T. S. Eliot and the School of Donne," Costerus, 3 (1972), 163-180.

3368 Leavis, F. R. "Approaches to T. S. Eliot," Scrutiny, 15, #1 (December, 1947), 56-67.

3369 __________. "Eliot and Pound," TLS, #3574 (August 28, 1970), 950; #3576 (September 11, 1970), 998.

3370 __________. "'English'--Unrest and Continuity," TLS, #3509 (May 29, 1969), 569-572.

3371 __________. "Mr. Eliot and Lawrence," Scrutiny, 18, #1 (June, 1951), 66-73.

3372 __________. "Mr. Eliot and Milton," SR, 57, #1 (January, 1949), 1-30.

3373 __________. "T. S. Eliot," New Bearings in English Poetry.

London: Chatto & Windus, 1932, pp. 75-132; Ann Arbor: Michigan U. P., 1964, pp. 75-132.

3374 __________. "T. S. Eliot and the Life of English Literature," MassR, 10 (Winter, 1969), 9-34.

3375 __________. "T. S. Eliot's Later Poetry," Scrutiny, 11, #1 (Summer, 1942), 60-71; repr., in Education and the University. London: Chatto & Windus, 1943, pp. 87-104.

3376 __________. "T. S. Eliot's Stature as a Critic," Commentary, 26 (November, 1958), 399-410; repr., in Anna Karenina and Other Essays. New York: Pantheon Bks., 1968, pp. 177-195.

3377 Lebois, André. "T. S. Eliot, les Imagistes et Jean de Boschère," RLC, 26 (July-September, 1952), 365-379.

3378 Lebowitz, Martin. "Thought and Sensibility," KR, 5, #2 (Spring, 1943), 219-227.

3379 LeBreton, Georges. "T. S. Eliot et la dialectique d'Héraclite," MdF, 353 (March, 1965), 518-523.

3380 LeBrun, Philip. "T. S. Eliot and Henri Bergson," Part I, RES, 18 (May, 1967), 149-161; Part II, (August, 1967), 274-286.

3381 Lee, Young Gul. "Other Echoes: Source Studies on the Poetry and Plays of T. S. Eliot," DAI, 31 (St. Louis: 1971), 4125A.

3382 Lees, F. N. "The Dissociation of Sensibility: Arthur Hallam and T. S. Eliot," N&Q, 14, #8 (August, 1967), 308-309. Eliot's concept of "dissociation of sensibility" anticipated by Arthur Hallam.

3383 __________. "T. S. Eliot and Nietzsche," N&Q, 11 (October, 1964), 386-387.

3384 Lehmann, John. "The Other T. S. Eliot," List, 51 (January, 1954), 178-182. Eliot's many interests.

3385 Lehmann, Timgard. "Begegnung mit T. S. Eliot," NZ, 1, #3 (1949), 63-66.

3386 Leighton, Lawrence. "Eliot and Dante," H&H, 3, #3 (April, 1930), 442-444.

3387 __________. "A Note on the Poems," HA, 125, #3 (1938), 10, 48.

3388 Leitch, Vincent B. "Religious Desolation in the Poetry of

Southwell, Herbert, Hopkins and Eliot," DAI, 34 (Florida: 1973), 278A.

3388a ________. "Religious Vision in Modern Poetry: Uku Masing Compared with Hopkins and Eliot," JBalS, 5 (1974), 281-294.

3389 Lelièvre, F. J. "Parody in Juvenal and T. S. Eliot," CP, 53, #1 (January, 1958), 22-26.

3390 LeMaster, J. R. "Stevens and Eliot on the Mind of the Poet," ForumH, 10, #3 (1972), 27-30.

3391 Lenhart, Charmenz S. Musical Influence on American Poetry. Athens: Georgia U. P., 1956, passim.

3392 Lento, Thomas Vincent. "The Epic Consciousness in Four Romantic and Modern Epics by Blake, Byron, Eliot and Hart Crane," DAI, 35 (Iowa: 1974), 7911A.

3393 Lerner, M. "Toward a Definition of T. S. Eliot," NR, 120 (May 9, 1949), 22-23.

3394 Levi, Albert W. "Three," The Hidden Harmony: Essays in Honor of Philip Wheelwright. Oliver Johnson, et al, eds. New York: Odyssey, 1966, pp. 73-91.

3395 Levi, Peter, S. J. "The Death of Poets," Month, 33 (1965), 114-119.

3395a Levin, Harry. Ezra Pound, T. S. Eliot and the European Horizon. Oxford: Clarendon Press, 1975.

3396 Levý, Jirí. "Ideový základ tvurcí metody T. S. Eliot," [The Foundation of the Creative Method of T. S. Eliot], CMF, 32 (1949), 139-142.

3397 ________. "Rhythmical Ambivalence in the Poetry of T. S. Eliot," Anglia, 77 (Heft 1, 1959), 54-64.

3398 ________. "Synthesis of Antitheses in the Poetry of T. S. Eliot," EIC, 2 (October, 1952), 434-443.

3399 Levy, William Turner and Victor Scherle. Affectionately, T. S. Eliot: The Story of a Friendship, 1947-1965. New York: Lippincott, 1968.

3400 ________. "The Idea of the Church in T. S. Eliot," ChS, 41, #4 (December, 1958), 587-600.

3401 ________. "Letter to the Editor: A Memoir of T. S. Eliot," NYTBR, 114, #39,084 (January 31, 1965), 34-35.

3402 Lewis, Anthony. "T. S. Eliot and Animal Farm," NYTB (January 26, 1969), 14-16.

3403 Lewis, Wyndham. "First Meeting with T. S. Eliot," Blasting and Bombardiering. 2nd ed. Berkeley: California U. P., 1967, pp. 282-289.

3404 ________. "T. S. Eliot (Pseudoist)," Men without Art. London: Cassell, 1934, pp. 64-100; reissued: New York: Russell & Russell, 1964.

3405 ________. "To T. S. Eliot," The Letters of Wyndham Lewis. W. K. Rose, ed. Norfolk, Conn.: New Directions, 1963, passim.

3406 Leyris, Pierre. "Rencontres avec T. S. Eliot," FL (Paris), 3, #1 (November 13, 1948).

3407 Licht, Merete. "What Is the Meaning of Happening?" OL, 14 (Spring, 1959), 19-32.

3408 Liebowitz, Martin. "Sense and Sensibility," KR, 5, #2 (1943), 219-227.

3409 Lindberger, Örgan. "Modern anglosaxisk litteraturkritik," BLM, 18 (December, 1949), 784-794.

3410 Lindsay, Jack. "Déchéance de T. S. Eliot," LetF, 8, #1 (November 11, 1948), 1.

3411 Link, Franz H., ed. Amerika: Vision und Wirklichkeit. Frankfurt am Main: 1968.

3412 ________. "Das christliche Schauspiel T. S. Eliots," Literatur und Sprache der Vereinigten Staaten: Aufsatze zu Ehren von Hans Galinsky. Hans Helmcke, et al, eds. Heidelberg: Winter, 1969, pp. 165-179.

3413 Linton, Calvin D. "The Emergence of Christian Themes in the Early Poetry of T. S. Eliot," GordonR, 6, #4 (Winter, 1962-63), 140-150.

3414 Litz, A. Walton, ed. Eliot in His Time. Princeton: Princeton U. P., 1973.

3415 Livesay, Dorothy. "London Notes," CanF, 38 (November, 1958), 171-172.

3416 Lobb, Randolph Edward. "T. S. Eliot and the English Critical Tradition," DAI, 35 (Princeton: 1974), 3750A.

3417 Loesch, Katharine. "A Dangerous Criminal Still at Large," N&Q, 6 (January, 1959), 8-9.

3418 Lohner, Edgar. "Gottfried Benn und T. S. Eliot," NDH, Heft 26 (1956), 100-107.

3419 Lombardo, Agostino. "Dall scuola di Eliot a quella di Auden," FLe, 21 (May 18, 1952), 1-2.

3420 ______. Realismo e Simbolismo: Saggi di Letteratura Americana Contemporanea. (Biblioteca di Studi Americani, No. 3.) Rome: Edizioni di Storia e Letteratura. 1957.

3421 Lonkon, Richard. "T. S. Eliot's Recent Work," ConR, #1039 (July, 1952), 34-37.

3422 Lorentzatos, Zisimos. Meletes. Athina: Ekdoseis Galaxia, 1966. On T. S. Eliot, Seferis, and others.

3423 Loring, M. L. S. "T. S. Eliot on Matthew Arnold," SR, 43, #4 (December, 1935), 479-488.

3424 Lo Schiavo, Renato. "Poesie minori di T. S. Eliot," SA, 5 (1959), 191-217.

3425 Lotringer, Sylvère. "T. S. Eliot à rebours," LetF, 1066 (February 4-10, 1965), 6-7.

3426 Low, Anthony. "The Friendly Dog: Eliot and Hardy," AN&Q, 12 (1974), 106-108.

3427 Loya, Arieh. "al-Sayyáb and the Influence of T. S. Eliot," MW, 61 (1971), 187-201.

3428 Lu, Fei-Pai. T. S. Eliot: The Dialectical Structure of His Theory of Poetry. Diss. Chicago: 1965.

3429 ______. T. S. Eliot: The Dialectical Structure of His Theory of Poetry. Chicago and London: Chicago U. P., 1966.

3430 Lucas, F. L. "Criticism," L&L, 3, #18 (November, 1929), 433-465.

3431 Lucy, Seán. T. S. Eliot and the Idea of Tradition. New York: Barnes & Noble; London: Cohen & West, 1960.

3432 Ludowyk, E. F. C. "T. S. Eliot in Ceylon," T. S. Eliot: A Symposium. Richard March, et al, comps. Freeport, N. Y.: 1968, pp. 103-105.

3433 Ludwig, Richard M. "Eliot," American Literary Scholarship: An Annual/1974. James Woodress, ed. Durham, North Carolina: Duke U. P., 1976, pp. 110-121.

3434 ______. "T. S. Eliot," Fifteen Modern American

Authors: Jackson R. Bryer, ed. Durham, N.C.: Duke U.P., 1969, pp. 139-174.

3435 __________. "T. S. Eliot," Sixteen Modern American Authors: A Survey of Research and Criticism. Jackson R. Bryer, ed. New York: Norton, 1973, pp. 181-182.

3436 Lund, Mary Graham. "The Androgynous Moment: Woolf and Eliot," Renascence, 12 (Winter, 1960), 74-78.

3437 __________. "The Eliotian Cult of Impersonality," TQ, 9 (Spring, 1966), 164-167.

3438 __________. "The Social Burden of T. S. Eliot," Discourse, 9, #4 (Autumn, 1966), 450-455.

3439 __________. "T. S. Eliot's 'Book of Happenings,'" ForumH, 4, #12 (1967), 39-42.

3440 Luzi, Mario. "Grandezza di Eliot," Approdo, 11, #1 (1965), 47-49.

3441 Lyman, Dean B., Jr. "Aiken and Eliot," MLN, 71 (May, 1956), 342-343.

3442 Lynd, Robert. "Mr. T. S. Eliot as Critic," Books and Authors. New York: Putnam, 1923, pp. 277-284; London: Cobden-Sanderson, 1922, pp. 248-255.

3443 Lynen, John B. "Selfhood and the Reality of Time: T. S. Eliot," The Design of the Present: Essays on Time and Form in American Literature. New Haven, Conn.: Yale U.P., 1969, pp. 341-441.

3444 McAuley, James. "In Regard to T. S. Eliot," [poem], Surprises of the Sun. Sydney: Angus & Robertson, 1969, p. 55.

3445 MacCarthy, Desmond. "New Poets," NSt, 16 (January 8, 1921), 418-420; repr., as "T. S. Eliot (1921)," in Criticism. New York: Putnam, 1932, pp. 89-97.

3446 McCarthy, Harold E. "T. S. Eliot and Buddhism," PE&W, 2 (April, 1952), 31-55.

3447 McClanahan, Billie. "A Surprising Source for Belladonna," TSEN, 2 (Spring, 1975), 2.

3448 Maccoby, Hyam. "The Anti-Semitism of T. S. Eliot," Midstream, 19, #5 (1973), 68-79.

3449 McCreadie, Marsha Anne. "T. S. Eliot and the Romantic Poets: A Study of the Similar Poetic Themes and Methods

Used by Eliot and Wordsworth, Coleridge, Keats, Byron, and Shelley," DAI, 34 (Illinois, Urbana-Champaign: 1973), 7713A.

3450 McCutchion, David. "Yeats, Eliot and Personality," Quest, 50 (July-September, 1966), 13-24.

3451 McElderry, B. R., Jr. "Santayana and Eliot's 'Objective Correlative,'" BUSE, 3 (Autumn, 1957), 178-181.

3452 __________. "T. S. Eliot on Poe," PN, 2, i-ii (1969), 32-33.

3453 McGill, Arthur C. The Celebration of Flesh: Poetry in Christian Life. New York: Association Pr., 1964.

3454 McGreevy, Thomas. Thomas Stearns Eliot: A Study. London: Chatto & Windus, 1931. Said to be the "first book entirely devoted to Eliot's work."

3455 McGregor-Hastie, Roy. "Incontro con T. S. Eliot," FLe, 13 (October 26, 1958), 5.

3455a MacKendrick, Louis K. "T. S. Eliot and the Egoist: The Critical Preparation," DR, 55 (1975), 140-154.

3456 MacKendrick, Paul. "T. S. Eliot and the Alexandrians," CJ, 49 (October, 1953), 7-13.

3457 McLuhan, Herbert M. "Mr. Eliot and the 'St. Louis Blues,'" AntigR, 18 (1974), 23-27.

3458 __________. "Mr. Eliot's Historical Decorum," Renascence, 2 (1949-50), 9-15; repr., Renascence, 25 (1973), 183-189.

3459 __________. "T. S. Eliot," (Radio Broadcast), CanF, 44, #529 (February, 1965), 243-244.

3459a McNeal, David Stuart. "T. S. Eliot's Impersonality: A Study of the Personae in Eliot's Major Poems," DAI, 37 (British Columbia, Canada: 1976), 4373A.

3460 MacNeice, Louis. "Eliot and the Adolescent," T. S. Eliot: A Symposium. Richard March and Tambimuttu, comps. Freeport, N.Y.: 1968, pp. 146-151.

3461 __________. Modern Poetry. London: Oxford U.P., 1938, passim.

3462 MacNiven, Ian S. "Hart Crane and T. S. Eliot on the Mod-City," RUCR, 36 (1973), 63-73.

3463 Magny, Claude E. "A Double Note on T. S. Eliot and

James Joyce," T. S. Eliot: A Symposium. Richard Marsh, et al, comps. Freeport, N. Y.: 1968, pp. 208-217.

3464 Malmberg, Bertil. "Hallucinationsrealism," BLM, 18 (January, 1949), 45-48.

3465 Manacorda, Guido. "Thomas Stearns Eliot," ICS, 42 (1959), 216-217.

3466 Mandell, Eli. "The Language of Humanity," TamarackR, 29 (Autumn, 1963), 82-89.

3467 Mandeville, Sandra C. "T. S. Eliot Still Speaks Out Loud," Kultur, LIT, #5 (1964), 24-30.

3468 Mangan, Sherry. "A Note: On the Somewhat Premature Apotheosis of Thomas Stearns Eliot," Pagany, 1, #2 (Spring, 1930), 23-36.

3469 Manning, Hugo. "Onorate l'Altissimo Poeta," T. S. Eliot: A Symposium. Nelville Braybrooke, ed. New York: 1958, pp. 181-184.

3470 March, Richard, and M. J. Tambimuttu, comps. T. S. Eliot: A Symposium. Freeport, N. Y.: Books for Libraries Press, 1968.

3471 Marcus, Philip L. "T. S. Eliot and Shakespeare," Criticism, 9 (Winter, 1967), 63-79.

3472 Margolis, John D. T. S. Eliot's Intellectual Development, 1922-1939. Chicago: Chicago U. P., 1972.

3473 __________. "Towards a New Beginning: The Development of T. S. Eliot's Thought, 1922-1939," DAI, 30 (Princeton: 1969), 1173-74A.

3474 Marion, Sister Thomas. "Eliot's Criticism of Metaphysical Poetry," Greyfriar (1961), 17-23.

3475 Marks, Emerson R. "T. S. Eliot and the Ghost of S. T. C.," SR, 72 (Spring, 1964), 262-280.

3476 Marsh, T. N. "The Turning World: Eliot and the Detective Story," EM, 8 (1957), 143-145.

3477 Marshall, Robert. "T. S. Eliot et le 'Baudelaire' de Swinburne," Bayou, #70 (Summer, 1957), 432-438.

3478 Martin, Graham, ed. Introduction. Eliot in Perspective: A Symposium. London: Macmillan; New York: Humanities, 1970.

3479 Martin, Jay. Conrad Aiken: A Life of His Art. Princeton: Princeton U. P., 1962, passim.

3480 Martin, Mildred A. "T. S. Eliot: The Still Point and the Turning Wheel," BuUS, 4 (1953), 51-68.

3481 Martin, P. W. Experiment in Depth: A Study of the Work of Jung, Eliot and Toynbee. London: Routledge, 1955; New York: Pantheon, n. d.

3482 Martin, W. D., et al. "The Critic Criticized," TLS (January 6, 1966), 9.

3483 Martinez Menchén, Antonio. "Una lírica de la cultura (T. S. Eliot)," CHA, 71 (1967), 47-81.

3484 Martz, Louis L. "The Wheel and the Point," The Poem of the Mind: Essays on Poetry, English and American. New York: Oxford U. P., 1966, pp. 105-124.

3485 ________. "The Wheel and the Point: Aspects of Imagery and Theme in Eliot's Later Poetry," SR, 55, #1 (Winter, 1947), 126-147; repr., in T. S. Eliot: A Selected Critique. L. Unger, ed. New York: 1948, pp. 444-462.

3486 Marx, Leo. "Mr. Eliot, Mr. Trilling and Huckleberry Finn," AmSch, 22, #4 (Autumn, 1953), 423-440.

3487 Mason, Eudo. Exzentrische Bahnen: Studien zum Dichterbewusstsein der Neuzeit. Göttingen: Vandenhoeck & Ruprecht, 1963.

3488 Materer, Timothy. "Wyndham Lewis's Portrait of T. S. Eliot," TSEN, 1, #1 (Spring, 1974), 4.

3489 Mateucci, Benvenuto. "La Madonna in T. S. Eliot," Humanitas, 6 (June, 1954), 527-546.

3490 Mathews, R. T. "The Journey of a Magus," Wingover, 1 (Fall-Winter, 1958-59), 32-33.

3491 Mathewson, George. "The Search for Coherence: T. S. Eliot and the Christian Tradition in English Poetry," DA, 23 (Princeton: 1962), 225-26.

3492 Matthews, Thomas Stanley. Great Tom: Notes Towards the Definition of T. S. Eliot. London and New York: Harper & Row, 1974. Cf., James Breslin, Rev.-art., VQR, 50 (1974), 632-637.

3493 Matthiessen, F. O. The Achievement of T. S. Eliot: An Essay on the Nature of Poetry. New York: Oxford U. P., 1935; revised and enlarged, 1947; 1959.

3494 ________. "American Poetry, 1920-40," SR, 55, #1 (1947), 24-55.

3495 ________. "A Dark Necessity: From Hawthorne to James and Eliot," American Renaissance. New York: Oxford U. P., 1941, pp. 351-368.

3496 ________. "T. S. Eliot after Strange Gods," T. S. Eliot: A Selected Critique. Leonard Unger, ed. New York: Rinehart, 1948, pp. 415-443.

3497 Mavroeidi-Papadaki, Sophia. "Ho Tomas S. Eliot kai to archaio drama," KP, 1 (1971), 333-340.

3498 Maxwell, D. E. S. "After The Waste Land," ISE, 1 (1969), 73-84.

3499 ________. The Poetry of T. S. Eliot. London: Routledge & Kegan Paul, 1952; New York: Hilary House, 1959.

3500 Maxwell, J. C. "Eliot and Husserl," N&Q, 11 (February, 1964), 74.

3501 Mayer, John Theodore, Jr. "The Dramatic Mode of T. S. Eliot's Early Poetry," DA, 25 (Fordham: 1964), 1918-19.

3502 Mayo, E. L. "The Influence of Ancient Hindu Thought on Walt Whitman and T. S. Eliot," AryP (Bombay), 29, #4 (April, 1958), 167-177.

3503 Mazzaro, Jerome. "Robert Lowell and the Kavanaugh Collapse," UWR, 5, i (1969), 1-24.

3504 Meanor, Patrick Hugh. "T. S. Eliot and Wallace Stevens: A Concurrence of Careers," DAI, 35 (Kent State: 1974), 7915A.

3505 Mégret, Hélène. "T. S. Eliot," Bull. de l'Assoc. des Eleves... de Sevres, 1931.

3506 Melchers, Hans Joachim. T. S. Eliot: Das 'Muster' und die Wirklichkeitsprobleme der Dichtung. Diss. Cologne: 1955.

3507 Melchiori, Giorgio. "Eliot and Apollinaire," N&Q, 11 (October, 1964), 385-386.

3508 ________. "Joyce, Eliot and the Nightmare of History," RLV, 40 (1974), 582-598.

3509 ________. The Tightrope Walkers: Studies of Mannerism in Modern English Literature. New York: Macmillan, 1936; London: Routledge & Kegan Paul, 1956.

3510 Mende, Georg. "Nobelpreis für einen Philister," Einheit (Leipzig), 4, #3 (1949), 281.

3511 Mendel, Sydney. "Dissociation of Sensibility," DR, 51, #2 (Summer, 1971), 218-227.

3512 Meoli Toulmin, Rachel. "Shakespeare e Eliot nelle versioni di Eugenio Montale," Belfagor, 26 (1971), 453-471.

3513 Messiaen, Pierre. "Le Sens de l'oeuvre poétique de T. S. Eliot," Etudes (Paris), (December, 1948), 383-385.

3514 Metwally, Abdalla A. Studies in Modern Drama. Beirut: Arab Univ., 1971.

3515 Meyerhoff, Hans. "Mr. Eliot's Evening Service," PartisanR, 15, #1 (January, 1948), 131-138. An account of T. S. Eliot's appearance at the Parish House of St. Thomas Church, Washington, D. C.

3516 Michaels, Walter Benn. "Writers Reading: James and Eliot," MLN, 91, #5 (October, 1976), 838-849.

3517 Miles, Josephine. Major Adjectives in English Poetry: From Wyatt to Auden. (Pubs. in Eng., 12, #3). Berkeley and Los Angeles: California U. P., 1946.

3518 Miller, James E., Jr. "Whitman and Eliot: The Poetry of Mysticism," SWR, 43 (Spring, 1958), 113-123; repr., in Quests Surd and Absurd: Essays in American Literature. Chicago & London: Chicago U. P., 1967, pp. 112-136.

3518a Miller, Joseph Hillis. The Disappearance of God. Cambridge, Mass.: Belknap Pr. of Harvard U. P., 1963, passim.

3519 ___________. "T. S. Eliot," Poets of Reality: Six Twentieth-Century Writers. Cambridge, Mass.: Harvard U. P., (Belknap), 1966, pp. 131-189.

3520 Miller, Stephen. "Studies in the Idea of the City in Western Literature," DAI, 31 (Rutgers: 1971), 6018A.

3521 Miller, Vincent. "Eliot's Submission to Time," SR, 84 (Summer, 1976), 448-464.

3522 ___________. "The Verities and the Wonder," NatlR 24, #8 (March 3, 1972), 225-226. Rev.-art., Russell Kirk, Eliot and His Age. Random House, 1972.

3523 Milner, Ian. "T. S. Eliot and the Avant-garde," PP, 11, #4 (1968), 203-208.

3524 "Milton Lost and Regained," TLS, #2356 (March 29, 1947), 140.

3525 Milward, Peter, S. J. "Sacramental Symbolism in Hopkins and Eliot," Renascence, 20 (Winter, 1968), 104-111.

3526 Mitra, S. N. "Notes Toward the Definition of T. S. Eliot's Classicism," Quest, #47 (Autumn, 1965), 17-26.

3527 Mizener, Arthur. "To Meet Mr. Eliot," SR, 65 (Winter, 1957), 34-49; repr., in T. S. Eliot: A Collection of Criticism. Linda Wagner, comp. New York: 1974, pp. 9-20.

3528 Mohrt, Michel. "T. S. Eliot, ce Baudelaire anglis," FLe, 20 (January 7-13, 1965), 4.

3529 Moloney, Michael F. "The Critical Faith of Mr. T. S. Eliot," Thought, 22, #85 (June, 1947), 297-314.

3530 __________. "Mr. Eliot and Critical Tradition," Thought, 21, #82 (September, 1946), 455-474.

3531 Monroe, Harriet. "Eliot and Sarett: A Contrast," Poets and Their Art. New York: Macmillan, 1926, pp. 100-108.

3532 Montale, Eugenio. "Eliot and Ourselves," T. S. Eliot: A Symposium. Richard March, et al, comps. Freeport, N.Y.: 1968, pp. 190-195.

3533 Monteiro, Adolfo Casais. "Teoria da impersonalidade: Fernando Pessoa e T. S. Eliot," TeM, 68 (1969), 204-209.

3534 Montgomery, Marion. "Eliot and the Meta-poetic," InR, 9, #1 (1973-74), 29-36.

3535 __________. "Eliot and the Particle Physicist: The Merging of Two Cultures," SoR, 10 (July, 1974), 583-589.

3536 __________. "Emotion Recollected in Tranquility: Wordsworth's Legacy to Eliot, Joyce, and Hemingway," SoR, 6, #3 (July, 1970), 710-721.

3537 __________. "Shadows in the New Cave: The Poet and the Reduction of Myth," SWR, 55, #3 (Summer, 1970), 217-223.

3538 __________. "The Shifting Sands of Ego and the Rock: Eliot's and Whitehead's 'Romantic Quest,'" TSEN, 1, #2 (Fall, 1974), 9-13.

3539 __________. T. S. Eliot: An Essay on the American Magus. Athens: Georgia U.P., 1969.

3540 __________. "Through a Glass Darkly: Eliot and the Romantic Critics," SWR, 58, #4 (Autumn, 1973), 327-335.

3541 ______. "Wordsworth, Eliot, and the 'Personal Heresy,'" SAB, 32, #4 (November, 1967), 17-20; repr., in The Reflective Journey Toward Order. Athens: Georgia U. P., 1973, pp. 235-245.

3542 Moody, A. D. "A Note on Hugh Kenner's 'Eliot Book,'" Meanjin, 20, #2 (July, 1961), 223-226.

3543 Moore, Marianne. "It Is Not Forbidden to Think," Nation, 142 (May 27, 1936), 680-681.

3544 ______. "A Virtuoso of Make-Believe," T. S. Eliot: A Symposium. Richard March, et al, comps. Freeport, N. Y.: 1968, pp. 179-180.

3545 Moore, Merrill. "Homage to T. S. Eliot," HA, 125, #3 (1938), 42, 45.

3546 Moore, Nicholas. "Three Poems for Mr. Eliot," [poems], T. S. Eliot: A Symposium. Richard March, et al, comps. Freeport, N. Y.: 1968, pp. 48-50.

3547 Moorman, Charles W. Myth and Modern Literature: A Study of the Arthurian Myth in Charles Williams, C. S. Lewis, and T. S. Eliot. Diss. Tulane: 1953.

3548 ______. "Order and Mr. Eliot," SAQ, 52 (January, 1953), 73-87.

3549 ______. The Precincts of Felicity: The Augustinian City of the Oxford Christians. Gainesville: Florida U. P., 1966, passim.

3550 ______. "T. S. Eliot," Arthurian Triptych: Mythic Materials in Charles Williams, C. S. Lewis, and T. S. Eliot. Berkeley and Los Angeles: California U. P., 1960, pp. 127-148.

3551 Mordell, Albert. T. S. Eliot--Special Pleader as Book Reviewer and Literary Critic: A Study of the Literary Leader of Intellectual, Political, Religious, and Philosophical Reaction.... Girard, Kansas: Haldeman-Julius Pubs., 1951.

3552 ______. "T. S. Eliot's Deficiencies as a Social Critic," Critic and Guide, 5 (May, 1951), 97-120.

3553 ______. T. S. Eliot's Deficiencies as a Social Critic. Girard, Kansas: Haldeman-Julius Pubs., 1951.

3554 More, Paul Elmer. "The Cleft Eliot," SatR, 9, #17 (November 12, 1932), 233-236.

3555 Moreh, Shmuel. "The Influence of Western Poetry and Particularly T. S. Eliot on Modern Arabic Poetry," AAS, 5 (1969), 1-50.

3556 Morris, David Buchan. The Poetry of Gerard Manley Hopkins and T. S. Eliot in the Light of the Donne Tradition. Bern: A. Francke, 1953. (Swiss Studies in English, No. 33.)

3557 Morris, J. A. "T. S. Eliot and Antisemitism," JES, 2 (1972), 173-182.

3558 Morrissette, Bruce A. "T. S. Eliot and Guillaume Apollinaire," CL, 5 (Summer, 1953), 262-268.

3559 Morrow, Felix. "The Serpent's Enemy: Mr. More as Social Thinker," Symposium, 1, #2 (April, 1930), 168-193.

3560 Morton, A. L. "T. S. Eliot: A Personal View," ZAA, 14, #3 (1966), 282-291.

3561 Mountain, John A. "The Search for an Absolute: The Influence of F. H. Bradley on T. S. Eliot," DAI, 31 (Univ. of Washington: 1971), 3558A.

3562 Mowat, John. "Samuel Johnson and the Critical Heritage of T. S. Eliot," SGG, 6 (1964), 231-247.

3563 Mudrick, Marvin. "The Two Voices of Mr. Eliot," HudR, 10 (Winter, 1957-58), 599-605.

3564 Mueller, W. R. "Psychoanalyst and Poet: A Note," Psychoanalyst, 5 (Summer, 1957), 55-66.

3565 Muhlberger, Josef. "T. S. Eliot als Lyriker," WuW, 11 (1956), 180, 182.

3566 Muir, Edwin. "Contemporary Writers: Mr. T. S. Eliot," Nation, (London), 37 (1925), 644-646; repr., in Transition. New York: Viking, 1926, 131-146.

3567 __________. "Mr. Eliot on Evil," Spectator, #5515 (March 9, 1934), 378-379.

3568 __________. "The Political View of Literature," Essays on Literature and Society. London: Hogarth Pr., 1965; enlarged and revised, Cambridge, Mass.: Harvard U. P., 1967, pp. 134-142.

3569 __________. "Some Letters of Edwin Muir," Encounter, 26, #1 (January, 1966), 3-10.

3570 __________. "A Tribute," T. S. Eliot: A Symposium.

Richard March, et al, comps. Freeport, N.Y.: 1968, pp. 152-153.

3571 Muir, Kenneth. "A Brief Introduction to the Method of Mr. T. S. Eliot," DUJ, 5 (June, 1944), 80-87.

3572 Murdoch, Iris. "T. S. Eliot as a Moralist," T. S. Eliot: A Symposium. Neville Braybrooke, ed. New York: 1958, pp. 152-160.

3573 Murphy, Russell Elliott. "The Tragic Quandary: Hart Crane and the Poetry of T. S. Eliot," DAI, 36 (Massachusetts: 1975), 881A.

3573a Murray, Byron D. "Tradition and the Eliot Critical Talent," ConnR, 9 (May, 1976), 2-15.

3574 Murry, John Middleton. "T. S. Eliot on Shakespeare and Seneca," Poets, Critics, Mystics: A Selection of Criticism Written between 1919 and 1955. Carbondale: So. Ill. U.P., 1970, pp. 9-14.

3575 __________. "Towards a Synthesis," Criterion, 5, #3 (September, 1927), 297-313.

3576 Musgrove, Sydney. "James Picot's Use of T. S. Eliot," Meanjin, 13 (Autumn, 1954), 88-95.

3577 __________. T. S. Eliot and Walt Whitman. Wellington: New Zealand U.P., 1952; New York: Haskell House, 1966.

3578 Muzina, Matej. "T. S. Eliot's Convictions Concerning the Use of Ideas in Literature," SRAZ, 24 (December, 1967), 127-135.

3579 Myers, William. "Aesthetic and Critical Judgments," EIC, 21 (1971), 107-108. Cf., John Lucas, EIC, 20 (1970), 497-50; and Bernard Bergonzi, EIC, 20 (1970), 382-385.

3580 Nageswara Rao, G. "A Famous Poet and Student of Sanskrit," LCritM, 8 (1967), 19-32.

3581 __________. "T. S. Eliot's Use of the Upanishads," AryP, 38 (1967), 266-271.

3582 Naik, M. K. "Wit and Humour in Eliot's Verse," JKU, 5 (June, 1961), 120-127.

3583 Naples, Diane C. "Eliot's 'Tradition' and The Sound and the Fury," MFS, 20 (Summer, 1974), 214-217.

3584 Narasimhaiah, C. D. "The Best I Have Read in Modern Poetry," LCritM, 3 (Summer, 1957), 106-113.

3585 __________. "To a Workshop for Research Scholars on T. S. Eliot," LCritM, 10, #3 (1973), 1-21.

3586 Nathan, Monique. "James Joyce et T. S. Eliot: Conjonctions et Divergences," CdMN, 6 (1950), 94-102.

3587 Nathan, Norman. "Eliot's Incorrect Note on 'C. i. f. London,'" N&Q, 5 (June, 1958), 262-263.

3587a Nathan, Robert. "The Pound-Eliot Controversy," SatR, 32 (July 9, 1949), 23-25.

3588 Necco, Giovanni. "Dal fine secolo a Eliot," FLe, 52 (December 31, 1950), 7.

3589 Negura, Neonila, and Sorin Piru. "T. S. Eliot si tragedia greaca" [T. S. Eliot and the Greek tragedy], Cronica, 5 (May, 1970), 22.

3590 Nelson, C. E. "Saint-John Perse and T. S. Eliot," WHR, 17 (Spring, 1963), 163-171.

3591 Nelson, Conny. "T. S. Eliot, Michelangelo, and John Webster," RSWSU, 38 (1970), 304-306.

3592 Nemoianu, Virgil. "Eseism şi estetism la Pater, Chesterton, Eliot," Calmul valorilor. [The Calm of the Values.] Claj: Dacia, 1971, pp. 124-146.

3593 Newton, F. J. "Venice, Pope, T. S. Eliot and D. H. Lawrence," N&Q, 5 (March, 1958), 119-120.

3594 Nicholson, John. "Musical Form and Preludes," T. S. Eliot: A Symposium. Neville Braybrooke, ed. New York: 1958, pp. 110-112.

3595 Nicholson, Norman. "Modern Verse-Drama and the Folk Tradition," CritQ, 2 (Summer, 1960), 166-170.

3596 __________. "Words and Imagery," T. S. Eliot: A Symposium. Richard March, et al, comps. Freeport, N.Y.: 1968, pp. 231-234.

3597 Nicoll, Allardyce. "T. S. Eliot and the Revival of Classicism," EJ, 23, #4 (April, 1934), 269-278.

3598 Nicolson, Harold. "My Words Echo," T. S. Eliot: A Symposium. Neville Braybrooke, ed. New York: 1958, pp. 34-35.

3599 Niedermayer, Franz. "T. S. Eliot: Der Dichter, Kritiker, Laientheologe," SdZ, 145 (1950), 88-98.

3600 Nimkar, B. R. "T. S. Eliot: The Interpreter of the Intellectual Crisis," ModRev, 117, (February, 1965), 148-150.

3601 Nims, John Frederick. "Greatness in Moderation," SatR, 46, #42 (October 19, 1963), 25-27.

3602 Ninomia, Takamichi. "Eliot no Hamlet Ron," Oberon, 14 (1973), 20-30.

3603 Nishiwaki, Junzaburo. T. S. Eliot. Kenkyusha, 1956.

3604 Nojima, Hidekatsu. Exiles' Literature: A Study of James Joyce, D. H. Lawrence and T. S. Eliot. Tokyo: Nanundo, 1964.

3605 Noonan, James. "Poetry and Belief in the Criticism of T. S. Eliot," QQ, 79, #3 (Autumn, 1972), 386-396.

3606 Nott, Kathleen. The Emperor's Clothes. Bloomington: Indiana U. P., 1954, passim.

3607 __________. "Whose Culture?" List, 67 (1962), 631-632, 677-678.

3608 Novykova, Marija. "'Objektyvnist' i maska objektyvnosty," Zovten, 23, #1 (1972), 132-140.

3609 Nowottny, Winifred. "'The Common Privileges of Poetry,'" PBA, 52 (1966), 61-86.

3610 Nuhn, Ferner. "Orpheus in Hell: T. S. Eliot," The Wind Blew from The East. New York: Harper, 1942, pp. 205-215.

3611 Nuttall, A. D. A Common Sky: Philosophy and the Literary Imagination. Berkeley: California U. P., 1974, passim.

3612 Obertello, Alfredo. "Eliot, premio Novel 1948," Studium, 45 (January, 1949), 17-21.

3613 O'Brien, M. N. "Lines on T. S. Eliot," [poem], CanF, 13 (November, 1932), 62.

3614 O'Donnell, G. M. "Homage to T. S. Eliot," HA, 125, #3 (1938), 17-18.

3615 Oestreich, Marianne. Das Problem der Schuld bei T. S. Eliot. Diss. Berlin: 1955.

3616 Ohashi, Isamu. "Hiru to Yoru to Tasogare to," [Daylight, Darkness, Twilight], EigoS, 115 (1969), 354-356.

3617 __________. "Jikan no Seishiten," [Still Point of Time], EigoS, 115 (1969), 296-298.

3618 ________. "T. S. Eliot no Shiron," [Eliot's Poetic Theory], EigoS, 115 (1969), 413-415.

3619 Okerlund, Arlene N. "Literature and Its Audience: The Reader in Action in Selected Works of Spenser, Dryden, Thackeray, and T. S. Eliot," DAI, 30 (Calif., San Diego: 1969), 1991A.

3620 Okubo, Junichiro. "Wakaki Eliot ni okeru Sosaku to Hihyo," EigoS, 116 (1970), 465-467. [Creation and Criticism in the young Eliot.]

3621 Olderman, Raymond M. Introduction. Beyond the Wasteland. New Haven, Conn.: Yale U. P., 1972, pp. 1-29.

3622 Olson, Elder. "The Achievement of T. S. Eliot by F. O. Matthiessen," Poetry, 50 (April, 1937), 54-56. Rev.-art.

3623 O'Nan, Martha. "T. S. Eliot's 'Le Directeur,'" Symposium, 21 (Spring, 1967), 61-66.

3624 Ong, Walter J., S. J. "Only Through Time," Poetry, 108 (July, 1966), 165-268.

3625 Oras, Ants. The Critical Ideas of T. S. Eliot. Tartu, Estonia: K. Mattieson, 1932.

3626 Orsini, Napoleone. "Nota in margine ad una poesia di T. S. Eliot," Letteratura, 9 (March-April, 1947), 110-112.

3627 Osowski, Judy. "T. S. Eliot on Poe the Detective," PN, 3 (1970), 39.

3628 Österling, Anders. "Anförande vid Nobelfesten 1948," Prisma (Stockholm), 1 (1948), 18-24.

3629 Otake, Masaru. "T. S. Eliot: The Lyric Prophet of Chaos," SELit, 16 (October, 1936), 542-554.

3630 Otto, Wilhelm. Eugene O'Neill, T. S. Eliot und die griechische Tragödie. Diss. Frankfurt: 1950.

3631 Oyama, Tokiko. "A Study of Bird, Flower, and Colour Images in T. S. Eliot," E&S(T), 7 (Summer, 1959), 103-128.

3632 Page, Charles. "T. S. Eliot and F. H. Bradley," Delta (Summer, 1963), 40-42.

3633 Page, L. Alun. "T. S. Eliot a'i Athroniaeth," YGen, 15, #2 (Spring, 1965), 308-313.

3634 Palette, Drew B. "Eliot, Fry, and Broadway," ArQ, 11 (Winter, 1955), 342-347.

3635 Palmer, Leslie. "Animal, Man, and Angel: A Study of T. S. Eliot's Beast-Imagery," ForumH, 11, #1 (Spring, 1973), 47-52.

3636 Palmer, Richard Edward. A Study of Existentialism in Certain Poems by Charles Baudelaire, R. M. Rilke, and T. S. Eliot. Diss. Redlands Univ: 1959.

3637 Panaro, Cleonice. "Il problema della communicazione nella poesia di T. S. Eliot," SA 14 (1968), 193-245.

3638 Panella, Sergio. "E. Montale e T. S. Eliot," Galleria (Italy), 4 (December, 1954), 244-256.

3639 Panichas, George A. "Notes on Eliot and Lawrence, 1915-1924," The Reverent Discipline: Essays in Literary Criticism and Culture. Knoxville, Tenn.: Tenn. U. P., 1974, pp. 135-156.

3640 __________. "T. S. Eliot and the Critique of Liberalism," ModA, 18 (1974), 145-162.

3641 Panicker, Geevarghese T. A Whole of Feeling: A Study of the Place of Emotion and Feeling in the Poetic Theory of T. S. Eliot. Diss. Catholic Univ. of America: 1959.

3642 Paris, Jerome M. "Poetry and the Uses of Stoicism: Motives of Consolation in Matthew Arnold and T. S. Eliot," DAI, 33 (Cornell: 1973), 5742A.

3643 Parkes, H. B. The Pragmatic Test. San Francisco: Colt Pr., 1941, pp. 178-186.

3644 Parkinson, R. N. "The Secret Garden," N&Q, 2 (January, 1955), 6.

3645 Parkinson, Thomas. "Intimate and Impersonal: An Aspect of Modern Poetics," JAAC, 16, #3 (March, 1958), 373-383.

3646 Parsons, I. M. "T. S. Eliot's Reputation," CritQ, 8 (1965), 180-182. Cf., George Watson. "The Triumph of T. S. Eliot," CritQ, 7 (Winter, 1965), 328-337; and CritQ, 8 (1965), 180-182.

3647 Partridge, A. C. "T. S. Eliot," Pubs. of Univ. of Pretoria, Series #3, #4 (1937), 16.

3648 Patterson, Gertrude. T. S. Eliot: Poems in the Making. Manchester: Manchester U. P.; New York: Barnes & Noble, 1971.

3649 Pattinson, John Patrick. "A Study of British Poetic Criticism between 1930 and 1965 as Exemplified in the Critics of Yeats, Pound, and Eliot," DAI, 30 (NYU: 1970), 4460A-61A.

3650 Peacock, Ronald. "T. S. Eliot on Goethe," The Discontinuous Tradition. Peter F. Ganz, ed. Oxford: Oxford U. P., 1971, pp. 67-78.

3651 Pearce, Roy Harvey. "Eliot: The Poetics of Myth," The Continuity of American Poetry. Princeton U. P., 1961, pp. 306-309.

3652 Pearce, T. S. T. S. Eliot. (Literary Critiques Series.) London: Evans Bros., 1967.

3653 Pearson, Gabriel. "Eliot: An American Use of Symbolism," Eliot in Perspective: A Symposium. Graham Martin, ed. New York: 1970, pp. 83-101.

3654 Peetz, D. W. "Eliot's Politics," NSt (September 30, 1966), 477-478.

3655 Pellizzi, Camillo. "Eliot e Bridges cercano la bellezza," FLe, #50 (December 17, 1950), 1, 6.

3656 Pérez Gállego, Cándido. "Las etapas espirituales de T. S. Eliot," Arbor, #64 (1966), 283-290.

3657 __________. "Notas a los Occasional Verses de T. S. Eliot," FMod, (October-January, 1965), 75-81.

3658 Perloff, Marjorie. "The Poet and His Politics," NR, 170 (March 16, 1974), 21-23.

3659 Perselli, Luciano. "Relativo e assoluto nel mito di Eliot," FLe, 30 (July 27, 1952), 8.

3660 Peschmann, Hermann. "The Significance of T. S. Eliot," Wind and the Rain (London), 6 (Autumn, 1949), 108-123.

3661 Peter, John. "Eliot and the Criterion," in Eliot in Perspective. Graham Martin, ed. New York: 1970, pp. 252-266.

3662 Peyre, Henri. "T. S. Eliot et le classicisme," RHL, #3-4 (May-August, 1969), 603-613.

3663 Phillips, C. W. "Our Literary Intellectuals," Cw, 27 (February 18, 1938), 470.

3664 Phillips, W. "Mr. Eliot and Notions of Culture: A Discussion," PartisanR, 11, #3 (Summer, 1944), 307-309.

3665 Piazzola, Marino. "T. S. Eliot poeta cattolico," FLe, 14 (January 11, 1959), 3-5.

3666 Piebinga, H. Tj. "Ta de poëtyske gerontology fan T. S. Eliot," Flecht op 'e koai: Stúdzjes oanbean oan Prof. Dr. W. J. Buma ta syn sechstichste jierdei. (Fryske Akad. 382.) Groningen: Wolters-Noordhoff, 1970, pp. 337-341.

3667 Piercy, Marge, and Dick Lourie. "Tom Eliot Meets the Hulk at Little Big Horn: The Political Economy of Poetry," TriQ, No. 23-24 (1972), 57-91.

3668 Pietersma, H. "The Overwhelming Question," Folio, 2 (Summer, 1956), 19-32.

3669 Plutzik, Hyam. "For T. S. Eliot Only," AmSch, 24 (Spring, 1955), 183-185.

3670 Poirier, Richard. "T. S. Eliot and the Literature of Waste," NR, 156 (May 20, 1967), 19-25. Rev.-art., Allen Tate, ed. T. S. Eliot: The Man and His Work.

3671 Policardi, Silvio. La Poesia di T. S. Eliot. Anno Accademico, 1948-49. Milano: La Goliardica, [1949?].

3672 Politi, Francesco. "Due traduzioni delle poesie di T. S. Eliot," Belfagor (March, 1951), 221-223.

3673 Pons, Christian. "T. S. Eliot ou la critique moderne: critique et metacritique," CdSud, 52, #381 (1965), 116-120.

3674 Popovici-Teodoreanu, Liliana. "A treia voce a lui T. S. Eliot," ["T. S. Eliot's Third Voice,"], AnUBLUC, 18-2, (1969), 123-132.

3675 Porter, Katherine Anne. "From the Notebooks of Katherine Anne Porter--Yeats, Joyce, Eliot, Pound," SoR, 1, #3, n. s., (Summer, 1965), 570-573.

3676 __________. "On First Meeting T. S. Eliot," Shenandoah, 12, #3 (Spring, 1961), 25-26.

3677 Porteus, Hugh Gordon. "Resurrection in the Crypt," T. S. Eliot: A Symposium. Richard March, et al., eds. New York: 1968, pp. 218-224.

3678 Post, Robert M. "Auditory Imagination, Mythic Consciousness, and the Oral Interpreter," JWS, 34 (1970), 203-211.

3679 Poulsen, Søren R. "Milton's stil i Paradise Lost: Et litteratur-kritisk problem. En redegørelse og diskussion med saerligt henbilk pa T. S. Eliot og F. R. Leavis' Milton-kritik," Extracta, 4 (1972), 177-179.

3680 Pound, Ezra. The Letters of Ezra Pound, 1907-1941. D. D. Paige, ed. New York: Harcourt, Brace, 1950, passim; repr., Norfolk, Conn.: New Directions, pp. 418-422.

3681 __________. "Mr. Eliot and Mr. Pound," TLS (July 26, 1957), 457.

3682 __________. "Mr. Eliot's Mare's Nest," NewEW, 4, #21 (March 8, 1934), 500.

3683 __________. "Prefatio Aut Cimicium Tumulus," and "Mr. Eliot's Solid Merit," Polite Essays. Norfolk, Conn.: New Directions, 1937, pp. 35-52, 98-105.

3684 __________. "Sagt om Eliot," Prisma (Stockholm), 1, (1948), 25.

3685 __________. "T. S. Eliot," Poetry, 10, #5 (1917), 264-271.

3686 __________. "T. S. Eliot and Others," London Chapbook, No. 27 (July, 1922).

3687 Powell, Dilys. "The Poetry of T. S. Eliot," L&L, 7 (December, 1931), 386-419.

3688 __________. "T. S. Eliot," Descent from Parnassus. New York: Macmillan, 1935, pp. 55-100.

3689 Power, Sister Mary James. "T. S. Eliot Emerges from the Waste Land," Poets at Prayer. Freeport, New York: Bks. for Libraries Pr., 1938, pp. 125-136.

3690 Pratt, Linda R. "'The Neutral Territory between Two Worlds': A Comparative Study of Alfred Tennyson and T. S. Eliot," DAI, 32 (Emory: 1972), 4017A.

3691 Pratt, William C., Jr. "Revolution without Betrayal: James, Pound, Eliot and the European Tradition," DA, 17 (Vanderbilt: 1957), 2600.

3692 Praz, Mario. James Joyce, Thomas Stearns Eliot, due maestri dei moderni. Torino, Italy: ERI, 1967.

3693 __________. "La scuola di Eliot," FLe (Italy), (November 28, 1948).

3694 __________. "T. S. Eliot and Dante," SoR, 2, #3 (Winter, 1937), 525-548; repr., in The Flaming Heart. Garden City, New York: Doubleday, 1956.

3695 __________. "T. S. Eliot and Eugenio Montale," T. S. Eliot: A Symposium. Richard March, et al, ed. Freeport, N.Y.: 1968, pp. 244-248.

3696 ___________. "T. S. Eliot as a Critic," SR, 74, Special Eliot Issue (Winter, 1966), 256-271.

3697 ___________. "T. S. Eliot e Dante," Let, 1, #2 (July, 1937), 3.

3698 ___________. "T. S. Eliot e il Simbolismo," Il Simbolismo letteratura Nord-Americana. (Pubblicazioni dell'Ist. di Studi Americani, U. degli Studi di Firenze, 1.) Firenze: La Nuova Italia, 1965, pp. 1-27.

3699 ___________. "Thomas Stearns Eliot," TP, #2 (1965), 87-163.

3700 ___________. "What Is a Classic?" Modern Miscellany. T. E. Lawrenson, et al, eds. New York: Barnes & Noble, 1969, pp. 195-202.

3701 Preston, Priscilla. "A Note on T. S. Eliot and Sherlock Holmes," MLR, 54 (July, 1959), 397-399.

3702 Preston, Raymond. "T. S. Eliot as a Contemplative Poet," T. S. Eliot: A Symposium. Neville Braybrooke, ed. New York: 1958, pp. 161-169.

3703 Pritchard, William H. "On Wyndham Lewis," PartisanR, 35, #2 (Spring, 1968), 253-267.

3704 Pritchett, V. S. "'Our Mr. Eliot' Grows Younger," NYTMS (September 21, 1958), 15, 72-73.

3705 Prokosch, Frederick. "Homage to T. S. Eliot," HA, 125, #3 (1938), 41.

3706 Puckett, Harry. "T. S. Eliot on Knowing: The Word Unheard," NEQ, 44, #2 (June, 1971), 179-196.

3707 Puhalo, Dusan. "Pesnik velikih fragmenata," Savremenik, 11 (June, 1960), 614-631.

3708 ___________. "Poezija T. S. Eliota," Savremenik, 6 (Beograd), (1956), 688-711.

3709 ___________. "T. S. Eliot kao knjizevni kriticar," Letopis Matice Sprske, Novi Sad, 1957, pp. 3-31.

3710 Pujals, Esteban. "Un poeta con misión: T. S. Eliot, 1888-1964," Nuestro Tiempo, 36, #149 (1966), 484-501.

3710a Purcell, Victor William S. [Myra Buttle, pseud.] The Sweeniad. New York: Sagamore Pr.; London: Secker & Warburg, 1958. A satire of T. S. Eliot. Cf., Edmund Wilson. "'Miss Buttle' and 'Mr. Eliot,'" NY, 34 (May 24, 1958), 119-150.

3711 Quennell, Peter. "Mr. T. S. Eliot," L&L, 2, #10 (March, 1929), 179-190.

3712 Quiller-Couch, Arthur. "Tradition and Orthodoxy," *The Poet as Citizen and Other Papers*. New York: Macmillan, 1935, pp. 44-65.

3713 Quinn, Sister M. Bernetta. "Eliot and Crane: Protean Techniques," *The Metamorphic Tradition in Modern Poetry*. New York: Gordian Pr., 1966, pp. 130-167.

3714 Qureshi, I. H. "Eliot and Our Culture," Venture, 5, #1 (June, 1968), 4-6.

3715 Qvamme, Börre. "T. S. Eliot," Edda (Oslo), 43 (January-March, 1943), 23-33.

3716 Rago, Henry. *T. S. Eliot, A Memoir and a Tribute*. Chicago: Chicago Univ. Printing Dept., 1965.

3717 Rahman, K. "The Mystic as a Critic," Venture, 5, #1 (June, 1968), 38-42.

3718 Rahme, Mary. "T. S. Eliot and the 'Histrionic Sensibility,'" Criticism, 10 (Spring, 1968), 126-137.

3719 Rahv, Philip. "T. S. Eliot," Fantasy, 2 (1932), 17-20.

3720 Raina, M. L. "T. S. Eliot as Thinker," JML, 3 (1973), 134-142.

3721 __________. "T. S. Eliot's Criticism of the Novel," RSWSU, 40 (1972), 81-94.

3722 Raine, Kathleen. "The Art of T. S. Eliot," Britain Today, #164 (1949), 14-18.

3723 __________. "Besök i tjugonde seklet," BLM, 21 (October, 1952), 599-600.

3724 __________. "The Poet of Our Time," *T. S. Eliot: A Symposium*. Richard March, et al, eds. Freeport, N.Y.: 1968, pp. 78-81.

3725 Rajan, B[alachandra]. "The Constant Core," E-WR, 3 (Summer, 1967), 113-125.

3726 __________, ed. *T. S. Eliot: A Study of His Writings by Several Hands*. London: Dennis Dobson, 1947, 1966.

3727 Rajasekharaiah, T. R. "Pride and Prejudice: A Note on T. S. Eliot's Criticism," Jour. of Karnatak Univ., 5 (June, 1961), 136-147.

3728 Rajasundaram, C. F. "Western Influence in Modern Tamil Poetry," R. E. Asher, ed. Proceedings of the Second International Conference of Tamil Studies, Madras, India, January, 1968, 2 vols. Madras: Internatl. Assn. of Tamil Research, 1971, II, 97-106.

3729 Raleigh, John H. "The New Criticism as an Historical Phenomenon," CL, 11 (Winter, 1959), 21-28.

3730 __________. "Revolt and Revaluation in Criticism, 1900-1930," The Development of American Criticism. Floyd Stovall, ed. Chapel Hill: North Carolina U. P., 1955, pp. 59-198.

3731 Ralston, William H., Jr. "That Old Serpent," SR, 81 (1973), 389-428.

3732 Ram, Tulsi. "Milton and the Language of Ideality: A Supplement to T. S. Eliot," IJES, 7 (1966), 42-56.

3733 Rama, Murthy. T. S. Eliot: Critic. Allahabad, India: Kitab Mahal, 1968.

3734 Ramamrutham, J. V. "T. S. Eliot and Indian Readers," LHY, #1 (January, 1960), 46-54.

3735 Ramsey, Warren. Jules Laforgue and the Ironic Inheritance. New York and London: Oxford U. P., 1953.

3736 __________. "The Oresteia Since Hofmannsthal: Images and Emphases," RLC, 38 (1964), 359-375.

3737 Ransom, John Crowe. "Criticism as Pure Speculation," The Intent of the Critic. Donald A. Stauffer, ed. Princeton: Princeton U. P., 1941; repr., 1963, pp. 89-124.

3738 __________. "Eliot and the Metaphysicals," Accent, 1, #3 (Spring, 1941), 148-156.

3739 __________. "The Inorganic Muses," KR, 5, #2 (Spring, 1943), 278-300.

3740 __________. "The Poems of T. S. Eliot: A Perspective," NR, 127 (December 8, 1952), 16-17.

3741 __________. "T. S. Eliot: A Postscript," SoR, n. s., 4 (Summer, 1968), 579-597.

3742 __________. "T. S. Eliot: The Historical Critic," New Criticism. Norfolk: New Directions, 1941, pp. 135-208.

3743 Rao, G. Nageswara. "T. S. Eliot's Use of the Upanishad," AyrP, 38, #6 (June, 1967), 266-271.

3744 Rao, K. S. Narayana. "Addendum on Eliot and the 'Bhagavad-Gita,'" AmQ, 16 (1964), 102-103.

3745 __________. "T. S. Eliot and the 'Bhagavad-Gita,'" AmQ, 15 (1963), 572-578.

3746 Rascoe, Burton. "Pupils of Polonius," The Critique of Humanism. C. Hartley Grattan, ed. New York: Brewer & Warren, 1930, pp. 109-130.

3747 __________. "Shreds and Tatters," Newsweek, 13 (April 3, 1939), 40.

3748 Rawler, J. R. "T. S. Eliot et Paul Valéry," MdF, 341 (March, 1961), 76-101.

3749 Ray, Mohit. "Eliot's Search for a Critical Credo," Rajasthan Jour. of Eng. Stud, 1 (July-December, 1974), 12-15.

3750 __________. "T. S. Eliot and Irving Babbitt: A Question of Critical Influence," University of Rajasthan Studies in English No. 4. R. K. Kaul, et al, eds. Jaipur: Univ. of Rajasthan Dept. of Eng., 1969, pp. 97-102.

3751 Rayan, Krishna. "Rasa and the Objective Correlative," BJA, 5 (1965), 246-260.

3752 __________. "Suggestiveness and Suggestion," EIC, 19, #3 (July, 1969), 309-319.

3753 __________. "When the Green Echoes or Doesn't," MalR, #14 (April, 1970), 30-38.

3754 Read, Herbert. Form in Modern Poetry. London: Sheed & Ward, 1932, passim.

3755 __________. "A Point of Intensity: T. S. Eliot," The True Voice of Feeling. London: Faber & Faber, 1953, pp. 144-145.

3756 __________, and Edward Dahlberg. "Robert Graves and T. S. Eliot: Correspondence between Herbert Read and Edward Dahlberg," TC, 166 (August, 1959), 54-62.

3757 Rebora, Piero. "T. S. Eliot e la poesia possible," L'Ultima, 3 (November, 1948), 23-30.

3758 Reckford, K. J. "Heracles and Mr. Eliot," CL, 16 (Winter, 1964), 1-18.

3759 Redman, Ben R. "T. S. Eliot: In Sight of Posterity," SatR, 32, (May 14, 1949), 9-11, 30-31.

3760 Reed, Henry. "Chard Whitlow (Mr. Eliot's Sunday Evening Postscript)," A May of Verona. London: Reynal, 1947. A poem--parody.

3761 Rees, Garnet. "A French Influence of T. S. Eliot: Rémy de Gourmont," RLC, 16, #4 (October, 1936), 764-767.

3762 Rees, Thomas Richard. "The Orchestration of Meaning: A Study of the Relationship between Form and Meaning in T. S. Eliot's Early Poetry (1910-1922)," DA, 27 (Tulane: 1966), 484A-485A.

3763 __________. "T. S. Eliot, Rémy de Gourmont, and Dissociation of Sensibility," Studies in Comparative Literature. Waldo F. McNeir, ed. (La. State Univ. Studies, Humanities Series, No. 11.) Baton Rouge: La. St. U. P., 1962, pp. 186-198.

3764 __________. "T. S. Eliot's Early Poetry as an Extension of the Symbolist Technique of Jules Laforgue," ForumH, 8, #1 (Winter-Spring, 1970), 46-52.

3765 __________. The Technique of T. S. Eliot: A Study of the Orchestration of Meaning in Eliot's Poetry. (De Proprietatibus Litterarum, Ser. Practica, No. 39). The Hague and Paris: Mouton, 1974.

3766 Reeves, James. "Cambridge Twenty Years Ago," T. S. Eliot: A Symposium. Richard March, ed. Freeport, N.Y.: Bks. for Libraries Pr., 1968, pp. 38-42.

3767 "Reflections," Time, 55, #10 (March 6, 1950), 22-26.

3768 Regnery, Henry. "Eliot, Pound and Lewis: A Creative Friendship," ModA, 16, #2 (Spring, 1972), 146-160.

3769 Rehak, Louise Rouse. "On the Use of Martyrs: Tennyson and Eliot on Thomas Becket," UTQ, 33 (October, 1963), 43-60.

3770 Reid, Benjamin L. The Man from New York: John Quinn and His Friends. New York: Oxford U.P., 1968, passim.

3771 Reid, David, and Mark Turner. "A Conversation with Hugh Kenner," Occi, 7, #1 (1973), 18-48.

3772 Reid, John T. "Contemporary North American Lyric Poetry," Estudios Americanos, 15 (March-April, 1958), 45-155.

3773 Reiss, Hans. "Tradition in Modern Poetry: T. S. Eliot and Rainer Maria Rilke; a Comparison," Proceedings of the 4th Congress of the International Comparative Literature Association. Francois Jost, ed. Fribroug: 1964, II, 1122-27.

3774 Renner, Stanley. "A Note on Joseph Conrad and the Objective Correlative," Conradiana, 6 (1974), 53-56.

3775 Restivo, Giuseppina. "Il primo Eliot: Scritti critici dal 1914 al 1919," Studi e Ricerche di Letterature Inglese e Americana. Claudio Gorlier, ed. II. Milan: Cisalpino-Goliardica, [1969], pp. 135-187.

3776 Revol, Enrique Luis. "Permanencia de T. S. Eliot," Torre, 65, 17 (July-September, 1969), 43-52.

3777 Rexroth, Kenneth. American Poetry in the Twentieth Century. New York: Herder & Herder, 1971, pp. 56-63, passim.

3778 Richards, I[vor] A[rmstrong]. "Appendix B: The Poetry of T. S. Eliot," Principles of Literary Criticism. New York: 1934, pp. 289-295.

3779 ___________. Discovering Poetry. New York: Norton, 1933, passim.

3780 ___________. "Mr. Eliot and Notions of Culture: A Discussion," PartisanR, 11, #3 (Summer, 1944), 310-312.

3781 ___________. "Mr. Eliot's Poems," NSt, 26 (February 20, 1926), 584-585. Repr., in LivAge, 329 (April 10, 1926), 112-115.

3782 ___________. "On T. S. Eliot," T. S. Eliot: The Man and His Work. Allen Tate, ed. New York: 1966, p. 5.

3783 ___________. "On T. S. Eliot: Notes for a Talk at the Institute of Contemporary Arts, London, June 29, 1965," SR, 74 (Winter, 1966), 21-30.

3784 Rickman, H. P. "Poetry and the Ephemeral: Rilke's and Eliot's Conceptions of the Poet's Task," GL&L, 12 (April, 1959), 174-185.

3785 Ricks, Christopher B. Tennyson. (Masters of World Lit. Ser.) New York: Macmillan, 1972, passim.

3786 Rickword, Edgell. "The Modern Poet," Toward Standards of Literature. F. R. Leavis, ed. London: Wishart, 1933, pp. 100-106.

3787 Riding, Laura, and Robert Graves. A Survey of Modernist Poetry. Garden City, N. Y.: Doubleday, Doran, 1928, pp. 50-53, 167-174, 211-215, passim.

3788 Ridler, Anne. "Eliot, 1888-1965," English Poetry. A. E. Dyson, ed. New York: 1971, pp. 360-375.

3789 __________. "I Who Am Here Dissembled," [a poem], T. S. Eliot: A Symposium. Richard March, et al, eds. Freeport, New York: 1968, p. 189.

3790 __________. "A Question of Speech," Focus Three: T. S. Eliot, A Study of His Writings by Several Hands. B. Rajan, ed. London: Dennis Dobson, 1947, pp. 107-118.

3791 Rillie, John A. M. "Melodramatic Device in T. S. Eliot," RES, 13, #51 (August, 1962), 267-281.

3792 Rillo, Lila E. Aldous Huxley and T. S. Eliot. Buenos Aires: Talleres gráficos Contreras, 1943. (Argentine Assn. of English Culture. English Pamphlet Series.)

3793 Ritter, Joachim. "Poetry and Through," Subjektivität. Frankfurt: Suhrkamp, 1974.

3794 Rizzardi, Alfredo. "Eliot minore," Aut Aut, 33 (May, 1956), 239-244.

3795 Robbins, Rossell H. The T. S. Eliot Myth. New York: Henry Schuman, 1951.

3796 __________. "The T. S. Eliot Myth," Science & Society, 14 (1950), 1-28.

3797 Roberts, Michael. "The Poetry of T. S. Eliot," LonMerc, 34 (May, 1936), 38-44.

3798 Robinson, David. "Eliot's Rose Garden: Illumination or Illusion?" CSR, 4 (1975), 201-210.

3799 Robson, W. W. "Eliot's Later Criticism," Rev, #4 (November, 1962), 52-58.

3800 __________. "T. S. Eliot as a Critic of Dr. Johnson," New Rambler (June, 1965), 42.

3801 __________. "The Unread Eliot," PartisanR, 40 (1973), 136-141.

3802 Roby, Robert C. T. S. Eliot and the Elizabethan and Jacobean Dramatists. Diss. Northwestern: 1949.

3803 Rochat, Joyce. "T. S. Eliot's 'Companion' Poems: Eternal Question, Temporal Response," ConR, 227 (August, 1975), 73-79.

3804 Roche, Paul. "After Eliot: Some Notes Toward a Reassessment," EvergreenRev, 10, #39 (February, 1966), 84-92.

3805 __________. "Since Eliot: Some Notes Toward a

Reassessment," PoetryR, 59, #1 (Spring, 1968), 123-125. Cf., Frederick Grubb. "Reply," PoetryR, 59 (1968), 123-125.

3806 Rochester, Howard. "En Torno a 'La Tierra Baldia,'" Revista americano, Nos. 45, 46 (September, October, 1950).

3807 Rodgers, Audrey T. "Dance Imagery in the Poetry of T. S. Eliot," Criticism, 16 (1974), 23-38.

3807a __________. "Eliot in the 70's: A Mosaic of Criticism," TSER, 2, #1 (1975), 10-15.

3807b __________. "Mythic Vision in the Art of T. S. Eliot and Dante: A Study in Correspondences," DA, 28 (Pennsylvania State: 1967), 4143A-44A.

3808 Roeffaers, H. "Gedichten van T. S. Eliot in Vertaling," Streven, 28 (1975), 527-533.

3809 Roman, Christine Marie. "Patterns of Recurrence in the Long Poems of Carlos Williams and T. S. Eliot," DAI, 37 (Minnesota: 1975), 300A.

3810 Rømhild, Lars P. "Efterslaet af Eliot," Laesere: Artikler og Foredrag. (Munksgaardserien 42.) Kobenhavn: Munksgaars, 1971, pp. 11-18.

3811 Roos, Alarik. "Gunnar Björling, T. S. Eliot och litteraturhistorisk metodik," SoF, 17 (1960), 170-174.

3812 Rosales, Rodulfo S. "Some Dantesque Images in the Works of Thomas Stearns Eliot," SLRJ, 1 (1970), 473-502.

3813 Rosario, Salvatore. "Postilla al pensiero critico di Eliot," FLe (Italy), (November 14, 1948).

3814 __________, ed. Thomas S. Eliot: Nobel Prize, 1948. Milan: Club degli editori, 1970.

3815 Rose, Alan. "The Impersonal Premise in Wordsworth, Keats and Eliot," DAI, 30 (Brandeis: 1969), 2547A-48A.

3816 Rosenberg, John. "Anatomist and Poet," T. S. Eliot: A Symposium. Neville Braybrooke, ed. New York: 1958, pp. 187-189.

3817 Rosenthal, M. Louis. The New Poets: American and British Since World War II. New York: Oxford U.P., 1967, passim.

3818 __________. "T. S. Eliot and the Displaced Sensibility," The Modern Poets: A Critical Introduction. New York: Oxford U.P., 1960, pp. 75-103.

3819 Ross Williamson, Hugh. The Poetry of T. S. Eliot. New York: Putnam, 1933; repr., Folcroft, Pa.: Folcroft Lib. Editions, 1971.

3819a ___________. "T. S. Eliot and His Conception of Poetry," Bookman, 79, #474 (March, 1931), 347-350.

3820 Rosseaux, André. "Mort d'une Revue (The Criterion). Sur un texte de T. S. Eliot," Revue Universelle, 76 (March 15, 1939), 748-750.

3821 ___________. "Poésie et poétique de T. S. Eliot," FL (Paris), 5 (May 20, 1950), 2.

3822 Rothbard, Lorraine. "Eliot," Diameter, 1 (March, 1951), 31-38.

3823 Rother, James. "Modernism and the Nonsense Style," ConL, 15 (1974), 187-202.

3824 Rottiers, A. K. "Bij de Dood van een Dichter: T. S. Eliot," V1G, 49, #3 (March, 1965), 200-203.

3825 Rougemont, Denis de. "Religion and the Mission of the Artist," Spiritual Problems in Contemporary Literature. Stanley Romaine Hopper, ed. New York: Institute for Rel. & Soc. Studies, distr. by Harper, 1952, pp. 173-186.

3826 Rowland, John. "The Spiritual Background of T. S. Eliot," New-Church Mag, 61 (January-March, 1942), 52-62.

3827 Rowland, Thom. "Post-Romantic Epiphany as Apocalyptic Reversal: A Reconsideration of Hopkins and Eliot," Nassau Rev, 2, #3 (1972), 62-82.

3828 Rozsa, Olga. "T. S. Eliot's Reception in Hungary," HSE, 8 (1974), 35-44.

3829 Ruban, Jonathan. "Silent Buds," NSt, (March 27, 1970), 447-448.

3830 Rubin, Louis D., Jr., ed. Ill Take My Stand: The South and the Agrarian Tradition. New York: Harper, 1930, passim.

3831 Ruland, Richard. The Rediscovery of American Literature: Premises of Critical Taste. Cambridge, Mass.: Harvard U.P., 1967, pp. 173-177, 231-272, passim.

3832 Ruland, Vernon. Horizons of Criticism: An Assessment of Religious Literary Options. Chicago: American Lib. Assn., 1975, passim.

3833 Rupp, Barbara. Der Begriff der gesellschaftlichen Reprasentanz am Beispiel der Lyrik Thomas Stearns Eliots und seine Ortsbestimmung innerhalb der "Geschichte der écriture," (EurH 9.) Bern: Lang, 1973.

3834 Russell, Bertrand. The Autobiography of Bertrand Russell, 1914-1944. 2 vols. Boston: Little, Brown, 1968, II, passim.

3835 Russell, Francis. "Some Non-encounters with Mr. Eliot," Horizon, 7 (Autumn, 1965), 36-41.

3836 Russell, Walter Sanders, Jr. "Stravinsky and Eliot: Personality, Poetics, and Cultural Politics," DAI, 37 (Emory: 1976), 2485A-86A.

3837 Ryan, Krishna. "Suggestiveness and Suggestion," EIC, 19 (July, 1969), 309-319.

3838 Sabbadini, Silvano. Una salvezza ambigua: Studio sulla prima poesia di T. S. Eliot. (Biblioteca di Studi Inglesi 22.) Bari: Adriatica, 1971.

3839 Sackton, Alexander. "T. S. Eliot at Texas," LCUT, 8 (Spring, 1967), 22-26.

3840 __________. The T. S. Eliot Collection at the University of Texas. Austin: (Humanities Research Center Biblio. Ser.) Texas U. P., 1975.

3841 Sahal, K. L. "The Objective Correlative and the Theory of Rasa," CalcR, 2, #2 (October-December, 1970), 237-240.

3842 Sampley, Arthur M. "Quiet Voices, Unquiet Times," MidwQ, 4, #3 (Spring, 1963), 247-256.

3843 __________. "The Woman Who Wasn't There: Lacuna in T. S. Eliot," SAQ, 67, #4 (Autumn, 1968), 603-610.

3844 Sando, Ephriam G. Against the Philistines: Literary Orthodoxy in the Criticism of T. S. Eliot. Diss. UCLA, 1962.

3845 Sanesi, Roberto. "Gli alberi di Natale di T. S. Eliot," Aut Aut, 30 (November, 1955), 517-519.

3846 Sarkar, Subhas. "The Hinterland of Eliot's Poetry," CalcR, 168 (July, 1963), 21-30.

3847 __________. "The Impact of Indian Philosophy on T. S. Eliot," ModRev, #761 (May, 1970), 366-368.

3848 Sastri, P. S. "T. S. Eliot and the Contemporary World," ModRev, 83 (March, 1953), 233-236.

3849 Savage, D. S. "The Orthodoxy of T. S. Eliot," The Personal Principle. London: Routledge, 1944, pp. 91-112.

3850 Savelli, Giovanni. "Eliot premio Nobel," Humanitas, 3 (December, 1948), 1223-1227.

3851 Scarfe, Francis. "Eliot and Nineteenth-century French Poetry," Eliot in Perspective. Graham Martin, ed. New York: 1970, pp. 45-61.

3852 Schaar, Claes. "Främmande gudar," BLM, 17 (March, 1950), 205-208.

3853 Schaeder, Grete, und Hans Heinrich Schaeder. Ein Weg zu T. S. Eliot. Hameln: Verlag der Buchsterstube Fritz-Seifert, 1948.

3854 Schäfer, Hans Dieter. "T. S. Eliot: Gesammelte Gedichte, 1909-1962," NDH, 3, #139 (1973), 131-134. Rev.-art.

3855 Schappes, Morris. "The Irrational Malady," Symposium, 1, #4 (October, 1950), 518-530.

3856 Schmidt, Gerd. "'Et Vera Incessu Patuit Dea': A Note on Eliot, Pound, and the Aeneid," TSEN, 1, #2 (Fall, 1974), 4.

3857 __________. "T. S. Eliot: Unveröffentlichte Gedichte, Vorträge, Briefe. Ein Beitrag zur Bibliographie," JA, 14 (1969), 219-241.

3858 Schmied, Wieland. "T. S. Eliot und Ezra Pound als Kritiker," WZ, 5, 11 (1959), 44-46.

3859 Schneider, Elisabeth W. T. S. Eliot: The Pattern in the Carpet. Berkeley and Los Angeles: Calif. U. P., 1975.

3860 Schneider, Karl. "T. S. Eliots Poetische Technik," GRM, Neue Folge, 3 (1953), 57-71.

3861 Schoeck, R. J. "T. S. Eliot, Mary Queen of Scots, and Guillaume de Machaut," MLN, 63 (March, 1948), 187-188.

3862 Schöne, Annemarie. "Beruhrungspunkte zwischen Nonsense-Dichtung und Metaphysischem Humor in T. S. Eliots Scherzgedichten," GRM, 36 (1955), 40-52.

3863 Schröder, Franz Rolf. "T. S. Eliot und Harald der Strenge," GRM, 41 (1960), 345-347.

3864 Schuchard, Ronald. "Eliot and Hulme in 1916: Toward a Revaluation of Eliot's Critical and Spiritual Development," PMLA, 88, #5 (October, 1973), 1083-1094.

3864a ________. "'First Rate Blasphemy': Baudelaire and the Revised Christian Idiom of T. S. Eliot's Moral Criticism," ELH, 42, #2 (Summer, 1975), 276-295.

3865 ________. "T. S. Eliot's Early Religious and Curious Classicism," DA, 31 (Texas (Austin): 1970), 1812A.

3866 Schulte, Edvige. "Ritmi yecci e nuovi nella poesia inglese moderna," Annali, Sezione germanica, 2 (1959), 191-238.

3867 Schwartz, Delmore. "The Criterion: 1922-1939," KR, 1, #4 (Autumn, 1939), 437-449.

3868 ________. "The Literary Dictatorship of T. S. Eliot," PartisanR, 16, #2 (February, 1949), 119-137.

3869 ________. "T. S. Eliot as the International Hero," PartisanR, 12, #2 (Spring, 1945), 199-206.

3870 ________. "T. S. Eliot's Voice and His Voices," (I and II), Poetry, 85 (December, 1954), (Part III), Poetry 85 (January, 1955), 170-176; 232-242.

3871 Scott, E. "There Is Humor in T. S. Eliot," CSMM, 36, (January 11, 1944), 6.

3872 Scott, John S. "Aspects of the Problem of Structure in Modern American Poetry and Philosophy," DAI, 33 (UCLA: 1973), 4431A-32A.

3873 Scott, Nathan A., Jr. "Eliot and the Orphic Way, JAAR, 42 (June, 1974), 203-231.

3874 ________, ed. Man in the Modern Theatre. Richmond, Va.: John Knox Pr., 1965, passim.

3875 ________. Modern Literature and the Religious Frontier. New York: Harper, 1958, passim.

3876 ________, ed. The New Orpheus: Essays Toward a Christian Poetic. New York: Sheed and Ward, 1964, passim.

3877 ________. Rehearsals of Discomposure: Alienation and Reconciliation in Modern Literature. New York: King's Crown Pr., 1952, passim.

3878 Scott, Peter D. The Social and Political Ideas of T. S. Eliot. Diss. McGill: 1955.

3879 Scott-Moncrieff, George. "Eliot Remembered," SR, 80 (1972), 632-638. Rev.-art. Russell Kirk's Eliot and His Age. 1971.

3879a Scruggs, Charles E. "T. S. Eliot and J.-P. Sartre Toward the Definition of the Human Condition," ApSTC (1965), 24-29.

3880 Seferis, George. "Letter to a Foreign Friend," Poetry, 105 (October, 1964), 50-59. [Nanos Valaoritis, tr.]

3881 ________. "T. S. Eliot in Greece," [Nanos Valaoritis, tr.] T. S. Eliot. Richard March, et al, eds. Freeport, N.Y.: 1968, pp. 126-135.

3882 Seidel, Frederick. "The Art of Poetry," ParisR, 7, #25 (Winter-Spring, 1961), 57-95.

3883 Seif, Morton. "The Impact of T. S. Eliot on Auden and Spender," SAQ, 53 (January, 1954), 61-69.

3884 Seldes, Gilbert. "T. S. Eliot," Nation, 115 (1922), 614-616.

3885 Semaan, Khalil I. H. "T. S. Eliot's Influence on Arabic Poetry and Theater," CLS, 6, #4 (December, 1969), 472-489.

3886 Semmler, Clement. "Slessor and Eliot: Some Personal Musings," Southerly, 31 (1971), 267-271.

3887 Sen, Jyoti P. The Progress of T. S. Eliot as Poet and Critic. New Delhi: Orient Longman, 1971; Port Washington, New York: Kennikat, 1971.

3888 ________. "The Theory of the 'Objective Correlative,'" IJES, 11 (1970), 99-111.

3889 Sen, Mihir Kumar. "Eliot's 'Objective Correlative,'" Visvabharati Qt, 22 (Winter, 1956-57), 206-220.

3890 ________. Inter-War English Poetry: With Special Reference to Eliot's 'Objective Correlative' Theory. Burdwan, India: Burdwan Univ., 1967.

3891 Sen, Sunil Kanti. Metaphysical Tradition and T. S. Eliot. Calcutta: Mudhopadhyay, 1965; Folcroft, Pa.: Folcroft, 1965.

3892 Sena, Vinod. "Henrik Ibsen and the Latest Eliot," LCritM, 6, #4 (1965), 19-25.

3893 Sencourt, Robert. T. S. Eliot: A Memoir. Donald Adamson, ed. London: Garnstone Pr.; New York: Dodd, Mead, 1971.

3894 Senior, John. "The Detail of the Pattern: Eliot," The Way Down and Out: The Occult in Symbolist Literature. Ithaca,

New York: Cornell U. P., 1959; New York: Greenwood Pr., 1968, pp. 170-198.

3895 Serpieri, Alessandro. "Arabesco metafisico eliotiano," LeS, 5 (1970), 435-45; 6, 1-14.

3896 __________. "La poesia di T. S. Eliot: Dalla Terra Desolata alla Terra Promessa," Il Ponte, 15 (July-August, 1959), 935-948.

3897 __________. T. S. Eliot: Le Strutture Profonde. Saggi, #124. Bologna: Il Mulino, 1973.

3898 Serpieri, Sandro. "La fuga di Eliot dal tempo," SA, 7 (1961), 411-428.

3899 Servotte, Herman. "T. S. Eliot (1888-1965): Een Inleiding," DWB, 110 (1965), 403-422.

3900 Sewell, Elizabeth. "Lewis Carroll and T. S. Eliot as Nonsense Poets," T. S. Eliot. Neville Braybrooke, ed. New York: 1958, pp. 49-56.

3901 Seymour-Smith, Martin. "The Revolutionaries," Spectator, #7133 (March 12, 1965), 331. Rev.-art. Herbert Howarth's Notes on Some Figures Behind T. S. Eliot. 1964.

3902 Seyppel, Joachim H. T. S. Eliot. (Mod. Lit. Monographs Ser.) Berlin: 1963; tr. from German by author: New York: Ungar, 1972.

3903 Shanahan, C. M. "Irony in Laforgue, Corbière, and Eliot," MP, 53 (November, 1955), 117-128.

3904 Shankar, D. A. "T. S. Eliot, I. A. Richards, and the New Critics," LCritM, 5, #4 (1963), 32-41.

3905 Shapiro, Leo. "The Medievalism of T. S. Eliot," Poetry, 56 (July, 1940), 202-213.

3906 __________. "Modern Poetry as a Religion," AmSch, 28, #3 (Summer, 1959), 297-305.

3907 __________. "The Persistence of Poetry," Poetry, 76 (May, 1950), 89-91.

3908 __________. "T. S. Eliot: The Death of Literary Judgment," SatR, 43, Pt. 1 (February 27, 1960), 12-17, 34-36; repr., in In Defense of Ignorance. New York: Random House, 1972, pp. 35-60; The Poetry Wreck: Selected Essays, 1950-1970. New York: Random House, 1975, pp. 3-28.

3909 Sharma, H. L. The Essential T. S. Eliot: A Critical Analysis. Mystic, Conn.: Verry, 1971.

3910 Sharma, Jitendra Kumar. "Achilles' Spear: A Phenomenological Exploration of the Problem of Time and Consciousness in T. S. Eliot," DAI, 35 (Toronto, Canada: 1970), 1061A.

3911 Sharma, Mohan Lal. "The Spiritual Quest in the Poetry of T. S. Eliot," Variations on American Literature. Darshan Singh Maini, ed. New Delhi: U. S. Educ. Foundation in India, 1968, pp. 26-37.

3912 Sharrock, Roger. "The Critical Revolution of T. S. Eliot," ArielE, 2, #1 (1971), 26-42.

3913 Shaw, Sam. "T. S. Eliot's Theory of Tradition," DA, 25 (New York: 1964), 1924-25.

3914 Sheehan, Donald G. "The Poetics of Influence: A Study of T. S. Eliot's Use of Dante," DAI, 30 (Wisconsin: 1969), 2043A-44A.

3915 Shiga, Masaru. "Reason and Belief: An Essay on T. S. Eliot," SEL, 14 (1934), 43-57.

3916 Shillito, Edward. "The Faith of T. S. Eliot," ChrC, 51 (1934), 994-995.

3917 Shulman, Robert. "Myth, Mr. Eliot, and the Comic Novel," MFS, 12 (Winter, 1966-67), 395-403.

3918 Shuttle, Penelope. "T. S. Eliot: An Appreciation," AylR, 7 (1965), 45-47.

3919 Siegel, Daniel G. "T. S. Eliot's Copy of Gatsby," Fitzgerald/Hemingway Annual, 1971. Matthew J. Bruccoli and C. E. Frazer Clark, Jr., eds. Washington, D. C.: NCR/Microcard Eds., pp. 291-293.

3920 Siegel, Eli. "T. S. Eliot and W. C. Williams: A Distinction," UKCR, 22 (Autumn, 1955), 41-43.

3921 Silvi, Valeria. "Appunti per una definizione della cultura," Il Ponte, 9 (February, 1953), 225-226. Concerns the Italian translation of Eliot's work.

3922 Simons, J. W. "Eliot and His Critics," Cw, 58 (February 27, 1953), 515-516.

3923 Simpson, Louis. Three on a Tower: The Lives and Works of Ezra Pound, T. S. Eliot, and William Carlos Williams. New York: William Morris, 1975.

3924 Singh, D. P. The Influence of F. H. Bradley on T. S. Eliot. Diss. Patna: 1964.

3925 Sinha, K. N. "Imagery and Diction in Eliot's Later Poetry," IJES, 1 (1960), 79-90.

3926 Sitwell, Edith. Aspects of Modern Poetry. London: Duckworth, 1934, passim.

3927 __________. "For T. S. Eliot," [poem], T. S. Eliot: A Symposium. Richard March, et al, comps. Freeport, N. Y.: 1968, pp. 33-34.

3928 __________. "Lecture on Poetry since 1920," L&L, 39 (1943), 86-93.

3929 Sitwell, Osbert. Laughter in the Next Room. Boston: Little, Brown & Co., 1951, pp. 34n, 37-39. An early description of T. S. Eliot.

3930 Skinner, A. E. "New Acquisitions: Rare Book Collections: T. S. Eliot," LCUT, 6 (Spring, 1958), 46-50.

3931 Slack, R. C. "Victorian Literature as It Appears to Contemporary Students," CE, 22 (February, 1961), 344-347.

3932 Slochower, Harry. No Voice Is Wholly Lost. New York: Creative Age Pr., 1945, pp. 181-183.

3933 Smidt, Kristian. The Importance of Recognition: Six Chapters on T. S. Eliot. Tromso: Peter Norbye, 1973.

3934 __________. "Lyrikeren, T. S. Eliot," Spektrum (Oslo), No. 4 (1947), 181-197.

3935 __________. Poetry and Belief in the Work of T. S. Eliot. Oslo: J. Dybwad, 1949; revised: London and New York: Humanities Pr., 1961.

3936 __________. "Point of View in Eliot's Poetry," OL, 14 (Spring, 1959), 38-53.

3937 __________. "T. S. Eliot and W. B. Yeats," RLV, 31, #6 (November-December, 1965), 555-567.

3938 __________. "T. S. Eliot: tiden og teatret," Minerva's Kvartalsskrift, 9 (1965), 452-466.

3939 __________. "T. S. Eliot, William Archer, and Henrik Ibsen," Seyersted, Brita, ed. Americana-Norvegica. Vol. IV: Norwegian Contributions to American Studies Dedicated to Sigmund Skard. Oslo: Universitetsforlaget, 1973, pp. 89-106.

3940 Smith, Bernard. *Forces in American Criticism.* New York: Harcourt, Brace, 1939, pp. 358-359, 382-387.

3941 Smith, Chard P. "Semi-Classical Poetry and the Great Tradition," MassR, 3 (Autumn, 1961), 41-61.

3942 Smith, Dane Farnsworth. "Neither 'Snow-Bound' nor Moribund," NMQ, 12 (May, 1942), 154-161.

3943 Smith, Grover, Jr. "Charles-Louis Philippe and T. S. Eliot," AL, 22, #2 (November, 1950-51), 254-259. Charles-Louis Philippe's *Bubu de Montparnasse* "exerted upon Eliot's poetry a *conspicuous influence* in 1910 and 1911."

3944 __________. "Getting Used to T. S. Eliot," CE, 49, #1 (January, 1960), 1-10, 15.

3945 __________. "The Poems of T. S. Eliot, 1909-1928: A Study in Symbols and Sources," Microfilm Abstr, 10, #4 (1950), 233-235.

3946 __________. "T. S. Eliot and Sherlock Holmes," N&Q, 193 (October 2, 1948), 431-432.

3947 __________. "T. S. Eliot's Lady of the Rocks," N&Q, 194 (March 19, 1949), 123-125. Various possible sources.

3948 __________. *T. S. Eliot's Poetry and Plays.* Chicago: Chicago U. P., 1956.

3949 Smith, James. "Notes on the Criticism of T. S. Eliot," EIC, 22 (October, 1972), 333-361.

3950 Smith, Janet Adam. "T. S. Eliot and *The Listener*," List, (January 21, 1965), 105; repr., in SR, 74 (January-March, 1966), 327-330; and in *T. S. Eliot: The Man and His Work.* Allen Tate, ed. New York: 1966, pp. 333-336.

3951 Smith, Marcus, and Landry Slade. "T. S. Eliot as a Chemist," AN&Q, 12 (1974), 158.

3952 Smith, R. G. "An Exchange of Notes of T. S. Eliot: A Critique," Theol Today, 7 (January, 1951), 503-506.

3953 Sobreira, Alberto. "T. S. Eliot: Um Humanista," Brotéria, 80 (1965), 322-328.

3954 Soldo, John J. "The American Foreground of T. S. Eliot," NEQ, 45, #3 (September, 1972), 355-372.

3955 __________. "Knowledge and Experience in the Criticism of T. S. Eliot," ELH, 35, #2 (June, 1968), 284-308.

3956 __________. The Tempering of T. S. Eliot, 1888-1915. Diss. Harvard: 1972.

3957 Southam, B. C. A Guide to the Selected Poems of T. S. Eliot. New York: Harcourt, Brace & World, 1969.

3958 __________. "Whispers of Immortality," TLS, 22 (June, 1973), 720-721. Eliot's literary borrowing from Alan Seeger.

3959 Southworth, J. G. "The Poetry of T. S. Eliot," Sowing the Spring. Basil Blackwell, ed. Oxford: 1940, pp. 76-91.

3960 Speaight, Robert. "Un attore parla di T. S. Eliot," Idea, 6, (June 27, 1954), 3.

3961 __________. "The Later Poetry of T. S. Eliot," DubR, 216 (April, 1945), 152-159.

3962 __________. "T. S. Eliot, O. M.: A Birthday Tribute," List, 60 (September 25, 1958), 455-457.

3963 __________. "T. S. Eliot ou l'intelligence d'une sensibilité," RGB, #3 (May, 1965), 943-952.

3964 Spears, Monroe K. Dionysus and the City: Modernism in Twentieth-Century Poetry. New York: Oxford U. P., 1970, passim.

3965 Spears-Brooker, Jewel. "Whether and How: A Study of the Relation of Aesthetic Form to Contemporary History in T. S. Eliot's Poetry," DAI, 37 (So. Florida: 1976), 4377A.

3966 Spector, Robert Donald. "Eliot, Pound, and the Conservative Tradition," HINL, 3, #2 (1957), 2-5.

3967 Spencer, Theodore. "The Poetry of T. S. Eliot," Atl, 151 (January, 1933), 60-68.

3968 Spender, Stephen. "The Influence of Yeats on Later Poets," TriQ, 4 (1965), 82-89.

3969 __________. "La Londra di Eliot," FLe, 4 (May, 1967), 11-13.

3970 __________. "Meeting T. S. Eliot," The English Speaking World, 33, #2 (1951), 13-15.

3971 __________. "Remembering Eliot," Encounter, 24, #4 (1965), 3-14.

3972 __________. "Rilke and the Angels, Eliot and the Shrines," SR, 61 (Autumn, 1953), 557-581; repr., in The Creative

Element: A Study of Vision, Despair and Orthodoxy among Some Modern Writers. New York: British Bk. Center, 1954, pp. 56-76.

3973 __________. "Speaking to the Dead in the Language of the Dead," T. S. Eliot: A Symposium. Richard March, et al, Freeport, N.Y.: 1968, pp. 106-110.

3974 __________. T. S. Eliot. Frank Kermode, ed. (Modern Master Ser.) New York: Viking, 1975.

3975 __________. "T. S. Eliot in His Poetry" and "T. S. Eliot in His Criticism," The Destructive Element. New York: Houghton Mifflin, 1936, pp. 132-149, 153-167.

3976 __________. World within World: The Autobiography of Stephen Spender. London: Hamish Hamilton, 1951, pp. 145-148, passim.

3977 Sperna Weiland, J. "De vreemdeling bij T. S. Eliot," Wending, 19 (July-August, 1964), 306-317.

3978 Spiller, Robert, ed. "Poetry," Literary History of the United States. New York: Macmillan, 4th ed., 1974, passim.

3979 __________. The Third Dimension: Studies in Literary History. New York: Macmillan, 1965, pp. 146-148, passim.

3980 __________. "The Uses of Memory: Eliot, Faulkner," The Cycle of American Literature. New York: Macmillan, 1957, pp. 210-216, passim.

3981 Spinucci, Pietro. "T. S. Eliot e Hart Crane," SA, 11 (1965), 213-250.

3982 Spivey, Ted R. "The Apocalyptic Symbolism of W. B. Yeats and T. S. Eliot," Costerus, 4 (1972), 193-214.

3983 __________. "Archetypal Symbols in the Major Poetry of T. S. Eliot and Conrad Aiken," IJSym, 2, #3 (1971), 16-26.

3984 Spratt, P. "Eliot and Freud," LHY, 1, #1 (January, 1960), 55-68.

3985 Squires, J. Radcliffe. "Literary Intelligence: Harvard," WestR, 15 (Spring, 1951), 197-199.

3986 Stamm, Rudolf. "Rebellion und Tradition im Werke T. S. Eliots," Univ, 22 (1967), 725-742.

3987 __________. "T. S. Eliot zum siebzigsten Geburtstag," Der Bund (September, 1958), 26.

3988 Standop, Ewald. "A Note on the Dramatic Verse of T. S. Eliot," LWU, 5 (1972), 33-36.

3989 __________. T. S. Eliots Kulturkritik. Diss. Münster, 1949.

3990 Stanescu, Nichita. "T. S. Eliot: Un menhir de aer," [T. S. Eliot: A Menhir in the Open Air], Luceafãrul, #35 (August, 1969), 6.

3991 Stanford, Derek. "Concealment and Revelation in T. S. Eliot," SWR, 50, #3 (Summer, 1965), 243-251.

3992 Stanley, John M. "Church and World: A Critical Evaluation of the Corpus Christianum Approach in the Thought of John Baillie, V. A. Demant, and T. S. Eliot," DAI, 30 (Columbia: 1969), 1628A.

3993 Stapleton, Laurence. "T. S. Eliot: The Dialogue of the Writer," The Elected Circle: Studies in the Art of Prose. Laurence Stapleton, ed. Princeton: Princeton U. P., 1973, pp. 233-267.

3994 Stead, C. K. "'Classical Authority' and 'The Dark Embryo': A Dichotomy in T. S. Eliot's Criticism," AUMLA, No. 22 (November, 1964), 200-207.

3995 __________. The New Poetic: An Investigation into Certain Common Problems Evident in the Work of English-Speaking Poets of the Twentieth Century, the Study Confined Mainly to the Literary Scene in England from 1900 to 1930, and Paying Special Attention to the Work of W. B. Yeats and T. S. Eliot. Diss. Bristol: 1962.

3996 __________. The New Poetic. London: Hutchinson; New York: Hillary House, 1964, passim.

3997 Steadman, John M. "Eliot and Husserl: The Origin of the 'Objective Correlative,'" N&Q, 5, #6 (June, 1958), 261-262.

3998 Stein, William B. "Santayana and Literary Tradition," MLN, 73 (January, 1958), 23-25. Prints a letter from Santayana discussing Eliot's views on tradition.

3999 Steinmann, Martin, Jr. "Coleridge, T. S. Eliot, and Organicism," MLN, 71 (May, 1956), 339-340.

4000 Stephane, Nelly. "T. S. Eliot et Baudelaire," Europe, #456 (April, 1967), 244-246.

4001 Stephenson, Ethel M. T. S. Eliot and the Lay Reader. London: Fortune Press, 1944; 2nd ed., 1946; repr., 1948.

4002 Stevens, Wallace. "Homage to T. S. Eliot," HA, 125, #3 (December, 1938), 41ff.

4003 Steward, Diana. "A Contrast of Landscapes: 'Virginia' and 'Usk,'" T. S. Eliot: A Symposium. Neville Braybrooke, ed. New York: 1958, pp. 108-110.

4004 Stewart, Randall. American Literature and Christian Doctrine. Baton Rouge: Louisiana U.P., 1958, passim.

4005 ________. Regionalism and Beyond: Essays of Randall Stewart. George Core, ed. Nashville: Vanderbilt U.P., 1968, passim.

4006 Stock, Noel. "The Precision of T. S. Eliot," NatlRev, 14, #4 (January 29, 1963), 76-78.

4007 ________. "Reflections on Eliot and the Art of Readings," PoetA, 49 (1973), 50-56.

4008 Stonier, G. W. "Eliot and the Plain Reader," FnR, 138 (November, 1932), 620-629.

4009 Storey, Robert F. "Pierrot: A Critical History of a Mask," DAI, 33 (UCLA: 1973), 5751A. "...A Chapter devoted entirely to Pierrot's role in the poetry of Jules Laforgue leads to a final discussion of his appearance, under various pseudonymous guises, in the work of T. S. Eliot and Wallace Stevens."

4009a Storm, Leo. "J. M. Robertson and T. S. Eliot," JML, 5 (April, 1976), 315-321.

4010 Stormon, E. J., S.J. "Some Notes on T. S. Eliot and Jules Laforgue," EFL, #2 (1965), 103-114.

4011 Strachey, John. The Coming Struggle for Power. New York: Modern Library, 1935, pp. 224-228.

4012 Strandberg, Victor H. "Eliot's Insomniacs," SAQ, 68, #1 (Winter, 1969), 67-73.

4013 ________. "Whitman and Eliot: Two Studies in the Religious Imagination," FQ, 22, #2 (Winter, 1973), 3-18.

4014 Straumann, Heinrich, and Cyril Connolly. "T. S. Eliot--der Grosse Dichter der zeitgenössischenenglischen Literatur," Univ, 20 (1965), 571-578.

4015 Strickland, G. R. "Flaubert, Pound, and T. S. Eliot," CamQ, 2 (Summer, 1967), 242-263.

4016 Strong, Robert. "The Critical Attitude of T. S. Eliot," Lon Qt, and HolbornR, 158 (October, 1933), 513-519.

4017 Stuart, D. R. "Modernistic Critics and Translators," PULC, 11 (Summer, 1950), 177-198. Borrowings from the classics by Eliot and others.

4018 Styler, W. E. "T. S. Eliot as an Adult Tutor," N&Q, 19, #2 (February, 1972), 53-54.

4019 Stühnel, Rudolf. "Die Literarischen Voraussetzungen von Joyce's Ulysses," GRM, n. s., 12, #2 (April, 1962), 202-211. Comparison of Joyce with Pound and Eliot.

4020 ________. "T. S. Eliots Stellung zum Humanismus," NS, 8 (July, 1959), 303-314.

4021 Sullivan, Sheila, ed. Critics on T. S. Eliot: Readings in Literary Criticism. (RLitC, 14) London: Allen & Unwin, 1973.

4021a Sullivan, Zohreh Tawakuli. "Memory and Meditative Structure in T. S. Eliot's Early Poetry," Renascence, 29 (Winter, 1977), 97-105.

4022 Sutton, Walter. American Free Verse: The Modern Revolution in Poetry. New York: New Directions, 1973, pp. 35-39, passim.

4023 Sweeney, Frances. "In Memoriam: T. S. Eliot," America, 112, #4 (January 23, 1965), 120-121.

4024 Swinnerton, Frank. The Georgian Literary Scene. London: Heinemann, 1935, pp. 509-514.

4025 Symes, Gordon. "T. S. Eliot and Old Age," FnR, 61 (March, 1951), 186-193.

4026 Symons, Julian. "The Criterion," LonMag, 7, #8 (November, 1967), 19-23.

4027 Sypher, Wylie. Rococo to Cubism in Art and Literature. New York: Vintage Bks., 1960, pp. 265-266, 283-285, 313-317, passim.

4028 "T. S. Eliot Goes Home," LivAge, 342, #4388 (May, 1932), 234-236.

4029 Takayanagi, Shunichi. "The Garden and the City: An Attempt to Overcome Schizophrenia in T. S. Eliot's Poetry," ELLS, 11 (1974), 27-45.

4029a ________. "Search after the Whole: F. H. Bradley and T. S. Eliot," ELLS, 5 (1968), 12-69.

4030 __________. "Virgil Theodor Haecker and T. S. Eliot," ELLS, 8 (1971), 37-63.

4031 Tambimuttu, [Thurairajah]. "O What a Beautiful Morning (from Natarajah: a poem for Mr. Eliot)," T. S. Eliot: A Symposium. Richard March and Tambimuttu, comps. Freeport, N.Y.: Bks. for Libraries Pr., 1968, p. 77.

4032 Tanner, Stephen L. "T. S. Eliot and Paul Elmer More on Tradition," ELN, 8 (1971), 211-215.

4033 Tate, Allen. "Homage to T. S. Eliot," HA, 125, #3 (1938), 41.

4034 __________. "A Poetry of Ideas," NR, 47, #604 (June 30, 1926), 172-173.

4035 __________. "Postscript by the Guest Editor," SR, 74, #1, A Special Eliot Issue (January-March, 1966), 383-387.

4036 __________. "T. S. Eliot, 1931," On the Limits of Poetry. New York: Swallow Pr., 1948, pp. 341-349.

4037 __________, ed. T. S. Eliot: The Man and His Work. New York: Delacorte Pr., 1966.

4038 __________. "Taste and Mr. Johnson," NR, 68, #827 (August, 1931), 23-24.

4039 Taupin, René. "The Classicism of T. S. Eliot," Symposium, 3, #1 (January, 1932), 64-84.

4040 __________. "The Example of Rémy de Gourmont," Criterion, 10, #41 (July, 1931), 614-625.

4041 __________. L'Influence du Symbolisme Francais sur la Poesie Americaine, 1910-1920. Paris: Honore Champion, 1929, passim.

4042 Tello, Jaime. "El concepto del tiempo y del escapio en la poesía de Eliot," RNC, 116 (1956), 113-122.

4043 __________. "Eliot and Sitwell," RNC, 27 (January-June, 1965), 168-169.

4044 Tentori, F. "Lorca, Hopkins, Eliot: misure difficili della poesia moderna," FLe, #11 (March 12, 1950).

4045 Terada, Takehiko. T. S. Eliot. Tokyo: Kenkyusha, 1964.

4046 __________. "T. S. Eliot: The Fundamental Problems of His Later Works," REngL, 9 (March, 1961), 118-152.

4047 Terrell, Carroll Franklin. "The Bone on the Beach: The Meaning of T. S. Eliot's Symbols," DA, 19 (New York: 1959), 3310.

4048 Thatcher, David S., ed. "Richard Aldington's Letters to Herbert Read," MalR, 15 (July, 1970), 5-44.

4049 Theall, Donald F. Communication Theories in Modern Poetry: Yeats, Pound, Eliot, Joyce. Diss. Toronto: 1955.

4050 Theoharis, Zoe George. "The Concepts of Noesis and Pathos in Ancient and Modern Criticism: Longinus and T. S. Eliot on the Dissociation of Sensibility," DAI, 36 (Indiana: 1975), 5272A.

4051 Thomas, Caleekal Thomas. "Views of History in the Works of T. S. Eliot," DA, 31 (Michigan: 1969), 769A.

4052 Thomas, R. Hinton. "Culture and T. S. Eliot," ModQt, n. s. 6, #2 (Spring, 1951), 147-162.

4053 Thomas, Wright, and Stuart Gerry Brown. Reading Poems: An Introduction to Critical Study. New York: Oxford U. P., 1941, pp. 716-731, 749-751.

4054 Thompson, Eric. "'Dissociation of Sensibility,'" EIC, 2 (April, 1952), 207-213.

4055 ________. "The Problem of Literary Interpretation," OUR, 8 (1966), 54-72.

4056 ________. T. S. Eliot: The Metaphysical Perspective. With Preface by Harry T. Moore. Carbondale: Southern Illinois U. P., 1963.

4057 Thompson, Katharine S. "The Lost Lilac and the Lost Sea Voices: Old Essex in New Writing," EIHC, 92 (1956), 18-25. Discussion of Eliot and others.

4058 Thompson, Marion C. The Dramatic Criticism of T. S. Eliot. Diss. Cornell: 1953.

4059 Tillotson, Geoffrey. "The Critic and the Dated Text," SR, 68 (Autumn, 1960), 595-602.

4060 Tillyard, E. M. W. "The Personal Heresy in Criticism: A Rejoinder," Essays and Studies by Members of the English Assn., 20 (1934), 7-20.

4061 Tindall, William York. "Exiles: Rimbaud to Joyce," AmSch, 14 (Spring, 1945), 351-355.

4062 ________. Forces in Modern British Literature, 1885-

1956. New York: Knopf, 1947, passim; Vintage Bks., 1956, passim.

4063 ________. "T. S. Eliot in America: The Recantation of T. S. Eliot," AmSch, 16, #4 (Autumn, 1947), 432-437. Eliot's change of attitude toward Milton.

4064 Todd, Oliver. "T. S. Eliot contre l'humain," TM, 7 (April, 1952), 1858-79.

4065 Todd, Ruthven. "A Garland for Mr. Eliot," T. S. Eliot: A Symposium. Richard March, et al, eds. Freeport, New York: 1968, p. 235.

4066 Tomlin, E. W. F. "T. S. Eliot and His Work," EigoS, 111 (April, 1965), 214-219.

4067 Tordeur, Jean. A la rencontre de Thomas Stearns Eliot, un classique vivant. Brussels: La Sixaine, 1946.

4068 Torrens, James, S. J. "Charles Maurras and Eliot's 'New Life,'" PMLA, 89 (March, 1974), 312-322. The influence of Maurras and Dante on Eliot's work in the late 1920's.

4069 ________. "T. S. Eliot and the Austere Poetics of Valéry," CL, 23 (Winter, 1971), 1-17.

4070 ________. "T. S. Eliot and the Contribution of Dante Towards a Poetics of Sensibility," DA, 29 (Michigan: 1968), 916A-17A.

4071 Trilling, Lionel. "Mr. Eliot's Kipling," Nation, 157, #16 (October, 1943), 436-442.

4072 ________. "T. S. Eliot Talks about His Poetry," CUF, 2 (Fall, 1958), 11-14.

4073 Trompeo, P. P. "Cicerone di Eliot," FLe, (November 14, 1948).

4074 Tuohy, Frank. "The World of T. S. Eliot's Early Poetry," EigoS, 111 (May, 1965), 312-313.

4075 Turnell, G. M. "Tradition and Mr. T. S. Eliot," Colosseum, 1, #2 (June, 1934), 44-54.

4076 Ueda, Tamotsu. "On T. S. Eliot's Literary Criticism," HR, 6 (September, 1959), 15-32.

4077 ________. "T. S. Eliot as a Poet," HR, 6 (October, 1960), 37-44. Study of Eliot's poems as reflections of the restless contemporary world.

4078 Unger, Leonard. "Laforgue, Conrad, and T. S. Eliot," The Man in the Name. Minneapolis: Minnesota U. P., 1956, pp. 190-242.

4079 __________. "T. S. Eliot," Poems for Study. New York: Holt, Rinehart & Winston, 1953, pp. 618-635.

4080 __________. "T. S. Eliot," Seven Modern American Poets. Minneapolis: Minnesota U. P., 1967, pp. 191-227.

4081 __________. T. S. Eliot. (Pamphlets on American Writers, No. 8) Minneapolis: Minnesota U. P., 1967.

4082 __________. T. S. Eliot: A Selected Critique. New York: Rinehart, 1948.

4083 __________. "T. S. Eliot, 1888-1965: Viva il poeta!" MassR, 6 (Winter-Spring, 1965), 408-410.

4084 __________. T. S. Eliot: Moments and Patterns. Minneapolis: Minnesota U. P., 1966, 2nd pr., 1967.

4085 __________. "T. S. Eliot's Images of Awareness," SR, 74, #1 (January-March, 1966), 197-224.

4086 __________. "T. S. Eliot's Rose Garden: A Persistent Theme," SoR, 7 (Spring, 1942), 667-689.

4087 __________. "A Tribute. T. S. Eliot: The Intimate Voice," SoR, 1, n. s., #3 (Summer, 1965), 731-734.

4088 Untermeyer, Louis. "The Cerebralists: T. S. Eliot," American Poetry Since 1900. New York: Holt, 1923, pp. 350-362.

4089 __________. "Irony de Luxe," Freeman, 1 (June 30, 1920), 381-382.

4090 Vaish, Y. N. "T. S. Eliot and the East," ModRev, #761 (May, 1970), 329-337.

4091 Valette, Jacques. "A propos de T. S. Eliot," MdF, 322 (September, 1954), 151-154.

4092 __________. "Fortunes d'un apophtegme," MdF, #1061 (January, 1952), 149-151.

4093 __________. "On parle de T. S. Eliot," MdF, 342 (July, 1961), 518-520.

4094 __________. "T. S. Eliot, Milton et la póesie anglais," MdF (August, 1948), 747-749. Eliot's debt to Milton.

4095 __________. "Une vue conservatrice de la culture," MdF, #1029 (May 1, 1949), 162-174.

4096 Valverde, José María. "T. S. Eliot, desde la poesía americana," Insula, 4 (August 15, 1950), 1-2.

4097 Vance, Thomas. "Wallace Stevens and T. S. Eliot," DCLB, 4, #3 (December, 1961), 37-44.

4098 Van der Vat, D. G. "The Poetry of T. S. Eliot," ES, 20 (June, 1938), 107-118.

4099 Van Doren, Mark. "England's Critical Compass," Nation, 112, #2913 (May, 1921), 751.

4100 __________. "First Glance," and "Mr. Eliot Glances Up," The Private Reader. New York: Henry Holt & Co., 1942, pp. 131-133, 212-216, passim.

4101 __________. The Happy Critic and Other Essays. New York: Hill & Wang, 1961, pp. 2-5, 23.

4102 Vania, Rhoda. "The American in T. S. Eliot," Venture, 5, #1 (June, 1968), 12-20.

4103 Verma, Rajendra. Royalist in Politics: T. S. Eliot and Political Philosophy. London: Asia Pub. House, 1968.

4104 Vickery, John B. "Golden Bough: Impact and Archetype," VQR, 39, #1 (Winter, 1963), 37-57.

4105 __________. T. S. Eliot and "The Golden Bough": The Archetype of the Dying God. Diss. Wisconsin: 1956.

4106 __________. "T. S. Eliot and The Golden Bough: The Archetype of the Dying God," SDD-UW, 16 (1956), 560-561.

4107 __________. "T. S. Eliot's Poetry: The Quest and the Way," Renascence, 10 (Autumn, 1957), Part I, 3-10, 31; Part II (Winter, 1958), 59-67.

4108 Vigée, Claude. "Les artistes de la faim," CL, 9 (Spring, 1957), 97-117.

4109 Vinograd, Sherna S. "The Accidental: A Clue to Structure in Eliot's Poetry," Accent, 9 (Summer, 1949), 231-238.

4110 Viswanathan, K. "Matthew Arnold and T. S. Eliot," NewR, (India), 29 (April, 1949), 255-267.

4111 Viswanathan S. "Eliot and Shelley: A Sketch of Shifts in Attitude," ArielE, 2, #1 (January, 1971), 58-67.

4112 Vivas, Eliseo. Creation and Discovery. New York: Noonday Pr., 1955, pp. 75-76, passim.

4113 ______. "Literary Criticism and Aesthetics," Mon/TuMS, # 10 (1970), 13-39.

4114 Vizioli, Paulo. "Eliot e Wagner: O processo de composição poética," ESPSL, 3 (November, 1974), 1.

4115 Voight, F. A. "Milton, Thou Shouldst Be Living...," NineC, 130 (October, 1941), 211-221.

4116 Voight, G. P. "Has the Pendulum Started Back?" LuthChQt, 9 (1936), 149-155.

4117 Von Phul, Ruth. "Query about Joyce's Relationship with Eliot," JJQ, 8 (1971), 178-179.

4118 Von Wellsheim, Mother Anita. "Imagery in Modern Marian Poetry," Renascence, 10 (Summer, 1958), 176-186.

4119 Vordtriede, Werner. "Der junge T. S. Eliot," NDH, 120 (1968), 47-64.

4120 Waggoner, Hyatt Howe. The Heel of Elohim: Science and Values in Modern American Poetry. Norman: Oklahoma U. P., 1950, passim.

4121 ______. "Thomas Stearns Eliot," American Poets: From the Puritans to the Present. Boston: Houghton Mifflin, 1968, pp. 409-427.

4122 Wagner, C. Roland. "Conversation with Santayana, 1948: A Letter to a Friend," AL, 40, # 3 (November, 1968), 340-351. Description of an interview with George Santayana in which he discussed Eliot and others.

4123 Wagner, Linda W., comp. T. S. Eliot: A Collection of Criticism. (Contemp. Studies in Lit.) New York: McGraw-Hill, 1974.

4124 Wagner, Robert D. "The Meaning of Eliot's Rose-Garden," PMLA, 69 (1954), 22-33.

4125 Wain, John. "On T. S. Eliot," LanM, 59, # 3 (May-June, 1965), 115-119.

4126 ______. "Poetry," The Twentieth-Century Mind: History, Ideas, and Literature in Britain. C. B. Cox, et al, eds. London: Oxford U. P., 1972, II, 307-72.

4127 ______. "The Prophet Ezra v. 'The Egotistical Sublime': On Pound, Eliot, Joyce," Encounter, 33, # 2 (August, 1969), 63-70.

4128 ________. "T. S. Eliot," Encounter, 24, #3 (March, 1965), 51-53.

4129 ________. "A Walk in the Sacred Wood," LonMag, 5 (January, 1958), 45-53. On Eliot as a critic.

4129a Wajima, Shiro. "T. S. Eliot to Nishida Kitaro," EigoS, 121 (1975), 4-8.

4130 Waldron, Philip. "T. S. Eliot, Mr. Whiteside and 'The Psychobiographical Approach,'" SoRA, 6 (1973), 138-147.

4131 Waldson, C. M. "T. S. Eliot," NZ, 1, #2 (1949), 46-50.

4132 Wall, Bengt V. "Möte med T. S. Eliot," BLM, 26 (November, 1957), 774-778.

4133 Wallace, Ronald Henry. "Religious Development in the Poetic Works of T. S. Eliot," DAI, 35 (McGill (Canada): 1974), 6686A.

4134 Walmsley, D. M. "Unrecorded Article by T. S. Eliot," BC, 9 (Summer, 1960), 198-199.

4135 Walton, Geoffrey. "The Age of Yeats or the Age of Eliot? Notes on Recent Verse," Scrutiny, 12, #4 (Autumn, 1944), 310-321.

4136 Ward, David E. "The Cult of Impersonality: Eliot, St. Augustine, and Flaubert," EIC, 17, #2 (April, 1967), 169-182.

4137 ________. "Il culto dell'impersonalità: Eliot, Sant'Agostino e Flaubert," Verri, 31 (1969), 83-95.

4138 ________. "Eliot, Murray, Homer, and the Idea of Tradition: 'So I Assumed a Double Part....'" EIC, 18, #1 (January, 1968), 47-59.

4139 ________. T. S. Eliot Between Two Worlds: A Reading of T. S. Eliot's Poetry and Plays. London and Boston: Routledge & K. Paul, 1973.

4140 Warncke, Wayne. "George Orwell on T. S. Eliot," WHR, 26, #3 (Summer, 1972), 265-270.

4141 Warren, Austin. "Continuity and Coherence in the Criticism of T. S. Eliot," Connections. Ann Arbor: Michigan U. P., 1970, pp. 152-183.

4142 ________. "Continuity in T. S. Eliot's Criticism," E-WR, 1, #1 (Spring, 1964), 1-12.

4143 __________. "Eliot's Literary Criticism," SR, 74 (Winter, 1966), 272-292.

4144 Wasser, Henry. "Note on Eliot and Santayana," BUSE, 4 (Summer, 1960), 125-126.

4145 Wasserstrom, William. "T. S. Eliot and The Dial," SR, 70 (Winter, 1962), 81-92.

4146 Wasson, Richard. "'Like a Burnished Throne': T. S. Eliot and the Demonism of Technology," CentR, 13 (Summer, 1969), 302-316.

4147 __________. "T. S. Eliot's Antihumanism and Antipragmatism," TSLL, 10 (Fall, 1968), 445-455.

4148 Watanabe, Nancy Ann. "Creative Destruction: The Irony of Self-Betrayal in the Psychosymbolic Monologue: Browning, Poe, Eliot, Kafka, and Camus," DAI, 36 (Indiana: 1975), 5289A-90A.

4149 Waterman, A. E. "Conrad Aiken as Critic: The Consistent View," MissQ, 24, #2 (Spring, 1971), 91-110. "...He saw early the importance of Eliot's poetry...."

4150 Waters, Leonard. Coleridge and Eliot: A Comparative Study of Their Theories of Poetic Composition. Diss. Michigan: 1948.

4151 Watkins, Floyd C. "T. S. Eliot," The Flesh and the Word: Eliot, Hemingway, Faulkner. Nashville, Tenn.: Vanderbilt U. P., 1971, pp. 13-91, passim.

4152 __________. "T. S. Eliot's Painter of the Umbrian School," AL, 36 (March, 1964), 72-75.

4153 Watkins, Vernon. "Ode" [poem], T. S. Eliot: A Symposium. N. Braybrooke, ed. New York: 1958, pp. 24-26.

4154 __________. "To T. S. Eliot," [poem], T. S. Eliot: A Symposium. Richard March, et al, comps. Freeport, N. Y.: 1968, p. 243.

4155 Watson, George. "Quest for a Frenchman," SR, 84 (Summer, 1976), 465-475.

4156 __________. "The Triumph of T. S. Eliot," CritQ, 7, #4 (Winter, 1965), 328-337. Cf., I. M. Parsons, CritQ, 8 (1965), 180-182.

4157 Watt, F. W. "The Critic's Choice," CanL, 19 (Winter, 1964), 51-54. Rev.-art. Northrop Frye's T. S. Eliot. 1963.

4158 Watts, Harold H. "The Tragic Hero in Eliot and Yeats," CentR, 13 (Winter, 1969), 84-100.

4159 Weatherby, Harold L. "Eliot and Mystical Wisdom," The Keen Delight: The Christian Poet in the Modern World. Athens: Univ. of Georgia Pr., 1975, pp. 99-122.

4159a ________. "Old-Fashioned Gods: Eliot on Lawrence and Hardy," SR, 75 (Spring, 1967), 301-316.

4160 ________. "Two Medievalists: Lewis and Eliot on Christianity and Literature," SR, 78 (Spring, 1970), 330-347.

4161 Weathers, Winston. "An exemplary Theory of Communication in Modern Literature," Communication Theory and Research. Lee Thayer, ed. Springfield, Ill.: Charles C. Thomas, 1966-67, pp. 149-173.

4162 Webber, B. G. "Lucasta Angel," N&Q, 202 (March, 1957), 133.

4163 Weber, Alfred. "Ein Beitrag zur Chronologie und Genesis der Dichtung T. S. Eliots," JA, 3 (1958), 162-191.

4164 ________. "Ein Briefwechsel mit T. S. Eliot," JA, 16 (1971), 204-212.

4165 ________. Der Symbolismus T. S. Eliots. Versuch einer neuen Annäherung an moderne Lyrik. Diss. Tübingen: 1953-54.

4165a ________. "T. S. Eliot: Auflehnung und Ordnungsidee eines modernen Traditionalisten," Englische Dichter der Moderne: Ihr Leben und Werk. Rudolf Sühner and Dieter Riesner, eds. Berlin: Schmidt, 1971, pp. 252-268.

4166 Webster, Grant T. "T. S. Eliot as Critic: The Man Behind the Masks," Criticism, 8 (Fall, 1966), 336-348.

4167 Wecter, Dixon. "The Harvard Exiles," VQR, 10, #2 (April, 1934), 244-257.

4168 Weidlé, Vladimir. "L'Oeuvre critique d'un poète," Critique (Paris), 6 (December, 1950), 220-228.

4169 Weigand, Elsie. "Rilke and Eliot: The Articulation of the Mystic Experience," GR, 30 (October, 1955), 198-210.

4170 Weimann, Robert. "New Criticism und bürgerliche Literaturwissenschaft Geschichte und Kritik Neuerer Strömungen," ZAA, 8 (January, 1960), 29-74, 141-170.

4171 Weinberg, Kerry. T. S. Eliot and Charles Baudelaire. (Studies in Gen. and Comp. Lit. 5.) The Hague: Mouton, 1969.

4172 Weintraub, Stanley. "The Private Life of a Dead Poet," NR, 170 (March 23, 1974), 27-28.

4172a Weisberg, Robert. "T. S. Eliot: The Totemic-Mosaic Dream," Bulletin of the Midwest Modern Language Association, 8, #2 (1975), 24-44.

4173 Weiss, Charlotte. Die Sprachkunst in T. S. Eliots dichterischen Werken. Diss. Hamburg: 1956.

4174 Weiss, Theodore. "The Nonsense of Winter's Anatomy," QRL, 1 (Summer, 1944), 212-234; 300-318.

4175 __________. "T. S. Eliot and the Courtyard Revolution," SR, 54, #2 (Spring, 1946), 289-307.

4176 Weitz, Morris. "T. S. Eliot: Time as a Mode of Salvation," SR, 60 (Winter, 1952), 48-64.

4177 Wellek, René. "The Criticism of T. S. Eliot," SR, 64, #3 (Summer, 1956), 398-443.

4178 __________. "The Main Trends of Twentieth-Century Criticism," YR, 51, #1 (October, 1961), 102-118.

4179 __________. "Thomas Stearns Eliot," Listy pro umeni a kritiku, 1 (June, 1933), 285-286.

4180 Wells, Henry W. New Poets from Old: A Study in Literary Genetics. New York: Russell & Russell, 1964, pp. 70-76, passim.

4181 Wentraub, Dennis A. "Auden's 'To T. S. Eliot on His Sixtieth Birthday,'" Expl, 31 (May 9, 1973), Item 75.

4182 West, Anthony. "The Last Puritan. Edmund Wilson vs. T. S. Eliot," Sun Times (August 3, 1958), p. 7.

4183 Wheelwright, Philip. "A Contemporary Classicist," VQR, 9 (January, 1933), 155-160.

4184 __________. "Eliot's Philosophical Themes," T. S. Eliot: A Study of His Writings by Several Hands. B. Rajan, ed. London: 1966, pp. 96-106.

4185 Whitaker, Thomas R. "Voices in the Open: Wordsworth, Eliot and Stevens," IowaR, 2, #3 (Summer, 1971), 96-112.

4186 White, Gina. "Modes of Being in Yeats and Eliot," MoOc, 1, #2 (Winter, 1971), 227-237.

4187 Whiteside, George. "Eliot and Psychobiography," SoRA, 6, #3 (September, 1973), 253-256.

4188 ________. "T. S. Eliot: The Psychobiographical Approach," SoRA, 6, #1 (March, 1973), 3-26. Cf., Philip Waldron. "T. S. Eliot, Mr. Whiteside and 'The Psychobiographical Approach,'" SoRA, 6, #2 (June, 1973), 138-147.

4189 ________. "T. S. Eliot's Character and Work up to The Waste Land," DA, 31 (Columbia: 1969), 1820.

4190 ________. "T. S. Eliot's Dissertation," ELH, 34 (September, 1967), 400-424.

4191 ________. "T. S. Eliot's Doctoral Studies," AN&Q, (1973), 83-87.

4192 Whitfield, J. H. "Pirandello and T. S. Eliot: An Essay in Counterpoint," EM, 9 (1958), 329-357.

4193 ________. "Pirandello e T. S. Eliot: Identita e contrasti," Pel. 4 (1962), 5-30.

4194 Whitford, Ruth H. "Alienation and Reconciliation in the Works of T. S. Eliot," DA, 28 (N.Y.U.: 1967), 1519A-20A.

4194a Whitlark, James S. "More Borrowings by T. S. Eliot from The Light of Asia," N&Q, 22 (1975), 206-207.

4195 Whitman, Peter. "Poetry in the First Half of the Twentieth Century," European, 12 (October, 1958), 104-110.

4196 Wienhorst, Sue E. "Some Recent Christian Responses to Literature," Cresset, 36, #3 (January, 1973), 11-17. Rev-art. Helen Gardner, Religion and Literature. Oxford U.P., 1971.

4197 Wilbur, Robert Henry Hunter. "George Santayana and Three Modern Philosophical Poets: T. S. Eliot, Conrad Aiken, and Wallace Stevens," DA, 26 (Columbia: 1964), 2228.

4198 Wilder, Amos N. "Mr. T. S. Eliot and the Anglo-Catholic Option," Spiritual Aspects of the New Poetry. New York: Harper, 1940, pp. 205-216.

4199 ________. Modern Poetry and the Christian Tradition: A Study in the Relation of Christianity to Culture. New York: Scribner, 1952, passim.

4200 ________. Theology and Modern Literature. Cambridge: Harvard U.P., 1958, pp. 88f, passim.

4201 Wildi, Max. "Eine literarische Sensation. Zum Auftauchen von T. S. Eliots fruhen Manuskripten," NZZ (November 24, 1968), 51.

4202 Williams, Charles. "T. S. Eliot," Poetry at Present. Oxford: Clarendon Pr., 1930, pp. 163-173.

4203 Williams, Margaret, R. S. C. J. "T. S. Eliot and Eastern Thought," TkR, 2, #1 (1971), 175-194.

4204 Williams, Philip. "T. S. Eliot as American Poet," EigoS, 111 (May, 1965), 316-319.

4205 ________. "T. S. Eliot on Poetry and Belief," E-WR, 3 (Summer, 1967), 126-136.

4206 ________. "Whitman and Eliot: Two Sides of One Tradition," Hikaku Bungaku, 15 (1972), i-xxv.

4207 Williams, Philip Eugene. "The Biblical View of History: Hawthorne, Mark Twain, Faulkner, and Eliot," DA, 25 (Pa.: 1965), 4159-60.

4208 Williams, Raymond. "Eliot and Belief," Manchester Guardian (December 9, 1960), p. 6.

4209 ________. "Second Thoughts: T. S. Eliot on Culture," EIC, 6, #3 (July, 1956), 302-318.

4210 Williams, William Carlos. "Homage to T. S. Eliot," HA, 125, #3 (December, 1938), 42.

4211 ________. "Pagany," Autobiography. New York: New Directions, 1967, pp. 174-175.

4211a ________. "T. S. Eliot, or Religion," Three on a Tower: The Lives and Works of Ezra Pound, T. S. Eliot and William Carlos Williams. New York: William Morrow & Co., 1975, pp. 93-191.

4212 Williamson, George. A Reader's Guide to T. S. Eliot: A Poem-by-Poem Analysis. New York: Farrar, Straus & Cudahy, 1953; Noonday Pr., 1955.

4213 ________. "T. S. Eliot, 1888-1965," ModA, 9 (Fall, 1965), 399-407.

4214 ________. "The Talent of T. S. Eliot," 35 (July, 1927), 284-295.

4215 ________. The Talent of T. S. Eliot. (University of Washington Chapbooks, No. 32, Glenn Hughes, ed.) Seattle: Washington Univ. Bk. Store, 1929.

4216 Williamson, Mervyn Wilton. "A Survey of T. S. Eliot's Literary Criticism: 1917-1956," DA, 18 (Texas: 1958), 2131.

4217 Wills, Garry. "No Habitation, No Name," ModA, 8, #1 (Winter, 1964), 89-92. Rev.-art., Carol H. Smith. T. S. Eliot's Dramatic Theory and Practice. 1963.

4218 Wilson, Colin. "Existential Criticism," ChiR, 18 (Summer, 1959), 152-181.

4219 Wilson, Edmund. "'Miss Buttle' and 'Mr. Eliot'" NY, 34, #14 (May 24, 1958), 119-150. Discussion of Victor Purcell's satire on Eliot, The Sweeniad by Myra Buttle [My Rebuttal].

4220 __________. "Mr. More and the Mithraic Bull," NR, 91, #1173 (May, 1937), 64-68.

4221 __________. "Mr. More and the Mithraic Bull," The Triple Thinkers. New York: Oxford U. P., rev. and enlarged ed., 1948, pp. 3-14.

4222 __________. "T. S. Eliot," NR, 60 (November 13, 1929), 344ff; repr., in Axel's Castle: A Study in the Imaginative Literature of 1870-1930. New York: Scribner's; repr., 1959, pp. 93-131. "...the first important critical estimate of Eliot's work."

4223 __________. "T. S. Eliot and the Church of England," NR, 58, #751 (April 24, 1929), 283-284; repr., in The Shores of Light. New York: Farrar, Straus & Young, 1952, pp. 437-441.

4224 Wilson, Frank. Six Essays on the Development of T. S. Eliot. London: Fortune Pr., 1948.

4225 Wilson, Gary H. "The Shakespearian Design of T. S. Eliot's Poetry," DAI, 34 (Temple: 1973), 794A-95A.

4226 Wilson, Richard. "The Continuity of T. S. Eliot," KanoS, #1 (1965), 24-32.

4227 Wilson, Roderick. "Eliot and Achebe: An Analysis of Some Formal and Philosophic Qualities of No Longer at Ease," ESA, 14, #2 (September, 1971), 215-223.

4228 Wimsatt, W. K. "Eliot's Weary Gesture of Dismissal," MassR, 7 (1966), 584-590.

4229 __________. The Verbal Icon: Studies in the Meaning of Poetry. New York: Noonday Pr., 1960, passim.

4230 __________, and Cleanth Brooks. Literary Criticism: A Short History. New York: Random House, 1967, passim.

4231 Winkler, R. O. C. "Crumbs from the Banquet," Scrutiny, 10, #2 (October, 1941), 194-198; repr., in The Importance of Scrutiny. Eric Bentley, ed. New York: 1964, pp. 291-294.

4232 Winston, George P. "Washington Allston and the Objective Correlative," BuR, 11 (1962), 95-108.

4233 Winters, Yvor. "T. S. Eliot: The Illusion of Reaction," KR, 3 (Winter, 1941), 7-30; (Spring, 1941), 221-239; repr., in The Anatomy of Nonsense. Norfolk, Conn.: New Directions, 1943, pp. 120-167. Cf., Theodore Weiss. "The Nonsense of Winter's Anatomy," QRL, 1 (1943-44), 212-234; 200-318.

4234 Wolff, Erwin. "Einheit und Kontinuität in T. S. Eliot's Entwicklung als Lyriker," GRM, 8, #4 (October, 1958), 401-416.

4235 Wollheim, Richard. "Eliot and F. H. Bradley: An Account," Eliot in Perspective. Graham Martin, ed. London: Macmillan, 1970, pp. 169-193.

4236 __________. "Eliot, Bradley and Immediate Experience," NSt, 67 (March 13, 1964), 401-402.

4237 Wollner, Craig Evan. "Modernization and Discourse: T. S. Eliot, B. F. Skinner, and Herbert Marcuse as Studies in the Social Foundations of Intellectual History Since 1890," DAI, 36 (New Mexico: 1975), 3946A.

4238 Wood, Frank. "Rilke and Eliot: Tradition and Poetry," GR, 27 (December, 1952), 246-259.

4239 Wood, Grace. "Crime and Contrition in Literature," ConR, 198 (July, 1960), 391-397.

4240 Woodard, Charles R. Browning and Three Modern Poets: Pound, Yeats, and Eliot. Diss. Tenn.: 1953.

4241 Woodberry, Potter. "T. S. Eliot's Metropolitan World," ArQ, 22, #1 (Spring, 1966), 53-66.

4242 Woolf, Leonard. The Journey Not the Arrival Matters: An Autobiography of the Years 1939-1969. New York: Harcourt, Brace & World, 1969, passim.

4243 __________. "Modern Nightingale," Essays on Literature. Freeport, New York: Bks. for Libraries Pr., 1970, pp. 91-105.

4244 Worthington, Jane. "The Epigraphs to the Poetry of T. S. Eliot," AL, 21 (March, 1949), 1-17.

4245 Wren-Lewis, John. "The Passing of Puritanism," CritQ, 5 (Winter, 1963), 295-305.

4246 Wrenn, C. L. "T. S. Eliot and the Language of Poetry," Thought, 32 (Summer, 1957), 239-254; repr., in FordUQ, 32, # 125 (Summer, 1957).

4247 Wright, George T. "Eliot: The Transformation of a Personality," The Poet in the Poem: The Personae of Eliot, Yeats, and Pound. Berkeley and Los Angeles: Calif. U.P., 1962, pp. 60-87.

4248 Wright, Keith. "Rhetorical Repetition in T. S. Eliot's Early Verse," REL, 6, # 2 (April, 1965), 93-100.

4249 __________. "Word-Repetition in T. S. Eliot's Early Verse," EIC, 16 (1966), 201-206.

4250 Wright, Nathalia. "A Source for T. S. Eliot's 'Objective Correlative,'" AL, 41 (January, 1970), 589-592. Notes that Washington Allston used the term "objective correlative" in his Lectures on Art, and Poems, 1850.

4251 Wynn, Dudley. "The Integrity of T. S. Eliot," Writers of Our Years. A. M. I. Fiskin, ed. Denver: Denver U.P., 1950, pp. 59-78.

4252 Yamada, Akihiro. "Eliot and Webster," ES, 52 (February, 1971), 41-43.

4253 __________. "Seneca, Chapman, Eliot," N&Q, 17 (1970), 457-458.

4254 Yamada, Mitsuko. "The Problem of Religion and Humanism in Irving Babbitt and T. S. Eliot," Annual Reports of Studies, Vol. 21. Kyoto: Doshisha Women's College, 1971, pp. 366-387.

4255 __________. "The Relation between Religion and Literature in T. S. Eliot," Annual Reports of Studies, Vol. 22. Kyoto: Doshisha Women's College, 1971, pp. 228-245.

4256 Yamada, Shoichi. "Jijitsu o Noberu koto: T. S. Eliot no 'Ogon no Koeda' Hyoka," Oberon, 34 (1971), 2-22. Evaluation of Eliot's "Golden Bough."

4257 __________. "Personality ni tsuite" [T. S. Eliot and Rémy de Gourmont: on Personality], SELit, 47 (August, 1970), 41-52.

4258 Yamoto, Sadamiki. "Shinwa no Bigaku--Pater to Eliot," EigoS, 119 (1974), 752-754.

4259 Yarros, Victor S. "Phoenix Nest," SatR, 31 (August 7, 1948), 40.

4260 Yeats, W. B. "Introduction," The Oxford Book of Modern Verse. New York: Oxford U. P., 1936, pp. xxi-xxiii.

4261 Yeomans, W. E. "T. S. Eliot, Ragtime, and the Blues," UKCR, 34, #4 (June, 1968), 267-275.

4262 Zabel, M. D. "Poets of Five Decades," SoR, 2, #1 (1936), 168-171.

4263 ________. "The Still Point," Poetry, 41 (December, 1932), 152-158.

4264 ________. "T. S. Eliot," Literary Opinion in America. New York: Harper, 1951, pp. 91-97.

BIBLIOGRAPHY

4265 Arms, George, and Joseph M. Kuntz. "Eliot," Poetry Explication: A Checklist List of Interpretation Since 1925 of British and American Poets. New York: Swallow, 1950; rev. ed., 1962, pp. 97-114.

4266 Austin, Allen. "An Annotated Bibliography," T. S. Eliot: The Literary and Social Criticism. (IUHS 68.) Bloomington: Indiana U. P., 1971, pp. 105-123. "...includes all of Eliot's books on criticism, all articles that he [Eliot] collected in book form," and what Austin considers Eliot's "most significant articles (in periodicals) and introductions to books."

4267 Beare, Robert L. "Notes on the Text of T. S. Eliot: Variants from Russell Square," SB, 9 (1957), 21-49.

4268 Bentz, Hans Willi. Thomas Stearns Eliot in Übersetzungen. Frankfurt am Main, 1963. Provides listings of Eliot in translation, giving place, publisher, date and price of 222 translations into nineteen languages.

4269 Bergonzi, Bernard. "A Select Bibliography," T. S. Eliot. New York: Macmillan Co., 1972, pp. 150-173, 193-195.

4270 Bradbrook, Muriel Clara. "A Select Bibliography," T. S. Eliot. London: Longmans, Green, 1965.

4271 Braun, Elisabeth. T. S. Eliot als Kritiker. Diss. Freiburg, 1963.

4272 Caretti, Laura. T. S. Eliot in Italia: saggio e bibliografia, (1923-1965). Bari: Andriatica, 1968.

4273 Cheney, Frances. "A Preliminary Check List," Sixty American Poets: 1896-1944 by Allen Tate. Washington: 1945; rev. ed. prepared by Kenton Kilmer, 1954.

4274 Clark, David R., comp. "Selected Bibliography," Twentieth Century Interpretations of Murder in the Cathedral: A Collection of Critical Essays. Englewood Cliffs, N. J.: Prentice-Hall, 1971, pp. 117-118.

4275 Clemen, Wolfgang. "Kurze bibliographische Übersicht," Deutsche Beitrage. (II. Heft 6, 1948).

4276 Crowder, Richard. "Poetry: 1900 to the 1930's, T. S. Eliot," American Literary Scholarship. An Annual/1973. James Woodress, ed. Durham, North Carolina: Duke U. P., 1975, pp. 311-316.

4277 Fry, Varian. "A Bibliography of the Writings of Thomas Stearns Eliot," H&H, 1 (March, 1928), 214-218; (June, 1928), 320-324.

4278 Gallup, Donald C. A Bibliographical Check-list of the Writings of T. S. Eliot, Including His Contributions to Periodicals and Translations of His Work into Foreign Languages. New Haven: Yale U. P., 1947, rev. and extended, New York: Harcourt, Brace, 1969; repr., 1970.

4279 __________. A Catalogue of English and American First Editions of Writings by T. S. Eliot, Exhibited in the Yale Univ. Library February 22 to March 20, 1937. New Haven [Portland, Me., Southworth-Anthoensen Pr.,], 1937.

4280 __________. "The 'Lost' Manuscripts of T. S. Eliot," TLS, #3480 (November 7, 1968), 1238-1240; also BNYPL, 72 (December, 1968), 641-652.

4281 __________. T. S. Eliot: A Bibliography. London: Faber & Faber, 1952; New York: Harcourt, Brace, 1953; rev. and extended, New York: Harcourt, Brace & World, 1969.

4282 Greene, Edward J. "Bibliography," T. S. Eliot et la France. Paris: Boivan, 1951.

4283 Gunter, Bradley. The Merrill Checklist of T. S. Eliot. Columbus, Ohio: Merrill Pub. Co., 1970.

4284 Hirai, Masao. "Bibliography," T. S. Eliot: A Tribute from Japan. Masao Hirai and E. W. F. Tomlin, eds. Tokyo: Kenkyusha, 1966.

4285 Jones, Joseph. "Rare Book Collections: T. S. Eliot," LCUT, 6 (Spring, 1958), 46-50.

4286 Katsimbalis, G. K. Ellēnikē Bibliographia. Athens: 1957.

4287 Kenner, Hugh, ed. T. S. Eliot: A Collection of Critical Essays. Englewood Cliffs, N. J.: Prentice-Hall, 1962.

4288 Kleinstück, Johannes Walter. "Bibliography," T. S. Eliot in Selbstzeugnissen und Bilddokumenten. Reinbek bei Hamburg: Rowohlt, 1966, pp. 167-188.

4289 Lal, P., ed. "Useful Articles and Books on T. S. Eliot by Indians and Pakistanis," T. S. Eliot: Homage from India. Lake Gardens, Calcutta: Writers Workshop, 1965, pp.

227-228. A commemorative volume of fifty-five essays and elegies.

4290 Leary, Lewis. Articles on American Literature, 1900-1950. Durham: Duke U. P., 1954, pp. 79-86.

4291 __________. "T. S. Eliot," Articles on American Literature, 1950-1967. Durham: Duke U. P., 1970, pp. 124-146.

4292 Lu, Fei-Pai. T. S. Eliot: The Dialectical Structure of His Theory of Poetry. Chicago: Chicago U. P., 1966.

4293 Lucy, Sean. "Bibliography," T. S. Eliot and the Idea of Tradition. New York: Barnes & Noble, 1960, pp. 210-216.

4294 Ludwig, Richard M. "T. S. Eliot," Fifteen Modern American Authors: A Survey of Research and Criticism. Jackson R. Bryer, ed. Durham, N. C.: Duke U. P., 1969, pp. 139-174.

4295 __________. "T. S. Eliot," Sixteen Modern American Authors: A Survey of Research and Criticism. Jackson R. Bryer, ed. Durham: Duke U. P., 1974, pp. 182-222.

4296 Malawsky, Beryl Y. "T. S. Eliot: A Checklist: 1952-1964," BB, 25, #3 (May-August, 1967), 59-61, 69.

4297 Martin, Mildred. A Half-Century of Eliot Criticism: An Annotated Bibliography of Books and Articles in English, 1916-1965. London: Kaye & Ward, 1965; repr., Lewisburg, Pa.: Bucknell U. P., 1972.

4298 Matthews, T. S. "Selected Bibliography," Great Tom: Notes Towards the Definition of T. S. Eliot. New York: Harper & Row, 1974, pp. 207-209.

4299 Monteiro, George. "Addenda to Gallup's Eliot," PBSA, 66, #1 (1st Qt., 1972), 72. Adds three items to the section on translations.

4300 Nicholls, Norah. "A Bibliography of T. S. Eliot," Bookman (London), 82, #492 (September, 1932), 309.

4301 __________. "A Preliminary Check-List of T. S. Eliot," ABC, 3 (February, 1933), 105-106.

4302 Nilon, Charles H. Bibliography of Bibliographies in American Literature. London; New York: R. R. Bowker, 1970, p. 193.

4303 Patterson, Gertrude. "Bibliography," T. S. Eliot: Poems in the Making. New York: Barnes & Noble, 1971, pp. 186-191.

4304 Rajan, B. "A Check List of T. S. Eliot's Published Writings," T. S. Eliot: A Study of His Writings by Several Hands. London: Dennis Dobson, 1947, pp. 139-153.

4305 Rozsa, Olga. "T. S. Eliot's Reception in Hungary," HSE, 8 (1974), 35-44.

4306 Schneider, Elisabeth. "Notes on Texts and References," T. S. Eliot: The Pattern in the Carpet. Berkeley; Los Angeles: California U. P., 1975, pp. 214-221.

4307 Schwartz, Jacob. "Eliot, Thomas Stearns," 1100 Obscure Points: The Bibliographies of 25 English and 21 American Authors. London: Ulysses Bookshop, 1931; Folcroft Pa.: Folcroft Pr., 1969, pp. 51-52.

4308 Skinner, Aubrey E. "Rare Book Collections: T. S. Eliot," LCUT, 6 (Spring, 1958), 46-50.

4309 Smith, Carol H. "Bibliography," T. S. Eliot's Dramatic Theory and Practice. Princeton U. P., 1963, pp. 241-246.

4310 Spiller, Robert Ernest, et al. Literary History of the United States. New York: Macmillan, 1962, pp. 488-492; Supplement, pp. 111-115.

4311 "T. S. Eliot Comes Home," Bookman, 75 (1932), 449-451.

4312 Tate, Allen. "Thomas Stearns Eliot, 1888," Sixty American Poets: 1896-1944. Washington: Lib. of Congress & Biblio. Div., 1954, rev. ed., pp. 24-39.

4313 Taylor, Walter Fuller. A History of American Letters. Boston: American Bk. Co., 1936, pp. 593-595.

4314 Unger, Leonard, ed. "Bibliography," T. S. Eliot: A Selected Critique. New York: Holt Rinehart & Winston, 1948, pp. 463-478.

4315 ________. "Selected Bibliography," T. S. Eliot: Moments and Patterns. Minneapolis: Minnesota U. P., 1966, pp. 189-192.

4316 Vigliano, Gabriele. "Eliot in Italia," ICS (June, 1949).

4317 Wagner, Linda W. "Selected Bibliography," T. S. Eliot: A Collection of Criticism. New York: McGraw Hill, 1974, pp. 141-145.

4318 Williamson, George. "Bibliographical Note," A Reader's Guide to T. S. Eliot. 2nd ed., London: Thames & Hudson, 1967, pp. 245-246.

4319 Wilson, Frank. "Select Bibliography," Six Essays on the Development of T. S. Eliot. London: Fortune Pr., 1948, p. 66.

TOPICAL INDEX

Absolute, search for 3561
Absurd, drama of 539, 708a
Absurdities 1494
Action 468, 680
Adams, Henry 1234, 1441
Aeneid 1603, 3856
Aeschylus 636
Aesthetics, Eliot's 2913, 3060, 3579, 4113
Age see Old age
Aiken, Conrad 1405, 2570, 3441, 3479, 4149, 4197
Alcestis 102, 137, 139
Aldington, Richard 3321, 4048
Alexandrians 3456
Alienation 4194
Allegory 187, 2958
Allston, Washington 4232, 4250
al-Sayyāb 3427
Ambiguities 664
Ambivalence 465, 3397
Anarchy 3331
Andrewes, Bishop Lancelot 1259
The Androgynous Moment 3436
Anglicanism 3130
Anglo-Catholicism 2790a, 3277, 4198
Animal Farm 3402
The Anonymous 3295; tradition of 1700
Anouilh, Jean 343, 361, 394, 411, 424, 428, 448, 458
Antihumanism 4147
Antipragmatism 4147
Antisemitism 861, 3448, 3557
Antitheses 3398
Apollinaire 1761, 1998, 3507, 3558
Apollo 3159
April ("cruelest month") 1657, 1877, 1912, 1988a, 3074
Aquinas, Thomas 2667
Arabic and modern Arabic Poetry 3555, 3885, 3895
Archer, William 3939
Archetype (see also Imagery) 1274, 1630, 4104
Argument 910
Aristocracy 2189
Aristotle 2256
Arnold, Sir Edwin 353
Arnold, Matthew 406, 1415, 1784, 1811, 2137, 2503, 2711, 2888, 3109, 3331, 3423, 3642, 4110
Art, Eliot's impersonal theory of 2957
Arthurian theme 1803
Arthurian triptych 1781
Artifice 2963
Asian culture 3068
Athene 2012
Auden 393, 480a, 3419, 3883, 4181
Augustine, Saint 4136, 4137
Autobiography 1644, 1660, 1940, 1941, 1956
Autonomy 127
Awareness 4085

Babbitt, Irving 142, 2582, 2851, 2921, 2998, 3750, 4254
Barbarism, Christian 2768
Barry, Philip 85
Bartenders 2852
Bateson, F. W. 1524
Baudelaire 805, 1525, 1560, 1944, 2990, 3168, 3477, 3528, 3864a, 4000, 4171
Beardsley 2002
Becket, Thomas 361, 394, 452, 505, 2583, 3769; plays about

448, 464, 361, 473, 498
Beethoven 966, 978, 1036, 1092, 1131, 1161, 3117, 3222
Behavior 906, 907
Belief (see also Faith) 2920, 3147, 3605, 3915, 4208
Belladonna 3447
Bengali criticism, Eliot's influence on 2952
Benn, Gottfried 2970, 3418
Benson, Arthur Christopher 1200, 1316, 1356, 2767
Bergson 316, 3380
Bestiary, Eliot's 1306, 2774
Bhagavad-Gita 928, 948, 1049a, 1506a, 1507, 3248, 3744, 3745
Bible (the Biblical View) 111, 4207
Biology, social 2196
Birth 833, 1136
Bishop, John Peale 832, 950
Blake 778, 1946a
Blank verse 626, 3286
Boschère, Jean de 3377
"Bourgeois line" [of criticism] 3331
Bourget, Paul 2109a
Bowers, Edgar 832
Bradley, F. H. 920, 944, 2166, 2167, 2622, 2626, 2649, 2762, 2967, 3002, 3014a, 3079, 3561, 3611, 3632, 3924, 4029a, 4235, 4236
Brecht 2958
British poetry [modern] 3169
British Order of Merit 2499
Browning 255, 868, 1081, 1271, 1320, 1371, 1452, 1594, 1832, 2853, 2973, 3312, 4148, 4240
Brownson, Orestes Augustus 3132
Buddhism 146, 928, 1190, 1809, 1836, 2637, 3216a, 3446
Butler, Samuel 1081, 1271, 1594, 2853
Byzantium (see also Coleridge) 918
Calendar (Christian) 1039
Calvinism 1199
Cambridge 3766
Camus 4148
Carroll, Lewis 3900
Catholic liturgy and allusion(s) 808, 1199
Catholicism 808
Catholicity 1331, 2123
Cawein, Madison 1815
Celtic theme(s): 1803
Censorship 2076
The Cerebralists 4088
Change, theme of (see also Time) 790, 1434
Chapman, George 462, 1258, 4253
Character(s) 1870
Chaucer 1664, 1988a, 2852
Chesterton, G. K. 3592
Children 919, 2659, 2664
Chivalry 877a
Chorus 350, 375, 487, 493, 520, 585, 730, 1094
Christ and Christology 822, 1107, 1205, 1987, 3159
Christianity (see also Eliot's Idea of a Christian Society) 487, 576, 579, 785, 1670, 2141, 2142, 2144, 2189, 3413, 4160
Christian(s) 1300a, 1494, 3149
The Church 2141, 3400; Church of England 4223
Churchmanship, Eliot's 3256
Cicero 4073
The Circle [motif] 377, 1091
The City in Western literature 3520
Class(es) [social] 2181, 2206, 2209
The Classics and classicism 2504a, 2855, 2942, 2959, 2969, 3526, 3597, 3662, 3865, 3994, 4017, 4039, 4067, 4183
Clough, Arthur Hugh 1404
Coherence 2812, 3491, 4141
Coleridge 454, 1601, 1746, 2208, 3475, 3999, 4150
Collections of Eliot materials 3358, 3839, 3840
Comedy 742, 743, 1641
Commerce 1677
Communication 4049

Communion 2160
Compton-Burnett, Ivy 252
Conan Doyle 331, 354, 390, 434, 470, 1309, 1310, 1311, 2775
Conrad 1081, 1266, 1271, 1278 1281, 1594, 1634, 2005, 2853, 3774, 4078
Consciousness 843, 885, 1014, 1791, 2045, 2134, 2195, 3346, 3347, 3678, 3910
Consistency 1592
Consolation 3642
Continuity 2812, 4141, 4142, 4226
Contrition 321, 4239
Corbière, Tristan 1193, 1319, 1436, 1887, 2701, 3903
Cosmology 961
Coward, Noel 84
The Crab, image of 1439, 1441
Crane, Hart 1589, 2485, 2846, 3462, 3573, 3713, 3981
Crime 321, 4239
The Criterion 2647, 2799, 2875, 3226, 3661, 3820, 3867, 4026
The Critic 2578a, 3742 (historical)
Criticism Literary 1868, 4113; existential, 4218; new criticism, 1093, 1588, 3257, 3729, 3904; twentieth-century 1588, 4178
Croce, Benedetto 3127, 3129
Crowing Weathercock 1717
Cubists 1715
Culture (see also *Notes Toward a Definition of Culture*) 1984, 1985, 2159, 2181, 2183, 2185, 2190, 2191, 2192, 2197, 2198, 2202, 2205, 2206, 2209, 2210, 2213, 2216, 2217, 2218, 2221, 2222, 2223, 2591, 2598, 2609, 2847, 2908, 3331, 3664, 3714, 3780, 3921, 4052, 4095, 4209
Cummings, Edward Estlin 2966
Curtius, Ernst Robert 1626
Cynicism, Eliot's 1711

Dadaists 1715
Dante Alighieri (see also Eliot's *Dante* and *Selected Essays*) 210, 755, 761, 788, 798, 1010, 1142, 1189, 1218, 1279, 1290, 1338, 1341, 1388, 1403, 1443, 1462, 1566, 1599a, 1645, 1774, 1813, 1874, 2057, 2062, 2247, 2541, 2542, 2547, 2699, 2699a, 2789, 2790, 2949, 2951, 3059, 3092, 3127, 3129, 3175a, 3190, 3218, 3294, 3386, 3694, 3697, 3812, 3914, 4068, 4070
Davies, Sir Thomas 1110a
Death 833, 1058, 1128, 1251, 1269, 1283, 1561, 1634, 1637; "Death by Water," 2013; death-rebirth motif, 1612; death-in-life, 839
Decadence 1334, 1562, 2474, 2726
Decorum, Eliot's 3458
Defeatism 1579, 1579a
Degradation 1484
The Deity 1670, 2696
Democracy 889, 2121
Desire 621, 1325, 1898, 3241
Desolation, religious 3388
Despair 756
Destiny 1058
The Detective story 1101, 1308, 3476, 3627
Deussen, Paul 1691
The Dial 1589, 1945, 3272a, 4145
Dialect 1842; babylonish, 3304
Dialectic, moral 775, 1162, 3296, 3428, 3429
Dickens 1468
Diction 498a, 747a, 1363, 2961, 3925
Dies Irae 386
Disgust 3265
Disintegration 307
Dissertation, Eliot's 4190
Dissertations [and abstracts] 119, 237, 351, 411, 424, 450, 536, 554, 580, 601, 608, 610a, 610b, 618a, 637, 660, 670, 677, 688, 698, 700, 704, 708, 716, 733, 734a, 744, 746, 780, 898, 911, 918a, 959, 964, 985, 988, 1010a, 1026, 1029, 1032, 1046, 1053, 1064, 1066, 1074a, 1076, 1094, 1500, 1537a,

1572, 1651, 1665, 1689, 1710, 1725a, 1726, 1788a, 1811, 1955, 1957, 2104, 2450, 2484, 2485, 2501, 2542, 2550, 2551, 2554, 2568, 2583, 2586, 2613, 2621, 2631, 2652, 2672, 2698, 2699, 2708, 2711, 2715, 2744, 2771, 2805, 2836, 2851, 2858, 2874, 2888, 2902, 2963, 2967, 3025, 3057, 3060, 3070, 3073, 3077, 3079, 3084, 3092, 3095, 3103, 3113, 3116, 3130, 3137, 3169, 3178, 3209, 3213, 3216a, 3229, 3246, 3250, 3266, 3269, 3276, 3291, 3329a, 3359, 3381, 3388, 3392, 3416, 3428, 3449, 3459a, 3473, 3491, 3501, 3504, 3506, 3520, 3547, 3561, 3573, 3615, 3619, 3630, 3636, 3641, 3642, 3649, 3690, 3691, 3762, 3802, 3808, 3809, 3815, 3836, 3844, 3865, 3872, 3878, 3910, 3913, 3914, 3924, 3956, 3965, 3989, 3992, 3995, 4009, 4047, 4049, 4050, 4051, 4058, 4070, 4105, 4133, 4148, 4150, 4165, 4173, 4189, 4194, 4197, 4207, 4216, 4225, 4237, 4240
Dissimulatio 3324
Doctrine 977
The "Dog" 1711, 1995
Domesticity of T. S. Eliot 2938
Donne 2452, 2628, 3367
Dos Passos 1731
Dostoevsky 1308, 1419, 1420
Doubt 1357, 2770, 2920
Douglas Keith 2779, 2995, 3094, 3259
Dramatic unities 269
Dreiser 1675a
Droste-Hulshoff, Annette von 1469a
Drought 1968
Dryden 3018

The East and Eastern thought 4090, 4203
Education 2075, 2188, 2543, 2544, 2944, 3235
Education of Henry Adams 1441
Ego 2693
The Egoist 3455a
Ekelöf, Gunnar 2933
The Elizabethans 1831
Elyot, Sir Thomas 1034
Emerson 1357, 1360, 1501, 1503, 2618, 2770
Emotion 3641
Epic tradition 979
Epigraph(s) 882, 1304, 1341, 1505, 1975
Epiphany 973
The Esotericism of T. S. Eliot 1787
Eternal life 1623, 1786
Eternity 920
Eumenides 253, 270
Euripides 74, 96, 129, 137, 139, 173, 175, 319, 544, 545, 2505, 2506
Evans, Donald 2963
Everyman 360, 404, 1666, 3335
Evil 2053, 3567
Exiles 4061; Harvard exiles 4167
Existentialism 291, 1165, 3636, 4218
Expatriate poet 3041
Experience (see also Eliot's Knowledge and Experience...) 2164, 2165, 2166, 3955, 4169
Expressionism 701, 2947

Faith (see also Belief) 453, 1019, 1834, 2139, 3529, 3916
Fascism 1808, 2717
Faulkner 1600, 1625, 1659a, 1689, 1764a, 2400, 2955, 3583, 3980, 4151, 4207
Fear 605
Feeling 966, 1043, 1092, 1131, 1161, 3117, 3641
Fertility 1284, 1484
Fitzgerald, Edward 1200, 1316, 1349, 1356
Fitzgerald, F. Scott 1319, 1689, 1697, 1844, 3919
Fixity 2771
Flaubert 1754, 4015, 4136
Flowering Judas 3093
Fluchère, Henri 373
Flux 2771
The Fool 1348, 1382

Form (see also Structure) 731, 818, 921, 1242, 1665, 3116
Formalism 3164
The Fortuneteller 1896
Francesca, Piero della 1303
Freud 1222, 1385, 1938, 2578, 3984
Frost 3160, 3173
Fry, Christopher 343, 361, 411, 428, 436, 458, 572, 599, 657, 701, 739, 2700, 2729, 3262, 3634
Frye, Northrop 406
Futurists 1715

Gaiety 1312
García Lorca 4044
Germany (Eliot and) 2818
Gielen, Josef 443
Glasgow, Ellen 1389
Goal 1993
God (see also Deity) 2696
Goethe 105, 2379, 2574, 3180
The Golden Bough 1600, 4104, 4105, 4106, 4256
Gourmont, Rémy de 2705, 3761, 3763, 4040, 4257
Grace 910
The Grail [motif] 1432, 1824
Grammar 1868
Graves, Robert 1850, 2826
Graveyard poetry 1277a, 1704
Greece, Eliot in 3881
Greene, Graham 195a, 1166
Guillén, Jorge 2992
Guilt 734a, 1955

Haecker, Virgil Theodor 4030
Hallam, Arthur 2172
Hamlet (play and character) 277, 1382, 1435, 2094-2109a, 3172, 3602
Hardy 3426, 4159a
Harvard (Eliot at) 2371
Hawthorne 1744, 4207
Hazlitt 2487
The Hearth 615
Heine 883b
Hell 1338, 1410
Hemingway 1509, 1653, 1689, 1788, 2968, 4151
Heracles 3758
The Heraclitean element 932, 3379
Hero 335; international 3869; tragic 335, 349, 411, 553, 4158
Herrick, Robert 1657
Hindu sources and usages 1663, 2637, 3216a, 3502
History and the historical 1073 1221, 1868, 2602, 2692, 2922, 3116, 3118, 4051, 4207, 4237
Hodgson, Ralph 1295
Hofmannsthal, Hugo von 3220
Holmes, Sherlock (see also Conan Doyle) 434, 471, 1310, 1311, 1450a, 3260, 3701, 3946
The Holy Grail 1432, 1824
Homer 4138
Hood, Thomas 877a
Hopkins, Gerard Manley 2345 2485, 2935, 3250, 3274, 3525, 3827, 4044
Horace 1989, 3252
The "Horned Gate" 1472, 1496
Howells, William Dean 1692
Huckleberry Finn 3486
Hulme, T. E. 316, 2831, 2834, 3864
Human nature 3197, 3229
Human relations 618
Humanism 2704, 2855, 2888, 3187, 4020, 4147, 4254
Humanist influence 610, 2851
Humanity 2184, 3466
Humility 1921
Humor (see also Comedy) 3582, 3862, 3871
Hungary, Eliot's reception in 3828
Huret, Gaston 3148
Husserl, Edmund (Gustav Albrecht) 3500, 3997
Huxley, Aldous 1118, 1416, 1775, 1896, 3236, 3792
The "Hyacinth Girl" 1992

Ibsen 228, 2866, 3892, 3939
The Ideal 845
Ideality 3732
Ideas, use of 3578
Identity 634

Illumination 3798
Illusion 3798
Imagery (see also Imagism) 377, 420, 763, 827, 851, 1046, 1102, 1274, 1363, 1439, 1450, 1630, 1690, 1717, 1762, 2987, 3025, 3134, 3485, 3596, 3925, 4118; beast 3635; bird, flower, and color 3631; dance 959, 1429, 3807; fire 1010; primodial 2786, 2988, 3736; religious 2836, 3025; water, 1391, 2597
Imagination 621, 1596, 3241, 3678; auditory 1083, 1596; religious 4013, 4222
Imagism and imagists 1687, 2777, 3377
Imitation of Christ 431
Immortality 1251, 2020, 2021, 2022, 2772, 3958
Impact 4104
Impersonality 3303, 4136, 4137
Impotence 2968
Impressionism 1323, 1340
The Inarticulate 3156
Incarnation 830, 859, 920, 1008, 1177
Indian thought and culture (see also The East Hindu) 960, 1009, 1506, 1507, 1793, 2752, 2900, 3070, 3248, 3340, 3356, 3734, 3847
Integrity of Eliot 747, 4251
Intuition 2788
The Irish King Sweeney 1489
Irony 604, 1319, 1436, 1921, 3903, 4089, 4148

James, Henry 525, 865, 1399, 2581, 3209, 3210, 3211, 3516
James, William 783
Japanese poetry 1915
Jargon 1358
Jazz see Rhythm(s)
The Jews 527, 861, 1219, 1229, 1300a, 3017
Job 464
John-of-the-Cross 958, 1091, 3063
Johnson, Samuel 2888, 3562, 4038
Jonson, Ben 1830
The Journey 603, 613, 615, 989, 3490
Joyce 1224, 1518a, 1522a, 1591, 1631, 1726, 1728a, 1730, 1762, 1892, 1942, 2483, 2485, 2850, 3138, 3310, 3321, 3463, 3508, 3586, 4019, 4061, 4117, 4127
Judgment 1888, 3579, 3908
Jung 1608, 3269
Juvenal 3389

Kafka 4148
Karma 3069, 3070a
Keats 3815
The Kerygma 1107
Kierkegaard 99
Kipling 283, 836, 1314, 2477, 2488, 2953, 3230, 4071
Knowledge 3955
Korean Poetry 3072, 3311
Krishna [Hinduism] 948

The Lady of the Rocks 1899, 3947
Laforgue, Jules 863, 1300a, 1319, 1362, 1374, 1436, 1694, 1887, 2793, 3105, 3735, 3764, 3903, 4009, 4010, 4078
Lamb, Charles 1192, 1831
Landscape(s) 767, 770, 1377, 1826, 2434, 3052, 3145, 3153, 3154, 3173, 4003
Language 746, 789, 885, 1064, 1100, 1225, 1280, 1791, 1868, 1999, 2345, 2500, 2501, 2551, 3008; of the dead 3973; of drama 598; of Eliot's plays 746; of Humanity 3466; of liturgy 1280; of poetry 1196, 4246
The Laodiceans and Eliot 2861
Larisch, Countess Marie 1784
Laughter (see also Comedy; Humor) 2475
Lawrence, D. H. 861, 870, 900, 1001, 1002, 2051, 2448, 2469, 2552, 2616, 2757, 3040, 3371, 3593, 3639, 4159a
Lazarus 1339, 1365, 1370
Lear, Edward 1192, 2761
Lewis, Wyndham 2051, 2447,

3488, 3703, 3768
Liberal and liberalism 3149, 3640
Life (see also Eternal life) 1623, 1634
Limbo 1988
Linguistics (see also Language) 2551, 3274
The Listener 3950
The "Little Preacher" 28, 3225
Liturgy (see also Catholic) 688, 771, 789, 808, 885, 1280, 3080
London 1590, 3969
Loneliness 609, 2160
Lorca 4044
"Lost" manuscripts of Eliot 3045
The Lotus 1001, 1002
Love 210, 804, 1063
Lowell, Robert 3503
Loy, Nina 2963
Lucian 1298
Ludwig II 1710
The Lyric 1610, 2890

Macbeth, Lady 3212
McGreevy, Thomas 1757, 3454
Machaut, Guillaume de 935, 3861
Magus, the American magus 3539
Magus, Eliot's 827a
Man, image of 547, 2555, 3204; the City Man 1590; the "Man of Feeling," 3110
The Mango 1260
Mannerism(s) 3509
Manuscripts (Eliot's) 3358, 3839, 3840
Marion poetry 4118
Maritain, Jacques 776
Marlow, Fanny 2619
Marlowe 1315, 1599
Marvel 1204, 1227a, 1395, 1448, 2803
Marxism 2044, 2716
Mary Queen of Scots 3861
The Mass (see also Catholicism) 751, 808
Maurras, Charles 798, 1927, 4068
Meaning 921, 931, 1028, 1046, 1086, 1242, 1659a, 3151, 3167, 3765, 4229
Medievalism 461, 3905
Meditation 1243
Melancholy 1511
Memory 1325, 1898, 3980
Menander 174
Mercy 782
The Mermaids 1350, 1361
Metaphor(s) 985, 1014a, 1460, 1954, 3276, 3329
Metaphysical poetry 121, 122, 3474, 3534, 3738, 4056
Metaphysics 2608
Meter and metrics 890, 1030
Metropolitan world (see also City) 4241
Michelangelo 3591
Miller, Arthur 274, 349
Milton 462, 850, 1513, 2467, 2495, 2629, 2999, 3018, 3221, 3372, 4063, 4094, 4115
Mimetic principle 474
The mind of the poet 3390
Mirrlees, Hope 1518
The Mithraic bull 4220, 4221
Modernism and modernization 2104, 3181, 3823, 4237
Monologue, dramatic 849, 2586, 3312, 4148
Montale, Eugenio 1825, 3228a, 3512, 3638, 3695
Moore, Marianne 2992, 3057
Moral(s) and morality 658, 2076, 2194, 2236, 3024, 3051, 3572
Moral dialectic (see also Dialectic) 398, 775, 860, 3060
Morality plays 660
More, Paul Elmer 4032
Morris, William 1649
Motive and motivation 3000
Mount Carmel 934
Mountains 1785
Muses 3739
The Musgrave Ritual 331, 471, 434
Music and musical forms 923, 939, 957, 966, 1032, 1056, 1092, 1127, 1131, 1161, 1166, 1265, 1325a, 1444, 1565, 1675, 1894a, 3117, 3391
Mute speech 1545

The Mystic and mysticism 920, 1003, 1004, 3517; Islamic mysticism, 2507; mystic as critic, 3717; mystic experience, 1119
Myth 559, 1545, 1551, 1659a, 1670, 1782, 1817, 1890, 1949, 2865, 2956, 3027, 3282, 3537, 3917; Arthurian 3547; Greek myth, 296; mythical method 2983; mythic perspective 1168; mythic vision 3808; Naturalistic myth 1670
Mythology 160

The Naked Lady 2012
Names 869, 1245, 1699, 1784
Narcissus 2955a
Nativity of Christ 822
The Netherlands 2631
New Humanism 142
Newman, John Henry, Cardinal 1235, 1263
Nietzsche 1724, 3383
The Nobel Prize and Eliot 2906, 3850
Noesis [exercise of reason] 4050
The Nonsense poets 3900
Nonsense style 3823
Norris, Frank 1904
The Novel, comic 1890, 3917

The Objective correlative 771, 808, 1386, 2107, 2356, 2519, 2798a, 2813, 2854, 2870, 2891, 3002, 3264, 3451, 3751, 3774, 3837, 3841, 3888, 3889, 3890, 3997, 4232, 4250
Obscurity 3106
O'Casey 546
Occult 2940
Old age 796, 1050, 1074a, 1248, 1286, 1445, 4025
O'Neill 312, 712, 3630
Onomatopoeia 1154
Operatic allusions 1606
Orchestration 2809
Order 907, 3548
The Orestes theme 253a, 312, 321, 712, 3736
Organicism 3999
Original sin 284, 2041
Orpheus 183, 1805, 3873
Orthodoxy 2697, 3712, 3849
Orwell 4140
The "Overwhelming Question" 1319, 1418, 1424, 1425, 1426, 1454, 1455, 1840

Pagan society 2153
Painting 1690
Pakistani viewpoint of Eliot 2508
Palgrave, Francis Turner 1831
Palimpsest technique 1189
Parody 3076, 3389; of Eliot 3710a, 4219
Pater, Walter 1081, 1271, 1372, 1594, 2503, 2614, 2853, 2854, 3244, 3592
Pathos 4050
The Peach 1260
"Permanent Things" 3317
Perse, Saint-John 779, 821, 2450, 2915, 2915a, 3590
Petronius 1516, 1723
Philippe, Charles-Louis 1327, 1471, 3943
Philosophy 1059, 3245, 3246
The Phoenician sailor 1649
Picot, James 3576
Pierrot 4009
Pirandello 4192, 4193
Pizzetti, Ildebrando 380, 504
Places 1784
Plato 170
Poe 1779, 3452, 3627, 4148
Point of view 3936
Political philosophy, Eliot's 1936, 2431, 3878, 4103
Politics 3010a, 3020, 3654, 3658, 4103
"Polyphiloprogenitive" 1300
The Pomegranate 1260
Pope, Alexander 870, 1139, 1346, 1581, 2483, 3161, 3593
Porter, Katherine Anne 1218
Pound 1317, 1369, 1378, 1564, 1610, 1638, 1643, 1680, 1728a, 1773, 1774, 1801, 1814, 1852, 1916, 1917, 1967a, 2081, 2082, 2083, 2462, 2541, 2553, 2577,

2602, 2699, 2792, 2803a, 2824, 2825, 2840, 2873, 2890, 2946, 2963, 3007, 3046, 3089, 3184, 3191a, 3195, 3209, 3210, 3266, 3300, 3316, 3349, 3369, 3587a, 3649, 3768, 3856, 3858, 3923, 3966, 4015, 4127
The "Little Preacher" 28, 3225
The Present 1567
Pride 324
Primitives 3271
Prophecy in Old and New Testaments 1693
Proust 1631
Pseudonym (of Eliot) 2619
Psyche 2388
Psychoanalyst, Eliot as 288
Psychobiography 1940, 1941, 1956, 4130, 4187, 4188
Psychology 1342, 1343, 1465, 1881, 1940, 1941, 1956, 2539, 3212, 3564
Puritanism 168, 4182, 4245

Quest 603, 1288, 1786, 1937, 4107; personal 3025; romantic 3538; spiritual 3911

Railway, the London Underground 909
Reaction, illusion of 4233
Reactionaries 3158
Reader's Guide(s) 1963, 4212
Realism 382, 618a, 673, 2461, 3212
Reality 733, 769, 811, 968, 1480, 1668, 1954, 2894
Reason 3915
Rebellion 1614, 1737, 3986
Rebirth 1269
Reconciliation 4194
The Red Rock 1987, 1997
Regeneration 843
Relativity 1631
Religion 1038, 1436a, 2181, 2198, 2844, 3906, 4254, 4255
Religious themes and thought 286, 430, 716, 1261, 1306, 1478, 3825; religious development 4133
Reminiscence 1590
Repetition 376, 1255; rhetorical 4248; word 4249
Resignation, tragic 495
Rhetoric and rhetorical 317, 729, 1064, 1624, 1999, 2963, 3213
Rhyme 626, 1154, 1720, 2746, 3018, 3286
Rhythm(s) 876, 2746, 3016; Jazz Rhythms 526, 1635, 3016
Richards, Ivor 406, 3095, 3147, 3904
Rilke 1041, 1049, 1119, 1682, 2579, 3773, 3784, 3972, 4169
Rimbaud 4061
The "Ring Dance" 1284
Ritual 382, 1659
Robertson, J. M. 4009a
Roethke 1537a
Romance 1659
The Rose (see also Rose garden) 1001, 1002, 1010
The Rose garden 315, 803, 893, 1019, 1060, 1079, 1097, 1105, 1109, 1110a, 1116, 1117, 1121, 1150, 1171, 1186, 1250, 1933, 3052, 3798, 4086, 4124
Rossetti 2541
Rouault, Georges 927, 2725
Russell, Bertrand 1296a, 3155a, 3203, 3834

Sacrament(s) and sacramental 3525
Sacrifice 2956
St. Louis, Mo. 1108, 1377, 1393, 1407, 1411, 1442
Saints, lives of 1576
Salah 'Abd al-Sabur 699
Salinger, J. D. 1689
Salvation 348, 627, 927, 1067, 1161a, 1168, 1460, 1659, 3070a, 4176
Sandburg 1427
Sanskrit 3580
Santayana 1290, 3451, 3998, 4122, 4144, 4197
Sarett, Lew 1771

Sartre 151, 312, 712, 2422, 3879a
Satire and satiric theme 396, 889, 3265, 3710a, 4219
The Satyricon 1559, 1723
Science 901, 2502
Scotland Yard 1308
Sea (see also Imagery, water) 1391
Seeger, Alan 3958
The Seer 1951
Seferis, George 1631a, 3288, 3289
Self 1014a, 1772; Self-betrayal 4148
Seneca 844, 850, 1258, 3574, 4253
Sense 3408
Sensibility 1784a, 2171, 2172, 2487; poetic 3273; 3306, 3350, 3378, 3382, 3408, 3511, 3763, 3818, 3963, 4054, 4070; histrionic 3763
Setting (see also Landscapes) 380
The Seven-branched candelabra 1519
Sex 1343
Shackleton, Sir Ernest 1843
Shakespeare 393, 462, 719, 844, 1230, 1276, 1372, 1373a, 1675, 2050, 2104, 2305, 2445, 2604, 3313, 3471, 3512, 3574; Antony and Cleopatra 2006; The Tempest 1919; Symbolistic Shakespeare 3231, 3232; Shakespeare design of Eliot's poetry 4225
Shaw 72, 3042
Shelley 4111
Sherman, Stuart P. 2351a
Shrines 3972
Silence 757
Simplicity 613, 3186
Sin (see also Original sin) 273, 280, 284, 910, 2041
Sitwell, Edith 111, 4043
Smith, Pamela Coleman 1769
Smog 1313, 1450
Social and social criticism 2061, 2360, 2491, 2814, 3438, 3878
Society 2128, 2129, 2223, 2545
Sociology 2196, 2199
Sonnet(s) 1656, 2010
Sophocles 217
Sosostris, Madame 1699, 1712, 1714, 1775, 1896; source of name 1575, 1986, 1991, 2011
Sound 747a
Sound and effect 1393
Source(s) 869, 873, 1326, 1470, 1986, 1991, 1996, 2002
The South Seas 2662, 2663
Speech (see also Diction; language 3790
Spengler 1522, 1787
Spiritual center 629
Spiritual death 2013
Spiritual life 915
Spiritual progress 2858
Steinbeck 1652
Sterne 1354, 1382
Stevens, Wallace 973, 2259, 2963, 3390, 4009, 4185, 4197
Stevenson, Robert Louis 1328
Still, Colin 1919
The "Still Point" (see also Wheel) 948, 1079, 1102, 1103, 2787, 2909, 3216a, 3480, 3484, 3485, 4263
Stoicism 1811, 3642
Stoker, Bram 1859
Stravinsky 3836
Stream of consciousness 1791
Strenge, Harald der 3863
Structure 580, 698, 772, 881, 917, 922, 953, 1076, 1132, 1252, 1262, 1307, 1318, 1417a, 1593, 1683, 1701, 1849, 1865, 1964, 2018, 2486, 3872, 4021a, 4109
Style 400, 1325b, 2895, 2928
The Sublime 4127
Suffering 468
Suggestion 3837
Suicide 1877
Sullivan, J. W. N. 978, 3223
Surrealists 1715
Sweeney, the Irish King 1489
Swift 874, 984, 1182, 3265
Swinburne 1874, 3477
Symbolism 909, 917, 1318, 1343, 1484, 1549, 1762,

1953, 2018, 2572, 2597, 3027, 3039; American, use of 3653; apocalyplic 3982; archetypal, 3983; French 3169, 3761, 3851, 4041; gestic 954, 1275, 1343, 1484, 1640, 3039; great cats 3009; rock 792, 1987, 1997, 3538; sacramental 3525; symbolist Shakespeare 3232; theological 3092; topographical 1153; water 1949; white horse 824, 838

Tamil 3728
Tarot 1655, 1714, 1769
Tchelitchew, Pavel 949, 2991, 2993
Teaching 971
Technique(s) 1307, 1346, 2809, 2954, 4146
Tennyson 366, 411, 436, 452, 857, 873, 1438, 1458, 1464, 1755, 1824, 1832, 2502, 3690, 3769, 3785
Testaments, Old and New 1693
Thatcher shipwreck 1167
Theatre, experimental 646; of the mind 700
Theme(s) 154, 420, 559, 580, 609, 734a, 839, 856, 893, 922, 925, 964, 1046, 1102, 1116, 1132, 1156, 1177, 1250, 1262, 1269, 1294, 1328, 1376, 1434, 1665, 1717, 1744, 1803, 1955, 2787, 4184
Theology and the theological 714, 1306, 3229, 4200
Thinking (symbolic) 1910
The Thirties 633, 721, 744, 1983, 3019, 3035
Time 592, 790, 805a, 920, 974, 994, 995, 1014, 1016, 1027, 1063a, 1067, 1094, 1165, 1213, 1227, 1357, 1387, 1460, 1812, 2770, 2902, 3037, 3073, 3077, 3137, 3200, 3443, 3521, 3624, 3910, 4042, 4176
The Time-world of Eliot 316
Timelessness 1165, 1387, 3073
Tiresias 1874, 2012, 3178
Tolstoy 1678
Topography 1153
Totalitarianism 889, 2149
Tourneur, Cyril 1193
Tradition 1396, 1572, 2103, 2115, 2127, 2337-2356, 2378, 2714, 2715, 2874, 3001, 3143, 3181, 3239, 3280, 3416, 3530, 3573a, 3583, 3712, 3773, 3913, 3941, 3986, 4032, 4075, 4138, 4238; American 3201, 3202; Anglaise 3088; Christian 4199; Conservative 3966; Democratic 2845; Folk 667, 3595
Tragedy 348; Greek 319, 3589
Transfiguration 545
Translation, Russian 1982
Translator, Eliot as 2806
Triptych Arthurian 3550
Tristan 1712, 1724
Turgenev 1785
Twain, Mark 1154, 3486, 4207
The Twenties 1638a, 1685, 1742, 1958, 3206

The Unconscious 2947
The Unities [dramatic] 269
Unity 793, 1243, 1683, 1721, 1782, 3142
The Universe of Eliot 2283, 2284, 3003, 3004, 3005
Untermeyer, Louis 1589, 2846
The Upanishads 1663, 1792, 3581, 3743
Urdu literature 3284

Valéry 2625, 3366, 3748, 4069
Venclova, Tomas 1695
Venice 870, 3593
Verbal pattern 1195
Verse 707, 708
Vielé-Griffin, Francis 2813
Vision(s) 814, 977, 1156, 1357, 1595, 2770, 3808; transcendental 1156
Vocabulary 1762, 2809
Voice 1718, 3086, 3090, 4087

Wagner, Richard 1675, 1710, 4114

Waite, Arthur E. 1655, 1769
Wallant, Edward Lewis 757
Warren, Robert Penn 1627, 3085
Waugh, Evelyn 2743
Webster, John 1563, 3591, 4252
Weil, Simone 2925
Wells, H. G. 2575
Weston, Jessie Laidlay 166, 1973
The Wheel (see also "Still Point") 377, 420, 602, 1102, 1103, 3480, 3484, 3485
Whibley, Charles 1298
White, William Hale 118
Whitehead, Alfred North 3538
Whitlow, Chard 3760
Whitman 1003, 1004, 1300, 1401, 1980, 3201, 3279, 3329a, 3517, 3577, 4013, 4206
Wilder 2958, 3187, 3343
Will Power 2902
Williams, Charles 140, 154, 2940
Williams, William Carlos 1692a, 3809, 3920, 3923
Wilson, Edmund 4182
Winters, Yvor 2963, 2989, 3087, 4174
Wish 621, 3241
Wolfe, Thomas 1679, 2423, 3436
Women (Characters) 1870
The "Word without Flesh" 1061
Words (see also Diction; language) 3151, 3596
Wordsworth 962, 1177a, 2351, 2379, 2589, 3536, 3815, 4185
The Wryneck 1756
Wycherley, William 3161

Yeats 281, 554, 615, 832, 1127a, 2468, 2613, 2923, 2924, 3012, 3313, 3332, 3450, 3649, 3937, 3968, 3982, 3995, 4135, 4158, 4186

INDEX OF CRITICS

A. D. 1508
Abel, Darrel 1328
Abel, Richard O. 821, 2450, 2450a
Abrams, M. H. 897
Acton, H. B. 2181
Adair, Patricia M. 323
Adams, J. Donald 2451
Adams, John F. 324
Adams, Richard P. 1509
Adams, Robert M. 1329, 1510, 2452
Adell, Alberto 2453, 2454
Adler, Jacob H. 72
Aguilar, A. 2455
Ahearn, W. B. 1330
Aiken, Conrad, 1, 2, 3, 4, 506, 1323, 1331, 1332, 1468, 1511, 2036, 2066, 2084, 2241, 2357, 2456, 2457, 2458, 2459, 2460, 2461
Aldington, Richard 5, 2242, 2462, 2463
Allan, Alexander 1333
Allan, D. Mowbray 2464, 2465
Allen, Walter 2466
Alpers, Paul J. 2467
Alt, Helmut 2396
Alter, Robert 861
Alvarez, Alfred 1512, 2468, 2469, 2470, 2471
Amery, Carl 2473
Ames, Russell M. 1334, 2474
Amis, Kingsley 2475
Ana, Masahito 2476
Anand, Mulk Raj 2477
Anant, Victor 2478
Anceschi, Li 2479
Anceschi, Luciano 2480, 2481, 2482
Anderson, Chester G. 2483
Anderson, Paul Victor 898, 2484
Andreach, Robert Joseph 1513, 2485, 2486
Andrews, J. R. 2487
Anér, Kerstin 73, 2488
Angioletti, G. B. 2489
Anthony, E. 247
Anthony, Mother Mary 1075
Antrim, Harry T. 2500, 2501
ApIvor, Denis 1265
Appia, H. 172
Appleman, Philip 2502
Arakawa, T. 2503
Arbasino, Alberto 2504
Arden, Eugene 1338, 1339
Arms, G. W. 862, 4265
Arns, Karl 2067a
Arrowsmith, William 74, 74a, 173, 174, 175, 543, 544, 545, 2504a, 2505, 2506
Arvin, Newton 326
Ashraf, A. S. 2507, 2508
Askew, Melwin W. 818
Astre, Georges-Albert 2185, 2509, 2510, 2511
Atkins, Anselm 1299
Auden, Wystan Hugh 6, 327, 2186, 2512, 2513, 2514, 2515
Auffret, E. 1998
Austin, Allen 2111, 2128, 2161, 2187, 2246, 2339, 2360, 2516, 2517, 2518, 2519, 2520, 2521, 2522, 4266
Avadenei, Stefan 2523, 2524, 2525
Avery, Helen P. 248
Aylen, Leo 2527
Ayling, Ronald 546

B. D. 1340
B. M. K. 2023
Bacon, Helen H. 1516, 2528
Baeröe, Per Richard 2529

Bagg, Robert 2530, 2531
Bailey, Bruce 1517, 1518, 1518a
Bailey, Ruth 1197
Bain, Donald 75, 899
Baker, Carlos 2532
Baker, Howard 2533
Baker, James V. 2534
Baker, John Ross 1519
Balakanian, Nona 210, 2535
Baldi, Sergio 1520, 2536
Baldini, Gabriele 2537, 2538
Baldridge, Marie 2539
Balfour, Michael 1521
Balota, Nicolae 2540
Banerjee, Ron D. 1341, 2541, 2542
Bantock, G. H. 2188, 2276, 2315, 2340, 2543, 2544, 2545
Barber, C. L. 249, 2039, 2546
Barfoot, Gabrielle 2247, 2547
Barilli, Renato 2548
Barker, George 522, 2549
Barnes, T. R. 250, 328
Barnes, W. J. 843
Barnett, Gail Z. 2550
Barnhill, Viron Leonard 2551
Baron, C. E. 900, 2552
Barrett, William 76, 523, 2189
Barry, Iris 2553
Barry, John 1522
Barry, John B. 1984, 1985
Barry, Sister Mary Martin, O. P. 2554
Barry, Michael 77
Barry, Peter 1522a
Barth, J. Robert 547, 2555
Bartlett, Phyllis 1315, 2556
Barucca, Primo 2557
Basler, Roy P. 1342, 1343, 1472, 1488
Bassi, Emma 548
Basu, N. K. 2558
Bates, Ernest Sutherland 2559
Bates, Ronald 1523, 1999, 2560
Bateson, F. W. 863, 875, 879, 1524, 2561, 2562, 2563, 2564, 2565
Battenhouse, Henry M. 329, 549, 2566
Battenhouse, Roy W. 251, 329
Baumgaertel, Gerhard 2567
Bayley, John 78, 550, 2568, 2569
Beach, Joseph Warren 2570, 2571, 2572
Beare, Robert L. 330, 2573, 2574, 4267
Beatty, Richard Croom 1544
Beaufort, John 176
Beaver, Joseph 901
Becker, Mary L. 2575
Bedi, Jatinder 1344
Beer, Ernst 2576
Beer, J. B. 2577
Beery, Judith A. 1525
Beharriell, Frederick J. 2578
Behrmann, Alfred 2578a
Bejenaru, Cornelia 2579
Beker, Miroslav 2580, 2581
Belgion, Montgomery 1526, 2361, 2582
Belgion, W. R. 2040
Bell, Bernard I. 2129
Bell, Clive 7, 1527, 1528
Bell, Vereen M. 1345
Bellis, William Ward 2583
Bellow, Saul 177
Benét, William Rose 1529, 2041, 2584, 2585
Bengis, Nathan L. 331
Bennett, Joan 2362
Bennett, Mitchell Bruce 2586
Benson, Donald R. 1266
Bentley, Eric 2587
Bentz, Hans Willi 4268
Benziger, James 2588, 2589
Bergdahl, David L. 1076
Bergel, Lienhard 2590
Bergonzi, Bernard 8, 902, 1530, 1531, 2057, 2086, 2096, 2112, 2130, 2248, 2249, 2277, 2308, 2316, 2341, 2363, 2591, 2592, 2593, 4269
Bergsten, Staffan 903, 2594, 2595
Beringause, A. F. 1532
Beringause, Arthur 2596
Berland, Alwyn 1346
Bernadette, Jose A. 2597
Berry, Francis 1533
Berti, Luigi 2598, 2599
Betjeman, John 2600, 2601
Bevington, Helen 1174

Bewley, Marius 904, 2602
Bhattacharyya, Debiprasad 2603, 2604
Bille, Finn 905
Binse, Harry L. 2131
Birley, Robert 1534
Birrell, Augustine 2249a
Birrell, Francis 551
Bischoff, Dietrich 332
Bishop, Virginia C. 2132
Bissett, William 905
Bittner, Anton 333
Blackburn, Thomas 2505
Blackmur, R. P. 9, 334, 552, 749, 750, 906, 907, 1198, 1267, 1347, 1535, 2014, 2019, 2024, 2042, 2043, 2133, 2190, 2191, 2278, 2342, 2606, 2607, 2608, 2609, 2610, 2611, 2612
Blamires, Harry 908, 1077, 1125, 1152, 1175
Bland, D. S. 252, 335, 553, 909
Blanshard, Brand 10
Blau, Herbert 554, 2613
Blissett, William 910, 2614, 2615
Bloom, Harold 2616
Bloomberg, Lawrence 2617
Bloomfield, B. C. 555
Bluestein, Gene 2618
Bluestein, Mary Kate 911
Blum, Margaret Morton 1348
Blum, Walter, C. 2250
Blumenberg, Hans 556
Bly, Robert 1536
Boardman, Gwenn R. 211, 751, 1268, 2619
Bodelsen, C. A. 752, 912, 913, 914, 1078
Bodelsen, Merete 752
Bodgener, J. H. 915
Bodkin, Maud 253, 253a, 1537
Bogan, Louise 2620
Bogen, Donald Howard 1537a
Bohnsack, Fritz 2621
Boie, M. 2025
Bolgan, Anne C. 1538, 1539 2015, 2016, 2622
Bollier, Ernest Philip 883, 2251, 2343, 2623, 2624, 2625, 2626, 2627, 2628, 2629, 2630
Boonstra, Harry 2631
Bordwell, Harold 2397, 2632
Bornstein, George 2633
Boschere, Jean de 2634
Bose, Amalendu 2635
Bottomore, T. B. 2636
Bottorff, William K. 2637
Bottrall, Ronald 2638
Boulton, J. T. 336
Bovey, J. A. 2639
Bowers, Frederick 2640
Bowers, John L. 337
Bowra, C. W. 916
Bowra, E. M. 1540
Boyd, Ernest A. 2641
Boyd, John D. 1153, 2642
Boynton, Grace M. 2643
Brace, Marjorie 2644
Bracker, Jon 1349
Bradbrook, Muriel Clara 557 558, 1541, 1542, 1543, 2113, 2252, 2645, 2646, 4270
Bradbury, John M. 917
Bradbury, Malcolm 2647
Bradford, Curtis B. 918, 1126, 2648
Bradley, Francis Herbert 2649
Bradley, Sculley 1544
Brady, Ann Patrick 918a
Brandabur, Edward 1545, 2650
Brandell, Gunnar 2651
Branford, W. R. G. 559
Bratcher, James T. 1350
Braun, Elisabeth 2652, 4271
Braybrooke, Neville 11, 12, 338, 560, 889a, 919, 2653, 2654, 2655, 2656, 2657, 2658, 2659, 2660, 2661, 2662, 2663, 2664, 2665, 2666
Bredin, Hugh 2667
Bredvold, Louis I. 2668
Breit, Harvey 13, 2279, 2398, 2669
Brenner, Rica 561, 2670
Breslin, James E. 2671
Breslin, Paul Robert 2672
Brestin, James 14
Brett, R. L. 920, 921, 2673
Bridges, G. A. 2674
Brien, Alan 212
Brinnin, John Malcolm 765,

952, 1089, 1216, 1639, 3021
Broes, Arthur T. 822
Brombert, Victor H. 2675, 2676
Brooke, Nicholas 178
Brooks, Cleanth 254, 339, 753, 1351, 1469, 1546, 1547, 1548, 1549, 1550, 1551, 2192, 2364, 2430, 2677, 2678, 2679, 2680, 2681, 2682, 2683, 2684, 4230
Brooks, Harold F. 255, 922, 1269, 1552
Brooks, Van Wyck 2685
Brophy, Robert J. 2686
Brotman, D. Bosley 923, 1127, 2687
Brown, Alec 1296, 1553, 2688
Brown, Calvin S., Jr. 1469a, 2689
Brown, Christopher 1127a
Brown, E. K. 1554, 2690, 2691
Brown, John Mason 79, 340, 2691a
Brown, Lloyd W. 2692
Brown, R. D. 823
Brown, Ray C. B. 79a
Brown, Robert M. 1199
Brown, Spencer 179, 562
Brown, Stuart Gerry 1446, 1923, 4053
Brown, Wallace Cable 860c, 1473, 2253, 2693
Browne, Elliott Martin 80, 80a, 180, 181, 213, 256, 257, 341, 342, 343, 344, 345, 346, 347, 509, 563, 564, 565, 566, 567, 568, 569, 570, 571
Browning, Gordon 1352
Bruno, Francesco 2694
Bryer, Jackson R. 4294, 4295
Buck, Gerhard 1555
Buck, Philo M., Jr. 2695
Buckley, Vincent 2696, 2697
Budel, Maria 2698
Bugge, John 1154
Bullaro, John Joseph 2699, 2699a
Bullough, Geoffrey 2700, 2700a
Burch, Francis F. 2701
Burgess, Anthony 1556, 2702
Burke, Kenneth 2703, 2704
Burke, Sister Margaret, Jr. 2280
Burne, Glenn S. 2705
Burney, S. M. H. 2706
Bush, Douglas 2193, 2707
Butler, John F. 348
Buttle, Myra [pseud.] (see also Purcell, V. W. W. S.) 1474, 3710a
Butz, Hazel E. 2708

Caffi, Andrea 2709
Cahill, Audrey F. 2710
Cahill, Daniel Joseph 2711
Cajetan, Brother 1557, 2712
Calder, Angus 2713
Calinescu, Matei 2714
Callahan, Elizabeth Amidon 349
Calliebe, Gisela 2715
Calverton, V. F. 2044, 2716
Cambon, Glauco 924, 1558
Cameron, Elspeth 844, 925
Cameron, H. D. 1559
Cameron, J. M. 2717, 2718
Campbell, Harry M. 2719
Campbell, Roy 2720
Cantwell, Robert 2721
Capellán Gonzalo, Angel 926
Caprariu, Al 2722
Caretti, Laura 2723, 2724, 4272
Carew, Rivers 927, 2725
Carey, John, O. F. M. 1079
Carey, Sister M. Cecilia, O. P. 1560
Cargill, Oscar 1561, 1562, 2726, 2727, 2728
Carnell, Corbin S. 572, 2729
Carne-Ross, D. S. 258, 2730
Carpenter, Charles 572a
Carrier, Warren 1367
Carruth, Hayden 2162
Carson, Herbert L. 1353, 2731
Carter, Barbara B. 2732
Carter, Paul J. 81
Casey, Thomas C. 1500
Catlin, George 2194, 2733
Cattaui, Georges 2734, 2735, 2736, 2737, 2738, 2739, 2740
Causley, Charles 2741
Cauthen, Irby B., Jr. 1354, 1563

Cazamian, L. 182, 259
Cecchi, Emilio 2742
Ceechin, Giovanni 2743
Chace, William M. 1564, 2045, 2134, 2195, 2744, 2745
Chalker, John 2746, 2747
Chancellor, Paul 1565
Chang, Wang-Rok 350
Chaning-Pearce, M. 1176
Chapin, Katherine Garrison 2748
Chapman, Robert E. 351
Charity, A. C. 1566, 2749
Charvat, William 847, 1080, 1202
Chase, Richard 1567, 2750, 2751
Chatterji, Minai 2441
Chaturvedi, B. N. 928, 2752
Cheney, Frances 4273
Chew, Samuel C. 1568, 2281, 2753
Chiari, Joseph 573, 754, 810, 929, 1270, 1355, 1569, 1570, 1571, 2754
Chiaromonte, Nichola 574
Chiereghin, Salvino 2755
Child, Ruth C. 2756
Chinol, Elio 575, 2757, 2758, 2759
Chmielewski, Inge 2760
Christian, Henry 1294
Christie, Erling 930, 930a
Christopher, J. R. 2761
Church, Margaret 824
Church, R. W. 2762
Church, Richard 2763, 2764
Ciardi, John 2765
Ciarletta, Lalla 576
Cimatti, Pietro 2766
Claas, Dietmar 1572
Clark, David R. 352, 4274
Clark, John Abbot 1200, 1316, 1356, 2767
Clark, Marden J. 1177
Clark, Richard C. 2768
Clausen, Christopher 353, 1177a
Clemen, Wolfgang 2769, 4275
Clendenning, John 1357, 2770
Cleophas, Sister M. [Costello] 755, 931, 2020, 2771, 2772
Closs, Anthony 2773
Clowder, Felix 1306, 2774
Clubb, Merrel D., Jr. 932
Clutton-Brock, Alan 354, 2775
Clutton-Brock, Arthur 2097
Coats, R. H. 933
Coblentz, Stanton A. 2776
Coffman, Stanley K. 2777
Coghill, Nevill 82, 524
Cohen, J. M. 2778
Cohen, Savin 1358
Colby, Robert A. 83, 183
Coleman, Antony 2779
Collin, W. E. 2780, 2781
Collingwood, R. G. 1359, 1573
Colum, Mary M. 355, 356, 2068
Colum, Padraic 2782
Combecher, Hans 889b, 1128, 2783
Common, Jack 2046
Connolly, Cyril 2785, 4014
Conrad, S. 260
Cook, Albert 1574, 2008
Cook, Harold E. 845
Cook, Robert G. 1360, 1501
Cookman, A. V. 577
Coomaraswamy, Ananda K. 2786
Corder, Jim 1361
Cormican, L. A. 2196
Cornwell, Ethel F. 2787
Corrigan, Matthew 2788
Cossu, Nunzio 2789, 2790
Costello, Sister M. Cleophas see Cleophas
Cotten, Lyman A. 1575, 1986
Coulon, H. J. 2790a
Counihan, Sister Bernadette 934
Cowley, Malcolm 1362, 1576, 2026, 2135, 2791, 2792, 2793, 2794, 2795, 2796, 2797, 2798
Cowley, V. J. E. 2798a
Cox, Charles B. 846, 1577, 1578, 2799, 2800
Coxe, Louis O. 2801
Craig, David 1579, 1579a
Crane, R. S. 2802
Creaser, John 2803
Crewe, J. V. 2169
Crick, Bernard 2803a
Cronin, Anthony 2804

Cronin, Francis C. 2805
Cronin, Vincent 2806
Cross, Gustav 1580, 1987
Crowder, Richard 4276
Cruttwell, Patrick 2807
Cruz, Juan M. de la 2808
Cuddy, Lois A. 1154a
Culbert, Taylor 1201
Cummings, E. E. 2809
Cunliffe, John W. 2810
Cunliffe, Marcus 2811
Cunningham, A. M. 1129
Cunningham, Adrian 2812
Cunningham, J. S. 1581
Cunningham, J. V. 2225
Cunningsworth, A. J. 2813
Curtis, Anthony 2814
Curtius, Ernst-Robert 1582, 2815, 2816, 2817, 2818, 2819, 2820
Cutts, John P. 357
Czamanske, Palmer 2197, 2821
Czerniawski, Adam 2822

D., A. 1583, 1584
D., J. 2823
D. W. H. 2136
D'Agostino, Nemi 2824, 2824a
Dahlberg, Edward 1850, 2825, 2826, 3756
Daiches, David 847, 1080, 1202, 1203, 2827, 2828, 2829, 2830, 2831, 2832, 2833
Dale, Peter 1585
Daley, A. Stuart 2833a
Dallas, Elizabeth S. 935
Danby, John F. 578
Daniells, Roy 510, 579
Daniels, Edgar F. 1204
Daniels, J. R. 2834
Daniels, Roy 2835
Darby, James M. 2836
D'Arcy, M. C. 2837
Darrell, Sherry Bevins 580
Dasgupta, Rabindrakumar 358
Daus, Hans-Jürgen 2838
Davani, Maria Carmela Coco 581
Davenport, Gary T. 84
Davidson, Arthur 1586
Davidson, Clifford 756
Davidson, James 1475
Davie, Donald 936, 936a, 1155, 1587, 2839, 2840, 2841, 2842
Davies, Hugh Sykes 15, 2365
Davies, M. B. 2843
Davis, Jack L. 1156
Davis, Robert Gorham 1588, 2198, 2844, 2845
Davis, William V. 757
Davison, Richard 1589, 2846
Dawson, Christopher 2847
Dawson, N. P. 2848
Day, Douglas 2849
Day, Robert A. 1590, 1591, 2850
Day Lewis, C. 16, 1362a, 1591a, 2850a
Dean, Leonard F. 359
Deane, Paul 1592
De Arment, Warren Earl 2851
De Biassio, Giordana 1593
Deeney, John J. 1363
Degroote, Gilbert 360
Delasanta, Rodney 2852
De Laura, David J. 1081, 1271, 1594, 2853, 2854, 2855
Delpech, Jeanine 2856
De Masirevich, Constance 937, 1082, 1130, 1157, 1178
Dembo, L. A. 2857
Demers, Pierre E. 2858
DeMott, Benjamin 1595
Department of English, Washington U., St. Louis, Mo. 17
De Sola Pinto, Vivian 938
De Stasio, Marina 2859
Desternes, Jean 2399
Deutsch, Babette 848, 939, 940, 1083, 1476, 1596, 1597, 2069, 2860, 2861, 2862
DeVote, Bernard 1598
Dey, Bishnu 2863
Dick, Bernard F. 1599, 1599a
Dickerson, Mary Jane 1600
Dickinson, Donald H. 85, 582, 2864
Dickinson, Hugh 2865
Dierickx, J. 361, 583, 2866
Diggle, Margaret 1601
Dijkhuis, Dirk W. 2867
Dillon, George 2868
Dinwiddy, Hugh 2869
DiPasquale, Pasquale, Jr. 2870
Dobrée, Bonamy 18, 184, 185,

Fabricius, Johannes 2947
Fain, John T. 2948
Fairchild, Hoxie Neale 1212, 2949
Falck, Colin 2200, 2950
Falconieri, John V. 2951
Fallon, Gabriel 89
Faraque, Muhammad 2952
Farber, Marjorie 2953
Farenc, J. 367
Farmer, A. J. 2070, 2226
Farooqui, M. A. 2954
Farrell, William J. 1624
Farrelly, James 1213
Fasel, Ida 1625, 2400, 2955
Fausset, Hugh I'Anson 2432
Feder, Lillian 2955a, 2956
Felstiner, John 945
Fergusson, Francis 187, 262, 368, 369, 370, 2087, 2098, 2367, 2433, 2957, 2958
Fernandez, Ramon 2959
Ferrara, Fernando 263, 371
Ferris, Bob 2960
Ferry, David 2961
Ficimi, Fausto 2962
Fields, Kenneth W. 2963
Fieling, Keith 2071
Findlater, Richard 188, 590, 2964, 2965
Fink, Ernst O. 1626
Finn, H. Seth 2966
Fish, Clifford J. 1370
Fishbein, Michael 2967
Fisher, Ruth 1627
Fitz, Reginald 2968
Fitzgerald, Robert 2969
Fiumi, Annamaria B. 2970
Fiumi, Fausto 2971
Fleisher, Boel 2401, 2972
Fleisher, Frederic 2401, 2972
Fleissner, Robert F. 1308, 1371, 1372, 1373, 1373a, 2973, 2974, 2975
Fleming, Rudd 219
Fletcher, J. G. 946, 2976
Flint, R. W. 947
Floersheimer, Stephen 264
Fluchère, Henri 90, 372, 373, 591, 2977, 2978, 2979, 2980, 2981, 2982
Foltinek, Herbert 2983
Forster, E. M. 1628, 2201, 2984, 2985, 2986
Fortenberry, George 1374
Fortin, René E. 1629
Foster, Genevieve W. 763, 827, 851, 1274, 1630, 2987, 2988
Foster, Steven 1631
Fowler, D. C. 2017
Fowler, Helen 2989
Fowler, Rowena 1631a
Fowler, Russell T. 948
Fowlie, Wallace 949, 1632, 2990, 2991, 2992, 2993, 2994
Foxall, Edgar 2995
Franciosa, M. 2996
Franck, Jacques 2997
Frank, Armin Paul 1214, 2998, 2999, 3000, 3001, 3002
Frank, Joseph 950, 2317
Frank, Waldo 2283, 2284, 3003, 3004, 3005
Frankenberg, Lloyd 592, 891, 951, 1215, 1375, 1633, 3006
Franklin, Rosemary F. 827a, 1634
Franzen, Erich 3007
Fraser, G. S. 3008, 3009, 3010, 3010a, 3011, 3012
Frattini, Alberto 3013
Freddi, Giovanni 3014
Freed, Lewis 3014a, 3015
Freedman, Morris 526, 527, 593, 1635, 3016, 3017, 3018
Freeman, John 2114
Freimarck, Vincent 764
French, A. L. 1636, 1637, 1638, 3071
French, Warren 1638a, 3018a, 3019
Friar, Kimon 765, 952, 1089, 1216, 1639, 3020, 3021
Friedman, Alan Warren 1217
Friend, A. C. 3022
Frise, Adolf 3023
Frohock, W. M. 3024
Fry, Edith M. 594
Fry, Varian 4277
Fry, William A. 3025
Frye, Northrop 20, 3026, 3027, 3028, 3029
Fryxell, Donald R. 1376
Fukase, Kikan 3030
Fukase, Motohiro 3031, 3032
Fukuda, Rikutaro 766

Fuller, John 1307, 3033
Fuller, Roy 3034, 3035, 3036
Funato, Hideo 3037
Furbank, P. N. 2318
Fussell, B. H. 953
Fussell, Edwin S. 3038
Fussell, Paul, Jr. 954, 1275, 1276, 1640, 3039

G. R. B. R. 2368
Galinsky, Hans 374, 3040, 3041, 3042, 3043
Gallego, Cándido Pérez 3044
Gallivan, Patricia 1641
Gallup, Donald C. 1642, 1643, 2137, 3045, 3046, 4278, 4279, 4280, 4281
Galvin, Brendan 1305
Gamberini, Spartaco 595, 3047
García Lara, Jose 3048
Garçon, Maurice 20a, 3049
Gardner, Colin O. 1090
Gardner, Helen 91, 92, 92a, 93, 189, 189a, 190, 220, 375, 596, 596a, 597, 598, 767, 955, 956, 957, 1377, 1644, 1645, 1646, 1647, 1648, 2402, 3050, 3051, 3052, 3053, 3054, 3055, 3056
Garelick, Judith Spritzer 3057
Garetti, Laura 3058
Garrett, John 265
Gary, Franklin 2958, 3059
Gaskell, Ronald 266
Gassner, John 94, 267, 599, 600
Geier, Norbert Joseph 3060
Gent, Margaret 891a, 1649
George, Arapura G. 3061
George, R. E. Gordon 20b
Geraldine, Sister M., C. S. J. 376
Gerard, Martin 3062
Gerard, Sister Mary 958, 1091, 3063
Gerber, Richard 21
Germer, Rudolf 268, 828, 829, 1650, 1651, 3064, 3065, 3066
Gerstenberger, Donna 377, 601, 602, 1652, 1653
Gerster, M. 3067
Gervais, Terence White 3068
Ghose, Sisirkumar 1654
Ghosh, Damayanti B. 3069, 3070, 3070a
Ghosh, P. C. 378
Giannone, Richard J. 1317, 1378
Gibbons, Tom 1655
Gibbs, A. M. 3071
Gibbs, Barbara 3086
Gibson, William M. 1656, 2010
Gielgud, Val 379
Gil, Kim Jong 1379, 3072
Gilbertson, Philip N. 3073
Giles, Richard F. 1657, 3074
Gillet, Louis 3075
Gillett, Eric 95
Gillis, Everett A. 1277, 1478, 3076
Giroux, Robert 22
Gish, Nancy K. D. 830, 859, 3077
Giudici, Giovanni 191, 3078
Glaser, Michael S. 3079
Glass, Malcolm S. 3080
Glaza, James F. 1380, 3081
Glazier, Lyle 1658, 1988
Glenn, I. E. 865a
Glicksberg, Charles I. 603, 604, 3082, 3083
Gluck, Barbara 1380a
Gohdes, Clarence 2369
Goheen, Robert F. 866
Golden, William F. 3084
Goldfarb, Russell M. 3085
Goldman, Michael 605
Goldmann, Wilhelm 96
Goléa, Antoine 380
Golffing, Francis 3086
Göller, Karl Heinz 1659
Gomme, Andor 3087
Good, Thomas 2227, 3088
Goodwin, K. L. 3089
Gordon, Elizabeth 3090
Gordon, George S. 3091
Gordon, Lois 1659a
Gordon, Lyndall Felicity 22a, 1660, 3092
Gordon, Sarah Ellen 959
Gorman, William J. 768
Gottfried, Leon 1218, 3092
Gowda, H. H. Annian 960
Graham, Desmond 3094

Graham, Don B. 1661
Graham, James C. 3095
Grahn, Heinz 831
Grasmuck, Gloria 3096
Graves, Robert 606, 871, 1479, 1860a, 3097, 3098, 3787
Green, David Mason 1662
Greenbaum, Leonard 3100
Greenberg, Clement 2202, 3101, 3102
Greene, Edward J. H. 1381, 3103, 3104, 3105, 4282
Greenhill, Eleanor S. 961
Greenhut, Morris 3106
Greenwell, Tom 2403, 3107
Greenwood, E. B. 3108
Greenwood, Ormerod 268a
Gregor, Ian 3109
Gregory, Horace 269, 381, 962, 2047, 2228, 2370, 3110, 3111
Grenander, M. E. 1663
Grennen, Joseph E. 1664
Grierson, H. J. C. 3112
Griffith, Clark 1219
Grigorescu, Irina 963
Grigsby, Gordon Kay 964, 1665, 3113
Grigson, Geoffrey 3114
Grobler, P. du P. 23
Grochowiak, Stanislaw 3115
Gross, Harvey 965, 966, 1092, 1131, 1161, 1220, 1221, 1666, 1667, 3116, 3117, 3118
Gross, John 382
Gross, Seymour L. 1382
Grove, Robin 967
Grubb, Frederick 769, 811, 968, 1480, 1668, 3119, 3120
Grudin, Louis 3121
Grushow, Ira 1669
Guerin, Wilfred Louis 1670
Guidacci, Margherita 969
Guidi, Augusto 607, 3122, 3123, 3124, 3125, 3126
Guidubaldi, Egidio 3127, 3128, 3129
Gunter, J. Bradley Hunt 3130, 4283
Gupta, N. D. 3131
Gustafsson, Barbro 3131a
Guttmann, Allen 3132
Gwynn, Frederick L. 1383, 1481, 1482, 1483

H. J. M. 2099
Haas, Rudolf 3133
Habedank, Klaus 3133a
Hacikyan, A. 3134
Hager, Philip E. 2002
Hagger, Nicholas 3135
Hagstrum, J. H. 894
Hahn, Paul D. 1093
Hailey, Foster 2404
Hakac, John 1384
Hall, Donald 24, 2405, 3136, 3136a
Hall, Ian Roger 3137
Hall, Vernon, Jr. 895
Halper, Nathan 3138
Halverson, John 1222, 1385
Hamada, Kazuie 970
Hamalian, Leo 97, 270, 608, 3139, 3140
Hamburger, Michael 3141, 3142
Hamilton, Elizabeth 971
Hamilton, George Rostrevor 3143
Hamilton, Ian 98, 1671, 1672, 2406
Hamilton, K. M. 1673
Hancock, C. M. 3144
Hansen, Erik Arne 3145
Hanshell, Deryck 3146
Hanzo, Thomas 99
Hara, Ichiro 3147
Hardenbrook, Don 3148
Harding, D. W. 100, 192, 271, 512, 609, 1180, 1674, 2027, 2138, 2371, 3149, 3150, 3151
Harding, Joan N. 610
Hardy, John Edward 101, 3152
Hargrove, Nancy D. 770, 3153, 3154
Harlow, Agda Gronbeck 610a
Harmon, William 3155, 3155a, 3156
Harrex, S. C. 3156a
Harris, Bernard 1675
Harris, Warren Meredith 610b
Harris, Wendell V. 3157
Harrison, John 3158
Hart, Jeffrey P. 3159, 3160, 3161

Harter, Carol Clancy 1675a
Hartley, Anthony 192a, 3162
Hartley, L. P. 3163
Hartman, Geoffrey H. 3164
Harvey, C. J. D. 3165
Harvey, Versa R. 1386
Harvey-Jellie, W. 3166
Hasegawa, Mitsuaki 3167
Hassall, Christopher 611
Hassan, Ihab H. 3168, 3169
Hathaway, Richard D. 1676
Häusermann, Hans W. 272, 1132, 1133, 3170, 3171
Hawkins, Desmond 25, 2372, 3172
Hayakawa, S. Ichiye 2048
Hayman, Ronald 612
Hays, Peter L. 1677, 3173
Hayward, John 972, 3174, 3175
Hazlitt, Henry 2285
Headings, Philip Ray 1678, 2059, 3175a, 3176, 3177, 3178
Heath-Stubbs, John 3179
Heilman, Robert B. 102
Heines, Henry 613
Heller, Erich 2100, 3180, 3181
Helmcke, Hans 1679
Henderson, Philip 3182
Henn, Thomas Rice 614
Hennecke, Hans 3183
Hentz, Ann Louise 2345
Herdeck, Donald E. 1680, 3184
Hernigman, Bernard 973
Hertz, Karl 2197, 2821
Hesse, Eva 1223, 1681
Hesse, Walter 1682
Hester, Sister Mary 771
Hewes, Henry 26, 193, 221, 2407, 2408, 2409, 3185, 3186
Hewitt, Elizabeth K. 772, 1683
Heywood, Robert B. 103
Hicks, Granville 3187
Hidden, Norman 3188
Higgins, Bertram 3189
Higgins, David H. 3190
Higinbotham, R. N. 1181
Hildebrand, K. G. 3191
Hildesheimer, Wolfgang 3191a
Hill, Brennan 3192
Hillyer, Robert 1684, 2286, 3193, 3194, 3195
Hilton, Charles 3196
Hinchliffe, Arnold P. 1578
Hirai, Masao 3197, 3198, 3199, 4284
Hirsch, David H. 974, 1387, 3200
Hirsch, Foster L. 615
Hivnor, Mary 194
Hobsbaum, Philip 3201
Hobson, Harold 104, 616, 617
Hochwald, Ilse E. 105
Hodgson, R. A. 3202
Hodin, J. P. 2410, 3203, 3204
Hoellering, George 383, 384
Hoffman, Frederick J. 1685, 2319, 3205, 3206
Hogan, J. P. 3207
Holbrook, David 3208
Holden, Raymond 975
Holder, Alan 3209, 3210, 3211
Hollahan, Eugene 1388
Holland, Joyce M. 106, 195, 222, 618, 976
Holland, Norman N. 3212
Holland, Robert 1389
Holliday, Howard J. 3213
Hollis, Christopher 107
Holloway, John 1686
Holmes, John Haynes 385, 2028, 2139
Holroyd, Michael 27
Holroyd, Stuart 3214
Holt, Charles L. 528
Holthusen, Hans Egon 3215
Homan, Richard Lawrence 618a
Homann, Elizabeth R. 1484
Hombitzer, Eleonore 860a
Hönninghausen, L[othar] 386
Hook, Sidney 2203, 3216
Hoover, Judith Myers 3216a
Hopwood, V. G. 2346
Horton, Philip 273
Hosek, Chaviva 2287
Hoskot, S. S. 3217
Hough, Graham 977, 1687, 3218
House, Humphrey 3219
Hovey, Richard P. 108
Howard, Brian 773
Howarth, Herbert 28, 29, 619, 978, 1688, 2140, 2204, 3220, 3221, 3222, 3223, 3224, 3225, 3226

Howarth, R. G. 3227
Howell, John Michael 1689
Howes, A. B. 877
Hubbell, Jay B. 3228
Hübner, Walter 387, 620
Huffman, Claire 3228a
Huisman, David Arthur 3229
Humphries, Rolfe 1161a, 2072
Hungiville, Maurice 3230
Hunt, John Dixon 1690
Hunter, George K. 3231, 3232
Husain, S. M. 3233
Husain, Syed Sajjad 3234
Hutchins, Robert M. 3235
Huxley, Aldous 3236
Hyams, C. Barry 1988a
Hyman, Stanley Edgar 1485, 1486, 2347, 3237, 3238, 3239, 3240
Hynes, Sam 195a

Ingalls, Jeremy 979
Inge, W. Motter 109
Inserillo, Charles R. 274, 621, 3241
Instone, Ralph 1134
Iribarren Borges, Ignocio 1390
Irvine, Lyn 3242
Isaacs, Edith J. R. 388, 389
Isaacs, I. 390
Isaacs, Jacob 622, 3243
Isaacs, Jennifer I. 275
Isani, Mukhtar Ali 1691
Iser, Wolfgang 980, 3444
Ishak, Fayek M. 3245, 3246
Iwasaki, Soji 3247
Iyengar, K. R. Srinivasa 981
Isso, Carlo 1692

Jack, Peter Monroe 276, 391, 982, 2029, 2073, 2288, 2373
Jackson, James L. 1391
Jacobs, Arthur 392
Jähagirdar, C. J. 983
Jain, Narendra K. 852
Jain, Sushil Kumar 3248
Jameson, R. D. 3249
Jamil, Maya 277, 2101
Jankowsky, Kurt R. 3250, 3251
Janoff, Ronald W. 1989, 3252
Janssens, G. A. M. 3253
Jarrell, Randall 3254
Jarrett-Kerr, Martin 623, 3255, 3256
Järv, Harry 3257
Jay, Douglas 3258
Jayne, Sears 529
Jenkins, Harold 3259
Jenkins, William D. 3260
Jennings, Humphrey 393
Jennings, Paul 3261
Jha, Akhileshwar 3262
John, K. (Mrs.) 2049
Johnson, A. E. 3262a
Johnson, Geoffrey 3263
Johnson, Kenneth 1692a
Johnson, L. Eric 3264
Johnson, Maurice 984, 1182, 3265
Jolivet, Philippe 394
Jones, Dan L. 3266
Jones, David E. 110, 196, 223, 278, 395, 513, 530, 624
Jones, E. E. Duncan 774
Jones, Florence 1693, 3267
Jones, Genesius 3268
Jones, Howard Mumford 2074, 2141
Jones, Joseph 4285
Jones, Joyce Maria Meeks 3269
Jones, P. Mansell 1694
Joost, Nicholas 3270, 3271, 3272, 3272a
Jordan, Roland Carroll, Jr. 1094
Joselyn, Sister M., O. S. B. 832
Joseph, Brother, F. S. C. 3273
Joshi, B. N. 3274
Jouve, Pierre Jean 3275
Judelevicius, Dovydas 1695
Juhasz, Suzanne H. 985, 3276
Julian, Constance 3277
Jungman, Robert E. 1695a
Jury, C. R. 1696

Kagiya, Yukinobu 3278
Kahn, Sholom J. 1300, 3279
Kameyama, Masako 3280, 3281
Kane, Patricia 1697
Kantra, Robert A. 396
Kaplan, Charles 1487
Kaplan, Robert B. 625, 833, 1224
Karanikas, Alexander 3282

Karlin, Ken 3283
Kashfi, Abdul Khair 3284
Katsimbalis, G. K. 4286
Kaul, R. K. 626, 3285, 3286
Kayden, Eugene M. 2142
Kazin, Alfred 397, 2320, 3287
Kee, Howard C. 111
Keeley, Edmund 3288, 3289
Kelly, Bernard 279
Kelly, Brian 3292
Kelly, Gerald 3290
Kelly, Robert C. 3291
Kelly, Thomas 3292
Kemp, Lysander 1698, 1699, 1990, 1991, 2011
Kennedy, Andrew K. 626a
Kennedy, Eileen 1135
Kennedy, Richard S. 627
Kenner, Hugh 29a, 224, 398, 399, 775, 775a, 812, 834, 860, 890, 986, 1162, 1225, 1226, 1392, 1393, 1700, 1701, 1702, 1703, 1703a, 2030, 2205, 2229, 2321, 3293, 3294, 3295, 3296, 3297, 3298, 3299, 3300, 3300a, 3301, 3302, 4287
Keogh, J. G. 1277a, 1704
Kereaski, Rodica 3303
Kermode, Frank 225, 2031, 2060, 2088, 2230, 3304, 3305, 3306, 3307, 3308
Kerr, Walter F. 628, 3309
Kilgallin, Anthony R. 3310
Kim, Jong Gil 1394, 3311
Kincaid, Arthur N. 3312
King, Bruce 1395
King, S. K. 3313
Kinnamon, Rebeccah A. 776
Kinsman, Robert S. 1277b
Kintanar, Thelma B. 112
Kirby, J. P. 862
Kirk, Russell 30, 196a, 1227, 1396, 1705, 1706, 2143, 2206, 2255, 2322, 2348, 2374, 3314, 3315, 3316, 3317
Kirkup, James 3318
Kirschbaum, Leo 1472, 1488
Kitamura, Tsuneo 3319
Kittredge, Selwyn 3320, 3321
Kivimaa, Kirsti 400
Klatt, Heinz Günther 113
Kleinstück, Johannes Walter 4288
Kligerman, Jack 1136
Kline, George L. 3322
Kline, Peter 629
Klingopulos, G. D. 3323
Knapp, James F. 1397
Knickerbocker, William S. 3324
Knieger, Bernard 401, 630
Knight, G. Wilson 1707, 1708, 3325, 3326
Knight, W. F. Jackson 3327
Knights, L. C. 2050, 3328
Knoll, Robert E. 1709, 3329
Knowlton, Edgar C. 280
Knox, George A. 987
Knust, Herbert 531, 1489, 1710, 1711, 1712, 1713, 1714
Koch, Richard Earl 3329a
Koch, Vivienne 114
Koch, Werner, 2411
Kochetkova, I. K. 3330
Kogan, P[auline] 3331
Kohli, Devindra 3332
Kojecky, Roger 2061, 2144, 3333, 3334
Koppenhaver, Allen J. 402, 403, 777
Korg, Jacob 1715, 1716
Kornbluth, Martin L. 404, 3335
Kosok, Heinz 405
Kraemer, Konrad W. 3336
Krajewska, W. 631
Kramer, Dale 1717
Kramer, Hilton 115, 3337
Kramer, Kenneth P. 988
Krasavcenko, T. 3338
Kreymborg, Alfred 1398
Krieger, Murray 406, 407, 408, 409, 3339
Krishnamurti, S. 3340
Kronenberger, Louis 3341
Krutch, Joseph Wood 410, 2375, 3342
Kudo, Yoshimi 1399
Kuhn, Ortwin 3343
Kühnelt, Harro H. 3344
Kuin, J. 3345
Kuma, Franz 632
Kumar, Jitendra 3346, 3347, 3348
Kumashiro, Sobu 3349
Kuna, F. M. 2171, 3350
Kunst, Herbert 3351

Kuntz, Joseph M. 4265
Kytohonka, Arto 3352

L. L. S. 2003
L. W. 2256
Laboulle, M. J. J. 3353
LaChance, Paul R. 1718
Lair, Robert L. 3354
Lake, D. J. 3355
Lal, P. 3356, 4289
Lally, Sister Mary A. 411
Lalou, René 3357
Lambert, J. W. 633
Lancaster, R. Y. 989
Lancaster, Serena 3358
Langbaum, Robert 634, 1400, 1719, 2323, 3359, 3360, 3361
Langslet, Lars Roar 412, 990, 3362
Lannes, Roger 413
Lanza, Giuseppe 635
Larrabee, Ankey 3363
Laski, Harold J. 3364
Lasky, Melvin 991
Lasser, Michael L. 3365
Lattimore, Richmond 2376
Laurentia, Sister M. 1318
Lawler, James R. 3366
Lawlor, John 116
Lawlor, Nancy K. 1720
Lawrence, Seymour 116a
Lea, Richard 992
Leach, Elsie 1227a, 3367
Leary, Lewis 4290, 4291
Leavis, Frank Raymond 778, 778a, 853, 854, 855, 883a, 992a, 1095, 1138, 1163, 1164, 1183, 1228, 1721, 2051, 2075, 2089, 2231, 2257, 2258, 2377, 3368, 3369, 3370, 3371, 3372, 3373, 3374, 3375, 3376
Lebel, M. 636
Lebois, André 3377
Lebowitz, Martin 3378
Le Breton, Georges 3379
LeBrun, Philip 3380
LeClair, Thomas 1401/2
LeCroy, Anne 414
Lee, Jae Ho 1139
Lee, Young Gul 637, 3381
Lees, Francis N. 1722, 1723, 1724, 2163, 2172, 3382, 3383
Leggatt, Alison 117, 197
Lehmann, John 2412, 2413, 3384
Lehmann, Timgard 3385
Leighton, Lawrence 2062, 3386, 3387
Leitch, Vincent B. 3388, 3388a
Lelièvre, F. J. 3389
Lemarchand, J. 415
LeMaster, J. R. 2259, 3390
Lenhart, Charmenz S. 3391
Lensing, George S. 1725
Lento, Thomas V. 1725a, 3392
Lerner, Max 2207, 3393
Levi, Albert W. 3394
Levi, Peter 3395
Levin, Harry 1725b, 3395a
Levine, George 118
Levý, Jirí 3396, 3397, 3398
Levy, William Turner 31, 2444, 3399, 3400, 3401
Lewis, Anthony 3402
Lewis, Arthur O. 1096
Lewis, C. Day see Day Lewis, C.
Lewis, Janet E. O. 1726
Lewis, Wyndham 32, 33, 34, 35, 1402, 3403, 3404, 3405
Leyris, Pierre 3406
Licht, Merete 3407
Liebowitz, Martin 3408
Lightfoot, Marjorie J. 119, 120, 281, 638
Lindberger, Organ 3409
Lindenberger, Herbert 639
Lindsay, Jack 3410
Lindström, Göran 640
Link, Franz H. 3411, 3412
Linton, Calvin D. 3413
Little, Roger 779
Litz, A. Walton 1727, 1728, 1728a, 1729, 2324, 3414
Livesay, Dorothy 3415
Lobb, Kenneth Martyn 416, 641
Lobb, Randolph Edward 3416
Locke, Frederick W. 1403
Locke, James 1404
Locke, Louis G. 862, 867
Lodovici, C. V. 417
Loesch, Katharine 1309, 3417
Lohner, Edgar 3418

Lombardo, Agostino 3419, 3420
Long, E. Hudson 1544
Lonkon, Richard 3421
Lorch, Thomas M. 1730
Lorentzatos, Zisimos 3422
Loring, M. L. S. 3423
Lo Schiavo, Renato 3424
Lotringer, Sylvère 3425
Loucks, James F. 868, 877a
Lourie, Dick 3667
Lovell, Ernest J., Jr. 2260
Low, Anthony 3426
Lowell, R. T. S. 36
Lowenfels, Walter 36a
Lowry, E. D. 1731
Loya, Arieh, 3427
Lozano Mompo, Mercedes 780
Lu, Fei-Pai 3428, 3429, 4292
Lübker, Robert 993
Lucas, F. L. 1732, 3430
Lucas, John 1733, 1734
Lucy, Seãn 642, 1735, 2115, 2232, 2261, 2289, 2378, 3431, 4293
Ludowyk, E. F. C. 3432
Ludwig, Richard M. 37, 37a, 3433, 3434, 3435, 4294, 4295
Lumley, Frederick 643
Lund, Mary Graham 1736, 1737, 3436, 3437, 3438, 3439
Lundstöl, John 1165
Lunn, Hugh Kingsmill 2379
Luzi, Mario 3440
Lyman, Dean B., Jr. 1405, 3441
Lynd, Robert 2102, 2262, 2380, 3442
Lynen, John F. 3443

M. M. see Moore, Marianne
McAuley, James 3444
MacCallum, H. Reid 994, 1738
McCarron, William E. 995
MacCarthy, Desmond 3445
McCarthy, Harold E. 3446
McCarthy, Patrick A. 417a
McClanahan, Billie 3447
Maccoby, H. Z. 282, 283, 418, 781, 1097, 1098, 1099, 1739, 1740
Maccoby, Kyam 1229, 3448
McConnell, Daniel J. 1278
McCord, Howard 1741
McCreadie, Marsha Anne 3449
McCutchion, David 3450
McElderry, B. R., Jr. 2004, 3451, 3452
McGill, Arthur C. 3453
McGreevy, Thomas 1742, 3454
MacGregor-Hastie, Roy 1743, 2414, 3455
McKeever, Clare 1744
MacKendrick, Louis K. 3455a
MacKendrick, Paul 3456
Mackworth, Cecily 2415
McLauchlan, Juliet 1745
McLaughlin, John J., S. J. 122
MacLeish, Archibald 38, 644, 1746
McLuhan, Herbert M. 1259, 3457, 3458, 3459
McNeal, David Stuart 3459a
MacNeice, Louis 284, 1747, 3460, 3461
MacNiven, Ian S. 3462
Madeleine, Sister M. Claire 645
Madge, Charles 39
Madhusudan, Reddy V. 996
Magny, Claude E. 3463
Mahulkar, D. D. 1100
Mairet, Philip 40
Major, John M. 1230
Major, Minor W. 1407
Malawsky, Beryl Y. 4296
Male, Roy R., Jr. 1748
Malekin, P. 1749, 1749a
Malmberg, Bertil 3464
Mambrino, Jean 122
Manacorda, Guido 3465
Mandel, Eli 3466
Mandel, Oscar 646
Mandeville, Sandra C. 3467
Mangan, Sherry 3468
Mankowitz, Wolf 1231
Manning, Hugo 3469
Manuel, M. 285
March, Richard 3, 41, 647, 3470
Marcus, Philip L. 3471
Marder, Louis 2445
Margarey, Kevin 3071
Margolis, John D. 2052, 2063, 2090, 2116, 2145, 2263,

2349, 2381, 3472, 3473
Margolis, Joseph 1408, 1409
Marion, Sister Thomas 3474
Marks, Emerson R. 2146, 2208, 3475
Marsh, Florence 1750
Marsh, T. N. 1101, 3476
Marshall, Robert 3477
Marshall, William H. 1232, 1410, 1751
Martin, B. K. 869, 1411
Martin, Graham 2264, 2290, 2325, 2350, 2382, 3478
Martin, Jay 1752, 3479
Martin, Mildred A. 3480, 4297
Martin, P. W. 3481
Martin, Philip M. 782
Martin, W. D. 3482
Martin, W. R. 883b
Martinez Menchén, Antonio 3483
Martz, Louis L. 419, 420, 1102, 1103, 3484, 3485
Marx, Leo 3486
Mary Eleanor, Mother 835
Mason, Eudo C. 3487
Mason, H. A. 997
Mason, W. H. 421
Masters, Charlie 1104
Materer, Timothy 878, 3488
Mateucci, Benvenuto 3489
Mathews, R. T. 3490
Mathewson, George 3491
Matlaw, Myron 648
Matsuura, Kaichi 1105
Matthews, T[homas Stanley] 42, 3492, 4298
Matthiessen, Francis Otto 43, 422, 514, 649, 650, 998, 999, 1184, 1753, 1754, 3493, 3494, 3495, 3496
Mavroeidi-Papadaki, Sophia 3497
Maxfield, Malinda R. 424
Maxwell, D. E. S. 425, 651, 890a, 1755, 1756, 1757, 3498, 3499
Maxwell, J. C. 1000, 1166, 1758, 1759, 3500
Mayer, John Theodore, Jr. 3501
Mayo, E. L. 3502
Mazzaro, Jerome 3503
Meanor, Patrick Hugh 3504
Meckier, Jerome 2265
Mégret, Hélène 3505
Melchers, Hans Joachim 3506
Melchiori, Giorgio 198, 226, 426, 652, 653, 654, 655, 656, 1001, 1002, 1760, 1761, 1762, 3507, 3508, 3509
Mellers, W. H. 1140
Mende, Georg 3510
Mendel, Sydney 3511
Mendilow, A. A. 1324
Menning, Viiu 2287
Meoli Toulmin, Rachel 3512
Merchant, W. M. 657
Merritt, James D. 1763
Messiaen, Pierre 3513
Mesterton, Erik 1764
Meter, W. J. 2076
Metscher, Thomas 1106
Metwally, Abdalla A. 3514
Meyer, Christine 1260, 1261
Meyerhoff, Hans 3515
Michaels, Walter Benn 3516
Michel, Wolfgang W. 427
Miles, Josephine 3517
Miller, Arthur 658
Miller, James E., Jr. 1003, 1004, 1764a, 3518
Miller, Joseph Hillis 3518a, 3519
Miller, Milton 1765
Miller, Stephen 3520
Miller, Vincent 3521, 3522
Millett, Fred B. 1766
Milner, Ian 3523
Milstead, John 659
Milward, Peter 227, 1005, 1006, 1767, 3525
Mineo, Adinolfa 428
Mirsky, D. S. 1768
Mitchell, John D. 199
Mitra, S. N. 3526
Mizener, Arthur 1007, 1233, 1502, 3527
Moakley, Gertrude 1769
Moeller, Charles 286
Moffa, Marisa 228
Mohrt, Michel 3528
Moloney, Michael F. 3529, 3530
Monis, Patricio V. 659a
Monroe, Harriet 1770, 1771, 3531

Montale, Eugenio 3532
Monteiro, Adolfo Casais 3533,
Monteiro, George 1234, 1300a, 4299
Montgomerie, William 287, 1412, 3534
Montgomery, Marion 43a, 1325, 1413, 1772, 1773, 1774, 1775, 1992, 2351, 3534, 3535, 3536, 3537, 3538, 3539, 3540, 3541
Montgomery, Peter Cleghorn 660
Moody, A. D. 1776, 1777, 1778, 3542
Mooney, Stephen L. 1779
Moore, Dom Sebastian 1141
Moore, Harry Thornton 515
Moore, Marianne 429, 532, 1406, 2032, 2266, 3543, 3544
Moore, Merrill 1780, 3545
Moore, Nicholas 3546
Moorman, Charles 1781, 1782, 3547, 3548, 3549, 3550
Mordell, Albert 3551, 3552, 3553
More, Paul Elmer 1783, 2291, 3554
Moreh, Shmuel 3555
Morgan, Frederick 123
Morgan, Roberta 1414
Morison, Samuel E. 1167
Moriyama, Yasuo 766
Morley, Frank 44
Morris, David Buchan 3556
Morris, George L. K. 1784
Morris, J. A. 3557
Morris, Robert L. 2005
Morrison, Theodore 783
Morrissette, Bruce A. 3558
Morrow, Felix 3559
Morse, J. I. 1784a
Mortimer, Raymond 2117
Morton, A. L. 3560
Moseley, Edwin M. 430
Mosley, Nicholas 200
Motola, Gabriel 1785, 2018
Mountain, John A. 3561
Mowat, John 3562
Moynihan, William T. 1008, 1786, 1993
Mudford, P. G. 229, 661, 1490
Mudrick, Marvin 3563
Mueller, William R. 288, 431, 3564
Mühlberger, Josef 3565
Muir, Edwin 432, 1185, 2033, 2053, 2118, 2383, 3566, 3567, 3568, 3569, 3570
Muir, Kenneth 836, 3571
Munson, Gorham B. 1787, 2077
Munz, Peter 124
Murdoch, Iris 3572
Murphy, George D. 1788
Murphy, Russell Elliott 1788a, 3573
Murray, Byron D. 3573a
Murry, John Middleton 125, 125a, 289, 290, 662, 2091, 2267, 3574, 3575
Murshid, K. S. 1009
Musacchio, George L. 1010
Musgrove, Sydney 3576, 3577
Musurillo, Herbert 1789
Muth, John Barker 1010a
Muzina, Matej 3578
Myers, William 1790, 3579

Nagano, Yoshio 1791
Nageswara, I. G. 1792
Nageswara Rao, G. 3580, 3581
Naik, M. K. 230, 663, 664, 3582
Naples, Diane 3583
Narasimhaiah, C. D. 1793, 3584, 3585
Nath, Raj 1794
Nathan, George Jean 126
Nathan, Monique 3586
Nathan, Norman 1795, 3587
Nathan, Robert 3587a
Necco, Giovanni 3588
Negura, Neonila 3589
Nelson, Armour H. 1796
Nelson, C. E. 3590
Nelson, Conny 3591
Nelson, F. William 1797
Nemoianu, Virgil 3592
Neto, Maria A. 1798
Nevo, Ruth 1799
Newton, Frances J. 870, 3593
Nicholas, Constance 434
Nicholls, Norah 4300, 4301
Nichols, Dorothy 665
Nicholson, Harold 3598
Nicholson, John 1325a, 3594

Nicholson, Norman 435, 666, 667, 1800, 3595, 3596
Nicoll, Allardyce 668, 669, 3597
Niedermayer, Franz 3599
Niikura, Shunichi 1801
Nilon, Charles H. 4302
Nimkar, B. R. 3600
Nims, John 3601
Ninomia, Takamichi 3602
Ninomiya, Sondo 1011
Nirula, S. C. 436
Nishiwaki, Junzaburo 3603
Nitchie, George W. 1802
Nitze, William A. 1803
Nojima, Hidekatsu 3604
Noon, William T. 1012
Noonan, James 3605
Nott, Kathleen 1804, 3606, 3607
Novak, Robert 1415
Novykova, Marija 3608
Nowottny, Winifred 3609
Nuhn, Ferner 45, 1805, 3610
Nuttall, A. D. 3611

Oberg, Arthur K. 127
Obertello, Alfred 3612
O'Brien, M. N. 3613
O'Connor, Daniel 1013
O'Connor, William Van 1235
Oden, Thomas C. 784, 1107
O'Donnell, G. M. 3614
Oestreich, Marianne 670, 3615
Ohashi, Isamu 1014, 1806, 3616, 3617, 3618
Okenwa, Nnamdi 1415a
Okerlund, Arlene N. 3619
Okubo, Junichiro 3620
Okumura, Mifune 231
Olderman, Raymond M. 3621
Oldham, J. H. 2147
Olney, James 1014a
Olshin, Toby A. 516
Olson, Elder 1807, 3622
Olsson, Y. B. 856
O'Nan, Martha 3623
Ong, Walter J., S.J. 1108, 2326, 3624
Orage, A[lfred] R[ichard] 2082
Oras, Ants 2054, 3625
Orgel, Stephen 2173
Orsini, Gian Napoleone 671, 672, 1300b, 3626
Orwell, George 2209
Osotsi, W. 1808
Osowski, Judy 3627
Osterling, Anders 3628
Otake, Masaru 3629
Otten, Kurt 673
Otto, Wilhelm 3630
Ould, Herman 438
Owen, Guy 1416, 1808a
Ower, John B. 1491
Oxenford, Mabel A. 439
Oyama, Tokiko 3631
Ozu, Jiro 674

Packard, William 128
Pacuvio, Giulo 440
Padmanabha, Jayanta 1617, 1809
Page, Charles 3632
Page, L. Alun 3633
Pagnini, Marcella 1015
Pal, R. M. 2103
Palette, Drew B. 3634
Palmer, H. E. 1810
Palmer, Leslie 3635
Palmer, Richard E. 291, 3636
Panaro, Cleonice 3637
Panella, Sergio 3638
Panichas, George A. 3639, 3640
Panicker, Geevarghese T. 3641
Pankow, Edith 441
Papajewski, Helmut 232
Paris, Jerome Marvin 1811, 3642
Parkes, Henry B. 1492, 3643
Parkinson, R. N. 3644
Parkinson, Thomas 3645
Parsons, Geoffrey 128a
Parsons, I. M. 2292, 2293, 3646
Partridge, A. C. 3647
Patmore, Brigit 46, 47
Patrides, Constantinos A. 1016, 1812
Patterson, Gertrude 1813, 1814, 3648, 4303
Patteson, Richard F. 1815
Pattinson, John Patrick 3649
Paul, David 129

Paul, Leslie 233, 1816, 2417, 2418
Peacock, Ronald 130, 292, 293, 442, 675, 676, 3650
Peake, Charles 1503
Pearce, Roy Harvey 1817, 3651
Pearce, T. S. 3652
Pearson, Gabriel 3653
Pearson, Norman Holmes 1017
Peetz, D. W. 3654
Pellegrini, Allessandro 1018, 2419
Pellizzi, Camillo 3655
Pérez Gállego, Cándido 3656, 3657
Perkins, David 1019, 1109, 1186
Perloff, Marjorie 3658
Perret, Marion 1818, 2012
Perrine, L. 1417
Perselli, Luciano 443, 3659
Peschmann, Herman 131, 1020, 3660
Peter, John 132, 294, 444, 1819, 1819a, 3661
Peterson, R. G. 785, 1417a
Peterson, Sven 2268
Peyre, Henri 3662
Pfeffer, Franz 2420
Phillips, C. W. 3663
Phillips, Rowena S. 677
Phillips, William 2210, 3664
Piazzola, Marino 3665
Pick, John 133
Pickering, Jerry V. 445
Piebinga, H. Tj 3666
Piercy, Marge 3667
Pietersma, H. 678, 1418, 3668
Pinkerton, Jan 2351a
Pinto, Vivian de Sola 1820
Pîrvu, Sorin 3589
Plewka, Kurt 295
Plimpton, George 2421
Plutzik, Hyam 3669
Pocock, D. F. 2211
Poirier, Richard 1821, 1822, 3670
Policardi, Silvio 679, 3671
Politi, Francesco 3672
Pons, Christian 2422, 3673
Poore, Charles 2212, 2311
Pope, John C. 1419, 1420
Pope, Myrtle P. 1236
Popkin, Henry 134
Popovici-Teodoreanu, Liliana 3674
Porter, David H. 296
Porter, Katharine Anne 3675, 3676
Porter, M. Gilbert 1021
Porter, Thomas 134a
Porteus, Hugh Gordon 3677
Post, Robert M. 3678
Pottle, Frederick A. 297, 680, 786, 1237
Poulsen, Søren R. 3679
Pound, Ezra 47a, 1421, 1422, 1823, 2055, 2294, 2384, 2446, 3680, 3681, 3682, 3683, 3684, 3685, 3686
Powel, Harford Willing Hare, Jr. 48
Powell, Dilys 681, 3687, 3688
Power, Sister Mary James 3689
Powers, Lyall H. 1423
Pratt, Linda R. 1824, 3690
Pratt, William C., Jr. 3691
Praz, Mario 1825, 1826, 1827, 3692, 3693, 3694, 3695, 3696, 3697, 3698, 3699, 3700
Press, John 1828
Pressey, Benfield 488
Preston, Keith 2269
Preston, Priscilla 1310, 1311, 3701
Preston, Raymond 1022, 3702
Price, Fanny 1187
Prince, F. T. 1829
Pritchard, William H. 1830, 3703
Pritchett, V. S. 2233, 3704
Prokosch, Frederick 3705
Prosky, Murray 1831
Puckett, Harry 3706
Puhalo, Dusan 682, 3707, 3708 3709
Puhvel, Martin 1832
Pujals, Esteban 3710
Purcell, Victor William Saunders [Myra Buttle, pseud.] 3710a
Püschel, Brita 446
Putt, S. Gorley 447

Quennell, Peter 2295, 3711
Quiller-Couch, Arthur 3712

Quillian, William Howell 2104
Quin, I. T. 135
Quinn, Sister M. Bernetta 1023, 1833, 3713
Qureshi, I. H. 3714
Qvamme, Borre 3715

Rabut, Marguerite 448
Raditsa, Leo F. 2234
Raffel, Burton 1834
Rago, Henry 48a, 48b, 2213, 3716
Rahman, K. 3717
Rahme, Mary 3718
Rahv, Philip 683, 2327, 3719
Rai, Vikramaditya 1835
Raina, M. L. 3720, 3721
Raine, Craig 1836, 1837
Raine, Kathleen 1838, 3722, 3723, 3724
Rainer, M. L. 1839
Rajan, Balachandra 787, 1024, 1025, 1424, 1425, 1426, 1840, 1841, 1842, 3725, 3726, 4304
Rajasekharaiah, T. R. 3727
Rajasundaram, C. F. 3728
Raleigh, John H. 3729, 3730
Ralston, William H., Jr. 3731
Ram, Tulsi 3732
Rama, Murthy V. 3733
Ramamrutham, J. V. 3734
Rambo, Dorothy Ellen 1026
Ramsey, Jarold 1843
Ramsey, Warren 3735, 3736
Randall, Dale B. J. 1844
Ransom, John Crowe 298, 449, 684, 1238, 1845, 1846, 2174, 2175, 2352, 2353, 2385, 3737, 3738, 3839, 3740, 3741, 3742
Rao, G. Nageswara 533, 884, 1506, 3743
Rao, K. S. Narayana 1506a, 1507, 1663, 3744, 3745
Rascoe, Burton 3746, 3747
Ratner, Joseph 2148, 2149
Rauber, D. F. 1848
Rawler, J. R. 3748
Ray, Mohit 3749, 3750
Ray, Paul G. 2328
Rayan, Krishna 3751, 3752, 3753
Raybould, Edith 1849
Read, Herbert 49, 49a, 685, 1850, 2214, 2825, 2826, 3754, 3755, 3756
Rebmann, David R. 450, 1851
Rebora, Piero 3757
Rebora, Roberto 136
Reckford, Kenneth J. 137, 3758
Reckitt, Maurice 2150
Reddy, V. Madhusudan 1027
Redman, Ben Ray 2296, 3759
Reed, Henry 138, 2386, 3760
Reed, Kenneth T. 1427
Rees, Garnet 3761
Rees, Goronwy 2215
Rees, Richard 451, 2216
Rees, Thomas Richard 1028, 3762, 3763, 3764, 3765
Reeves, Gareth 1852
Reeves, George M. 2423
Reeves, James 3766
Reeves, Troy Dale 1428
Regnery, Henry 50, 3768
Rehak, Louise Rouse 452, 3769
Reibetanz, Julia 1029, 1030
Reichert, Karl H. 1988a
Reid, Benjamin L. 1853, 3770
Reid, David 3771
Reid, J. 1417
Reid, John T. 3772
Reinsberg, Mark 1031, 1110
Reiss, Hans 3773
Renner, Stanely 453, 3774
Restivo, Giuseppina 3775
Revol, Enrique Luis 3776
Rexine, John E. 139
Rexroth, Kenneth 3777
Rezzano de Martini, Maria Clotilde 299, 1238a
Rhoads, Kenneth W. 1032
Rice, Philip Blair 1854, 2078
Richards, I[vor] A[rmstrong], 51, 879, 880, 1855, 1856, 1857, 2217, 3778, 3779, 3780, 3781, 3782, 3783
Richardson, Joanna 52, 1858
Richman, Robert 53, 686
Richmond, Lee J. 1859
Richter, Dagny 1279
Rickey, Mary E. 454
Rickman, H. P. 3784
Ricks, Christopher B. 1187a, 2329, 3785
Rickword, Edgell 1860, 2297, 3786

Riding, Laura 871, 1860a, 3787
Ridler, Anne 1861, 1862, 1863, 3788, 3789, 3790
Rillie, John A. M. 3791
Rillo, Lila E. 3792
Ritter, Joachim 3793
Rizzardi, Alfredo 3794
Robbins, Rossell Hope 140, 141, 300, 686a, 3795, 3796
Roberts, Michael 301, 2298, 3797
Roberts, R. Ellis 2064
Robertson, J. M. 2105
Robinson, David 1110a, 3798
Robson, W. W. 2235, 3799, 3800, 3801
Roby, Robert C. 687, 3802
Rochat, Joyce Hamilton 1238b, 1428a, 3803
Roche, Paul 3804, 3805
Rochester, Howard 3806
Rodgers, Audrey T. 788, 1168, 1429, 1864, 3807, 3807a, 3807b,
Rodman, Selden 2236
Roeffaers, H. 3808
Rogers, Daniel John 688
Rogers, William N., II 1864a
Roman, Christine Marie 3809
Román, M. C. 455
Romer, Karen T. 789, 885, 1280
Romhild, Lars P. 3810
Roos, Alarik 3811
Rosales, Rodulfo S. 3812
Rosario, Salvatore 3813, 3814
Rosati, Salvatore 456, 689, 690
Rose, Alan 3815
Rose, W. K. 2447
Rosenberg, John 3816
Rosenthal, M. Louis 1033, 1169, 1188, 1239, 1430, 1865, 1866, 3817, 3818
Ross Williamson, Hugh 457, 1867, 1867a, 3819, 3819a
Rosseaux, André 3820, 3821
Rosu, Anca 1431
Rothbard, Lorraine 3822
Rother, James 3823
Rothwell, Kenneth S. 1868
Rottiers, A. K. 3824
Rougemont, Denis de 3825
Rowland, John 3826
Rowland, Thom 3827
Roy, Emil 458
Rozsa, Olga 3828, 4306
Ruban, Jonathan 3829
Rubin, Larry 2034
Rubin, Louis D., Jr. 3830
Ruland, Richard 3831
Ruland, Vernon 3832
Rumble, Thomas C. 1432
Rupp, Barbara 3833
Russell, Bertrand 54, 3834
Russell, Francis 55, 2424, 3835
Russell, Peter 141a, 302
Russell, Walter Sanders, Jr. 3836
Russi, Antonio 691
Ryan, Krishna 3837
Ryan, Lawrence V. 1285
Ryan, Marianna 1240, 1869

Sabbadini, Silvano 3838
Sachton, Alexander 3839, 3840
Sackville-West, V. 2299
Sahal, K. L. 3841
Salamon, Linda Bradley 1034, 1110b
Salmon, Christopher 233, 2387
Sampley, Arthur M. 201, 234, 1870, 3842, 3843
Sampson, Ashley 2388
Sampson, George 692
Sando, Ephriam G. 3844
Sanesi, Roberto 1871, 1872, 3845
San Juan, E[pifanio], Jr. 1241, 1242
Sansom, Clive 2436
Santoy, Peter Du 1873
Sarang, Vilas 1281
Sarbu, Aladár, 693
Sarkar, Subhas 3846, 3847
Sastri, P. S. 3848
Savage, D. S. 3849
Savelli, Giovanni 3850
Sayers, M. 459
Scalise, Anna Maria 837
Scarfe, Francis 2354, 3851
Schaar, Claes 1189, 3852
Schaeder, Grete 303, 460, 694, 695, 3853
Schaeder, Hans Heinrich 303,

460, 695, 3853
Schäfer, Von Hans Dieter 3854
Schanzer, Ernest 1301
Schappes, Morris U. 2300, 3855
Schenk, W. 1111
Scherle, Victor 31, 2444, 3399
Schlüter, Kurt 202, 235, 696
Schmidt, A. V. C. 885a, 1874
Schmidt, Gerd 697, 698, 1142, 1190, 1314, 3856, 3857
Schmied, Wieland 3858
Schneewind, J. B. 2165
Schneider, Elisabeth 534, 790, 813, 886, 1035, 1282, 1433, 1434, 1875, 2237, 2301, 2330, 2355, 2389, 3859, 4306
Schneider, Karl 3860
Schnetzer, Dean 1876
Schoeck, R. J. 3861
Schöne, Annemarie 3862
Schröder, Franz Rolf 3863
Schuchard, Ronald 2437, 2438, 2522, 3864, 2864a, 3865
Schulte, Edvige 3866
Schwalb, Harry M. 2006
Schwartz, Delmore 304, 1036, 1877, 1878, 3867, 3868, 3869, 3870
Schwartz, Edward 142
Schwartz, Jacob 4307
Schwarz, Daniel R. 1243
Scott, E. 3871
Scott, John S. 3872
Scott, Nathan A., Jr. 143, 305, 1143, 1879, 3873, 3874, 3875, 3876, 3877
Scott, Peter D. 3878
Scott-Moncrieff, George 3879
Scrimgeour, C. A. 306
Scruggs, Charles E. 3879a
Searl, Eva 1036a
Seelye, John 1880
Seferis, George 56, 2425, 3880, 3881
Seidel, Frederick 3882
Seif, Morton 3883
Seiler, Robert M. 1435
Seldes, Gilbert 2270, 3884
Semaan, Khali I. H. 699, 3885
Semmler, Clement 3886
Sen, Asoke 699a
Sen, Jyoti P. 3887, 3888
Sen, Mihir K. 1881, 1882, 3889, 3890
Sen, S. C. 1037
Sen, Sunil Kanti 3891
Sena, Vinod 144, 307, 3892
Sencourt, Robert 57, 791, 1883, 3893
Senior, John 3894
Sergeant, Howard 1038
Serpieri, Alessandro 1884, 1885, 1886, 3895, 3896, 3897
Serpieri, Sandro 1244, 3898
Servotte, Herman 3899
Sewell, Elizabeth 3900
Sexton, James P. 1039
Seymour-Smith, Martin 2331, 3901
Seyppel, Joachim H. 3902
Shahani, Ranjee 2426
Shanahan, C. M. 1319, 1436, 1887, 3903
Shand, John 1191
Shankar, D. A. 3904
Shapiro, Karl 1888, 2439, 3905, 3906, 3907, 3908
Shapiro, Leo 461
Sharma, H. L. 3909
Sharma, Jitendra Kumar 3910
Sharma, Mohan Lal 3911
Sharoni, Edna G. 462
Sharrock, Roger 3912
Shartar, I. Martin 700
Shaw, Sam 3913
Sheehan, Donald G. 3914
Shepherd, T. B. 1040
Sheppard, R. W. 1041
Sheppard, Richard 1889
Sherek, Henry 145
Shiga, Masaru 3915
Shillito, Edward 463, 3916
Short, Ernest 701
Short, M. H. 1325b
Shorter, Robert N. 464
Shulenberger, Arvid 1302
Shulman, Robert 1890, 3917
Shuman, R. Baird 146, 147
Shuster, George N. 2302
Shuttle, Penelope 3918
Sickels, Eleanor M. 792, 1891, 1994, 2007
Siddiqui, M. N. 465
Siegel, Daniel G. 3919
Siegel, Eli 3920

Silverstein, Norman 1892
Silvi, Valeria 3921
Simiot, Bernard 148
Simister, O. E. 1042
Simon, Irène 1893
Simons, John W. 1894, 3922
Simpson, Louis 1436a, 3923
Sinclair, May 1320, 1437
Singer, Glen W. 1504
Singh, D. P. 3924
Sinha, Krishna Nandan 1043, 1044, 1045, 1046, 3925
Sisson, C. H. 2218
Sitwell, Edith 535, 3926, 3927, 3928
Sitwell, Osbert 3929
Skinner, Aubrey E. 3930, 4308
Slack, Robert C. 1438, 3931
Slade, Landry 3951
Slattery, Sister Margaret Patrice 793
Slawińska, Irena 701a
Slochower, Harry 3932
Smailes, Thomas A. 838, 1894a
Smidt, Kristian 466, 702, 1047, 1895, 3933, 3934, 3935, 3936, 3937, 3938, 3939
Smith, A. J. M. 1188, 1239, 1430
Smith, Bernard 3940
Smith, Carol H. 149, 203, 236, 237, 308, 467, 517, 536, 537, 703, 704, 705, 2238, 4309
Smith, Chard P. 3941
Smith, Dane Farnsworth 3942
Smith, Francis J. 1144
Smith, Gerald 1439
Smith, Grover, Jr. 150, 204, 238, 309, 468, 469, 470, 471, 518, 538, 706, 794, 814, 887, 1048, 1112, 1192, 1193, 1245, 1246, 1283, 1326, 1327, 1470, 1471, 1896, 1897, 1898, 1899, 2013, 2390, 3943, 3944, 3945, 3946, 3947, 3948
Smith, J. C. 3112
Smith, James 1900, 3949
Smith, Janet Adams 3950
Smith, Marcus 3951
Smith, R. G. 150a, 3952
Smith, Ray 1901, 1995
Smith, Stevie 472
Sobreira, Alberto 3953
Sochatoff, A. Fred 473, 707
Soldo, John J. 58, 3954, 3955, 3956
Sorescu, Marin 1902
Sorial, F. I. 708
Southam, B. C. 815, 1440, 1903, 3957, 3958
Southworth, J. G. 3959
Spangler, George M. 1441, 1904
Spanos, William V. 310, 474, 539, 708a
Speaight, Robert 151, 475, 476, 477, 478, 709, 710, 711, 3960, 3961, 3962, 3963
Spears, Monroe K. 3964
Spears-Brooker, Jewel 3965
Spector, Robert Donald 3966
Spelvin, George 205
Spencer, Theodore 479, 872, 1905, 3967
Spender, Stephen 59, 60, 61, 61a, 61b, 61c, 151a, 311, 480, 519, 540, 795, 1049, 1906, 1907, 1908, 2092, 2151, 2152, 2176, 2219, 2303, 2332, 2333, 2391, 3968, 3969, 3970, 3971, 3972, 3973, 3974, 3975, 3976
Sperna Weiland, J. 3977
Sperry, W. L. 2153
Spiller, Robert Ernest 3978, 3979, 3980, 4310
Spinucci, Pietro 3981
Spivey, Ted R. 3982, 3983
Spratt, P. 3984
Sprich, Robert 1262
Squire, J. C. 1909
Squires, J. Radcliffe 3985
Srinath, C. N. 711a
Srivastava, Narsingh 1049a
Stallings, Laurence 2106
Stamm, Rudolf 312, 712, 3986, 3987
Standop, Ewald 713, 839, 1145, 3988, 3989
Stănescu, Nichita 3990
Stanford, Derek 239, 3991
Stanford, Donald L. 873, 1284
Stanley, John M. 3992
Stapleton, Laurence 3993
Starr, H. W. 1310a
Stauffer, Donald Alfred 1493, 1910, 1911

Stead, C. K. 3994, 3995, 3996
Steadman, John M. 3997
Steiger, Emil 152
Stein, Walter 153
Stein, William B. 3998
Steiner, George 1912
Steinmann, Martin, Jr. 3999
Stelzmann, Rainulf A. 714
Stemmler, Theo 860b
Stenger, G. L. 1113
Stepanchev, Stephen 1442
Stephane, Nelly 4000
Stephenson, Ethel M. 1913, 4001
Stevens, Wallace 62, 4002
Stevenson, David L. 2107
Steward, Diana 4003
Stewart, Randall 4004, 4005
Stock, Noel 63, 63a, 4006, 4007
Stone, Geoffrey 480a
Stonier, G. W. 1146, 1312, 1914, 4008
Storey, Robert F. 4009
Storm, Leo 4009a
Stormon, E. J. 4010
Strachey, John 4011
Strandberg, Victor H. 2021, 4012, 4013
Straumann, Heinrich 4014
Stravinsky, Igor 64
Strickland, G. R. 4015
Strong, L. A. G. 519a
Strong, Robert 4016
Strothmann, Friedrich W. 1285
Stroud, T. A. 819
Stuart, Duane R. 4017
Stuckey, William J. 1443
Styler, W. E. 65, 4018
Sugiyama, Yoko 1915
Sühnel, Rudolf 4019, 4020
Suhrkamp, Peter 313
Sullivan, Sheila 4021
Sullivan, Zohreh Tawakuli 4021a
Surette, P. L. 1444
Sutherland, James R. 2239
Sutton, Walter 1916, 4022
Sveino, Per 1247
Sweeney, Frances 4023
Sweeney, James J. 1147, 1194
Sweeney, John L. 1085, 1208, 1272
Swinnerton, Frank 4024
Sykes, Robert H. 1295
Symes, Gordon 796, 1050, 1248, 1286, 1445, 4025
Symons, Julian 4026
Sypher, Wylie 4027

Taborski, Boleslaw 715
Takaichi, Junichiro 1051
Takayanagi, Shunichi 1917, 1918, 2093, 4029, 4029a, 4030
Talley, Jerry B. 716
Tambimuttu, [Thurairajah] 3, 41, 647, 3470, 4031
Tamplin, Ronald 1919
Tanner, Stephen L. 4032
Taranath, Rajeev 888, 1920
Tardivel, Fernande 481
Tate, Allen 66, 66a, 797, 797a, 1921, 1922, 2012a, 2334, 4033, 4034, 4035, 4036, 4037, 4038, 4312
Taupin, René, 4039, 4040, 4041
Taylor, Walter Fuller 4313
Tbg [sic] 240
Tello, Jaime 1052, 4042, 4043
Tentori, F. 4044
Terada, Takehiko 4045, 4046
Terrell, Carol Franklin 4047
Thale, Mary 2177
Thatcher, David S. 4048
Theall, Donald F. 889, 4049
Theoharis, Zoe George 4050
Thomas, Caleekal Thomas 4051
Thomas, Henri 482, 717
Thomas, R. Hinton 4052
Thomas, Wright 1446, 1923, 4053
Thompson, A. C. 840
Thompson, Eric 1053, 1114, 1924, 2108, 2154, 2178, 2271, 2304, 4054, 4055, 4056
Thompson, Katharine S. 4057
Thompson, Marion C. 4058
Thompson, Ralph 2155
Thompson, T. H. 541, 1925
Thorlby, Anthony 1054
Thrash, Lois G. 154
Thurber, James 155
Tillotson, Geoffrey 1926, 4059
Tillyard, E. M. W. 4060

Tinckom-Fernandez, W. G. 67
Tindall, William York 4061, 4062, 4063
Tinsley, Molly Best 1307a
Tischler, Nancy M. 1494
Todd, Oliver 4064
Todd, Ruthven 4065
Tolhurst, Francesca 1148
Tomlin, E. W. F. 3199, 4066
Toms, Newby 156
Tordeur, Jean 718, 4067
Torrens, James 719, 798, 1927, 4068, 4069, 4070
Toth, Susan Allen 1928
Traversi, Derek 1055, 1928a, 1929
Trewin, J. C. 720, 721
Tribe, David 1495
Trigona, Prospero 1930
Trilling, Lionel 2156, 4071, 4072
Trompeo, P. P. 4073
Troy, William 2056
Troyat, Henri 483
Tschumi, Raymond 799, 1115, 1447, 1931
Tuohy, Frank 4074
Turnell, G. Martin 314, 4075
Turner, A. J. 484
Turner, Mark 3771
Turner, Richard C. 874
Turner, W. Arthur 1320a, 1448
Tynan, Kenneth 722

Ueda, Tamotsu 4076, 4077
Ullnaess, Sverre P. N. 520
Unger, Leonard 241, 315, 485, 723, 724, 800, 801, 802, 803, 892, 893, 1116, 1117, 1149, 1150, 1170, 1171, 1249, 1250, 1287, 1932, 1933, 1934, 2065, 2109, 2179, 4078, 4079, 4080, 4081, 4082, 4083, 4084, 4085, 4086, 4087, 4314, 4315
Untermeyer, Louis 1296a, 1321, 1449, 1935, 2035, 4088, 4089
Utley, Francis L. 1263

Vaish, Y. M. 4090
Vallette, Jacques 157, 725, 4091, 4092, 4093, 4094, 4095
Valverde, José Mariá 4096
Vance, Thomas 4097
Van der Vat, D. G. 4098
Van Doren, Mark 486, 2079, 2080, 2119, 2180, 2272, 2392, 4099, 4100, 4101
Vania, Rhoda 4102
Vassilieff, Elizabeth 158
Vaughn, Franklin H. 1313, 1450
Vergmann, Finn 804
Verheul, K. 1056
Verma, Rajendra 1936, 2220, 4103
Vickery, John Britton 1251, 1288, 1937, 1938, 1996, 4104, 4105, 4016, 4107
Vig, Jill 1450a
Vigée, Claude 726, 4108
Vigliano, Gabriele 4316
Villacañas Palomo, Beatriz 1057
Vincent, C. J. 159
Vinograd, Sherna S. 881, 1252, 4109
Virginia, Sister Marie 1058
Virsis, Rasma 487
Virtue, John 1451
Visentin, Giovanni 727
Viswanathan, K. 4110
Viswanathan, S. 4111
Vivas, Eliseo 2356, 4112, 4113
Vizioli, Paulo 4114
Voight, F. A. 4115
Voight, G. P. 4116
Voisine, Jacques 206, 242, 728
Vondersmith, Bernard J. 1452
Von Phul, Ruth 4117
Von Wellsheim, Mother Anita 4118
Vordtriede, Werner 4119
Voskuil, Duane 1059
Vyas, H. K. 857

Waggoner, Hyatt Howe 1172, 1289, 1453, 4120, 4121
Wagner, C. Roland 4122
Wagner, Linda W. 4123, 4317

Wagner, Robert D. 1060, 2448, 4124
Wain, John 1939, 2240, 2273, 4125, 4126, 4127, 4128, 4129
Wajima, Shiro 4129a
Walcutt, Charles Child 1454, 1496, 1504a, 2022
Waldoff, Leon 1454a
Waldron, Philip 1940, 1941, 4130
Waldson, C. M. 4131
Walker, Marshall 1253
Wall, Bengt V. 4132
Wall, Richard J. 833, 1224
Wallace, Ronald Henry 4133
Walmsley, D. M. 4134
Walton, Geoffrey 4135
Walton, James 1942
Walz, Rudolf 1455
Ward, Anne 316
Ward, David E. 1943, 4136, 4137, 4138, 4139
Ward, Nicole 1944
Warncke, Wayne 4140
Warren, Austin 1456, 2393, 4141, 4142, 4143
Warren, Robert Penn 68, 753, 1351, 1469
Wasser, Henry 1290, 4144
Wasserstrom, William 1945, 4145
Wasson, Richard 317, 729, 4146, 4147
Watanabe, Nancy Ann 4148
Waterman, A[rthur] E. 1457, 4149
Waters, Leonard Adrian 4150
Watkins, Floyd C. 1061, 1297, 1303, 1946, 4151, 4152
Watkins, Vernon 4153, 4154
Watson, C. B. 2305
Watson, E. Bradlee 488
Watson, George 2335, 4155, 4156
Watson-Williams, Helen 1946a
Watt, F. W. 4157
Watts, Donald 1118
Watts, Harold H. 1062, 4158
Weales, G. 243
Weatherby, Harold L. 4159, 4159a, 4160
Weatherhead, A. Kingsley 805, 1063
Weathers, Willie T. 1947, 1997
Weathers, Winston 4161
Weaver, Richard M. 2221
Webb, Eugene 805a, 1063a
Webber, B. G. 4162
Weber, Alfred 2449, 4163, 4164, 4165, 4165a
Webster, C. J. 730
Webster, Grant T. 4166
Webster, H. T. 1310a
Wecter, Dixon 1948, 4167
Weedon, William S. 2313
Weidlé, Wladimir 318, 4168
Weigand, Elsie 1119, 4169
Weightman, J. G. 207, 244
Weimann, Robert 4170
Weinberg, Kerry 4171
Weinig, Mother Mary Anthony 1064, 1195
Weinstein, Jacob J. 2157
Weinstock, Donald J. 1458
Weintraub, Stanley 4172
Weirick, Margaret C. 1949
Weisberg, Robert 4172a
Weiss, Charlotte 4173
Weiss, Klaus 1065, 1066
Weiss, Theodore 4174, 4175
Weisstein, Ulrich 160, 161, 731
Weitz, Morris 1067, 1459, 1460, 4176
Wellek, Rene 4177, 4178, 4179
Wells, Henry W. 732, 4180
Wentraub, Dennis A. 4181
West, Anthony 4182
West, Ray B., Jr. 1068
West, Rebecca 2306
West, William Channing 733
Wetzel, Heinz 1950, 1951, 1952
Wheeler, Charles B. 1461
Wheelwright, Philip Ellis 1069, 1120, 1151, 1173, 1254, 1953, 1954, 4183, 4184
Whicher, George F. 734
Whidden, R. W. 862
Whitaker, Thomas R. 4185
White, Alison 1121
White, Georgiana Donase 734a, 1955
White, Gina 4186
White, Robert 1462
Whiteside, George 893a, 1941, 1956, 1957, 4187, 4188, 4189, 4190, 4191

Whitfield, J. H. 1070, 4192, 4193
Whitford, Ruth H. 4194
Whitlark, James S. 489, 4194a
Whitman, Peter 4195
Widmer, Kinglsey 1958
Wienhorst, Sue E. 4196
Wilbur, Robert Henry Hunter 4197
Wilder, Amos N. 490, 4198, 4199, 4200
Wildi, Max 319, 491, 735, 4201
Wilhelm, Jean 492
Wilkinson, Burke 208
Wilks, A. John 1959
Williams, Charles 1071, 4202
Williams, Haydn Moore 1960
Williams, Helen 1961
Williams, Margaret 4203
Williams, Philip 4204, 4205, 4206
Williams, Philip Eugene 1072, 4207
Williams, Pieter D. 493
Williams, Raymond 162, 319a, 494, 495, 736, 737, 738, 2158, 2159, 2222, 2223, 4208, 4209
Williams, William Carlos 69, 806, 1962, 4210, 4211, 4211a
Williamson, Audrey 209, 320, 739
Williamson, George 542, 816, 820, 841, 1073, 1291, 1497, 1963, 1964, 1965, 1966, 4212, 4213, 4214, 4215, 4318
Williamson, Mervyn Wilton 1255 4216
Willingham, John R. 245
Wills, Garry 4217
Wills, John H. 842
Wilson, Colin 4218
Wilson, Edmund 740, 1498, 1967, 1967a, 1968, 1968a, 2120, 4219, 4220, 4221, 4222, 4223
Wilson, Frank 496, 741, 807, 820a, 1074, 1256, 1292, 1463, 1969, 4224, 4319
Wilson, Gary H. 4225
Wilson, James Southall 2394
Wilson, Richard 4226
Wilson, Roderick 4227
Wilson, Timothy 1970
Wimsatt, William K. 163, 742, 743, 1464, 2336, 4228, 4229, 4230
Wingate, Gifford W. 497, 744
Winkler, R. O. C. 4231
Winston, George P. 4232
Winter, Jack 164
Winters, Yvor 1971, 4233
Wiseman, James 165, 2160
Wohlstetter, Albert 1414
Wolff, Erwin 4234
Wollheim, Richard 2166, 2167, 4235, 4236
Wollner, Craig Evan 4237
Wood, Frank 4238
Wood, Grace 321, 4239
Woodard, Charles R. 4240
Woodberry, Potter 4241
Woodward, Daniel H. 1972, 2083
Woodward, Kathleen Middlekauff 1074a
Wool, Sandra 166, 1973
Woolf, Leonard S. 70, 71, 2274, 4242, 4243
Wooton, Carl 808
Wormhoudt, Arthur 1465
Worsley, T. C. 167, 246
Worth, Katharine 745
Worthen, John 1974
Worthington, Jane 858, 882, 896, 1122, 1257, 1264, 1293, 1298, 1304, 1322, 1466, 1499, 1509, 1975, 4244
Wren-Lewis, John 168, 4245
Wrenn, C. L. 1196, 4246
Wright, George T. 1976, 4247
Wright, Keith 4248, 4249
Wright, Nathalia 4250
Wyatt, Euphemia Van Rensselaer 169, 498
Wycherley, H. Alan 1467
Wylie, Elinor 1977
Wyman, Linda Lee 498a, 746
Wynn, Dudley 747, 4251

Yamada, Akihiro 1258, 4252, 4253
Yamada, Mitsuko 4254, 4255

Yamada, Shoichi 4256, 4257
Yamada, Yoichi 2168
Yamoto, Sadamiki 4258
Yarros, Victor S. 4259
Yasuda, Shoichiro 1123, 1978, 1979
Yeats, William Butler 499, 4260
Yen, Yuan-shu 747a
Yeomans, W. E. 4261
Yerbury, Grace D. 1980
Yokelson, Joseph B. 1199
Yoklavich, John M. 170
Young, Stark 500, 501
Young, Thomas D. 2948

Zabel, Morton D. 322, 502, 521, 748, 809, 817, 1981, 2395, 4262, 4263, 4264
Zanetti, Emilia 503
Zasurskii, Ya 1982
Zaturenska, Marya 3111
Zimmerman, Lester F. 1983
Zizola, Giancarlo 504, 505
Zolotow, Maurice 171
Zulli, Floyd, Jr. 2109a